Corporate Governing in Latin America

Jonathan Callund ·
Gonzalo Jiménez-Seminario · Neil Pyper
Editors

Corporate Governing in Latin America

The Importance of Scandals to Institute Change

palgrave
macmillan

Editors
Jonathan Callund
Callund y Compañía Ltda.
Santiago, Chile

Gonzalo Jiménez-Seminario
Pontificia Universidad Católica de Chile
Santiago, Chile

Neil Pyper
International Business, School of Business, Economics and Informatics
University of London
Birkbeck, UK

ISBN 978-3-030-85782-0 ISBN 978-3-030-85780-6 (eBook)
https://doi.org/10.1007/978-3-030-85780-6

This Palgrave Macmillan imprint is published by the registered company Springer Nature Switzerland AG
The registered company address is: Gewerbestrasse 11, 6330 Cham, Switzerland

Acknowledgments

Prof. Carlos Francisco Cáceres Contreras
Juan Andrés Camus Camus
Axel Christensen
Martin Costábal Llona
Mauro da Cunha Rodrigues
Prof. Stephen Davis
Prof. Alfredo Enrione Cáceres

The anonymous, local, academic and professional corporate governance specialists who we called on to review the respective country chapter.

Praise for *Corporate Governing in Latin America*

"This book is clearly the new reference on corporate governance research in Latin America. It has many layers to it. While it describes the main theoretical approaches, it also stimulates the reader by showing how different corporate scandals in Latin America have shaped these country's corporate governance practices. Then it turns to a systematic discussion of six countries' corporate governance systems based on its legal system and existing governance practices and it also has a sharp analytical perspective in forecasting what's in the future. Thus, this book is targeted to academic as well as practitioners who want to understand better the past, present and future of corporate governance in Latin America."

—Ruth Aguilera, *Brodsky Professor of Global Governance, Northeastern University, USA*

"*Corporate Governing in Latin America* offers a welcome perspective on how corporate governance policy reforms and practices are shaped in economies outside of the more advanced financial markets of North America and Western Europe, which tend to influence corporate governance policies and regulations globally. The variation of approaches taken in the six markets reviewed highlights the importance for credible market reforms to be tailored to the context of the local market and informed, where appropriate, by so-called internationally accepted best practices. As demonstrated, the process should be much more nuanced.

Kudos to the authors who provide an insightful assessment for policy makers, regulatory authorities, boards and directors, scholars and practitioners in evaluating approaches to good corporate governance which are both relevant and practical and not taken from a standard stereotype but shaped to the prevailing macroeconomic and institutional conditions. Many useful lessons are offered for emerging markets elsewhere in the world."

—Philip Armstrong, *Independent governance advisor and former Head, Global Corporate Governance Forum, South Africa*

"*Corporate Governing in Latin America* is a must read to better understand the evolution of corporate governance and its specificities in the context of Latin America. This book is of enormous benefit to company owners, managers, practitioners, and policy makers alike, in addressing the challenges of developing sustainable firms and consolidating their business governance structures. Written in plain English, the collection of papers explains the challenges and benefits of corporate governance through clear examples that illustrate the main ideas and conclusions, and the authors are able to lead us on an amazing journey and help navigate the complexity of corporate governance."

—Rodrigo Basco, *Professor, American University of Sharjah, Dubai, UAE*

"An understanding of the complex issues associated with improving Corporate Governance is becoming increasing important. For too long in the English language, there has been a Latin America sized gap in the corporate governance bookshelf until now with the arrival of *Corporate Governing in Latin America*. In its pages the authors make a thoughtful and original contribution in their examination of corporate governance in Latin America but also by identifying how it is often different from other geographies (notably North America, Europe and the UK). *Corporate Governing in Latin America* also covers how individual countries differ in their approach to the law, regulatory codes of practice and conduct as well as how the rules-based environment is changing. The authors have provided a readable and much-needed contribution to the subject of corporate governance."

—Gerry Brown, *Chairman of* NovaQuest Capital Management L.L.C. *and co-author (with Professor Randall S Peterson) of* Disaster in the Boardroom

"Harmony in any society is found in the subordination of its political and economic structures to moral reference points. Competition in a free market is essential to ensuring the efficient and correct allocation of scarce resources. Key to this, however, is also the prestige of the players – the corporations and agents – who effect these allocations and in just the pursuit of efficiency gains. Sustainable free market economies rely on their adherence to ethical behaviors such that society as a whole can achieve the common good.

The book *Corporate Governing in Latin America - The Importance of Scandals to Institute Change*, makes an important contribution in presenting multiple case studies flagging the behaviors of key actors in performing their corporate activities who give scant consideration to essential ethical parameters when carrying out their respective activities. The thumbnail cases draw on public accounts of malfeasances in Argentina, Brazil, Chile, Colombia, Mexico and Peru, while, providing testimonies of reprehensible conduct, open a space for analysis of both the lessons and concrete steps that can be taken to avoid their reoccurrence, specifically relating to management and board oversight of corporations, in both the private and public sectors.

This works is of great value! By reinforcing the essential nature of good conduct of those who participate in corporate life, confirming the subordination of efficiency criteria to moral principles that must dictate and illuminate all human action. There is no doubt that business activity has proven legitimate in terms of efficiency. However, ethical legitimacy can only be cultivated – day-by-day – through the behavior of its actors."

—Carlos Francisco Cáceres Contreras, *Professor, Director, former President of Chilean Central Bank, former Minister of Finance and Minister of Interior, Chile*

"A solid corporate governance practice is an essential factor for any company to be successful in the long term. In particular, it is even more important for family businesses, as they need to differentiate business issues from their family matters. This book provides extraordinary theoretical reflections on the principles that frame corporate governance practices in companies of six countries in Latin America. Moreover, its thumbnail studies of the authors' "top six" scandals in each of the leading countries in the region help derive practical lessons and the essential flags to doing business in Latin America. This superb study will inspire both academics and practitioners, business owners and legislators looking to innovate on old practices and produce institutional change. Founded on clear and insightful theoretical and empirical bases, the authors – and there are 21 – evolve a "theory of practice" for those looking to draw lessons in the development of better corporate governance in their own companies or countries."

—Jesús Casado Navarro-Rubio, *Secretary General, European Family Businesses, Belgium*

"Jonathan Callund, Gonzalo Jiménez and Neil Pyper the editors, have assembled an excellent collection of articles from 18 authors which cover critical theoretical aspects around Corporate Governing in Latin America. This is a major contribution to the field, a must read for academics, students, practitioners and those interested in corporate governance.

A unique and innovative part of the book is to show how thirty-six corporate scandal cases from six main countries in the region have forced a change in regulations and hence, have had a positive impact in changing public attitudes, board behaviors and relevant corporate practices.

This book is a must read for those interested in corporate governance and in Latin America."

—Lourdes Casanova, *Senior Lecturer and Gail and Rob Cañizares Director Emerging Markets Institute, Cornell S.C. Johnson College of Business, Cornell University, USA*

"A key challenge in learning about the intricacies and complexities of corporate governance is where to go to gain a deep theorical and practical understanding of this social and legalistic space. This book provides a unique grounding of the underlying theoretical premises of corporate governance, based on extensive and detailed first-hand experiences. Hitherto, as a supervisor of the financial markets, my job – and those of the rest of the market players – would have been that much easier had such a book existed in our day.

When reviewing the diverse and multiple cases of missteps, both here and across the region, I am heartened to see significant progress being made on all governing fronts, not least as a result of government, private and institutional reactions to these human failings.

This is a mammoth contribution and will help directors – new and old alike – in understanding the importance of what they do and how to do it better."

—Álvaro Clarke, *Founder & President, ICR Chile Credit Ratings, former Securities & Insurance Supervisor, Chile*

"First of all, I want to celebrate the initiative of the publishers in making *Corporate Governing in Latin America - The Importance of Scandals to Institute Change* a reality, which in my opinion had been long pending. I have read it with great interest and considerable nostalgia. In my different roles – as investment manager of the country's #1 pension fund, as a company director, and, most recently, as President of the merged bank, insurance and financial services regulator – I have first-hand knowledge of the people and circumstances narrated by Matías Zegers and Carla Rojas in their Chile chapter and, in particular, the six scandals they selected. In matters of corporate governance the role assumed by the pension funds was key, given the local market's low liquidity, hindering investors who were dissatisfied with a company's performance or governance to sell their positions without incurring large losses.

At the core of this book are the descriptions and lessons drawn from corporate scandals. This, however, should not be construed as yet another attribute of "Latin American magical realism", as scandals also abound in many developed economies. Maybe more striking is the dark side seen through the involvement of state-owned foreign multinationals. What is important are not the corporate scandals themselves, but more how these have been used – with widespread public support - as levers to close the differing legal and regulatory gaps in this regard. This is well documented in the book. In this context, Gonzalo Jiménez-Seminario also goes some way to closing the gap between the academic vision and the practice of corporate governing that are comprehensively addressed in his sections."

—Joaquín Cortez Huerta, *Director, former President Comisión para el Mercado Financiero, Chile*

"A comprehensive and unique description of the history of corporate governance and the multiple crises in key Latin America countries, delving into the evolution of each market's regulation, with pithy assessments and commentary. In flagging the current regulatory gaps, this book provides valuable policy and programmatic ideas at both a national and regional level on how to improve normative frameworks. *Corporate Governing in*

Latin America - The Importance of Scandals to Institute Change is an ideal primer for board members, executives, academics and regulators alike."

—Martin Costabal Llona, *Director and former Finance Minister, Chile*

"*Corporate Governing in Latin America, The Importance of Scandals to Institute Change* should become a definitive resource for analyzing CG in Latin America. It provides inciteful analyses on the past, present and future of CG developments in the six specific countries it examines as well as a regional view. This book will be useful for academics, practitioners, regulators as well as investors in emerging markets in Latin America. Regarding the latter, I find it a great resource particularly in determining contextual CG risk for the largest economies discussed in the book."

—Charles Travis Canfield, *Principal Corporate Governance Officer, IFC, USA*

"Like plane crashes, corporate scandals will only happen after a combination of factors. The recurring nature of such events in Latin America might lead to the depressing conclusion that they are an inherent fixture of the region. They need not be. This book offers hope and opportunity. Hope for those that believe in the construction of healthy capital markets as a tool for a better, more democratic, and more equal society. It will surely become a reference for academics and practitioners alike, given its rich interplay between theory, policy making and real life. But it also offers opportunity.

Corporate Governing in Latin America - The Importance of Scandals to Institute Change shows that corporate governance does not evolve linearly, but is rather a cyclical process of euphoria, hubris, reform and backlash. It allows us to see that not all investment cases are the same. Increasing regulation offers plenty of opportunities for box ticking, but problems keep popping up. Investors that go the extra mile and do the homework of understanding the true nature of corporate governance rather than its appearance in a checklist can be handsomely rewarded. Not least by avoiding the next scandal, but also by filling the gaps left open by other gatekeepers and taking advantage of the high cost of capital that such an environment creates. This book is an excellent companion for such a journey."

—Mauro Rodrigues da Cunha, *CFA, Independent Director, former President Brazilian Corporate Governance Institute (IBGC), Brazil*

"Most of the world's thriving businesses are owned by families or a state. But you wouldn't know that from the overwhelming focus of global corporate governance scholarship, which has for years been trained on the escapades of publicly traded enterprises in big developed markets. Finally, the aperture is widening, thanks in no small part to *Corporate Governing in Latin America - The Importance of Scandals to Institute Change*, edited by Callund, Jiménez-Seminario, Pyper.

The authors keep academics happy with solid theory about what distinguishes one market from another. For practitioners—that is, investors, companies, or executives—this book is a gold mine of real-world insights on how corporate governance works, or doesn't, across six Latin American markets. One key finding: Scandal, sometimes at monstrous scale, plays an outsized role in driving change in each country. But this makes the region a crucible of global significance: eruptions are what happens when entrenched power faces the shock troops of global capitalism in the form of foreign financial agents, international standards, probing media. The outcomes of such clashes are what now shape Latin America's corporate future. Callund, Jiménez-Seminario, Pyper, and their many chapter authors are the indispensable guides we need to understand and navigate it."

—Professor Stephen Davis, *Senior Fellow and Associate Director, Harvard Law School, Program on Corporate Governance, USA*

"Fascinating read on the catalytic effect of governance scandals and their power to mobilize for change. *Corporate Governing in Latin America - The Importance of Scandals to Institute Change* offers so many valuable insights!"

—Patrick Eamonn Dunne, *Chairman, Boardelta, Author of the award winning "Boards" and member of the Higgs Review, UK*

"*Corporate Governing in Latin America - The Importance of Scandals to Institute Change* is long overdue for academics and practitioners in the region. While the current literature would seem to suggest that the world is rife with dispersed ownership, efficient financial markets and strong institutional investors, we know that in most parts they are rather the exception. This book not only shows us the particularities of Latin America as a whole, but also the relevant differences between the six leading countries in the region. The collection of emblematic cases is a treasure trove for understanding the particular challenges and the adaptive solutions of regulators and other actors in each market. My congratulations and thanks to the authors!"

—Prof. Alfredo Enrione, *Director of the Corporate Governance Centre, ESE Business School, Universidad de los Andes, Chile*

"This is a comprehensive review of governance in Latin America and the influences and events that have shaped it. The analysis is developed with academic rigor and references, but will be of interest to academics and practitioners alike and explores overall themes and country by country analysis.

Corporate Governing in Latin America - The Importance of Scandals to Institute Change is essential reading for those who are involved with or, want to understand the Latin American landscape and compare and contrast it with Governance developments in the rest of the world."

—David Fairs, *Executive Director for Regulatory Policy, Analysis and Advice at The UK Pensions Regulator, UK*

"I have read *Corporate Governing in Latin America - The Importance of Scandals to Institute Change* with particular interest the aims, background and focus of this book, as well as those details relating to Chile, and I am taken by the exhaustive nature of its content and authors' prolific research. Although I am unable to comment on each chapter or the impacts on regulatory development deriving from corporate scandals in each of the six countries, I do recognize that they have indeed played a positive role in encouraging better corporate governance practices.

Moreover, the impact these scandals have had, and the feeble institutional reactions they have elicited serve to show the lack of appreciation of capitalism and the market economy in our society, as reflected in a substantial and continuous weakening of confidence in private enterprise. That said, I would also point out that the risks and consequences of bad corporate governance is not solely with private companies, but also with public corporations and institutions, as well as non-profit institutions, whose governing failures have understandably and drastically brought on the deep skepticism of our society and its confidence in them to solve problems, such as, in the cases of the pension fund industry, the management of private resources for old age."

—José Antonio Guzmán Matta, *Director, Past President, Enersis, ENDESA, AFP Habitat, Chile*

"*Corporate Governing in Latin America - The Importance of Scandals to Institute Change* is a balanced and comprehensive book about the state of the art and the challenges for corporate governance in Latin America. As the title suggests, it is an invitation to understand and assess the current situation learning from the past with an eye on the future. After introducing the reader with the theoretical framework - New Institutional Economics, Resource Dependency Theory, and Institutional Theory - an original chapter on corporate scandals in Argentina, Brazil, Chile, Colombia, Mexico and Peru follows. But the next chapters place the context for each country. In sum, theory illuminates reality, but practice also informs theory."

—Leonidas Montes, *Former Dean & Professor, Escuela de Gobierno, Universidad Adolfo Ibáñez. Director, Centro de Estudios Públicos (CEP), Chile*

"Latin America is a special case in corporate governance - arguably several special cases - and *Corporate Governing in Latin America - The Importance of Scandals to Institute Change* provides a way to see the problems from several different vantage points. The region has overlapping institutional arrangements - formal and informal - and political systems that are conscious of each other, while consciously different. The companies across the region copy each other - not always for the best - but also respond to local imperatives. Investment and share ownership involve both large, global players but also regional and local ones.

Corporate Governing in Latin America - The Importance of Scandals to Institute Change serves a valuable service in discussing the complexity but also the commonality across those four dimensions. It provides not just a critical overview but also abundant cases of scandals and malpractice that illustrate what we have learned about corporate governance in Latin America and where we need to learn more."

—Donald Nordberg, *Associate Professor of Corporate Governance, Bournemouth University, author of* "The Cadbury Code and Recurrent Crisis - A Model for Corporate Governance?", *UK*

"A systematic and detailed examination of the stories that have defined our understanding of the lacunae in corporate governance in Latin America, *Corporate Governing in Latin America - The Importance of Scandals to Institute Change* provides useful insights per country. Many of these learnings are translatable to the wider emerging markets scenario where governance, or the lack thereof, has created significant issues that individuals, businesses and governments have to contend with. To paraphrase a famous quote, the authors use their collective knowledge and experience to demonstrate how to 'never waste a good scandal'."

—Dr. Vinika D. Rao, *Executive Director, INSEAD Emerging Markets Institute, Gender Initiative & Africa Initiative, Singapore*

"I read *Corporate Governing in Latin America - The Importance of Scandals to Institute Change* with curiosity and interest. The book seeks to address the paradox of corporate governance scandals in juxtaposition with a historical aspiration to move beyond them to better practices. With summarized reviews of several academic literatures on corporate governance, the book is written for the thoughtful practitioner. Yet, it ends up inspiring the mindful policymaker through the depth of its concerns for building a better future for all corporations in Latin America.

The book is timely, engaging and full of insights explained through examples. An interesting side-effect of the book is that it provides a glimpse into the business histories of several countries in Latin America for those outside the continent."

—Saras Sarasvarthy, Paul M. Hammaker, *Professor of Business Administration, University of Virginia, Darden School, USA*

"A very interesting work providing a case-by-case review of corporate governance regulation in Latin America, following corporate scandals. *Corporate Governing in Latin America - The Importance of Scandals to Institute Change* invites an in-depth debate on corporate governance on two levels: (i) the concrete prospective improvements that are needed in a country's respective regulations given the risks of greenwashing and a general lack of transparency on corporate practices; and (ii) the innovations needed to improve "the process of creating regulations" to ensure better corporate governance, particularly in concentrated markets, dominated by business groups.

One lesson is that the business community and policy makers must not allow the future development of regulations to be dependent on the flow of new scandals –going from shock to shock. Rather, the book throws down the gauntlet, flagging the importance of the role and process of regulations in shaping future discussions and the evolution of markets. The history of capitalism shows that the regulations - so essential in the quest for better governance - normally arrive late, so engendering avoidable tensions in the economy and across the fabric of society. In addressing the problems inherent in the "process of regulation", the regulations themselves will necessarily improve, but so will the level of trust in capitalism. This is a strategic challenge especially now, when transformation of capitalism is needed to reward value creation, not value extraction. To design and implement the right governance structures for sustainable capitalism, based on competitve and more dinamic markets, is key for the future in this planet."

—Jeannette Von Wolfersdorff, *Director, Former President of the Corporate Governance & Sustainability Committee, at Santiago Stock Exchange, Author of* "Capitalismo", *Chile*

Contents

Part I Regional Chapters

Editors and Contributors

About the Editors

Jonathan Callund is *Independent Nominee Director* for IFC and financial services corporations in Europe and Latin America, CEO Callund y Compañía Ltda, Partner, MC^2 Salud.

Dr Gonzalo Jiménez-Seminario is *Professor of Governance, Strategy & Family Business* in the Engineering School at Pontificia Universidad Católica de Chile; *CEO*, Proteus Management, Governing & Effectuation; Independent Board Member.

Dr Neil Pyper is *Assistant Dean (Learning and Teaching), Senior Lecturer* in International Business, School of Business, Economics and Informatics, Birkbeck, University of London.

Contributors

Ismail Adelopo Faculty of Business and Law, University of the West of England, Bristol, UK

Verónica Ilián Baños-Monroy Tecnológico de Monterrey, Monterrey, Mexico

Andrés Bernal Governance Consultants, Bogotá, Colombia; iDirectores, Bogotá, Colombia

Jonathan Callund Callund y Compañía Ltda., Santiago, Chile

María de los Ángeles Lucero Bringas Faculty of Business and Economics, Universidad Católica de Córdoba, Córdoba, Argentina

Enrique Díaz Ortega ASCLA (Latin America Corporate Secretaries Association), Lima, Peru

Magdalena Díaz Le-Fort Chilean-Indian Chamber of Commerce, Vitacura, Chile;
Universidad del Desarrollo (UDD), Santiago, Chile

Hugo Gaggiotti Faculty of Business and Law, University of the West of England, Bristol, UK

Gonzalo Jiménez-Seminario Pontificia Universidad Católica de Chile, Santiago, Chile

Luiz Ricardo Kabbach de Castro School of Economics and Business, Universidad de Navarra, Pamplona, Spain

Dante Mendes Aldrighi Department of Economics, Universidade de São Paulo, São Paulo, Brazil

Carla Meza Morales Pontificia Universidad Católica de Chile, Santiago, Chile

Michelle Mora Governance Consultants, Bogotá, Colombia

Óscar Armando Pardo Aragón Faculty of Business Administration, Center of Studies in Comparative Governance, Universidad de Los Andes, Bogotá, Colombia

Edgar Rogelio Ramírez-Solís Tecnológico de Monterrey, Monterrey, Mexico

Catalina Rojas Governance Consultants, Bogotá, Colombia

Fernando Sandoval Institute of Business Families for Mexico and Latin America, Tecnológico de Monterrey, Monterrey, Mexico

Eulalia Sanín Kearney, Bogota, Colombia

Pablo Eugenio Souto is *Economist* from University of Buenos Aires, with graduate studies in Public Sector Economics at Universidad de San Andrés and International Economics at Kiel Institute for World Economics—Senior Associate at Global Outcomes.

Matias Zegers Ruíz-Tagle Pontificia Universidad Católica de Chile, Santiago, Chile

List of Figures

List of Tables

Chapter 6

Chapter 9

Chapter 11

CHAPTER 1

Introduction - Innovations & Drawbacks in Evolving Governing Practices

Gonzalo Jiménez-Seminario and Jonathan Callund

1 Setting the Theoretical Scene

Corporate governance refers to practices, theories, and dilemmas associated with the challenges of directing and controlling organizations (Bevir, 2011) in short *governing* them and, emphasizing the allocation of rights to information and decision-making among shareholders, board members, and the management team. The final purpose is to set the balance of empowerment and accountability to drive toward value creation by corporate leaders (directors and managers), while protecting an equitable distribution of the value created between internal and external stakeholders (Huse, 2007). However, corporate governance does not occur in a vacuum but more within distinctive institutional settings,

G. Jiménez-Seminario
Pontificia Universidad Católica de Chile, Santiago, Chile
e-mail: gjimenez@proteus.cl

J. Callund (✉)
Callund y Compañía Ltda., Santiago, Chile
e-mail: jonathan.callund@callund.cl

J. Callund et al. (eds.), *Corporate Governing in Latin America*,
https://doi.org/10.1007/978-3-030-85780-6_1

often characterized as *institutional logics* (Thornton & Ocasio, 1999), synthesizing the historical, cultural, and socio-political influences, which shape the practices, produce dilemmas, and engender theories to make greater sense of them. Moreover, such scenarios are not static in the slightest, but they are subject to the measures taken by *institutional entrepreneurs* pushing for change in these practices, often having themselves experienced the pain of limitations in the conventional espoused mental frameworks and theories. Thus, both academics and policymakers are confronted on their own with a need to update prevailing *theoretical lenses* in use and catch up with a permanently evolving arena.

This is particularly relevant in fast-changing environments, such as in emerging markets, which are logically inspired by the rapidly evolving practices of more advanced economies but are naturally constrained by swamped realities refusing to be boxed in by one-size-fits-all frameworks (Aguilera et al., 2018). Latin America faces these scenarios and has been struggling to combine modernity with historical concentrations of power. As such, it represents a fascinating landscape to study how the art of governing is being/has been (mis)applied, reformulated, and updated as a continuous and always turbulent process.

While the interplay between modernity and tradition is not exclusive to Latin America, the age-old patriarchal style of capitalism a recognized and distinctive feature of the subcontinent (Schneider, 2013). The commonplace business groups thrive in local markets, and global elites, well known to independent analysts, have been impressed by their dominion and influence over Chilean institutions (Rothkopf, 2008). As a consequence, studying how more democratic forms of governing fight for a new corporate deal, as well as, and, indirectly, for a new business-society deal, provides a fascinating window to observe the processes of institutional change, the reactions of the powers-that-be and the measures taken by daring institutional entrepreneurs.

Consequently, in this book, we discuss the continual evolution of corporate governance practices in Latin America. This evolution can be tied back to processes of adaptation to changing *institutional logics* embedded in distinctive socio-economic-political backgrounds over the last decades in Latin America. So, we pay special attention to *corporate governance innovations and drawbacks* in the largest Latin American countries,[1] describing the changing practices, the emerging dilemmas and the dominant institutional theories-in-use. For this purpose, we prefer inductive qualitative methods, such as case studies, interviewing key actors, and grounded theory methods to study how the practices are changing, and, consequently, how "*governing*" is evolving.

2 The Dilemmas

Since the beginning of the twenty-first century, the larger Latin American countries have seen an important and increasing frequency of corporate governance scandals that feature high profile industrialists and politicians from all sectors.

Naturally, the rising number of scandals might be taken as an indication of increased concern for governance matters, so making them more likely to come to light, higher levels of transparency, tighter, and more professional regulation, and a more informed public. Again, Latin America is far from being alone in experiencing such scandals, but that a tight-knit socio-economic system might be threatened or at least molested by government powers is new. But then, it would greatly surprise ancient statesmen to find that "small people" might feel powerful enough to dare to challenge "great people," and that the justice system would support such claims, the media would follow such stories and scandals become the subject of household small talk.

As a consequence, trust in private enterprise is at rock-bottom levels across the region,[2] leading to systematic questioning of large businesses, industrialists, wealthy families, and in more knowledgeable circles, the corporate governance of organizations and institutions, as well as their regulatory settings.

Cases of collusion, fraud, corporate abuses, and traffic of influence are commonplace in day-to-day conversations, and affairs have become well known (Undurraga, 2015). These developments have given shape

[1] In terms of population (2018) and GDP (2018) respectively, these are: Brazil (210 m/$3.530b), Mexico (126 m/$2,700b), Colombia (50 m/$790b), Argentina (44 m/900b), Peru (32 m/$490b) and Chile (19 m/$510b). Venezuela (29 m/$310b), Ecuador (17 m/$190b), Bolivia (11 m/$95b), and Uruguay (4 m/$90b) are not considered in this study.

[2] https://ourworldindata.org/trust.

to the idea that Latin American corporate governance is under increasing pressure (Agosín & Pastén, 2003; Aguilera et al., 2012).

However, this negative background contrasts with an increasing and widespread aspiration to incorporate best practices. For instance, a study by Acción, a CSR thinktank, finds that 70% of companies have redesigned their ESG norms over the last three years, that 86% of workers know them and 54% perceive their leaders foster a culture of ethics and probity (Acción,).[3]

These opposing trends converge into a paradox, raising the question of why corporate governance scandals keep appearing when there is in parallel a well-established trend to incorporate best practices. Greater understanding of corporate governance rules, actors, functions, and episodes in Latin America, are valuable both conceptually and in practice, acknowledging the past, present, and likely future evolution, facilitating understanding of these paradoxes, addressing the concerns of practitioners, and offering scholarly contributions.

In consequence, corporate governance scandals provide focal lenses through which to observe institutional changes in each country can be observed. We analyze how different institutional *rationales* are superimposed on the existing ones, so adding increasing layers of complexity. This research assesses the sources of corporate governance change in each country, associating them with transformations at institutional and societal levels. Finally, this book facilitates comparisons of corporate leaders' behaviors and attitudes towards both shareholders and stakeholders in each country, as well as their sensitivities in recognizing new governance imperatives. This cross-border investigation has allowed us to extract managerial and conceptual lessons, aiming at contributing practical guidance to entrepreneurs, investors, think tanks, regulators, multilateral agencies, and academics interested in discovering what "doing governance in Latin America" means and requires.

3 Attributes

In addition to its broad scope, perspective and conceptual perspective, the key attributes which make this book a distinctive contribution are:

[3] https://accionempresas.cl/herramientas/probidad-y-gobiernos-corporativos/.Accessed22 April 2022.

- An opportunity to understand, review and gain an updated perspective of the main governance models operating in the leading six countries in the region;
- Access to insider expertise in each country drawn from 21 experts, with unparalleled access to their respective governing elites, regulatory settings, and institutional logics;
- Its scholar-practitioner mix, combining rigor, and practical relevance;
- Its acting as a benchmark guide to corporate governance in emerging markets worldwide; and
- Its evolutionary perspective, allowing public policy designers and regulators to learn from eminently evolutionary governing processes and corporate crises in action.

Although this research is limited to Latin America, international researchers have made parallel claims that governance reforms seem to coexist with unsolved corporate issues. For example, Pound (1995) complained about corporate decision-making at the top in the USA; Carter & Lorsch (2003) called on directors to go "back to the drawing board" after the Enron and Andersen scandals; and Jaques (2003) warned that ethical curriculum changes in business schools would not solve the structural corporate governance problems, while making his own creative governance propositions. In the UK the pioneering *Cadbury Code* (1992) and its subsequent codification, namely the *Higgs Report Combined Code* (2003) and *UK Corporate Governance Code's* subsequent editions from 2010 to 2019,[4] have not stopped corporate scandals from continuing to happen. This has moved reformers to keep chasing what could be considered a moving target: first focusing on structural aspects, then targeting directors' independence, and finally attempting to modify behaviors, as proposed by Nordberg and McNulty (2013).

Implicit in this idea is the fact that paradoxes represent inflection points, inducing questioning processes, which might allow examination of the nature of a phenomenon when finding impossible to make sense of observations in terms of what is known about it. Thus, a paradox is an opportunity to start exploring "what we know we don't know" and in

[4] https://www.icaew.com/technical/corporate-governance/codes-and-reports/uk-corporate-governance-code.

the process to eventually find that "we don't know what we don't know" (Bourner & Pedler, 2005, p. 145).

In this book, the authors take on board Coglianese & Michael's suggestion in 2006 that "[d]eciding how to respond to corporate governance after the scandals will benefit from careful inquiry into how these scandals arose in the first place" (p. 20). Our rationale is that such endeavor seems both timely and useful for both scholars standing in the high ground of normative "good" governance, and practitioners immersed in the swamped realities of corporate governance practice happening on boards of directors of family business groups—the main kind of controlling owners in Latin America (Aldrighi & Postali, 2010; Fracchia et al., 2010; Hoshino, 2010; Lefort, 2010).

This book provides an overview of the comparative evolution of corporate governance practices across six Latin American countries, including an outlook of their foreseeable future, given the change agents and obstacles in place. Thus, this effort combining theory and practice shows what "governing in Latin America" looks like for interested and reflexive practitioners.

4 Aims

The purpose of this book is to explore how corporate governance has been understood, expressed, and configured in Latin America over the last two decades. Doing this involves exploring several more specific questions, including the following:

- How has corporate governance changed over time?
- What has driven these changes?
- Who are the change agents?
- Which challenges have they faced?
- What role have corporate scandals played in these changes?
- What can be learnt from these processes?

We review the trajectory of the developments in corporate governance in Latin America across an imaginary temporal axis involving the past, present, and future. We do so with the help of inductive tools drawn from diverse methodologies including case studies (Yin, 2009), legal analysis and grounded theory (Glaser & Strauss, 1967), among others. For this purpose, along with fellow co-editors, Gonzalo Jiménez-Seminario and Neil Pyper, we have engaged an extraordinary group of 18 scholar-practitioners, especially acquainted with the region's practices as well as the principal actors in the Latin American governance field. In their chapters, the authors explore the past and ongoing evolution of corporate governance, encouraging a systematic process of reflection, conceptualization, and learning.

The chapters have all been the subject of a rigorous double-blind review process, steered by Neil Pyper, and we acknowledge the work, critiques and suggestions of the many academics and professionals with deep experience in each of the territories under review; while keeping confidential their linkage to each specific chapter, all of whom will remain anonymous—you know who you are.... Many thanks! However, as editors we retain responsibility for the design and the structure of the book, the selection of its contents and the choice of authors and reviewers, as well as the coordination process.

A large part of this investigation has involved us in engaging with leading actors in the governing field in each territory and in Latin America as a whole, implying entering an arena of difficult access (Pettigrew, 1992), operating behind impassable gates (Carter & Lorsch, 2005). This has been facilitated by the scholar-practitioner status and networks of most authors, granting them a privileged window to observe governance from within. Thus, this endeavor represents a contribution to a field (governance) that is still in the process of becoming (Bevir, 2011)—justifying the use of the gerund, governing, and aspires to inform both academia and the professional practices of relevant actors—potentially stimulating behaviors that aim to increase accountability among key stakeholders.

5 What to Expect

As both editors and authors, as well as active practitioners in our own right, we hope this book will provide a useful guide for fellow practitioners, for business owners, directors and managers looking both to expand their local corporate governance background and innovate in the application of their own governance practices. We also expect this text to be of interest to regulators, stock exchanges, securities agents, trade associations and professionals in general in emerging markets and across the world.

Although not strictly the main nor unique target of this book, as expressed by the academic reviewers of this volume, we expect Academia to perceive this as a welcome addition to a knowledge void, namely, Latin American corporate governance practices. Theoretically, it goes some way to closing the gap between governance practices, institutional settings, and institutional entrepreneurship, so fostering the evolution of better practices. Therefore, we present this book as a contribution to knowledge creation covering a much-overlooked geographic region, where heady institutional changes are underway, both mirroring and expanding our understanding about the processes occurring in several other emerging markets around the world.

The next section provides a theoretical framework, helping to tie the practices and dilemmas back to existing theories. Practitioners may choose to skip this section and proceed directly to Chapter 3, which revisits emblematic Latin American corporate governance scandals, offering a lens to view the insights derived from such cases as seen by key governance practitioners in the region.

Chapter 4 provides a comparative regional overview of the main regulatory and self-regulatory developments of corporate governance in the countries under study, concluding with proposals for the prospective outlook of corporate governing in the region, proffering both conceptual and practical implications.

Building on these, Chapter 4 provides both theoretical and empirical contributions in exploring the past and current trajectories of corporate governing in Latin America, and, in the process, we formulate a tentative "theory of practice" framework for corporate governance practitioners to reflect on, update and eventually reassess their own work perspectives.

The subsequent chapters—6 to 9—drafted by territory specialists provide comprehensive assessments on corporate governance developments in each of the six countries under review.

References

Acción Empresas (2015/2022), https://accionempresas.cl/herramientas/probidad-y-gobiernos-corporativos/. Accessed 20 April 2022.

Agosin, M. R., & Pastén, E. (2003). Corporate governance in Chile. *Documentos De Trabajo (banco Central De Chile), 209*, 1–25.

Aguilera, R. V., Judge, W. Q., & Terjesen, S. A. (2018). Corporate governance deviance. *Academy of Management Review, 43*(1), 87–109.

Aguilera, R. V., Kabbach-Castro, L. R., Lee, J. H., & You, J. (2012). Corporate governance in emerging markets.

Aldrighi, D. M. & Postali, F. A. S. (2010). Business groups in Brazil. https://doi.org/10.1093/oxfordhb/9780199552863.003.0013

Alasuutari, P., & Qadir, A. (2014). Epistemic governance: An approach to the politics of policymaking. *European Journal of Cultural and Political Sociology, 1*(1), 67–84. https://doi.org/10.1080/23254823.2014.887986doi: 10.1080/23254823.2014.887986

Bevir, M. (2011). Governance as theory, practice, and dilemma. *The SAGE handbook of governance*, 1–16.

Bourner, T., & Simpson, P. (2005). Practitioner-centred research and the Ph.D. *Action Learning: Research and Practice, 2*, 133–151.

Cadbury, A. (2002). Corporate governance. In *EFMD Forum*, 2, 4–10.

Carter, C. B., & Lorsch, J. W. (2003). *Back to the drawing board: Designing corporate boards for a complex world.* Harvard Business Press.

Carter, C. B., & Lorsch, J. W. (2005). The role model of the board: A preliminary study of the roles of Icelandic boards.

Coglianese, C., & Michael, M. L. (2006). After the scandals: Changing relationships in corporate governance.

Council, F. R. (2012, September). The UK Corporate Governance Code.

Council, F. R. (2017). *Proposed revisions to the UK Corporate Governance Code.* FRC.

Council, F. R., & Britain, G. (2010). The UK Corporate Governance Code.

Fracchia, E., Mesquita, L., & Quiroga, J. (2010). *Business groups in Argentina.* The Oxford handbook of business groups.

Glaser, B. & Strauss, A. L. (1967). *The discovery of grounded theory: Strategies for qualitative research*, Transaction publishers.

Higgs, D. (2003). Higgs Report on Non-executive directors: Summary Recommendations. *January.* Available via the Internet: www.Berr.Gov.uk/files/file23012.Pdf

Hoshino, Taeko (2010). Business groups in Mexico, en A.M. Colpan, T.

Huse, M. (2007). *Boards, governance and value creation: The human side of corporate governance.* Cambridge University Press.

Jaques, E. (2003). Ethics for management. *Management Communication Quarterly, 17*(1), 136–142.

Lefort, F. (2010). Business Groups in Chile. In Oxford Handbook of Business Groups, edited by A. Colpan, T. Hikino, and J. Lincoln. Oxford: Oxford university Press, 2010. https://doi.org/10.1093/oxfordhb/9780199552863.003.0014

Nordberg, D., & McNulty, T. (2013). Creating better boards through codification: Possibilities and limitations in UK corporate governance, 1992–2010. *Business History, 55*(3), 348–374.

Nordberg, D. (2010). *Corporate governance: Principles and issues*. Sage.
Pettigrew, A. M. (2008). On studying managerial elites. In *The Value Creating Board* (pp. 179–207). Routledge.
Pettigrew, A., & Mcnulty, T. (1995). Power and influence in and around the boardroom. *Human Relations, 48*, 845–873.
Pound, J. (1995). The promise of the governed corporation. *Harvard Business Review, 73*(2), 89–98.
Rothkopf, D. (2008). *Superclass: The global power elite and the world they are making*. Farrar.
Schneider, Ben Ross. (2013). Hierarchical Capitalism in Latin America. Business, Labor and the Challenges of Equitable Development, p. 237. New York: Cambridge University Press.
Thornton, P. H., & Ocasio, W. (1999). Institutional logics and the historical contingency of power in organizations: Executive succession in the higher education publishing industry, 1958–1990 1. *American Journal of Sociology, 105*, 801–843.
Okike, E. (2019). Corporate governance in the United Kingdom. *Corporate Governance in Commonwealth Countries (S. 337–365)*.
Undurraga, T. (2015). Neoliberalism in Argentina and Chile: Common antecedents, divergent paths. *Revista De Sociologia e Política, 23*, 11–34.
Yin, R. K. (2009). Case study research: Design and methods (Vol. 5). Sage.
Yin, R. K. (2011). Applications of case study research. Sage.

CHAPTER 2

Theoretical Framework

Gonzalo Jiménez-Seminario

In this chapter, which draws heavily on the literature review and doctoral thesis of Jiménez-Seminario (2018), we conceptualize corporate governance and review relevant literature on governance, both in Latin America and more broadly; as well as placing it within the context of several high-level theoretical areas that we draw on collectively in the book, namely: *New Institutional Economics*, *Resource Dependence Theory* and (New) *Institutional Theory*. We then outline the country chapters as well as the findings emanating from them. Finally, we conclude with theoretical and practical implications.

1 Literature Review

Governance is a function that has been around for as long as humans have existed. Nonetheless, it remains difficult to define precisely, generally tending to be given a broad range of meanings across diverse academic disciplines (Bevir, 2011). However, despite such variety, *governing* can be

G. Jiménez-Seminario (✉)
Pontificia Universidad Católica de Chile, Santiago, Chile
e-mail: gjimenez@proteus.cl

J. Callund et al. (eds.), *Corporate Governing in Latin America*,
https://doi.org/10.1007/978-3-030-85780-6_2

taken to mean the making sense of what is going on, identifying a key theme, transforming such a theme into a vision, developing a strategy to achieve that vision, and using this insight consistently to direct, control, empower, and hold people (including rulers) to account, while retaining the ability to question the motivations, processes, roles, and outcomes (Bevir, 2011; Dean, 2010; Foucault, 1994).

However, given the many intangible facets of governance, it is only natural that some aspects may tend to become invisible in normal times and, consequently, be ignored or even forgotten. That is why it should not come as a surprise that, as Banner (1997) concluded, after studying "300 years of evidence," the "question of governance" systematically comes back to haunt us after every major crash.

Moreover, the focus, in terms of guilt and recriminations, tends to be placed on breaches in fiduciary governance (Chait et al., 2005). Several responsibilities are frequently missed, for instance, inadequate compliance with the *duty of care*[1], by not asking "what is the problem?," which is the most visible aspect of any crises. However, more in-depth analysis should point to faults in "generative governance" (Chait et al., 2005), i.e., questioning just "what is the purpose?" and "what are the values?" of the organization. Indeed, it is symptomatic that a common aspect of many scandals is the fact that nobody was able to question, in a timely manner, the raison d'être of the organization, nor notice that the common practices-in-use were often in direct opposition to the organization's espoused corporate ideals and values. And it appears as even more sinister that the strategic governance "plan" in place might just have implied particularly efficient ways to achieve a maligned purposes (Banner, 1997; Chait et al., 2005; Coffee, 2005).

The usual ex-post responses to such difficulties have tended to emanate from three flanks:

- *Governance*, when understood as best practices exemplified by Carter and Lorsch's (2003, p. 1) calls to go "back to the drawing board,"

[1] *Duty of care* is the requirement that directors be present, informed, and engaged, using good and independent judgment, consulting experts for their advice and trusted information where necessary and staying abreast of legal developments, good governance, and best practices that affect the company of which they are a board member—https://www.investopedia.com/terms/d/duty-care.asp.

that is, back to basics, recovering forgotten (or unknown) practices of good governing.
- *Governance*, when interpreted as a set of incorruptible values capable of overcoming individualism and unhealthy systemic interrelationships—often seen as the ultimate drivers of corporate governance scandals (Coglianese & Michael, 2006); and
- *Governance*, when seen as regulation "to rectify perceived governance weaknesses in [...] legal systems," especially after corporate collapses (Hill, 2012, p. 367).

However, such standard responses have all been tested, to some degree, have fallen short before the vast and amorphous dimensions of the challenge. Thus, a holistic governing perspective might prove more useful. In this context, Bevir (2011)'s proposition of governance as "...new theories of social coordination and new worlds of collective action..." appears to encapsulate the generative aspect mentioned above and has uses when looking at both the past and the future.

Unfortunately, as already mentioned, governance is far too common a term in a broad range of fields, particularly in economics, finance, management, geography, political science, sociology, public administration, and development studies (Bevir, 2011). What is more, "[e]ach discipline sometimes acts as if it owns the word and has no need to engage with the others" (Bevir, 2011, p. 1). Thus, governance is frequently studied from diverse perspectives, including: principles, policies and practices (Tricker, 2012), key concepts (Bevir, 2009), relationships (Coglianese & Michael, 2006), social coordination issues and practices of rule (Bevir, 2011), regulation (Horn, 2012), structures, roles and influence (McNulty et al., 2011), managerial incentives (Bos et al., 2013), incentives associated with economic institutions (North, 1990), and institutional logics (Westphal & Zajac, 2013), among many others.

However, a silo mentality, while useful in knowledge development in terms of focus and efficient reductionism, fails to pick up on important insights from neglected disciplines. Hence, a different mode of knowledge that is not limited by artificial boundaries and is needed to facilitate a broader range of insights to be integrated around the common challenge.

As made clear by Tricker (2012), the theoretical fundaments of corporate governance are often fragmented without a single shared integrative paradigm. Therefore, it would seem natural to stay open to the contributions from existing theories with the intention of gathering insights from diverse perspectives in an attempt to capture the elusive concept on the fly of practice.

Given such diversity, this chapter briefly reviews three theories, which appear to be most directly relevant to the investigations contained in this volume. Arguably, these theories are the most encompassing of macro and micro governance effects of direct interest to conceptualize this research: *New Institutional Economics*, *Resource-Dependence Theory*, and (New) *Institutional Theory*.

1.1 New Institutional Economics (NIE)

New Institutional Economics is a perspective originally derived from the work of Ronald Coase (1937), coined by Oliver Williamson in 1975 to extend neoclassical economic principles[2]—in particular, transactions costs theory—to institutional arrangements. NIE studies the effects of economic, social, and political institutions on economic behaviors and the performance of markets. Institutions are defined as "the humanly devised constraints that shape human interaction" (North, 1990, p. 3). Institutions "structure incentives in human exchange, whether political, social, or economic" and therefore institutions are key drivers of economic performance and development. Thus, for NIE, institutions are basically the rules of the game that economic agents play. Institutions are taken to be in permanent evolution and change due to the influence of external shocks and/or the action of institutional entrepreneurs; proactive, resourceful, and self-interested actors (North & Thomas, 1970). Because of such interplay, countries achieve either virtuous or vicious cycles of development, or stagnation (North, 1990).

NIE humanizes traditional economic theories, which tend to rely on under-socialized, highly rational actors pursuing their individual goals, directed by self-interest and personal risk inclinations, who are subject to information constraints and driven by incentives associated with stable preferences. The main governance mechanisms recognized by NIE are formal and informal incentives channeling behaviors and monitoring arrangements linked to economic and social goals. Failures of governance

[2] Neoclassical economics is a broad theory that focuses on supply and demand as the driving forces behind the production, pricing, and consumption of goods and services. It emerged in around 1900 to compete with the earlier theories of classical economics—https://www.investopedia.com/terms/n/neoclassical.asp.

systems, might lead to calls for greater regulatory attention, including contract-enforcement agencies and/or coercion-constraining institutions (Greif, 2008; Menard & Shirley, 2012).

NIE provides an initial theoretical framework by placing emphasis on the following aspects:

- Institutions, that reflect the rules of the corporate governance game played by actors and organizations.
- Rules, that might include both enforcing and coercion-constraining aspects, consequently, virtuous, or vicious cycles might derive therefrom; and
- Institutions, that change and evolve with the actions of institutional entrepreneurs.

However, NIE's (still) under-socialized nature of actors can be problematic. This theory is narrowly defined as self-interested actors only respond to positive or negative incentives. It can also put in doubt the purported and implicit fixed set of preferences of economic actors, given their institutional evolution; which, in turn, might transform these incentives, broaden the preferences, and mutate social attitudes; propelling a drive toward new, unintended, and unanticipated equilibriums. Such a process might be better explained through less economic but more social and informal mechanisms, as captured by socially embedded practices, beliefs, and attitudes (Pacheco et al., 2010).

Despite such weaknesses, the implicit paradigms adopted by governance policymakers in most of the six countries under review respond to such a logic, so NIE provides a useful initial perspective with which to frame the ideas set out in this book.

In this research, both Chile and Peru feature as *textbook* examples of NIE, in which self-interest, formalistic compliance and minimal adherence to the spirit of regulations seem to be the name of the game for some important actors. And so, hard law seems to be the critical institutional pillar fully respected; while cognitive and normative pillars are perhaps seen as optional or superfluous (Scott & Davis, 2007).

1.2 Resource Dependence Theory (RDT)

Resource Dependence Theory, proposed by Jeffrey Pfeffer and colleagues (Aldrich & Pfeffer, 1976; Salancik et al., 1978), combines an organizational theory of how organizations deal with their social environments with critical reflections on both intra-organizational and extra-organizational power. Their insights explain how organizations develop strategies to deal with resource dependencies (Pfeffer & Salancik, 2003). RDT has sometimes been characterized with the phrase: "when it came to explaining strategy, power often trumped profits" (Davis & Cobb, 2010, p. 5). Therefore, RDT might explain why certain organizations are able to harness more power than their counterparts because of different degrees of interdependence deriving from their positioning in socio-political networks, including the government and other social actors (Pfeffer & Salancik, 2003).

The main application of RDT centers around the formation of boards of directors and the formation of strategic alliances, as well as the relationships with political powers. Despite RDT's wide potential applicability and common-sense appeal, empirical studies over the last 30 years have not been very supportive of its tenets. This may in part be due to widely changing socioeconomic circumstances (Davis & Cobb, 2010).

RTD's main contributions in setting out a theoretical framework for this book are as follows:

- Environments affect organizations (and actors);
- Organizations (and actors) actively attempt to manage the external constraints on their environments; and
- External environmental constraints affect organizational dynamics.

The implication of these ideas is that, as Pfeffer (2003, p. 287) says, "corporate behavior can be more readily explained by resource dependence ideas than by ideas of efficient markets or even investor capitalism."

However, the relatively micro perspective of external environments under RDT can also give rise to problems, as it leaves some level of indeterminacy or ambiguity in its interpretation of the macro-sources of resource dependence—vis-à-vis institutional environments. For instance, Pfeffer & Salancik (2003) cite the studies by Fligstein (1997) and Thornton and Ocasio (1999) of the financial and publishing industries, respectively, as evidence supporting the search to secure external resources as proposed by RDT. However, in his argumentation, he does not assume the crux of *Institutional Theory* at the heart of these studies: the evolution of the macro-institutional logics determining most other properties in these industrial fields.

Pfeffer (2003) states that resource-dependence varies over time and that, consequently, environmental contexts should be researched systematically. This longitudinal sense-making perspective is illuminating for this research. Indeed, this book attempts precisely to do just that—to capture the institutional evolution on-the-fly and its influences in the current governing paradigm across the six countries.

It also makes sense to retain RDT's proposition of paying attention to non-market strategies, including active links developed by organizations with political, economic, and social activities. This last aspect points toward exploring the role played by power in business and society. Another well researched aspect by the authors in this volume.

For examples of this, see the Mexico and Brazil chapters. In Mexico power is tightly retained by controlling family elites, reluctant to accept limits being placed on their dominance and even less to share it with minority shareholders. In Brazil, we see the open struggle between the evangelists of modernization, pro-investment agencies, such as AMEC and the association of listed companies, ABRASCA, attempting to hold on to their historical advantages.

1.3 Institutional Theory (IT)

Institutional Theory sees institutions as social constructs formed by informal rules or cultural norms, generating practices, behaviors, and belief systems, thus, positing that cultural meaning encompass organizational structures, policies, and practices.

The heart of modern *Institutional Theory* is the prevailing institutional logic (Friedland & Alford, 1991) of the "organizing principles that furnish guidelines to actors as to how to behave" (Rao et al., 2003, p. 797). These logics go some way to explaining the basis for the configuring actors' social identity, including, but going beyond systems of incentives, and providing meaning to individual endeavors. Thus, existing theories of corporate governance, such as Agency Theory, might be seen as corresponding to "institutional logics" containing culturally meaningful social directions (Thornton & Ocasio, 2008; Thornton, Ocasio & Lounsbury, 2012; Westphal & Zajac, 2013).

Neo-institutional theorists have given a stronger emphasis to the role of individual agency and purposeful action in the generation and abandonment of institutions (DiMaggio, 1998; Fligstein, 1997; Oliver, 1991). As discussed above, new institutional theory (NIT) assumes that individuals are self-interested and act to transform their institutional environment by re-aligning it with their individual goals. Thus, the distinguishing factor of NIT is introducing the concept of the institutional entrepreneur as an actor, who manages, and mobilizes resources to bring about change and/or create new institutional structures (DiMaggio, 1998; Pacheco et al., 2010).

While institutional theory takes a broader macro-perspective on theories of corporate governance, proposing that firm-actor relationships are embedded in a larger sociocultural context (Westphal & Zajac, 2013), behavioral governance researchers have contributed to this institutional perspective by suggesting how organization-level social and political processes moderate the institutional influences on governance structures and policies (ibid.).

According to Westphal and Zajac (2013), there is a lack of studies on institutional change in corporate governance. They compare Friedland and Alford (1991), who define such evolutions as transformations at a societal level, affecting the institutional logics of organizations, with a more stringent definition by Fiss (2007); which includes transformations in the "institutional status" or in the social legitimacy of specific policies, structures, or forms (Fiss, 2007). And they add that most research does not satisfy Fiss's more constraining definition, as most researchers focus on institutionalization or de-institutionalization processes of governance procedures and configurations. An exception is Fligstein (1990)'s study of changing conceptions of control in the corporate field—a conceptualization that goes further than the traditional industrial setting. They also affirm that there have been even fewer serious studies of the sources of institutional evolution (Westphal & Zajac, 2013).

For the purposes of this book, we retain as relevant as part of the theoretical framework for this research the following insights from institutional theory:

- The relevance of cultural and meaning systems guiding social actions, structures, and policies, and the resulting impact in legitimacy (institutional status) of achieving a coherent alignment with such informal rules;
- The role of institutional entrepreneurs as proactive actors, generating institutional change; and
- The relevance of institutional logic as the cultural matrix defining organizing, behaving, and governing appropriate collective practices.

However, it can be argued that Institutional Theory tends to assign an overly generic perspective to the role of institutional entrepreneurs, and that the discipline of entrepreneurship might further enrich our understanding of entrepreneurs' roles, strategies, and their own logics, as argued by Pacheco et al. (2010). In addition, given the increasing role being played by social movements theories, NIT insights should be allied to the conceptualization of institutional entrepreneurs (Lounsbury, 2007). Thus, in this book, we maintain a state of alertness to observe and capture the relevant role of institutional entrepreneurship as catalyzers of institutional change.

The Colombian and Argentinian cases align well with NIT. In Colombia, business groups, such as Grupo Empresarial Antioqueño, through the mechanism of director interlocks, act as institutional entrepreneurs, favoring the dissemination of best governance practices among their participating companies while propelling a drive toward the incorporation of board evaluation as a key governance instrument. In the Argentinian cases, we are faced with the challenges posed by the lack of social trust and its implications in professionalization, delegation, and the development of the capital market.

2 Corporate Governing Evolution in Emerging Markets

In a study covering the realities of emerging and transition markets, Aguilera, Judge and Tejersen (2016) provide a bridge between institutional logics and national governance logics. They define institutional logics as the "socially-constructed assumptions, values, beliefs, formal and informal rules, and practices that equip organizations with a toolkit to interpret their experiences, direct their attention toward specific choices, define future goals, and limit their potential organizational choices" (p. 5).

We concur with the explicit assumption of Aguilera et al. (2016) that a multiplicity of logics exists in all countries. However, we remain doubtful about the predominance of a unique dominant governing logic delineating firms' conduct to obtain an "adequate level" of legitimacy—which these authors see as determined by both their internal corporate governance practices and their external governance influences. As some of the country chapters show, we have reason to remain more skeptical vis à vis their proposition that a single logic ends up dominating any of the others. In Peru, modernizing logics co-exist, and are in permanent tension, with traditional institutional settings. In Chile, Jiménez-Seminario (2018) has demonstrated the parallel influences of economic, political, and social logics. In Brazil, logic clashes quickly turn into legal fights between advocates of accountability and transparency versus sustainers of the status quo. In Colombia, we also see the same pressures of promoters of governing change and those defending traditional practices. However, in Argentina and Mexico, there is more evidence of dominant patriarchal logics, based on family control, imbalances of power, and resistance to the adoption of international best practices, so aligning with Aguilera and her colleagues.

Therefore, we are left with the question of how to take stock of the dynamics of those pushing for change and the forces opposing it. Thus, we need to look beyond Latin America to other emerging markets that are more advanced in considering and into account and assimilating updated corporate governance practices.

Park, Zhang and Keister (2020) propose viewing the multiplicity of governance practices as the consequence of innovation processes aimed at improving the alignment between "prototypical best practices" and the "idiosyncratic institutional or industry contexts." In their study, they research Chinese and Korean cases and conclude that innovation in governance is subject to both constraints and enablers, where the constraints take the form of relationships and culture through the companies in which they are embedded. Likewise, the enablers are factors such as the social positions and distinct experiences of "change agents" within a given organization. These two factors work in the following manner:

- **Embeddedness** contributes to *maintaining* and *adjusting* national governance practices embraced by companies in emerging nations, and
- **Agency** facilitates governance innovation initiatives by providing stimulus to adopt *new viewpoints generating novel governance practices*. The social status and specific experiences of directors and managers empower them to promote such innovative agencies. The agency of national managers encourages the adoption of global practices, renovating local governance.

Figure 1 illustrates Park, Zhang and Keister (2020) theoretical perspective on corporate governance innovation. The authors show that, while relational embeddedness might both restrict and facilitate governance innovation, cultural embeddedness tends to constrain—or even *decouple*—espoused practices from in-use practices.

Agency, on the other hand, constitutes an empowering influence to update companies' governance practices willingly (Emirbayer & Mische, 1998; Sewell, 1993). This is facilitated by its loose coupling with more established, local institutions. In other words, actors who are more on the periphery of networks and distant from elites are allowed greater

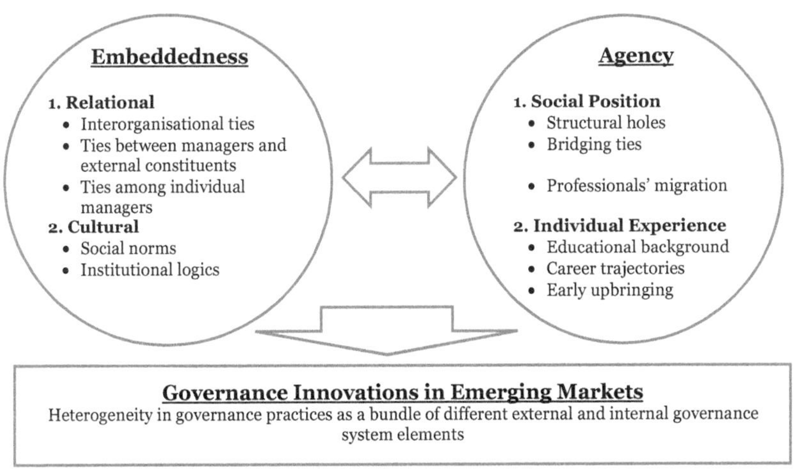

Fig. 1 Mechanisms of Governance Innovations in Emerging Markets (*Source* Park, Zhang and Keister [2020])

degrees of freedom to deviate from dominant national institutional logics. Similarly, higher degrees of freedom are enjoyed by organizations led by managers trained at global business schools, as well as those who have had experience working with multinational corporations.

Therefore, a focus on embeddedness and agency, again flagged by Park et al. (2020), provides a strong framework for understanding the diverse kinds of governance innovations. In their own words: "*from the decoupling of local practices from global rules to change agents' voluntary acceptance of and experimentation with new governance practices*" (p. 334). In addition, firms in emerging nations are profoundly influenced both by institutional logics related to the market economy, as well as by other logics deriving from the power of their "principals," home-based actors; chiefly among them founding families as well as State agencies.

From the previous flows, a natural alignment with the following definition of corporate governance innovation to help making sense of how organizations and people governance practices are evolving:

Corporate governance innovation is "*the reconfiguration of existing governance practice elements to balance the institutional demand* [for legitimacy] *of the external governance system and the efficiency requirements of internal governance activities*" (Park et al., 2020, p. 338).

In our six national chapters regulatory and institutional settings represent the external governance system, while ownership structures and owners' identities, forms of company control, and characteristics of management mirror the internal governing conditions.

Thus, Park et al. (2020) provide a dynamic perspective to research the evolution of corporate governance standards and offer a useful conceptual umbrella to situate the heterogeneous national arrangements of the six countries under study.

3 Main Findings: The Institutional Construction of Corporate Governing

The above conceptualization helps frame this research project—covering six primary Latin America countries in its attempt at exploring how the interactions between; exemplary global best practices; distinctive institutional and industry settings; and institutional entrepreneurs (Jiménez-Seminario, 2018) converge into a variety of governing practices. And thus, facilitate understanding these local practices as products of their respective parallel innovation processes—led by institutional innovators aiming at aligning global best practices—and national institutional or industry contexts (Park et al., 2020).

To illustrate this, we refer briefly to the prototype best practices; the idiosyncratic contexts, and the main institutional entrepreneurs driving corporate governance innovations in Latin America according to the six country chapters presented in the book.

Table 1 summarizes the preliminary ideas proposed by the authors of each national chapter.

Figure 2 places into general contexts the preliminary ideas researched by the authors of each national chapter.

As the figure shows, there exist tight-knit networks of powerful family business groups, accompanied by sets of loyal board members acting as interlocks between the largest companies. Those firms tend to exert large measures of control in concentrated markets. In small and closely held markets, the pool of qualified directors is shallow, and trust comes at a premium—cultivated and assured though dense, multiplexing professional, family, and educational ties. This age-old status is fast being eroded by more globalized financial, consumer, and production markets derived from a sustained internalization since early 90's. Another source of the breakdown in these traditional ties is the regular and more professionally and effectively enforced regulations introduced to enhance competitive market practices.

As will be seen, the emergence of the Chilean *Chicago Boys* in Chile was an important catalyzer of change in the region. Their example of liberalization was closely emulated—although not immediately, but over a decade or more—by the other five studied countries, among others. This precursory move was soon followed by thorough overhauls and updates to domestic securities commissions and anti-trust agencies, encouraging many of the countries to seek membership of the OECD and so greater exposure to international regulations, leading to standardized metrics and minimum audit requirements. Moreover, and as a source of some expectation, has been the gradual emergence of self-regulation, promoted by the domestic stock-exchanges, chambers of commerce, investors, and business associations alike, as seen through the positive development on interlocks in Colombia. International institutional investors, such as BlackRock, are also a valuable setter of higher corporate governance standards. Lastly, the COVID-19 pandemic brought an array of virtual remote connections, enabling faster knowledge sharing and further promoting the adoption of new practices.

Table 1 Institutional Context vs Institutional Entrepreneurs vs Best Practices

Institutional context	*Institutional entrepreneurs*	*Prototype best practices*[3]
Argentina • Underdeveloped capital market. • Dominant family lineages. • 'Trust', as an essential but scarce management attribute. • Families directly involved in management. • Scarcity of external managers, seen as a potential source of mistrust, partially mitigated by long-term friendships. • Lack of stable institutional conditions possibly fosters manipulation of rules and regulations. • Politicization of economic crime and repetitive corrupt practices.	• Mainly the regulatory agencies: National Securities Commission (CNV); Superintendency of Banking and Insurance (SBS). • Chief of Cabinet of Ministers promoting good corporate governance of State-owned enterprises.	• 2012, National Securities Commission regulates corporate governance practices to ensure "transparency" and "trust", requiring companies to incorporate a *Corporate Governance Code*, including the self-assessment of the board and their degree of compliance. • 2017, Superintendency of Banking and Insurance (SBS): regulation on Good Corporate Governance and Comprehensive Risk Management for financial entities and insurance companies, emphasizes board practices; risk control and management issues. • Public tender offer procedures established by CNV.

[3] For a comprehensive list of advancements seek.

Institutional context	*Institutional entrepreneurs*	*Prototype best practices*
Brazil		
• Governance of publicly traded companies biased in favor of controlling blockholders, frequently expropriating minority shareholders. • Poor legal protection and powerless watchdog (CVM)—empowered subsequently by a federal law. • Highly concentrated ownership exhibiting family control through control-enhancing mechanisms. • Controlling shareholders' association (ABRASCA) lobby vehicle. • Federal Government and its agencies as controlling or influential minority shareholders of major publicly traded companies. • Privatizations induced the formation of consortia formed by Brazilian business groups; foreign companies; and employees' pension funds of state-controlled enterprises, financed with subsidized loans from BNDES—the national development bank.	• São Paulo Stock Exchange (BOVESPA)'s private-led institutional innovation using *Deutsche Borse's Neuer Markt* as role model. • Global investors demand corporate accountability according to stricter governance standards than those legally mandated. • Changes in corporate and securities laws, empowering CVM, and its enforcement capabilities. • Multiple corporate wrongdoings, placing social, environmental, and ethical issues on center stage.	• Empowerment of CVM. • BOVESPA's Novo Mercado as a major institutional breakthrough, propelling a constant drive towards: - Protection of minority shareholders' rights. - Enhancement of transparency and disclosure requirements. - Creation of an Enforcement Office in 2008. • Constant revision of requirements to make insiders more liable to outside investors. • Independent directors required for companies listed on *Novo Mercado*. • Separation of the *CEO* and *Chairman* duties/positions. • Disclosure of insiders' securities trading policies.

(continued)

Table 1 (continued)

Institutional context	*Institutional entrepreneurs*	*Prototype best practices*
Chile • Family dominance and company control. • Market concentration. • 'Country Club' setting (Jiménez-Seminario, 2018). • Powerless regulation and weak enforcement. • Political changes (pro-market military dictatorship; pro-market social democracy; social unrest).	• Influence of Chicago-trained economists to impose a free market economy. • Role of Spanish MNCs as main foreign investors in regulated public sectors at moment of return of democracy. • Centre-left board members acting as government-business interlocks, facilitating interactions. • Social movements' reaction against political and business elites, catalyzed by corporate scandals. Entrance into OECD implied updates in regulation. • Scandals acted as catalyzers of new laws and practices. • Attempts by the Financial Market Commission (CMF) to generate changes through the "Comply or Not & Explain" system.	• Three subsequent institutional logics influencing corporate governance practices: - Shareholder value logic incorporated under economic (Friedman-inspired) institutional logic. From the early 70s onwards. - Corporate political behavior of politically exposed corporations under political institutional logic. From the early 90s onwards. - Corporate Social Responsibility practices are gaining predominance as a reaction to social unrest. Social institutional logic. From the 2010s onwards. • Corporate governance regulation embedded in law lacks flexibility and effective impact. • Ongoing debates about gender balance and worker representation in boards.

Institutional context	*Institutional entrepreneurs*	*Prototype best practices*
Colombia		
• Most companies have a controlling shareholder; typically, founding families. • Company crossholdings by corporate owners (business groups) controlling leading companies. • A network of ***interlocking*** board members, serving on multiple boards	• International and institutional investment of leading companies exposing them to governance standards of mature markets. • Evolution and sophistication of both securities' regulator and financial market regulator. • Competition Authority's prominent cases and large penalties, including penal responsibility of board members. • Voluntary adoption of external standards by leading companies (*Dow Jones Sustainability Index*) fostered the practice of external board *assessment*. • First ***external assessments*** spread to leading companies, via ***interlocking*** board members. • Demonstration effect, helped accelerate adoption.	• Initial regulation established by *Colombian Commerce Code* (CCC) of financial institutions. • Implementation of two rounds of *Código País* (voluntary corporate governance code; mandatory reporting for listed companies & bonds issuers). • Evolution in the design and composition of leading companies' boards and external evaluations of boards effectiveness. • Move away from "aesthetic" box ticking practices. • Voluntary adoption of *Dow Jones* ***Sustainability Index*** enhances recognition of ***external assessments*** of board performance. • Implementation of two rounds of *Código País* (voluntary corporate governance code). • Application to OECD implied changes to governance of State-owned enterprises: removal of conflicted Ministers and Regulators from boards and creation of a State Holding company to govern State investments.

(continued)

Table 1 (continued)

Institutional context	*Institutional entrepreneurs*	*Prototype best practices*
Mexico • Most firms are family businesses. • Regardless of size, dominant firms are founded, owned, and managed by families or their descendants. • Most board members linked to shareholders through family ties, friendships, business relationships, and employment contracts (53% of company managers are also managers of another company in the same group or are family relatives of executives of the same company).[4] • Chair is usually the main stockholder and CEO in most firms, 92% of chairs are family members. Independent board members create little opposition to chairs and have a limited role. • Just 30% of firms allow a majority of external members on boards and only where they are also involved with other companies within the same business group.[5]	• Mexican Stock Exchange. • The federal government agency: National Banking and Stock Commission (Comisión Nacional Bancaria y de Valores). • The private institution: Mexican Institute of Best Corporate Practices (*Instituto Mexicano de Mejores Prácticas Corporativas*). • The private association of Mexican entrepreneurs: Corporate Governance Best Practices Committee of the Business Coordinating Council (*Comité de Mejores Prácticas de Gobierno Corporativo del Consejo Coordinador Empresarial*). • The professional association: Committee of Best Corporate Practices of the Mexican Institute of Public Accountants (*Comité de Mejores Prácticas Corporativas del Instituto Mexicano de Contadores Públicos*).	• On the initiative of the Business Coordinating Council (CCE), the Committee of Best Corporate Practices was formed in 1999, which, together with the Mexican Institute of Public Accountants, and other industrial, government, financial and services organizations, prepared the Code of Principles and Best Practices of Corporate Governance (*Código de Principios y Mejores Prácticas de Gobierno Corporativo*). • The CCE asked the National Banking and Stock Commission to issue provisions. Companies listed on the Mexican Stock Exchange need to reveal their degree of adherence to suggested practices or explain them. • The Code's recommendations apply to all companies, whether of a civil, commercial, or social assistance nature, without distinguishing size, shareholding composition, or whether they are listed or not. This feature distinguishes this code from others that exist in the world.

[4] Husted, B., & Serrano, C. (2002). Corporate governance in México. *Journal of Business Ethics, 37*(3), 337–348.

[5] Espinoza Aguiló, T., & Espinoza Aguiló, N. (2012). Family business performance: Evidence from Mexico. *Cuadernos de Administración, 25*(44), 39–61.

Institutional context	*Institutional entrepreneurs*	*Prototype best practices*
• 69% of CEOs belong to the owner family; 85% of CEOs are also members of the Board; CEO duality is 38% in most prominent family firms listed. Mexico has lowest female representation on boards, 6%. Less managerial discretion in family firms than in non-family firms.[6] • Corporate systems similar to European or Latin-American governance models than with the Anglo-Saxon ones, given relatively concentrated ownership. • Only 34% of family businesses have boards.[7]		• Other particular best practices in this Mexican code include: - recommendations to incorporate women on the board - the selection, hiring, evaluation, and compensation of directors - the development of a ***Family Agreement*** for representation in governing bodies, and - a new Risk and Compliance function in one special committee of corporate governance.

(continued)

[6] Vázquez, P., Carrera, A., & Cornejo, M. (2020). Corporate governance in the largest family firms in Latin America. *Cross-Cultural & Strategic Management*, *27*(2), 137–163.

[7] Sandoval-Arzaga, F. (2021). *Radiografía de la Empresa Familiar Latinoamericana*. Estudio Preliminar. Instituto de Familias Empresarias para México y Latinoamérica, Escuela de Negocios, Tecnológico de Monterrey.

Table 1 (continued)

Institutional context	*Institutional entrepreneurs*	*Prototype best practices*
Peru		
• A general lack of independent directors in the listed companies and particularly in those companies recognized as GCG,[8] has not grown significantly. • This also leads to a practice that the same people are now being designated to the boards of different companies or are seen to rotate among said companies.	• Regulator initiatives to order and guide the corporate governance of companies through standards (practices) and regulations. • Regulator, CONASEV[9] *Special Task Force* to produce a *Code of Good Governance* for publicly traded corporations.	• Establishment of country code of conduct following guidelines of OECD 1999. • First CGG for companies published in 2003, since then many adjustments, most of them more formal than substantive. • Code obligated stock market (BVL[10]) listed companies, to apply the "comply or explain" approach.

[8] https://gcg.pe/ *Good Corporate Governance* (GCG) Certificate.

[9] Comisión Nacional Supervisora de Empresas y Valores (CONASEV)—Securities and Exchange Commission of Peru.

[10] Bolsa de Valores de Lima (BVL)—The Lima Stock Exchange.

Institutional context	*Institutional entrepreneurs*	*Prototype best practices*
• The slow dynamic in the appointment of new directors largely reflects the concentration of ownership. • A key element remains 'trust' or closeness with respect to controlling shareholders, when nominating board members. • Despite over 30 years of leadership in the local market, the AFPs (pension funds) have been unable to weaken this primordial situation. • A political environment marked by severe cases of corruption, involving several companies.	• Securities Commissioner indicative notes and answers provided disseminated as "relevant facts" to the market. • Regulatory supervision of company reports and warnings, as well as "enforcement" in relation to the Code. • BVL created and index for companies demonstrating good corporate governance standards, to promote best practices and recognize companies exhibiting high quality of corporate governance. • Market perception that the scheme was incomplete as it recognized companies that had had episodes contrary to BGC • To remedy this, the BVL incorporated the results of "*The Voice of the Market*" into the process, such that only companies with a positive market opinion in this survey are now recognized as GCG. • Companies exposed to international capital have received a favorable influence on corporate governance matters because they have had to adapt to the international market requirements.	• Publication of *self-assessments* led to periodic reviews with the intention of improving the quality of the information provided to the market. • In 2013 the scope of the *Good Governance Code* was expanded to include: risk; internal controls; and ethics. • Self-assessment measured against a stricter benchmark. • Indicative notes have been issued covering aspects, such as: board operations; independent directors; internal audit; codes of ethics; and related-party transactions. • This new practice has helped the SMV[11] detect self-evaluation reporting was neither informative nor complete and it has taken steps to correct this. • CG has emerged as a valuable way to enhance investor protections and help make the local market more attractive. • A decade after the implementation of IBGC, most listed companies do not qualify for *Good Corporate Governance* status; less than 10% submit to the validation process—and the trend is worsening.

(continued)

[11] Superintendencia del Mercado de Valores—Securities Market Superintendency.

Table 1 (continued)

Institutional context	*Institutional entrepreneurs*	*Prototype best practices*
	• Regulators (SMV) now focus on board composition in seeking to improve corporate governance standards: the role of independent directors, encouraging standardized definitions across companies and the incorporation of independent directors on the boards of regulated companies. • SMV stresses the importance of regular board member evaluations as a mechanism for promoting improvements in their performance and, through it, in the corporate governance of the company itself.	• The lack of eagerness by companies in seeking GCG recognition by the BVL is putting the very existence of the GCG index at risk. • Companies continue to be held to deficient corporate governance standards. • Exceptions are firms looking to differentiate themselves—often given exposure to more rigorous international markets. • Multiple formal displays seeking to reflect increasing adoption of corporate governance best practices but which, in most cases lack the substance to describe risks, which are inadequately disclosed or managed, representing uncontrolled exposures for investors and encouraging them to leave the local market.

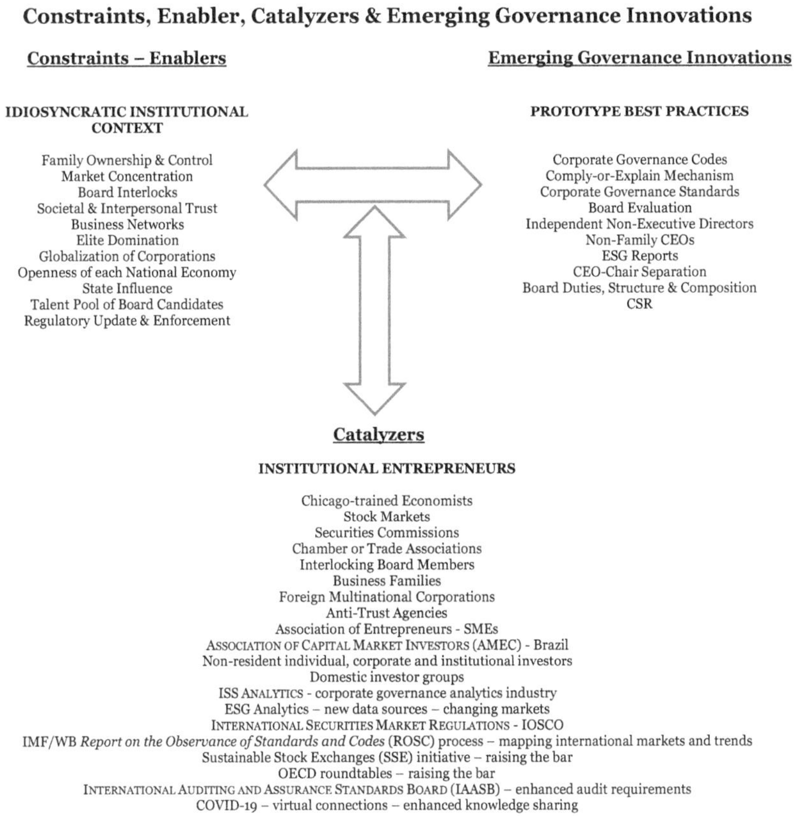

Fig. 2 Governing Innovations in Latin American Markets (*Source* Author's commentary on country practices – see external sources[12])

The depth and extension of innovations observed vary from country to country, but commonly accepted good practices in most countries include the adoption—some times, more officious than espoused—of corporate

[12] https://amecbrasil.org.br/?lang=en, https://www.issgovernance.com/solutions/iss-analytics/, https://www.esganalytics.ai/, https://www.iosco.org/about/?subsection=about_iosco, https://www.worldbank.org/en/programs/rosc , https://www.iaasb.org/, https://www.oecd.org/daf/ca/corporategovernance-regionalroundtablesandprogrammes.htm.

governance codes and standards (with the exception of Chile), comply-and/or-explain mechanisms, board evaluation procedures (enthusiastically embraced in Colombia), and the inclusion of outsiders, including non-executive ***independent directors*** or at least external board members, non-family CEOs, a timid but verifiable separation of the CEO and Chair positions (less frequent in Mexico), and proliferating ESG reports and CSR policies now seen among most large local and especially *Multilatina* corporations.

References

Aguilera, R.V. (2003). Are Italy and Spain Mediterranean sisters? A comparison of corporate governance systems. In corporate governance in a changing economic and political environment (pp. 23–70). Palgrave Macmillan.

Aguilera, R. V., Desender, K., Bednar, M. K., & Lee, J. H. (2015). Connecting the dots: Bringing external corporate governance into the corporate governance puzzle. *The Academy of Management Annals, 9*(1), 483–573. https://doi.org/10.1080/19416520.2015.1024503

Aguilera, R. V., Florackis, C., & Kim, H. (2016). Advancing the corporate governance research agenda. *Corporate Governance: An International Review, 24*(3), 172–180.

Aguilera, R. V., & Grøgaard, B. (2019). The dubious role of institutions in international business: A road forward. *Journal of International Business Studies, 50*(1), 20–35. https://doi.org/10.1057/s41267-018-0201-5

Aguilera, R. V., & Jackson, G. (2003). The cross-national diversity of corporate governance: Dimensions and determinants. *Academy of Management Review, 28*(3), 447–465. https://doi.org/10.5465/amr.2003.10196772

Aguilera, R. V., Judge, W. Q., & Terjesen, S. A. (2018). Corporate governance deviance. First published online July 2016. *Academy of Management Review, 43*(1), 87–109.

Aguilera, R. V., Kabbach-Castro, L. R., Lee, J. H., & YOU, J. (2012). Corporate governance in emerging markets. Capitalisms and Capitalism in the 21st century, pp. 319–344.

Aguilera, R. V., Marano, V., & Haxhi, I. (2019). International corporate governance: A review and opportunities for future research. *Journal of International Business Studies, 50*(4), 457–498.

Aldrich, H. E., & Pfeffer, J. (1976). Environments of organizations. *Annual Review of Sociology, 2*(1), 79–105.

Banner, S. (1997). What causes new securities regulation? 300 years of evidence. *Washington University Law Quarterly, 75*, 849.

Bevir, M. (2009). The construction of governance. *International Journal of Organization Theory & Behavior*.

Bevir, M. (2011). Governance as theory, practice, and dilemma. *The SAGE handbook of governance*, 1–16.

Bhaumik, S., Driffield, N., Gaur, A., Mickiewicz, T., & Vaaler, P. (2019). Corporate governance and MNE strategies in emerging economies. *Journal of World Business, 54*(4), 234–243.

Bos, S., Pendleton, A., & Toms, S. (2013, January 15). Governance thresholds, managerial ownership and corporate performance: Evidence from the UK. managerial ownership and corporate performance: Evidence from the UK.

Carter, C. B., & Lorsch, J. W. (2003). *Back to the drawing board: Designing corporate boards for a complex world*. Harvard Business Press.

Chait, R., Ryan, W., & Taylor, B. (2005). Leadership as governance. Cambridge.

Chua, J. H., Chrisman, J. J., & Steier, L. P. (2003). Extending the theoretical horizons of family business research. *Entrepreneurship Theory and Practice, 27*(4), 331–338.

Coase, R. (1937). The nature of the firm. *Economica. Blackwell Publishing, 4*(16), 386–405. https://doi.org/10.1111/j.1468-0335.1937.tb00002.x. JSTOR2626876

Coffee, J. C., Jr. (2005). A theory of corporate scandals: Why the USA and Europe differ. *Oxford Review of Economic Policy, 21*(2), 198–211.

Coglianese, C., & Michael, M. L. (2006). After the scandals: Changing relationships in corporate governance.

Davis, G. F., & Cobb, J. A. (2010). Resource dependence theory: Past and future. *Research in the Sociology of Organizations, 28*, 21–42.

Dean, M. (2010). Governmentality: Power and rule in modern society. Sage publications.

Dimaggio, P. (1998). The new institutionalisms: Avenues of collaboration. *Journal of Institutional and Theoretical Economics., 154*, 696–705.

Eisenhardt, K. M. (1989). Agency theory: An assessment and review. *Academy of Management Review, 14*(1), 57–74.

Emirbayer, M., & Mische, A. (1998). What is agency? *American Journal of Sociology, 103*(4), 963–1033.

Espinoza Aguiló, T., & Espinoza Aguiló, N. (2012). Family business performance: Evidence from Mexico. *Cuadernos De Administración, 25*(44), 39–61.

Fiss, P. C. (2007). Institutions and corporate governance. *The Sage Handbook of Organizational Institutionalism*, pp. 389–410.

Fligstein, N. (1990). *The Transformation of Corporate Control*. Harvard University Press.

Fligstein, N. (1997). Social skill and institutional theory. *American Behavioral Scientist, 40*, 397–405.

Foucault, M. (1994). La "Gouvernance." *Dits Et Écrits, III*, 635–657.

Friedland, R., & Alford, R. R. (1991, October 25). Bringing society back in: Symbols, practices and institutional contradictions. In Walter W. Powell, Paul J. Dimaggio (Eds.), *The New Institutionalism in Organizational Analysis*, pp. 232–263

Gao, C., Zuzul, T., Jones, G., & Khanna, T. (2017). Overcoming institutional voids: A reputation-based view of long-run survival. *Strategic Management Journal, 38*(11), 2147–2167.

Greif, A. (2008). *Commitment, coercion and markets: The nature and dynamics of institutions supporting exchange*. Springer.

Healy, R. (2014). Corporate political behavior: Why corporations do what they do in politics. Routledge.

Hill, J. G. (2012). Why did Australia fare so well in the global financial crisis? In Eilís Ferran, Niamh Moloney, Jennifer G. Hill, and John C. Coffee, Jr. (Eds.), *The Regulatory Aftermath of The Global Financial Crisis*, Cambridge University Press.

Horn, L. (2012). Corporate governance in crisis? The politics of EU corporate governance regulation. *European Law Journal, 18*, 83–107.

Husted, B., & Serrano, C. (2002). Corporate governance in México. *Journal of Business Ethics., 37*(3), 337–348.

Janis, I. L. (2008). Groupthink. *IEEE Engineering Management Review, 36*(1), 36.

Jiménez-Seminario, G. (2018). *Minding the corporate governance gap: The institutional construction of corporate governance in Chile*. University of Liverpool.

Kashwan, P., MacLean, L. M., & García-López, G. A. (2019). Rethinking power and institutions in the shadows of neoliberalism:(An introduction to a special issue of World Development). *World Development, 120*, 133–146.

Khanna, T., & Palepu, K. (1997). Why focused strategies. *Harvard Business Review, 75*(4), 41–51.

Lefort, F., & Walker, E. (2000). Corporate governance: Challenges for Latin America. *Abante, 2*(2), 99–111.

Lounsbury, M. (2007). A tale of two cities: Competing logics and practice variation in the professionalizing of mutual funds. *Academy of Management Journal, 50*, 289–307.

Mcnulty, T., Pettigrew, A., Jorome, G., & Morris, C. (2011). The role, power and influence of company chairs. *Journal of Management & Governance, 15*, 91–121.

Ménard, C., & Shirley, M. M. (2005). *Handbook of new institutional economics*. Springer.

Ménard, C. & Shirley, M. M. (2012). New institutional economics: From early intuitions to a new paradigm. *Working paper No 8*, September, 2012, Ronald Coase Institute.

North, D. C. (1990). *Institutions*. Cambridge University Press.

North, D. C., & Thomas, R. P. (1970). An economic theory of the growth of the Western World. *The Economic History Review, 23*, 1–17.

Oliver, C. (1991). Strategic responses to institutional processes. *Academy of Management Review., 16*, 145–179.

Pacheco, D. F., York, J. G., Dean, T. J., & Sarasvathy, S. D. (2010). The coevolution of institutional entrepreneurship: A tale of two theories. *Journal of Management, 36*, 974–1010.

Park, S. H., Zhang, Y., & Keister, L.A. (2020). Governance innovations in emerging markets. *Academy of Management Perspectives, 34*(2), 336–339. https://doi.org/10.5465/amp.3017.0177

Pfeffer, J., & Salancik, G. R. (2003). *The external control of organizations: A resource dependence perspective*. Stanford University Press.

Rao, H., Monin, P., & Durand, R. (2003). Institutional change in Toque Ville: Nouvelle cuisine as an identity movement in French gastronomy. *American Journal of Sociology, 108*, 795–843.

Salancik, G. R., Pfeffer, J., & Kelly, J. P. (1978). A contingency model of influence in organizational decision-making. *Pacific Sociological Review*, 239–256.

Sandoval-Arzaga, F. (2021). Radiografía de la Empresa Familiar Latinoamericana. Estudio Preliminar. Instituto de Familias Empresarias para México y Latinoamérica, Escuela de Negocios, Tecnológico de Monterrey.

Schneider, B. R. (2013). *Hierarchical capitalism in Latin America*. Cambridge University Press.

Scott, W. R. (2001). Institutions and organizations (2nd ed.). Sage.

Scott, W. R., & Davis, G. F. (2007). *Organizations and organizing: Rational, natural, and open systems perspectives*. Prentice-Hall.

Sewell, J. W. H. (1993). A theory of structure: Duality, agency, and transformation. *American Journal of Sociology, 98*(1), 1–39.

Simon, H. A. (1991, May 1). Organizations and markets. *Journal of Economic Perspectives, 5*(2), 25–44. https://doi.org/10.1257/jep.5.2.25. ISSN 0895-3309.

Thornton, P. H., & Ocasio, W. (1999). Institutional logics and the historical contingency of power in organizations: Executive succession in the higher education publishing industry, 1958–1990. *American Journal of Sociology, 105*, 801–843.

Thornton, P. H., & Ocasio, W. (2008). Institutional logics. *The Sage handbook of organizational institutionalism, 840*(2008), 99–128.

Thornton, P. H., Ocasio, W., & Lounsbury, M. (2012). The institutional logics perspective: A new approach to culture, structure and process. OUP Oxford.

Tricker, R. (2012). The evolution of corporate governance. *The SAGE Handbook of Corporate Governance*, pp. 39–61.

Vázquez, P., Carrera, A., & Cornejo, M. (2020). Corporate governance in the largest family firms in Latin America. *Cross-Cultural & Strategic Management, 27*(2), 137–163.

Westphal, J. D., & Zajac, E. J. (2013). A behavioral theory of corporate governance: Explicating the mechanisms of socially situated and socially constituted agency. *The Academy of Management Annals, 7*, 607–661.

Williamson, O. E. (1975). *Markets and hierarchies, analysis and antitrust implications: A study in the economics of internal organization.*

PART I

Regional Chapters

CHAPTER 3

Corporate Scandals in Latin America and Their Impact on the Corporate Governing Environment

Jonathan Callund and Gonzalo Jiménez-Seminario

Before proceeding with an assessment of the top national scandals, it is as well to assess the very concept of *scandal* itself, and how they might provide an interesting lens through which to view and assess corporate governance practices and malfeasance and the incentives that drive such patterns of behavior. In addition, we anticipate that reflecting on scandals and their implications in Latin America might also be a source of general interest for the readers of this book. Merriam-Webster provides a tongue-in-cheek definition of scandals, quoting a witty Samuel Johnson expression dated from his 1775 dictionary: "*Offense given by the faults of*

J. Callund (✉)
Callund y Compañía Ltda., Santiago, Chile
e-mail: jonathan.callund@callund.cl

G. Jiménez-Seminario
Pontificia Universidad Católica de Chile, Santiago, Chile
e-mail: gjimenez@proteus.cl

J. Callund et al. (eds.), *Corporate Governing in Latin America*,
https://doi.org/10.1007/978-3-030-85780-6_3

others". Beyond this irony, the etymology provides value in its own right that may help us decide on the best way to allude to such transgressions.

"Scandal" appears to be in ancient use, dating back to the beginning of the thirteenth century, deriving from the Latin *scandalum*, meaning "stumbling block" or "offense". The original meaning of scandal was associated more with the "discredit brought upon religion by unseemly conduct in a religious person" and used as a medieval goad to encourage hermits to behave appropriately. However, the word scandal was little used for the following several centuries. Although, by the end of the sixteenth century, the word had become substantially more common and expanded its range of meaning.[1] Thus, scandal is normally used as an indication of specific instances of conduct that is assumed to be socially or morally transgressive. Frequent mentions are typically concerned with sex, politics, or money issues—sometimes all of them, as suggested in Merriam-Webster. As a consequence, the term scandal seems to fully capture the three facets related to corporate governing[2]: normative theory on how things should work; real-world practice on how things actually work; and the concrete dilemmas arising in a corporate setting, as well as how each new dilemma sets the wheels in motion in reconsidering theories, illuminating best practices, and finding new ways to deal with emerging dilemmas. Bob Tricker exemplifies these in questioning just how far the *duty of care* goes and if an "I didn't know" is sufficient defense for a board member when facing a corporate scandal.[3]

In Anglo-Saxon settings, malfeasances tend to be connected with managers driven by perverse incentives within their established frameworks of absent, atomized, or negligent owners. Boards of directors are thus described as *dysfunctional* in these cases, due to: their subordination to the C-suite; imbalances in terms of their composition; their

[1] Merriam-Webster: A scandal may refer to specific circumstances or actions that offend established social mores ("*the congressman's arrest for bribery caused a scandal*") or can also refer more generally to a state of affairs ("*the state of our elections is a scandal*"). It can be used to refer to gossip (either true or false), and also has an archaic sense of "*a disgraceful usually baseless accusation or imputation*". One common thread with all of the word's definitions is that they tend to be concerned with meanings that most people would strongly prefer to not be associated with.

[2] Bevir, M. (2009). The construction of governance. *International Journal of Organization Theory & Behavior*.

[3] Tricker, R. (2012). The evolution of corporate governance. *The SAGE handbook of corporate governance*, pp. 39–61.

cultural mismatches and overarching inertia in confronting environmental changes; or as passive bystanders being dominated by managerial elites or blockholders[4], acting bureaucratically, and overall subject to high levels of conformity (Brown & Peters, 2022). As will be seen, boards in Latin America tend to display other motivations and behaviors. Despite displaying several of the same bad practices, the concentration of political, cultural, and economic considerations paints a different picture.

In Latin America, the corporate path is replete with many forms of scandal and, moreover is consistent with a long history of ineffective, or sometimes blatantly corrupt, institutions. However, despite their frequency and variety, scandals open up two important dimensions. On the one hand, in surprising or shocking us with established bad practices that are made known and reveal the scope of the day-to-day ugliness that is being taken for granted, in great measure through the realization that they have grown to be accepted as normal for a long time. This involves shaming, by throwing into relief the problematic nature of current habits, customs, and ways of carrying on. On the other hand, we see countries, such as, to some degree Brazil, without doubt in Chile, partially in Colombia, Mexico, and Peru, but less so in Argentina (unfortunately), steadily making progress in overcoming their local/national shortcomings, as revealed through the public airing of such scandals. Thus, scandals might be viewed as *markers*, flagging the advances in practices and policies, as well as social sensitivities. In general, Latin America has come to profit from having learnt such lessons the hard way.

This chapter looks at some of the most important *scandals* in each of the six countries under review, with a view to ascertaining just how they have affected the evolution of corporate government regulations and corporate practices over the last 20 years. The basis for this review has been the collation of the "top 6" national scandals in each country, as selected, researched, and prepared by the local authors. In each case, the summaries of the cases are supplemented by currently active dynamic links to provide further details and perspectives on the issues in each case.

[4] Blockholders is not strictly an academic term, but here is defined as shareholders who own at least 5% of a company's common shares. Consequently, they are influential shareholders who may gravitate in decisionmaking processes through board positions or act as holders of pivotal stakes required to approve or reject a board proposition at a Shareholder Meeting.

Given the sensitive nature of such cases, the authors only make use of public sources in preparing their narratives. Moreover, given that some cases have had years of judicial trials (and in a few cases these trials are still ongoing) and then there have been changes to the composition and scope of their boards, in drafting the cases and drawing up conclusions, all descriptions of the events and subsequent commentary focuses on typifying practices, and seek not to allude to any individual board members in particular, unless they figure prominently, given their family or leadership roles.

So, let's now investigate some of the most important cases in each territory asking the following questions:[5]

- What is the headline?
- Who were the key players?
- What happened?
- How did we find out?
- What was the fallout? and
- What have we learnt or done subsequently?

[5] Miller, B. & Uriegas F. (2019) Anti-Corruption Watch—Latin America's Biggest Corruption Cases: A Retrospective—From Mexico to Argentina, iconic scandals have reshaped politics. AQ examines their origins—and fallout.

1 Argentina

Pablo Eugenio Souto, Hugo Gaggiotti and
María de los Ángeles Lucero Bringas

For most of the second half of the twentieth century, the Argentinian financial markets have been shallow and have done little to support economic development. Macroeconomic instability and a weak institutional framework are at the root of this phenomenon. As in many other countries in the region, Argentina embarked on a set of economic reforms in the 1990s; these included the corporate and financial sectors.

In 2001, the Argentinian government issued Decree 677-01 which became the first piece of legislation where the concept of corporate governance was explicitly introduced for public listed companies. Since then, a number of other norms and regulations were passed encompassing different types of organizations ranging from the banking sector to institutional investors and from State-owned enterprises to firms participating in public procurement processes.

Over these last two decades, Argentina combined *comply-or-explain* regulations with mandatory practices to be implemented by firms. In most cases, international standards (such as the OECD Principles of Corporate Governance) served as the benchmark for the drafting of domestic regulations.

In Argentina, ownership concentration—usually in the hands of families—and corporate opaqueness are the norm, contract enforcement is weak, property rights are frequently violated with no major consequences, and many of the largest domestic firms have developed under an economic paradigm in which close ties with the government were the drivers for success. In such a context, the extrapolation of an Anglo-Saxon approach

P. E. Souto
University of Buenos Aires, Buenos Aires, Argentina
e-mail: psouto@hotmail.com

H. Gaggiotti
Faculty of Business and Law, University of the West of England, Bristol, UK
e-mail: hugo.gaggiotti@uwe.ac.uk

M. de los Ángeles Lucero Bringas
Faculty of Business and Economics, Universidad Católica de Córdoba, Córdoba, Argentina
e-mail: angeleslucerobringas@gmail.com

to a Continental law jurisdiction has been difficult and has had less success than expected.

The six cases presented below show how—although having in place relatively sound laws and regulations—the broader institutional framework and idiosyncratic characteristics of most Argentinian firms have limited any effective functioning of a good corporate governing framework. As it will be seen, compliance has largely been on paper only, and enforcement powers—being the Judiciary power and government regulators—have been either limited or non-existent. In that setting, a lack of a culture of ethics—both at the private and public sectors—has created a set of incentives favoring corrupt activities, corporate misbehaviors, and short-termism in the conduct of business. Overall, Argentina presents an interesting case to study in seeking to comprehend a *local* interpretation of global corporate corruption and the limits of corporate governance.

1.1 Desarrollo de Acuerdos Comerciales S.A. (DACSA)

Board integrity and initial public offering disclosure practices.

DACSA was a private company established in Argentina that operated a retail chain of sportswear stores located in the City of Buenos Aires and the province of Buenos Aires. The company was classified as a small and medium-size enterprise (SME) and wholly owned by local shareholders. In November 2006, DACSA became the first company to be listed in the recently created SMEs Panel at the Buenos Aires Stock Exchange, a listing segment developed to facilitate access to finance for SMEs through less stringent requirements and regulations. As of 2006, the firm had annual sales of USD3.7 million.

(a) What happened:
After successfully placing 20% of shares—equivalent to USD1.7 million—to finance expansion projects, the company subsequently failed to meet standard disclosure regulations. Its financial statements were incomplete, relevant facts were not disclosed among other breaches in capital market regulations. In May 2007, the company announced it was experiencing financial distress that finally led to bankruptcy procedures, after failing to secure agreements with its creditors. By the time the Buenos Aires Stock Exchange suspended DACSA stock trading, its value had fallen around 50% from its value

at the time of the IPO, i.e., six months earlier. A study[6] estimated that the share price had been overvalued by around 100% at the time of the IPO.

(b) How we found out:
Reports made to the capital markets regulator and mass media coverage.

(c) The fallout:
The capital markets regulator (Comisión Nacional de Valores) launched an investigation that concluded in 2010 with the imposition of a fine on DACSA's board members of USD125,000 each. The investigation concluded that: (i) the company had been involved in market manipulation practices through its own employees or related parties that had been buying the stock to artificially raise and stabilize the stock price; and (ii) board members had failed to discharge their duty of loyalty[7] and their duty of care, permitting opaque financial transactions and a general lack of adherence to principles of transparency. Overall, the company—through the board—had granted bonuses to staff who committed to buy the stock for themselves. Such a scheme was neither formalized nor disclosed.

(d) What we learnt or did subsequently:
This case brought to public discussion the trade-offs between easing certain regulations and protecting investors—and in particular, minority shareholders—when it comes to promoting SME participation in the capital markets. Furthermore, this case demonstrated the importance of enhanced transparency as a market discipline mechanism, showing how it can lead to the exposure of rogue managers or board members. As a conclusion, the (lack of) integrity of board members and senior management is as important a criteria as professional and business skills when it comes to due diligence procedures.

[6] Briozzo, A. (2011). Valuación de oferta pública inicial PyME: el caso de DACSA. Presented at the XXXI Financial Management National Conference. See public sources for the document.

[7] *Duty of loyalty* is the principle that directors and officers of a corporation, in making all decisions in their capacities as corporate fiduciaries, must act at all times in the best interests of their company and without personal economic conflict.

On the negative side, no sanctions were levied on other participants that had a responsibility in the case—the so-called gatekeepers—such as the comptrollers (*síndico*), the underwriters, and the market makers. It also flagged how poor accounting practices and weak internal control systems—which are critical elements of any governing structure—helped facilitate the circulation of deceptive and false accounts prior to the IPO.

The timing of the regulator's intervention as well as the inordinate time it took to deliver a final decision—over four years—did little to enhance public confidence in the capital markets, compounded by the trivial fines handed out in relation to damage suffered by investors.

(e) Public Sources:
All Retrieved on 14 July 2022:

https://www.cnv.gov.ar/descargas/sumarios/blob/95694aef-eb26-45ff-a7de-02e58f1ba4ef

https://abogados.com.ar/index.php/la-cnv-multo-con-500-mil-a-una-firma-por-manipulacion-de-mercado/6092

https://www.cnv.gov.ar/descargas/sumarios/blob/98b2a05c-cd83-4ae7-bf36-19e3b41af801

https://www.cnv.gov.ar/descargas/sumarios/blob/52f87684-de69-4df7-9fe0-f24f3bfeb29e

https://www.cronista.com/impresa-general/La-accion-de-Dacsa-finalmente-inauguro-el-Panel-Pyme-de-la-Bolsa-portena-20061201-0005.html

https://repositoriodigital.uns.edu.ar/bitstream/handle/123456789/4307/Valuaci%c3%b3n%20de%20oferta%20p%c3%bablica%20inicial%20pyme%20el%20caso%20de%20DACSA.pdf?sequence=3&isAllowed=y

1.2 YPF S.A.

Nationalization and statutory public tender offer procedures.

YPF S.A. (formerly Yacimientos Petrolíferos Fiscales) is in the exploration, production, and distribution of oil and gas businesses. The company is the largest Argentinian oil and gas company and has been an iconic organization since the early twentieth century. Initially a state-owned enterprise, it has experienced several ownership changes and is currently a company subject to private sector corporate law, albeit the Argentine Republic (both Federal and some provincial governments) currently holds a controlling interest—51% of the shares.

YPF is publicly listed on the Buenos Aires Stock Exchange and New York Stock Exchange and, as such, is subject to regulations applicable in both markets. The company primarily operates in Argentina, albeit with some production and exploration activities in Bolivia and Chile. As of 2021, the company had annual revenues of USD12 bn. and a market capitalization of USD3.3 bn.

(a) What happened:
As of 2012, Repsol—a Spanish company—owned approximately 57% of the company and a domestic investor—Petersen Energía—owned 25% of the shares.[8] At the time, the Argentine Republic was a minority shareholder, although it retained certain rights ("golden shares"). In May 2012, the Argentine Congress passed an expropriation law by which 51% of the company shares—all those owned by Repsol—were to be transferred to the Argentine Republic, hence making the latter the new controlling shareholder. Two years later, the Argentine Republic and Repsol reached an agreement on the amount of compensation for the expropriation and for Repsol to withdraw all the claims it had filed in relation to the company's nationalization.

(b) How we found out:
Reports to the capital markets regulator and corporate disclosures.

(c) The fallout:
The expropriation procedure followed by the Argentine Republic failed to adhere to the obligations set out in the initial public offering and the company's by-laws. As a publicly listed company, it is/was subject to procedures applicable in cases of hostile takeovers. These state that to carry out an acquisition that leads to a purchaser holding 15% or more of YPF capital stock or 20% or more of the outstanding Class D shares, then the purchaser must make a public offer for

[8] The mechanism used by Petersen Energía to acquire such 25% of YPF from Repsol in 2008 is also controversial and subject to investigation; this part of the YPF saga is beyond the scope of the present case analysis.

all of the outstanding shares and convertible securities. The Argentine Republic did not make such an offer to the other shareholders, and this triggered a lawsuit by Petersen Energía against the Argentine Republic and YPF in the US courts. The claim was filed in 2015 and a final resolution is still pending. Another former minority shareholder (Eton Park) filed a similar claim in 2017. The judiciary process turned out to be cumbersome, involving multiple courts, including the US Supreme Court, given that the company and the Argentine Republic are seeking to dismiss the claims, on grounds that the US Judiciary has no authority in the matter and that the case should only go forward under Argentinian law.

(d) What we learnt or did subsequently:
This case highlights the importance that the board and the effective functioning of a judiciary have in protecting the interests of minority shareholders.

First, at the time of the expropriation, the members of the board failed to discharge their duties towards all shareholders and, in particular, to protect the interest of the minority ones. For instance, they might have initiated legal action themselves, against the hostile buyer. They might have also taken steps to inform the shareholders of the damages and alternative redresses available to them were the expropriation to have gone ahead.

Secondly, as corporate governance is reflected through several contractual obligations, judicial procedures are critical in ensuring that such obligations are met and provide protection to the parties affected should such violations occur. This is even more important when it is the government that is prospectively seeking to violate minority shareholder rights.

Overall, where the rule of law is weak then corporate governing becomes an abstract set of norms and practices with limited means for their enforcement. It is, therefore, the institutional framework that is the basis for an effective corporate governance framework. Furthermore, the dispute over the US or Argentina jurisdiction flags the asymmetries in the institutional frameworks and how they protect creditors/shareholders' rights respectively, and ultimately serves to show the premium paid by domestic companies in the higher costs of raising capital locally.

(e) Public Sources:

All Retrieved on 14 July 2022:

https://www.ypf.com/english/investors/Lists/InformeAnualForm20/YPF-20F-2020.pdf

1.3 Benito Roggio E Hijos S.A.

Ethics and compliance when contracting with the government.

Benito Roggio e Hijos S.A. (BRH) operates in the construction, engineering services and road concessions businesses. The company was founded in Argentina in 1908 and is at the core of the Grupo Roggio, a conglomerate of firms operating in the transportation, water and waste management, tourism, and entertainment businesses, among others. The Group has subsidiaries in Brazil, Paraguay, Peru, and Uruguay.

Although a family-owned company, BRH is subject to the regime of public offerings since its controlling entity (CLISA) first issued bonds that are listed on the public domestic markets. As of 2021, the group reported USD600 million in revenues.

(a) What happened:

The construction business is heavily focused on infrastructure projects and contracts with all manner of public sector entities. Many other areas of its operations also involve dealings with the public sector. As such, the company has a heavy exposure to risks deriving from its participation in public procurement processes.

An investigation conducted by a local newspaper in August 2018 revealed a complex network of corruption in public sector works projects where private companies had been awarded contracts at above market prices in return for bribes paid to public officials. The schemes involved senior government officials (including the President) and many of the largest construction companies operating in Argentina. The case, known as "*Cuadernos*" (notebook) was based on the annotations made by a driver at the Ministry of Public Works in his day-to-day workplace dealings over a decade.

(b) How we found out:

Whistleblower action and mass media coverage.

(c) The fallout:
As soon as the investigation was made public, over 60 senior government officials and businessmen were accused of illicit association and bribery. The Chairman and largest shareholder of BRH (and CLISA) was one of those under investigation and a criminal case was brought against him. As a consequence, the reputational risk materialized and had significant effects on the company's daily operations, primarily in participating in new projects and its access to finance. As a measure to contain damages, the Chairman resigned from all his long-standing positions in the company and the Group. He agreed to collaborate with the judiciary officials and went public on having been part of the corruption network.

At the time of events, the company was found not to have a code of conduct/ethics or any compliance function, nor any policy on integrity or a framework for integrated risk management. No independent directors or an audit committee existed either. The whole internal control environment—a key component for an effective governing framework—and the checks-and-balances failed to prevent criminal activities occurring in a systematic way. The external auditors, credit rating agencies, regulators, etc. —the so-called gatekeepers—did little to strengthen or warn against the weaknesses in the company's internal control systems. These failures are even more evident when considering that a similar corruption scandal had already occurred and was still under review and as yet had no significant impact on the company's governing structures.

(d) What we learnt or did subsequently:
This case shows that corporate governance regulations are insufficient and that just by adhering to them on paper significantly raises operational risks; accountability and systems of checks-and-balances are needed, as well as a discrete set of corporate values embedded deep into the organization. The reputational and financial consequences this case had on the company was due in part to the impact it had on public opinion. The (sometimes) overlooked reputational risks soon materialized and prompted the company to take drastic action and in a very short period of time.

It showed just how a company—supposedly with higher-than-average corporate governance standards, as it is under the public listing regime—failed both to implement good practices in practice and then failed to hold its executives and board members accountable for breaching the existing practices. The response was a full-blown internal reform of the governing framework—and in particular the functions of the board. By 2019, the company had implemented a comprehensive *integrity* program, including a code of ethics, an anti-corruption policy, and strict protocols for the engagement with the public sector. In addition, independent directors had been appointed, audit and compliance committees created, and a compliance function was in place, established along international recommended best practices lines. This includes a whistleblower procedure. Contrary to the previous opaqueness in terms of the disclosure of information, the new policies were shared widely by the company and play a central role in the company's renewed website.

(e) **Public Sources:**
All Retrieved on 14 July 2022:
https://www.cnv.gov.ar/SitioWeb/Empresas/Empresa/30692239292
https://www.broggio.com.ar/programa-de-integridad/
https://chequeado.com/el-explicador/el-abc-de-la-causa-cuadernos-de-la-corrupcion/

1.4 Skanska

Internal controls and compliance.

Skanska is a multinational project development and construction group founded in 1887 and based in Sweden. The company operations are focused on three distinct streams: Construction, Commercial Development and Homes, with presence in Europe and the United States. The company is listed on the NASDAQ and Stockholm Stock Exchange and has a relatively diversified investor-base, with no controlling shareholder. As of 2021, the company reported USD14.7 billion in revenues and a market capitalization of USD10.3 billion. In the early 2000s, the company had operations in several countries in Latin America that represented approximately 4% of group revenues.

(a) What happened:

In Argentina—where the company had its regional headquarters—Skanska was awarded a contract for the construction of a gas pipeline; the contractors were two private companies, although the financing and oversight of the works were conducted by the government.

In 2005, an internal investigation on tax evasion by Skanska discovered the company had been using shell companies to which it allegedly paid for certain goods and services using false invoices. However, these practices were being used as a channel to pay bribes to public officials to ensure Skanska would be awarded the contract. The company carried out an internal investigation that confirmed the existence of accounting practices set up to evade taxes and, possibly, for paying bribes.

(b) How we found out:

Investigation by the tax authorities and whistleblower action.

(c) The fallout:

Overall, the investigation concluded that seven Argentinian executives had breached the corporate Code of Conduct and were consequently dismissed. To uncover any other potential events, the company hired an external consultancy firm to carry out a full investigation. As a result, Skanska paid all due taxes and handed over documents relating to the project to the Argentinian judiciary authorities in charge of the criminal case against the senior executives and government officials involved. Despite an admission of guilt to the payment of bribes by one senior executive, a ruling is still pending on the responsibilities of public officials.

(d) What we learnt or did subsequently:

At the time of these events, Skanska already had in place a number of good governance practices, including: a code of conduct and compliance practices; a corporate governance report with certifications by the board of directors of the functioning of key governing areas (internal controls and risks). However, these did not prevent the executives' misconduct and goes to highlight that ethics goes beyond formal compliance with existing rules and is more about the corporate values embedded in the executives and staff. Moreover, the internal control function failed to prevent these events. Subsequently, as indicated, the company has strengthened its processes relating to compliance with its code of conduct.

This event had a relatively minor direct financial impact on the company—the taxes only amounted to USD1.7 million—but clearly the larger impact came from the hit to Skanska's reputation and the global implications of these events. The company carried out a review of its risk exposure and risk appetite and was seen to divest its operations in the region. By 2015, the company had sold out of its operations in Argentina and a year later, the last part of Skanska's Latin America operations was shut down, when the construction business in Peru was sold to a local company.

(e) Public sources:

All Retrieved on 14 July 2022:

https://es.wikipedia.org/wiki/Caso_Skanska

https://www.infobae.com/tag/caso-skanska/

https://www.perfil.com/noticias/politica/despues-de-14-anos-elevan-a-juicio-oral-el-caso-skanska.phtml

https://www.telam.com.ar/tags/8216-caso-skanska/noticias

https://group.skanska.com/corporate-governance/corporate-governance-reports/

https://web.archive.org/web/20130321140010/, http://latinbusinesschronicle.com/app/article.aspx?id=1477

1.5 Vicentin SAIC

Conflicts of interest in official financing of private companies.

Vicentin SAIC is a family-owned holding company that was established in the Province of Santa Fé in 1927. The company's core business is oilseed crushing and grains trading but is also a producer of biodiesel and operates its own port. As of 2019, the company was among the country's ten largest exporters, and the group comprises thirty subsidiary companies with operations in Argentina, Uruguay, and Paraguay. In 2019, the company reported revenues of about USD4.2 billion.

(a) What happened:

Since 2003, the firm expanded aggressively and had seen its revenues increase tenfold over that period. This expansion was largely financed by taking on loans in US dollars taken out in both the local and international markets. As of 2019, the firm was heavily leveraged while the spread of the trading activities was narrowing, all of which led to significant financial stress. Banco Nación—a state-owned bank—was the largest single creditor, with outstanding lines of around USD300 million, followed by the International Finance Corporation (USD236 million) and the Nederlandse Financierings (USD132 million). Around 1,900 small-time grain producers—that had supplied their grains in advance to Vicentin—also comprised a large group of creditors.

(b) How we found out:
Mass media reports.

(c) The fallout:
In the second half of 2019, the company defaulted on its obligations and entered into receivership in February 2020, a process that is still developing in connection with criminal charges against the company's board members for fraud and related charges. Furthermore, the national government has acted to seize control of the company, launching a series of interventions and expropriation procedures, albeit with little success.

Preliminary investigations showed a number of malfeasances in the conduct of business. Firstly, loans extended by Banco Nación had been granted under irregular circumstances, given they represented over 10% of the bank's loanable capacity. Second, the company was found to have presented false financial statements to obtain the lines of credit. And third, assets that were tendered as collateral for some of the loans were subsequently found to have been reassigned through inappropriate related-party transactions away from the company to other entities allegedly controlled by the owners of Vicentin. The final report by the auditors—running to 225 pages—was published in October 2020 and forms part of the receivership legal process.

Consequently, the Federation of Grain Collectors requested the expulsion of Vicentin from the organization, concluding that the company's financial statements were unreliable with regard to the reporting of these loans.

(d) What we learnt or did subsequently:

The case flagged a number of corporate governing weaknesses, both from the standpoint of the company and the government. In the first case, the company failed to adhere to ethical standards in having an unsound risk management function, poor transparency practices and an ineffective audit function. The company's expansion plans were contested by external auditors whose performance was also put into question.

Although some of those policies had been in place,[9] adherence was only on paper, and accountability was lacking. In the second case—on the government side—the process revealed abuses of power and disregard for the rule of law and property rights, hence affecting the interest of other stakeholders, such as the small-time creditors. To be effective, corporate governance practices must be implemented within a well-defined institutional context that, in this case, proved to be lacking. In addition, the case casts doubt on the effective functioning of Banco Nación's corporate governance framework, including the role of the board, checks-and-balances, and internal controls. An internal investigation was subsequently launched to determine the responsibilities of senior officials. Yet, it is clear that it failed in dealing with conflicts of interest that are inherently present in the case of state-owned enterprises dealing with private firms with extensive links to political parties.[10]

(e) Public sources:

All Retrieved on 14 July 2022:

https://www.pagina12.com.ar/349394-caso-vicentin-informe-final

https://www.errepar.com/resources/descargacontenido/Suple-VICENTIN-ius.pdf

https://www.lanacion.com.ar/economia/el-credito-banco-nacion-vicentin-nunca-supero-nid2383780/

[9] In part because these policies are standard requirements by international creditors, such as the IFC.

[10] Vicentin had been a regular contributor to political parties.

https://www.cronista.com/negocios/bancos-acreedores-de-vicentin-piden-una-valuacion-independiente-de-la-cerealera/

https://disclosures.ifc.org/project-detail/SII/36265/vicentin-pre-exp

https://www.bna.com.ar/Downloads/MemoriayBalanceGeneralConsolidado2019.pdf

https://www.vicentin.com.ar

1.6 TGLT

Acquisitions and public offer procedures.

TGLT S.A is a real estate developer established in Argentina in 2005. The company quickly became one of the most dynamic firms in the sector, responsible for the development of large prime residential and commercial projects in Argentina; minor projects were also developed in Uruguay. The company went public in 2010 on the Buenos Aires Stock Exchange and is also listed over the counter in the US market (through *American Depository Receipts* - ADRs). The largest individual shareholder is another local real estate developer (IRSA) that holds 30% of the shares. The company reported revenues of about USD500 million in 2021.

(a) What happened:
In January 2018, TGLT announced the acquisition of 82% of the shares of Caputo SAIC.[11] This latter firm was one of the largest construction companies in Argentina and was also a publicly listed company, although the majority stake in the firm (82% involved in this transaction) was in possession of the members of the founding family. This transaction allowed TGLT to become an integrated constructor and developer, expanding also into the infrastructure sector. This transaction amounted of USD109 million, hence valuing the whole of Caputo in the order of USD132 million.

(b) How we found out:
Reports to the capital markets regulator.

[11] The timing and price at which TGLT acquired Caputo has also been a controversial issue.

(c) The fallout:

Both companies informed the public about the prospective transaction in a timely manner. However, the takeover procedure followed by TGLT failed to adhere to the legal and regulatory requirements that oblige the buyer to extend the offer to all shareholders prior to taking control of the acquired company. At the time of the announcement of the acquisition of Caputo, no such offer had been made. It took 9 days following the announcement for TGLT to inform about the prospective public offer for minority shareholders.

The inconsistencies that were apparent during the process triggered an abnormal trading of Caputo shares on the subsequent days, which prompted the securities market regulator (CNV) to suspend the trading of Caputo shares for a week, hence affecting minority shareholders. In August 2018, the public offer was finally formalized and extended to all minority shareholders. In April 2018, the CNV initiated a case against TGLT board members for violation of the public offer regulations that was concluded in November 2020, when fines were imposed.

(d) What we learnt or did subsequently:

The mandatory public offer regime is a governance device intended to protect the interest of minority shareholders in the case of a change in control of a company. This case clearly shows the importance of prompt action by the authorities when breaches come to light, to protect those rights. On the one hand, the board of directors of both TGLT and Caputo failed to comply with the duty of loyalty and duty of care. Moreover, TGLT board members contended that if breaches in legislation had occurred, then they should not be held accountable since their corporate legal team had cleared the transaction. On the other hand, the prompt intervention of the regulator may have accelerated the public offer process made by TGLT. Against this backdrop, the sanctions imposed on the board members of TGLT appear to be minor—each director was fined USD19,000—and took over two years to be settled. No investigations or legal actions has been taken in the case of Caputo.

(e) Public sources:

All Retrieved on 14 July 2022:

https://www.cnv.gov.ar/SitioWeb/Empresas/Empresa/30709282537?fdesde=02/11/2007
https://www.cnv.gov.ar/descargas/sumarios/blob/15e573b7-5d0f-44f7-a921-32395462f13e
https://www.sec.gov/edgar/browse/?CIK=1510178
https://docplayer.es/110603700-Tglt-s-a-oferta-publica-de-adquisicion-obligatoria-de-caputo-s-a-i-c-y-f.html
https://pagbam.com/noticias/tglt-recibe-autorizacion-para-lanzar-opa-sobre-resto-de-acciones-de-caputo/

1.7 Lessons from Argentina and Open Questions for Further Study

These cases reflect how corporate governing has acquired importance as a structural development, decision-making and control mechanism. These are underdeveloped practices among Argentine businessmen. Business School and other business educational institutions should be aware of this, so companies can start improving their internal practices and become attractive to negotiate and integrate into a globalized world.

1. A lack of rigor of those who implement the laws when penalizing fraudulent, opportunistic, and speculative conduct, as seen with DACSA, TGLT, and IRB. This is closely related to the lack of independence of powers, in breach of the Argentine National Constitution.
2. The intervention of powers, because of the lack of effective legal recourse, and the lack of respect for the rules discourages foreign investment.
3. The capital market is not developed because of the lack of transparency.
4. The implementation of good corporate governance practices is discouraged by the high degree of corruption in hiring.
5. The lack of regulation of conflicts of interest between shareholders and management, as seen in the cases of DACSA, TPF, and Vicentin.
6. In emerging economies, with high levels of inflation and poverty, where most companies (99.5%) are SMEs, unfair practices by large corporations or economic groups linked to their political powerbases, have tended to discourage the implementation of good government practices.

2 Brazil

Dante Mendes Aldrighi and Luiz Ricardo Kabbach de Castro

Albeit the results of the copious literature on the effect of sound governance practices on firms' performance are far from conclusive, the evidence available demonstrates that poor corporate governance can severely harm firms, shareholders, and other stakeholders.

In this section, we focus on six major corporate governance failures in Brazil. For the selection of the cases, we proceeded as follows: first, each of the coauthors indicated separately the six most relevant cases, of which four overlapped; the remaining two cases were defined by consensus after a thorough discussion on the potential candidates. We are convinced that these cases capture the main challenges underlying Brazil's corporate governance environment, such as corruption, insider trading, and related-party transactions.

2.1 Petrobras

"The oil is ours": crony capitalism, state-owned enterprise, and corruption.

Petrobras, the state-controlled oil company, is the largest Brazilian company (Fortune, 2021). In 2014, Federal public attorneys and the Federal Police unraveled an intricate corruption scheme involving the company's top management, the leading domestic construction companies, and politicians.

(a) What happened:

Officers of Petrobras as well as of some privately held companies, together with politicians were involved in a long-standing scheme of diversion of money from the state-owned company through over-invoiced public work contracts that fed political parties' coffers and

D. Mendes Aldrighi
Department of Economics, Universidade de São Paulo, São Paulo, Brazil
e-mail: aldrighi@usp.br

L. R. Kabbach de Castro
Department of Management, Universidad de Navarra, Pamplona, Spain
e-mail: lrkcastro@gmail.com

bribing of politicians and Petrobras' officers, fraudulent mergers and acquisition, biased procurement proceedings, money laundering, and evasion of foreign currency.

Officers of State-owned and privately held companies, coupled with politicians, were involved in a longstanding scheme to divert money from PETROBRAS through a scheme that over-invoiced public work contracts which, in turn, fed political parties' coffers and the bribery of politicians. Moreover, PETROBRAS' officers, were found to be involved in fraudulent mergers and acquisitions, biased procurement proceedings, money laundering, and the evasion of foreign currency regulations.

In addition, several Petrobras ' contractors were accused of bribing in exchange for contracts rents, including Odebrecht , Andrade Gutierrez, UTC, OAS, , Queiroz Galvao, Mendes Junior, and Engevix.

The Federal Police estimated the losses to Petrobras of around BRL42 billion (USD8.1 billion).

(b) How we found out:

A joint initiative embracing the Office of the Federal Public Prosecutor, the Federal Police, and the Federal Court—dubbed "*Operação Lava Jato*" ("*Operation Car Wash*")—brought to light the mechanisms whereby money was embezzled from Petrobras over seven years. The *Operation Car Wash Task Force* began work in March 2014, when the Federal Court located in Curitiba investigated the participation of public officials, businessmen, and money changers in Petrobras' over-invoiced contracts.

(c) The fallout:

The *Operation Car Wash* task force led to 295 arrests (including the arrest of the two former presidents Luiz Inácio Lula da Silva and Michel Temer, as well as many other leading politicians and businessmen), 278 convictions, and BRL4.3 billion (USD803 million) in ill-gotten gains over roughly seven years being returned to the Brazilian state. Moreover, Petrobras recovered BRL5.3 billion (USD1 billion), an amount that is close to around 85% of the estimated losses diverted by the fraudsters–BRL6.2 billion (USD1.19 billion).

In 2021, the Supreme Federal Court (STF) ruled that the then federal judge Sergio Moro, who had led Operation Car Wash task force, and who in 2019 became the Minister of the Justice in the Bolsonaro's administration, had not been impartial in coming to his rulings in the process that culminated in former president Lula da Silva's conviction.

In February 2021, the Attorney General's Office (PGR) transferred the Operation Car Wash investigations to the *Special Action Group to Combat Organized Crime* (Gaeco), closing down the task force.

(d) What we learnt or did subsequently:
The *Operation Car Wash* task force managed to probe and punish high-level corporate and political leaders allegedly connected to corruption. Nonetheless, its political support faltered when the STF revoked part of its decisions on the grounds that the task force had resorted to practices at odds with legal procedural formalities, prompting the reaction of politicians under its investigation. These political and judicial backlash ended up closing-down the task force as well as laxer legal changes, making it more difficult to fight corruption.

(e) Public sources:
All Retrieved on 14 July 2022:

https://www.reuters.com/article/us-brazil-corruption-idUSKBN2A4068

https://www.gazetadopovo.com.br/republica/lava-jato-dinheiro-recuperado-destino/

https://www1.folha.uol.com.br/poder/2021/06/supremo-confirma-decisao-que-declarou-moro-parcial-em-caso-de-lula.shtml

https://fortune.com/longform/biggest-companies-in-every-country-global-500/

2.2 *Odebrecht*

A multinational shadow division solely dedicated to buying political patronage.

Created in 1944, Odebrecht is a diversified family business group that operates in construction and engineering services, energy, transportation, and, through the subsidiary Braskem, in the petrochemical industry. In the 2000s, Odebrecht had managed to organize a multinational bribery scheme to obtain politicians' support for shaping legislative measures and rules for public contracts and bids in accordance with its own economic interests. The business group was at the core of the corruption schemes uncovered by *Operation Car Wash*. According to Valor Grandes Grupos, Odebrecht jumped from the 26th position in 2001 to the 6th in 2012 in the ranking of the largest business groups in Brazil, with gross revenues growing on average over the period by 15.9% p.a. ODEBRECHT currently trades as Novonor, having changed its name and corporate identity in December 2020.

(a) What happened:

The Operation Car Wash task force started a probe in 2014 into allegations of bribery involving Petrobras' high executives and politicians from parties of a wide ideological spectrum. The investigations revealed that Petrobras was the mainstay of a scheme of over-invoiced contracts with suppliers and engineering and construction services companies, of which Odebrecht was a key protagonist. The probe into "Petrolão", as the corruption case became known, uncovered that the business group had created a division specifically dedicated to pay bribes, euphemistically called *Division of Structured Operations* (*Departamento de Operações Estruturadas*).

Odebrecht used bribes to shape the terms of the government's auctions in its favor and to benefit from contract renegotiations (Campos et al., 2021). The group's bribing payments grew *pari passu* with its revenues—which jumped from BRL40.9 billion (USD17.5 billion) in 2008 to BRL107.7 billion (USD40.6 billion) in 2014—and internationalization. According to the US Department of Justice, between 2001 and 2015 Odebrecht paid USD788 million worth in bribes to former presidents (or their relatives) and high-ranked officials of Latin American and African countries (such as Peru, Venezuela, Panama, Mexico, Angola, and Mozambique), while Braskem, the group's petrochemical arm, paid a further USD250 million.

Odebrecht also financed electoral campaigns for candidates from different political parties in Brazil as well as in several other Latin American countries, e.g. Argentina, Colombia, Ecuador, Peru, Guatemala, and the Dominican Republic. In Peru, Odebrecht paid USD29 million in bribes to officials over many years, including the presidents Alejandro Toledo, Alan García, Ollanta Humala, and

Pedro Pablo Kuczynski. In Mexico, an ex-CEO of Pemex, the state-controlled oil company, acknowledged,[10] through a plea bargain, that he had received bribes from Braskem in exchange for favorable terms in an auction, on top of accusing three former Presidents (Peña Nieto, Carlos Salinas, and Felipe Calderón) of benefiting from such schemes. Odebrecht's foreign operations were strongly boosted by the Brazilian government system of subsidized export loans, which had financed 17 projects in countries such as Angola, Argentina, Cuba, Ecuador, Guatemala, Honduras, Mexico, Peru, and the Dominican Republic.

(b) How we found out:
Detailed media coverage.

(c) The fallout:
Odebrecht's CEO, Marcelo Odebrecht, was arrested in 2015 and sentenced to 19 years in prison. He remained in jail for just 30 months, being released in December 2017 after signing a plea agreement and assuming the alleged crimes. Based on the US Foreign Corrupt Practices Act, the US Department of Justice fined Odebrecht S.A. USD2.6 billion in 2016, the highest fine ever paid in a corruption case. Pursuant the US Department of Justice report of 21 December 2016, Odebrecht S.A. and Braskem agreed to pay global fines of USD3.5 billion to settle bribery charges with the Brazilian, Swiss, and US prosecutors.

The Odebrecht business group filed for bankruptcy protection in Brazil in June 2019 and for Chapter 15 bankruptcy in New York the following month. With a debt of USD25 billion, part of which was backed by Braskem's shares as collateral, the group had as its largest creditors the major Brazilian state-run banks (BNDES, Banco do Brasil, and Caixa). In the end of 2020, 13 affiliates of the group had gone into receivership.

Odebrecht was forced to transfer most of its main mature businesses as collateral to the reorganization process, among which are Braskem, Atvos (a sugar and ethanol company), and Ocyan (an oil exploration company). In 2020, the group's construction arm, OEC, reached an agreement with its bondholders to ratify the turnaround process. In 2021, Odebrecht (then rebranded as Novonor) announced they were searching for a potential acquirer to Braskem. At the beginning of the following year, Odebrecht and Petrobras, another large shareholder, released their intention to promote BRASKEM's financial restructuring through new issues of preferred shares.

(d) What we learnt or did subsequently:
By several metrics, Odebrecht business group's performance before the uncovering of the illicit practices was outstanding: fast growth in revenues, including those from exports of services to developed and developing countries, expertise in several businesses, subsidiaries in many countries, and strong commitments to social and environmental goals. In 2010, the Swiss business school IMD recognized Odebrecht as the world's best family business group (Campos et al., 2021). As with the case of Enron, a firm's outperformance may weaken the incentives for external monitoring and governance, paving the way to insiders' moral hazard behavior.

One potential explanation for Odebrecht's engagement in such a staggering corruption scandal without being detected by tax authorities and external auditors is the creation in 2006 of the dedicated unit (*Division of Structured Operations*) to deal with the purchase of political patronage through a complex bribery system reliant on a network of firms and financial institutions in tax havens, which resorted to shadow and off-book mechanisms of communications and accounting to undertake its tasks, under the leadership of Odebrecht's chief executive, Marcelo Odebrecht.

(e) Public sources:
Campos, N., Engel, E., Fischer, R. D., & Galetovic, A. (2021). The ways of corruption in infrastructure: Lessons from the Odebrecht case. *Journal of Economic Perspectives, 35*(2), 171–190.

Gaspar, M. (2020). A Organização: A Odebrecht e o Esquema de Corrupção que Chocou o Mundo. Companhia das Letras.

All Retrieved on 14 July 2022:

https://www.justice.gov/opa/pr/odebrecht-and-braskem-plead-guilty-and-agree-pay-least-35-billion-global-penalties-resolve

https://www.justice.gov/opa/press-release/file/919901/download

https://www.justice.gov/opa/press-release/file/919906/download

https://www.justice.gov/opa/press-release/file/919911/download

https://www.justice.gov/opa/press-release/file/919916/dow
nload

2.3 *JBS*

From national champion to global leader: Thriving under the support of political connections.

JBS S.A. is the Brazilian subsidiary of JBS Group, the world's biggest meatpacker. Investigated within the context of "*Operation Car Wash*", the holding company admitted to bribing hundreds of politicians and agreed to pay one of the largest fines for corruption in global corporate history.

(a) What happened:
The *Operation Car Wash* task force revealed that JBS' controlling shareholders transferred to politicians around BRL1 billion (USD192 million as of December 2020) for the sake of bribes and official and hidden campaign donations. In the plea bargaining the company's chairman reported that more than 1,800 politicians had been bribed. The business group had donated to electoral campaigns that managed to elect 179 Federal Deputies, 28 Senators, and 16 Governors, who were willing to favor the group's affiliates in issues related to tax breaks and regulatory bodies' decisions. CVM conducted several probes against the controlling shareholders for the use of insider information in foreign exchange transactions, abuse of controlling power, and self-interested related-party transactions.

Between 2005 and 2016, the Brazilian Development Bank (BNDES) heavily contributed to funding JBS Group's expansion and internationalization, through both subsidized loans and minority equity stakes. Although independent auditors found several instances wherein the bank's officers failed to comply with its lending guidelines, their conclusion was that the financing decisions were not driven to meet the group's interests at the expense of the bank.

(b) How we found out:
The *Operation Car Wash* task force and controlling shareholders' plea-bargaining agreements.

(c) The fallout:

The controlling shareholders were prosecuted and arrested in the aftermath of the investigations. In 2017, the controlling shareholders reached a plea bargain agreement with both the US and Brazilian prosecutors whereby the accusation was ceased. They were released after a short stay in prison and had to pay BRL250 million (equivalent to USD48.1 million in December 2020) in fines. The company in turn agreed to pay BRL10.3 billion (USD1.85 billion) in fines and social projects. In 2020, the Supreme Court ratified the renegotiation of the plea agreement, increasing the controlling shareholders' personal fines to BRL1 billion (USD192 million). By 2019, they had paid 20% of the original value.

In 2020, the holding company J&F Investimentos, which controls JBS, appealed to reduce the company's fines to BRL 1.3 billion, request that was rejected by the Institutional Council of the Federal Public Ministry (CIMPF) in February 2022.

(d) What we learnt or did subsequently:

The impact of plea-bargaining incentives should be considered, given that potential wrongdoers may find that crime pays if the chance of being detected are not high and punishment is limited to the payment of fines (Becker, 1968; Klimczak et al., 2021).

(e) Public sources:

Becker, G. (1968). Crime and punishment: An Economic approach. *Journal of Political Economy, 76*(2), 169–217.

All retrieved on 14 July 2022:

https://sistemas.cvm.gov.br/

https://veja.abril.com.br/brasil/stf-julga-a-validade-das-delacoes-de-joesley-e-wesley-batista/

https://www.bndes.gov.br/arquivos/agencia/relatorio-auditoria-cleary-gottlieb-resumo.pdf

Klimczak, K. M., Sison, A. J. G., Prats, M., & Torres, M. B. (2021). How to deter financial misconduct if crime pays? *Journal of Business Ethics*. Advance online publication.

All retrieved on 14 July 2022:

https://sistemas.cvm.gov.br/
https://veja.abril.com.br/brasil/stf-julga-a-validade-das-delacoes-de-joesley-e-wesley-batista/
https://www.bndes.gov.br/arquivos/agencia/relatorio-auditoria-cleary-gottlieb-resumo.pdf
https://www.reuters.com/article/us-j-f-brazil-crime-idUKKBN26Z2FZ
https://www.jdsupra.com/legalnews/brazilian-meatpacking-company-settles-7344845/

2.4 *Grupo EBX*

Boom and bust of one of the largest Brazilian business groups.

The Brazilian business group EBX operated in the businesses of oil and gas (OGX), energy (MPX), logistics (LLX), mining (MMX), and shipbuilding (OSX). After being convicted for insider trading and corruption, its controlling shareholder relinquished his stakes in most of the companies, either voluntarily or mandated by bankruptcy procedures.

(a) What happened:
Grupo EBX's controlling shareholder was prosecuted and convicted for paying bribes to politicians, insider trading, and market price manipulation in several affiliated firms. In 2011 and 2012, the Toronto Stock Exchange detected market price manipulations during the negotiations for the acquisition of the mining companies Ventura Gold and Galway by AUX Canada, an affiliated company of Grupo EBX, involving around USD70 million in each of the two cases. The controlling shareholder's objectives were to buy the mining companies at a lower price and reduce the minority shareholders' reluctance to the deal.

Market price manipulations also occurred in the São Paulo Stock Exchange (B3). First, fraudulent trading of shares of MPX Energia, an affiliate of Grupo EBX, was carried out between January and April 2013, amounting to BRL85 million (USD36 million in 2013). Second, MMX Mineração e Metálicos, another affiliate, had its share prices manipulated between March 2013 and January 2015, totaling BRL30 million (USD7.8 million).

In 2017, Grupo EBX's controlling shareholder was also charged for paying BRL16.5 million (USD5 million in 2017) in bribes to the former Governor of Rio de Janeiro in exchange for state construction contracts. In 2018, he was convicted and sentenced to 30 years in prison.

(b) How we found out:
Investigations led the asset manager Opus Investimentos' founder and controlling shareholders to sign plea-bargaining agreements whereby they paid BRL300 million (USD57.8 million in 2020) worth of fines as well as delivered USD9.2 million of Grupo EBX's controlling shareholder that was under their custody. The latter's plea bargaining agreement was connected to bribing politicians.

(c) The fallout:
The controlling shareholder was prosecuted and convicted for financial market crimes and corruption. By the sole clause disclosed of the plea-bargaining agreement with the Public Ministry and the Supreme Court, he agreed to pay BRL800 million (USD154 million in 2020) in fines.

(d) What we learnt or did subsequently:
The *Operation Car Wash* task force's rights and wrongs leave important lessons. An intelligence division well designed and equipped with appropriate financial and human resources to enforce the capital markets' legal and regulatory framework by conducting thorough probes to uncover offenders and submit them to fair judgments seem to be a promising avenue to inhibit white-collar crimes. Public support for its activities is likely to be decisive in achieving its goal and avoiding backlashes, which explains why enforcement institutions, at the multiple levels, must act in accordance with their formally assigned missions, so complying with all the legal and procedural formalities.

(e) Public sources:

All Retrieved on 14 July 2022:

https://agenciabrasil.ebc.com.br/justica/noticia/2019-08/entenda-os-crimes-atribuidos-eike-que-o-levaram-de-volta-prisao

https://www1.folha.uol.com.br/mercado/2020/11/ministra-rosa-weber-do-stf-homologa-delacao-premiada-de-eike-batista.shtml

2.5 *Brasil Resseguros (IRB)*

Boosting stock prices and executive pay by cooking the books: Monitors' failings and whistleblowing.

Created in 1939, the reinsurance company IRB Brasil Resseguros became a government-controlled company in 1996, was privatized in 2013, and went public in 2017. From its IPO to 2019, its stock prices increased by 400%. In January 2020, an asset manager released a report suggesting that the company had manipulated the financial statements, triggering a sharp fall in the stock price and the top management's replacement. Notwithstanding most monitors' omissions and failures, one active market monitor blew the whistle on an accounting fraud.

(a) What happened:
Following the IPO in July 2017, the share price of Brasil Resseguros (IRB) escalated sharply until peaking at over BRL40 at the end of January 2020, when an asset manager, Squadra Investimentos, released a report questioning IRB's accounting and casting suspicion on its recurring stellar financial performance. The share price plummeted afterwards, and the pandemic reinforced the nosedive.

On a conference call in early March 2020, IRB's CFO and CEO falsely reported that Berkshire Hathaway had raised its stake in the company, fostering a rally in the share price. Following a declaration by Warren Buffett's investment firm that it "*is not currently a shareholder of IRB, it has never been a shareholder of IRB and it has no intention of becoming a shareholder of IRB*", the share price resumed its fall, prompting the resignation of both the CEO and the CFO.

An internal audit carried out by an independent firm contracted by the new management concluded that the former executives had manipulated the financial statements, omitting BRL1.3 billion (USD250 million in 2020) worth of liabilities to artificially inflate profits and boost the share price. The bogus valuation entitled the top executive team to aggregate bonuses amounting to BRL60 million (USD11.6 million).

(b) How we found out:
The fund manager Squadra blew the whistle on IRB's wrongdoings, which were quickly echoed throughout the specialized media and news agencies.

(c) The fallout:
In 2020, IRB's share price fell from BRL40.88 on 27 January to BRL10.00 on 13 March and to 11.00 BRL on 30 July. On 30 November 2021, the price reached BRL4.20.

IRB sued the former management and sent and internal audit report to the Prosecutor's Office and to the CVM, which, on 31 May 2021, announced the initiation of proceedings and two enquiries. The first enquiry led to proceedings to probe IRB's irregular share trading in the three first months of 2020 and the sharp rise in its share price after Squadra Investimentos' reported IRB's false information regarding Berkshire Hathaway, as well as Squadra's conflicts of interest in holding short positions in IRB shares. The second enquiry arose from proceedings begun in December 2019 and looked into IRB's financial statements non-compliance with mandatory disclosure requirements, as raised by Squadra.

(d) What we learnt or did subsequently:
Ironically, in 2019 IRB had been awarded the "Discovery" company-of-the-year prize by three specialized firms in providing financial services of analysis, education, and data (InfoMoney, Ibmec, and Economatica, respectively). The prize was given to the best companies going public in the three previous years that excelled in profitability, share performance, and corporate governance. Indeed, IRB's reported return on net worth in 2018 was 32%—much higher than the average of 5.9% for the main global reinsurers.

Privatized in 2013, the case of IRB endorses the view that governance failures are not restricted to government-controlled companies. It fell to a fund manager, Squadra, holding and disclosing its short position in IRB, to take the initiative to denounce the illicit records in the reinsurer's accounting.

It is noteworthy that, albeit ITAU UNIBANCO and BaANCO BRADESCO, two leading Brazilian banks, had high equity stakes in IRB, both nonetheless failed to play their expected monitoring role. Another gatekeeper, the auditing firm BDO TREVISAN, also missed overseeing IRB's management misconduct. As Brooks (2018, p. 196) points out, "[...] leaving the critical task of checking the finances of the banks and companies [...] to what are essentially all-purpose management consultancies is a recipe for further disaster."

The Brazilian regulatory change that allowed plea bargaining as a mechanism to foster whistleblowing (Law 12.850/2013) seems to have been more effective in curbing corporate wrongdoings than expected monitors such as audit committees, auditing firms, and boards of directors.

(e) Public sources:

Brooks, R. (2018). Bean counters: The triumph of the accountants and how they broke capitalism. Atlantic Books.

All Retrieved on 14 July 2022:

Sontag, R. (2019). Para uma história da delação premiada no Brasil. *Revista Brasileira de Direito Processual Penal*, *5*(1), 441–468.

All retrieved on 14 July 2022:

https://www.infomoney.com.br/negocios/irb-brasil-re-a-ex-estatal-que-triplicou-de-valor/

https://valor.globo.com/financas/noticia/2020/09/21/irb-poderia-nao-ter-sobrevivido-a-fraudes.ghtml

https://www.reuters.com/article/us-irb-brasil-accounting-idUSKBN20R31C

https://www.nasdaq.com/articles/shares-in-brazil-irb-resseguros-sink-after-buffetts-berkshire-denies-owning-stake-2020-03

https://www.gov.br/cvm/pt-br/assuntos/noticias/informacoes-relativas-a-companhia-irb-brasil-resseguros-s-a

https://www.gov.br/cvm/pt-br/assuntos/noticias/informacoes-relativas-a-companhia-irb-brasil-resseguros-sa-863975920cdc4a5d8495986a57b5dbbe

2.6 AmBev

An ingenious (and stealthy) approach to corporate takeovers.

AmBev, the Brazilian subsidiary of the world's largest brewer, AB-Inbev, emerged in 1999 from the merger between two centenary domestic breweries (Brahma and Antarctica). It has been controlled by a shareholder agreement comprising three investors (Jorge Paulo Lemann, Carlos Alberto Sicupira, and Marcel Telles) and its employees' pension fund. In 2004, Lemann, Sicupira, and Telles took control of AmBev's through controversial stock options transactions, which later allowed them to carry out its merger with Interbrew, a Belgian brewery. CVM initiated an administrative proceeding to sanction the three investors, who subsequently offered to pay a penalty to settle the CVM charges.

(a) What happened:

In March 2004, AmBev, then and now Brazil's largest brewer, announced its merger with Interbrew. As of October 2002, AmBev had been controlled by a shareholder agreement between the holding company Braco—owned by Lemann, Sicupira and Telles—and a non-profit entity. As indicated, Braco's owners were also AmBev directors. According to the merger agreement, Interbrew should issue new shares to Braco's controlling shareholders in exchange for control. Given Braco's equity stake of 52.8% in AmBev's voting capital at the time of the deal, Interbrew *de facto* controlled AmBev. In addition, after the merger AmBev would have to issue new shares to Interbrew and assume debts of USD1.5 billion in exchange for Interbrew's North American operations.

A CVM commission confirmed that the deal discriminated against AmBev's minority shareholders, concluding that the new common shares were negotiated at a large premium, diluting the preferred shareholders' interests. The commission also accused Telles, who was one of the board co-chairmen, of trading on insider information in June 2003, when he sold a large block of preferred shares he had acquired through stock option plans to Ambev. Telles countered that he used all the proceeds from the sale to buy common shares, exercising his rights to stock options granted as part of previous compensation packages. However, it was shown that the stock option plans gave AmBev a priority to acquire the block of common shares at the average market price should Telles decide to sell it. Violating this clause, he transferred to Braco, both directly and through his two partners, that block of shares together with another block he already owned. Moreover, the price for which he sold the common shares to Braco was 30% lower than the price the company should have paid and 50% lower than the price he himself paid. The commission argued that Braco's owners undertook these private transactions to achieve *stealth control* of AmBev, as the block of shares that Telles acquired through stock option plans and transferred to Braco was pivotal for this company to reach a 52% stake in AmBev's voting capital. Furthermore, as Lemann, Sicupira, and

Telles were members of the AmBev board, the stock option plans were generously designed for them, with the strike price set at 90% of the average market prices in the three days before the date of granting, which was not previously determined and varied from year to year.

(b) How we found out:
CVM's sanctioning administrative resolution PAS 21/2005, media coverage and news agencies, such as Reuters.

(c) The fallout:
CVM's administrative resolution accused Telles, Lemann, and Sicupira of both abusing its controlling power and concealing their acquisition of a relevant equity stake in AmBev. As the company's directors, they were also liable for insider trading and breaches of the duty of loyalty to the company, as they undertook irregular trading of the shares acquired through stock option plans. All three submitted settlement offers to CVM whereby each would pay BRL1 million (USD430,000). The commissioner in charge of reviewing the proposal urged for its rejection, arguing that the imputed infractions were grave and that there were four other CVM on-going inquiries involving the three accused. After the board of commissioners turned the proposals down, Telles, Lemann, and Sicupira made a second proposal to pay BRL5 million (USD2.14 million) each. This offer was approved by the board.

(d) What we learnt or did subsequently:
The case draws attention to the sophisticated strategy the three investors conceived of to take control of the company—relying primarily on their dominant influence on the board of directors, the instance responsible for designing the stock option plans—as well as the harmful incentives entailed by the regulators' acceptance of the alleged wrongdoers' settlement proposal. The accused directors' payment of BRL5 million (USD2.14 million) to prevent the CVM from sanctioning administrative proceedings is likely disproportionate to the magnitude of economic and reputational benefits they obtained in acting as they did.

(e) Public sources:

The above account is drawn from Aldrighi (2011), who relied on reports from the *Term of Commitment Committee* and the *Amendment to the Proposal for the Term of Commitment*, both related to the PAS 21/2005 and which were available on 6 January 2011, but now are no longer to be found at http://www.cvm.gov.br/port/descol/respdecis.asp?File556342-0.htm

Aldrighi, D. M. (2011). Risks of wrongdoing in public companies and ways to cope with them. In S. Rose-Ackerman & T. Søreide (Ed.), *International handbook on the economics of corruption*, Vol. 2, Chapter 8, Edward Elgar Publishing.

Retrieved on 14 July 2022:

www.reuters.com/article/abinbev-brazil-fines-idUSN2418895020091224

2.7 *Lessons from Brazil and Open Questions for Further Research*

The quality and effectiveness of corporate governance effectiveness of corporate associated with the legal and regulatory framework, boards of directors, patterns of ownership (whether concentrated or dispersed, whether a controlling shareholder exist ...), shareholder activism, generally from institutional investors, and the market for corporate control. As discussed above, the institutional environment underlying capital markets in Brazil has improved significantly since 2000, mainly due to the legal reforms, the granting of enhanced power to CVM's in carrying out its mission as regulatory and enforcement authority with autonomy and independence, and the ongoing efforts of B3 to upgrade the listed companies' governance standards.

Nonetheless, corruption and corporate wrongdoings, such as those carried out in Petrobras and Odebrecht, were uncovered thanks primarily to the *Operation Car Wash*, a task force led by a team of public attorneys that managed the probe and lead successful court cases, that resolved against wealthy and powerful politicians and business leaders, some of whom went to jail. . Its reliance on unorthodox methods in carrying out its investigations and striking plea bargaining agreements with the accused executives and politicians, as well as the political ambitions of some of the *Operation Car Wash*'s main leaders, as revealed over subsequent years, has triggered backlash against the fight to curtail corruption.

These include recent legislative actions to limit the power of the Brazilian Department of Justice.

It should be noted that JBS, Grupo EBX's firms (e.g. MMX, OGX, MPX, and OSX), and IRB were all listed on the *Novo Mercado*, the listing segment requiring the most stringent corporate governance standards. Neither the *Novo Mercado*'s "seal" of governance quality nor the amended Corporate Law succeeded in precluding IRB's CEO and CFO from manipulating their public financial accounts. The IRB episode provides additional evidence of behavioral finance implications from investors' bounded rationality and the financial markets' fragility to rein in corporate insiders' unscrupulous self-interested decisions.

In the six cases reviewed, the boards of directors failed flagrantly to comply with their assigned roles as the first barrier against corporate mismanagement and undue practices. That internal corporate governance mechanism was submissive to controlling shareholders in the cases of Braskem, JBS, Grupo EBX, and AmBev, and neglectful in the cases of Petrobras and IRB.

It is also worth noting that, among the six cases of corporate wrongdoing in Brazilian firms, bribery and corrupt practices are present in Petrobras, Grupo EBX, JBS, and Odebrecht. Even though only the former is a state-controlled public company, all of them expropriated government resources—and thus those of taxpayers—through over-invoiced contracts for public works or the provision of services and inputs, influencing tax rules and legislation, and privileged access to public concessions. Those schemes benefited politicians, entrepreneurs, top executives, public servants, and controlling shareholders. In 2016, the Brazilian congress issued the Law 13,303/2016 (the so-called the "state-owned enterprise law"), which represents a landmark in the evolution of the governance practices in state-controlled companies, aiming at reducing the risk of rent extraction from state-owned companies by politicians and specific interest groups, responsible for notorious cases of corruption and the inefficient allocation of public resources.

Finally, as seen in the cases of Petrobras, JBS, Grupo EBX, AmBev, and Braskem (the only publicly traded company of the Odebrecht business group), ownership concentration, which is ubiquitous in Brazil (and in much of Latin America), inherently biases companies' internal corporate governance protocols and attitudes towards prioritizing controlling shareholders' interests, generally at the expense of the other stakeholders. To conclude, we suggest the following recommendations to contribute to improving the corporate governance environment in Brazil:

1. Attempts to design and enforce public policies to fight such corporate wrongdoings should consider the backlashes stemming from groups with vested interests groups from the very moment they are proposed in legislative and regulatory instances.
2. Just as corporate underperformance usually raises suspicion from investors, other stakeholders, and analysts, outperformance should equally require require systematic and thorough monitoring, as the cases of Odebrecht and IRB demonstrate.
3. As recurring cases of corporate wrongdoings engender negative externalities to the whole capital markets and the economy as a whole, regulatory and legal frameworks need to be strategically designed, implemented, and enforced to prevent such cases. In this sense, the laws aiming to combat corruption (12.850/2013) and to inhibit trusts and collusions (12.529/2011) appear to be on the right track.
4. Law enforcement is pivotal in providing capital market players with the right incentives to comply with the rules and regulations (e.g. Petrobras, Group EBX, and Odebrecht).
5. Market mechanisms, such as short selling, are positive, as they may contribute to creating economic incentives to catch and dissuade corporate misbehavior (e.g., Squadra in the case of IRB).
6. Activist institutional investors as well as financial analysts and investment advisors are well placed to put pressure on companies to be more transparent and to furnish the disclosure of the relevant information (e.g., IRB, AmBev, and Odebrecht).
7. Efforts and resources should be directed to prevent corporate misbehavior in the first place. Nonetheless, the design of effective dissuasive mechanisms remains a challenge to those engaged in enhancing corporate governance.
8. Authorities responsible for enforcing the capital markets' regulations should take stock of the perverse incentive implications of accepting pecuniary fines and payments from alleged fraudsters whose wealth is disproportionately higher in exchange for terminating their probes. The payoff for corporate crimes may in fact, be rewarding if the countervailing punishments are not adequately

designed (e.g., Odebrecht, JBS, and Ambev). A matter of concern is that even the executives and firms that struck plea-bargains with the prosecutors and attorney general offices, having agreed to pay huge amounts in fines to settle the accusation of corruption practices, are now trying to renegotiate the deal and alleviate the penalties.

3 Chile

Matias Zegers Ruíz-Tagle and Carla Meza Morales

Corporate governance structures and practices have changed dramatically in Chile over the last 20 years. As the following cases illustrate, in the late 1990s and early 2000s, the cases were more related to structural corporate governing issues, which showed up important misconceptions in how companies should be managed—primarily seen on the boards of listed companies—when moving from being closely held to, precisely, listed companies and, as a consequence the impact on emerging focus on directors' fiduciary responsibilities—their duties of care and loyalty and the management of conflicts of interest.

Over the last 10 years, the situation has again changed with the heightened awareness among all relevant stakeholders—including controlling shareholders and institutional investors—of the need for sound corporate governing structures, and as will be seen in practice, some fell short. There was some disconnect between the implementation of formal best practices and the real world, where sometimes lack of control or complex systems worked against the best interests of the organization. On top of all this, the emerging focus on ESG parameters has introduced significant pressures, which will likely lead to new situations and practices that will require further study.

M. Zegers Ruíz-Tagle
Faculty of Law, Pontificia Universidad Católica de Chile, Santiago, Chile
e-mail: mzegers@baz.cl

C. Meza Morales
Pontificia Universidad Católica de Chile, Santiago, Chile
e-mail: cbmeza@uc.cl

3.1 ENDESA Chile (Chispas)

Conflicts of interest and related-party transactions in the context of takeovers.

Empresa Nacional de Electricidad S.A. (ENDESA) was established by the State development corporation CORFO in 1943 with a capital of 500 million pesos with a view to developing the country's hydroelectric generation capacity as well as transmission and distribution. Despite initial problems, it came to manage over half of Chile's energy generation in the early 1970s and was a successful state-owned enterprise. However, given its large capital costs and sophisticated engineering scale, with the prevailing economic policies of the 1980s, it was key candidate and was privatized in 1987. This process involved selling equity to ENDESA employees in a process known as *capitalismo popular* together with the pension funds and other institutional investors, listing its stock on the Santiago Stock Exchange (SSE).[12] In 1994, it also issued ADRs on the NYSE.

Following its privatization, under the control of a small group of executives who, through their company ENERSIS, bought up the small holdings of stock, ENDESA quickly expanded throughout Latin America, becoming the largest private electricity generation utility in the region. In 1997, ENERSIS — now the largest owner of ENDESA Chile — negotiated its sale to ENDESA España.

(a) What happened:

The voids in the law at the time allowed the controlling shareholders of ENERSIS to obtain disproportionate rewards, receiving a substantial premium over and above the prevailing market price. These special conditions of sale were only possible given the existence of two classes of shares: Class A shares, with an entitlement to higher dividends, but no voting rights, and Class B shares, which could elect the majority of the board. In addition, holders of Class B shares also concurrently held positions on the ENERSIS board and/or were C-suite executives.

ENDESA España negotiated the terms of the sale directly with the controllers of ENERSIS. Class B shares were offered a price 840

[12] Bolsa de Comercio de Santiago (BCS).

times higher than the price offered for Class A shares, as well as the granting of extra benefits to its shareholders (the preferential price for ENDESA España shares and the grandfathering of employment contracts). For these reasons, the deal soon became known as "*the deal of the century*".

(b) How we found out:

The sale of ENERSIS was a public event, but it was mainly the AFPs (the asset managers representing the country's mandatory pension fund savings) who cried foul, in protest at the Class B minority the shareholders' (those of ENERSIS) disproportional benefits and the evident corporate governing issues.

(c) The fallout:

The AFPs, representing their members' pension funds, only held non-voting Class A shares and, from the outset, opposed the deal. The initial terms of the initial public offering (IPO or "OPA"[13] in Spanish) were struck down by the (Superintendency of Securities and Insurance or "SVS")—the market regulator, a decision that was subsequently upheld by the Supreme Court.

Subsequently, the SVS brought charges against the controllers, arguing primarily on grounds of a board members' breaches in their duty of loyalty. The courts sentenced all those involved and ordered them, in aggregate, to pay around USD75 million in fines.

(d) What we learnt or did subsequently:

The *Chispas* case arguably marked the turning point for corporate governance in Chile and—even 25 years after the event—it is still a landmark case that is studied and analyzed in corporate governance classrooms in Chile and abroad. As described in the Chile chapter, the scandal was the precursor of a law that specifically regulated publish tender offerings (Law No. 19,705). This law sought to improve transparency in the market, the protection of minority shareholders' rights, as well as laying down the terms and procedures for takeovers.

(e) Public sources:

All Retrieved on 14 July 2022:

[13] *Oferta pública de adquisición.*

https://www.cmfchile.cl/portal/prensa/615/articles-11934_doc_pdf.pdf

https://www.elmercurio.com/legal/movil/detalle.aspx?Id=903441&Path=/0D/C9/

https://www.ifc.org/wps/wcm/connect/topics_ext_content/ifc_external_corporate_site/sustainability-at-ifc/publications/publications_casestudy_cg-focus6

3.2 FASA

When a controlling shareholder doesn't consider the company's board.

Farmacias Ahumada S.A. (FASA) is the largest drugstore chain in Latin America and one of the largest in the world in number of outlets, with a network of around a thousand pharmacies in Chile, Peru, Brazil, and Mexico. It was founded in 1968 by a José Codner Chijneros when he established his first pharmacy in Santiago. He gradually expanded the network of the FASA outlets nationwide in the 1980s and 1990s, expanding to Peru in 1996, then to Brazil in 2000 and Mexico in 2002.

The retail drugstore sector in Chile is concentrated in three large players, FASA, Cruz Verde, and Salco Brand, with FASA currently controlling around 40% of the market.

(a) What happened:

2006 saw the culmination of an intense pricing war between the three largest retail pharmacy chains—FASA, Cruz Verde, and Salco Brand—leading to squeezed profit margins in the market. In 2008, following media reports of persistent rises in the prices of specific drugs and medicines and suspicion of a cartel, the antitrust authority (Fiscalía Nacional Económica or "FNE") initiated an under-cover investigation that led to large economic sanctions (in excess of USD20 million) against all three chains, having been found to be party to agreements to end the pricing war and agree on prices.

In 2009, the SVS fined all the directors of FASA for breaching their duty of monitoring and being informed about antitrust violations committed by its employees.

FASA management were informed of the FNE's investigation in April 2008, but this information was not passed on to the board until June that same year—and with scant detail. In December 2009, the

FNE presented the case to the antitrust Courts. An internal investigation was conducted in FASA—but the board was not told about this initiative—and, given the results (hard evidence of the collusion was substantiated), the administration of FASA began negotiations—on condition of leniency[21] (*delación compensada*)—to settle the case directly with FNE. These negotiations ended in March 2009 with a settlement that recognized the existence of antitrust practices. The settlement was only reported to the board on the day that it was filed with the antitrust Courts.

(b) How we found out:

Initially, the press sounded the alarm on the rises in pharmacy prices. Subsequently, the AFPs reported the corporate governance mistakes, including misinformation, nepotism, and the irrelevance of minority shareholders.

(c) The fallout:

In December 2009, the SVS fined the board for being in breach of their duty of care in not having insisted that management should provide a complete report of the antitrust requirements.

Besides the collusion scandal itself, the minority shareholders (primarily the AFPs) also denounced a series of corporate governance malpractices. At the time of the FNE investigation, the board of directors comprised the founder, controller, and CEO of the company, José Codner, four other directors, chosen through his controlling votes, two other directors elected by the minority shareholders and two other directors elected by the AFPs (pension fund managers). The minority shareholder directors accused José Codner of having hidden the investigations from the board and an abuse of his position as controller.

(d) What we learnt or did subsequently:

The FASA case highlighted the importance that board members are entitled to be informed, but that it is their duty to exercise such a right. While the corporate governance law of 2009 (Law No. 20,382) was primarily introduced to meet OECD membership requirements, following the FASA case, additional legal changes were introduced, most notably new protections for minority shareholders through enhanced transparency standards and mechanisms to address the (ab)use of privileged information.

(e) Public sources: All retrieved on 14 July 2022:
All Retrieved on 14 July 2022:

https://www.cmfchile.cl/portal/prensa/615/articles-13361_doc_pdf.pdf

http://www.fundinguniverse.com/company-histories/farmacias-ahumada-s-a-history/

https://www.cmfchile.cl/portal/prensa/615/w3-article-12084.html

https://www.latercera.com/noticia/actas-describen-como-se-gesto-el-quiebre-en-el-directorio-de-fasa-en-2009/

https://www.latercera.com/noticia/svs-multa-a-10-altos-directivos-de-fasa-por-incumplir-ley-de-s-a/

3.3 Pehuenche

Penalizing abuses in assigning contracts to parties in the same group that weakens the competitive environment.

Empresa Pehuenche was a subsidiary of ENDESA Chile, the holding company controlled through Spanish owner ENDESA España. Empresa Tricahue S.A., was a company incorporated by the employees of ENDESA CHILE who participated in the construction of the Pehuenche hydroelectric plant, with around 7% of equity in Empresa Pehuenche.

(a) What happened:
In 2007, Empresa Eléctrica Pehuenche signed an electricity supply contract with Empresa Tricahue, which did not follow the arm's length principle, but favored the major shareholder (which was also an ENDESA Chile subsidiary). The estimated damages of this contract to Empresa Tricahue—as assessed by the litigants—amounted to USD330 million.

(b) How we found out:
Minority shareholder activism, as the biggest minority shareholder (Inversiones Tricahue S.A.) filed a lawsuit against the majority shareholders with the SVS.

(c) The fallout:

Following accusations of the minority shareholders, in 2011 the SVS began to investigate and sanction Pehuenche directors based on an infraction of the duty of care when evaluating transactions with related parties. The Regulator found that Pehuenche's directors had not complied with the duty established in article 41 of the Company Act in so far as they had not taken the appropriate steps to ensure that the conditions of its supply contract with the parent were on competitive market terms. In addition, it went further in finding that the members of the Board Committee had not complied with the correct RPT procedures when approving the contract.

Six ENDESA Chile directors were fined UF300 (around USD12,000) each and additional fines of UF400 (around USD16,000) each were due from the members of the Board Committee.

The CEO of Pehuenche subsequently lost his job, presumably for having denied information to minority shareholders and agreed on the deal with ENDESA.

(d) What we learnt or did subsequently:

Following the SVS sanctions, ENDESA Chile settled its disagreements with Tricahue over Pehuenche by signing a new contract on market conditions.

The case also was a landmark for minority shareholders exercising their rights against a controller. It is important to note that more recently these same minority shareholders opposed a controversial merger deal to form ENEL (the name of the new company formed after Italian ENEL Group acquired Spain's ENDESA Group) allegedly because the terms of the merger only favored the controller.

At the time corporate governance law of 2009 (Law No. 20,382) had recently included enhancements to the regulation of Related-party Transactions, which has subsequently been reinforced in 2021 by Law No. 21,314 (2021).

(e) Public sources:

All Retrieved on 14 July 2022:

https://www.cmfchile.cl/documentos/res/res_2013_344.pdf

https://m.elmostrador.cl/mercados/2011/10/13/svs-sanciona-a-directores-de-endesa-en-pehuenche-por-vulnerar-la-ley-de-sociedades-anonimas/

https://www.revistaei.cl/2008/09/15/la-historia-detras-del-conflicto-entre-endesa-e-inversiones-tricahue/#

3.4 *Enersis*

Related-party transactions (RPT) when raising capital from institutional investors.

In July 2011, the holding of ENDESA Chile (ENDESA Spain – through ENDESA Latinoamérica, S.A.) proposed an unprecedented capital increase for ENERSIS (Chile's largest financial operation in recent times), amounting to USD8,020 million, to be paid for by ENDESA through "contributions in kind" (primarily through the transfer of shares that the ENDESA Group was holding in different subsidiary companies in South America), while the rest of the minority shareholders were required to make cash commitments.

In April 2015, ENDESA Chile informed the SVS of a proposal of ENEL (the final controlling group of ENDESA with Italian capital) of a restructuring process in ENERSIS with the purported intention of separating electricity generation and distribution activities in Chile from those of other Latin American countries, and with the subsequent merger of the non-Chilean businesses to constitute a new holding company that would also operate in Chile.

(a) **What happened:**

Enersis I

Should the minority owners elect not to participate in the capital increase, then new foreign capital would be sought and found, so further diluting their ownership in the company. This proposed restructuring came at a time when ENDESA Spain needed to liquidate assets due to the financial crisis that affected Spain in 2011.

Enersis II

This restructuring proposal went counter to the commitments assumed by ENDESA Group during the capital increase agreement of 2011. Again, these proposals were strongly resisted by the minority shareholders, mainly the AFPs.

(b) How we found out:
Public information provided by ENDESA to the SVS.

(c) The fallout:

Enersis I

The SVS considered the whole capital increase operation to be a transaction between related parties that consequently should comply both with rules regarding capital increase operations and operations among related parties, respectively. After a debate, ENDESA Chile accepted the SVS instructions and procedures regarding capital increases, applying the rules for RPTs.

As a last step in accepting the capital increase, ENDESA Spain issued a *Letter of Commitment*, granting guarantees to minority shareholders regarding all *Cono Sur*[14] operations carried out by the ENDESA Group, committing to ensure ENERSIS would be the sole vehicle used to promote growth, dividend policies, use of funds, and a promise to remain in the sub-region.

The terms of the capital increase were agreed in December 2011 with most minority shareholders signing and paying in the capital increases and receiving the new shares.

Enersis II

After a consultancy process with the SVS, promoted by the minority shareholders—the market authority ruled that this operation would not be treated as an operation between related parties. Regardless, the minority shareholders demanded stronger assurances for their respective positions and better conditions. Eventually, the minority shareholders agreed on the restructuring process.

(d) What we learnt or did subsequently:
Minority shareholders, especially institutional investors such as the AFPs, representing their pension funds, when organized can have a significant impact on corporate governing decisions vis-à-vis the controllers and ensuring that their rights are protected under the legal framework and quickly gaining the support of the market authority.

[14] *The Southern Cone* is a geographic and cultural region composed of the southernmost areas of South America, mostly south of the Tropic of Capricorn. Traditionally, it covers Argentina, Chile, and Uruguay, bounded on the west by the Pacific Ocean and on the east by the Atlantic Ocean.

(e) Public sources:

All retrieved on 14 July 2022:

https://www.cmfchile.cl/portal/prensa/615/w3-article-12323.html

https://www.enel.cl/en/investors/investor-enel-generacion/projects/corporate-reorganization-enel-generacion-chile.html

https://www.cepchile.cl/cep/opinan-en-la-prensa/leonidas-montes/las-lecciones-de-enersis

https://www.latercera.com/diario-impreso/caso-enersis-svs-falla-a-favor-de-minoritarios-y-obliga-a-rehacer-operacion/

https://www.latercera.com/noticia/guillermo-arthur-por-enersis-las-afp-no-han-sobrerreaccionado/

https://www.latercera.com/noticia/las-dos-decadas-cambios-llegar-enel-chile/

3.5 La Polar

Management fraud and board members' duty of care.

The Chilean retail industry is very competitive, which has led to retailers also establishing consumer lending businesses to offset the low margins. The retail market is dominated by four leading groups—Falabella, Cencosud, Ripley, and La Polar, all with branded department chain-stores and the former two also with grocery stores and home improvement centers. All the groups are public companies with deeply traded stocks on the Santiago Stock Exchange, being held by the AFPs, mutual funds, and other institutional investors. As a client loyalty tool, all the chains offer their clients branded store credit cards as non-bank retail credit is largely unregulated.

As the fourth largest retailer in Chile, when La Polar went public in 2003, it had 43 department stores, on the high streets of smaller regional towns, primarily selling clothing, white lines, and electronic goods to the lower economic segments of the population. Another key difference with the other groups is that La Polar, unlike most of the traded public companies in Chile, has no controlling shareholder.

(a) What happened:

In line with the market, La Polar offered its clients a store credit card (*Tarjeta La Polar*), which soon became good business and a key driver of its growth. The company was very aggressive in its credit policies, and with dispersed ownership, the executive team had significant levels of independence and trust from the board (the CEO won a "CEO of the decade" award in 2009) which came with a generous options plans if certain results were achieved.

The store credit card sector was deeply affected by the 2008 global financial crisis and by 2010, all retailers except La Polar were reporting declining revenues, increasing credit card failures, and high loan loss provisions. However, La Polar credit business was thriving, reporting high fees and interest income and low write-offs, delinquencies, and loan loss provisions. In what was later discovered, this apparent success was due to the illegal practice of unilaterally rolling-over and refinancing their customers store credit card debts, strongly incentivized by the needs of the management team to post strong results, and so vest their options, rolling millions of pesos of fees and arrears interest into the clients' balances due and then assigning impossible monthly payments to customers' unpaid cards, all without their knowledge or approval.

As in many other cases with clear agency issues, this case ended up with institutional investors (primarily AFPs and life insurance companies) footing the bill for the management team's misdemeanors. From a consumer standpoint, however, this system provided some real benefits: firstly as they were never declared in default with the credit rating agencies, so allowing them to show a clean record of being up to date in their payments and, secondly, as part of the final resolution much (if not all) of their debts were written down as non-recoverable, so ensuring the clients never had to pay.

(b) How we found out:

The scandal was unveiled by the office of Chile's consumer ombudsman Servicio Nacional del Consumidor or SERNAC, that began receiving complaints from La Polar's customers about the company's unilateral refinancing program. By May of 2011, the number of customer complaints had grown to such a level that a group of inority shareholders and SERNAC filed complaints with the securities regulator—then the SVS, today CMF—and called for a hearing to examine La Polar's credit card portfolio.

(c) The fallout:

La Polar informed the market in June 2011 that its financial reports had vastly under-provisioned its consumer credit card portfolio, that practices of its credit card portfolio were contrary to the company's parameters and standards, and that very high provisions were required to fix the situation. In one day, La Polar's share price dropped 42%. Trading was suspended for a week, after which the stock plunged more than 70%.

Criminal and civil charges were imposed by the courts. The SVS imposed fines on twelve executives, all—the highest individual fine being UF25,000 (USD1.16 million in March 2012) on the CEO—as well as the ten directors, and the auditing firm (PwC) and lead partner for breaching their fiduciary responsibilities and being in violation of Securities and Corporations Acts—a total of around USD5.6 million. Criminal and civil charges were also imposed by the courts. In addition to the fines, all five members of the management team were convicted and sentenced to up to 5 years in jail (although they were subsequently paroled, only serving real jail time while awaiting their convictions and the pronouncement of the sentences). As regards the auditors, the Supreme Court subsequently reached a decision in multiple cases that were brought by each of the institutional investors for over USD400 million in financial damages—primarily to the Pension Funds that the AFPs manage—and PwC has settled all its claims for around USD64 million.

(d) What we learnt or did subsequently:

La Polar was a huge scandal in the financial sector which led to several changes, which many stakeholders still consider to be "insufficient":

- The SVS pushed for greater financial disclosure by retailers operating in the finance sector. This has since led to some retailers reorganizing these aspects of their businesses, obtaining a banking license, or entering out-sourcing agreements with existing banks.
- There was a focus on the financial consumer with SERNAC establishing a specialized branch—"SERNAC Financiero"—and enhancements were made to the consumer protection act.

- The SVS raised standards on audit firms and risk-rating agencies.

After several cases (FASA; Pehuenche, Enersis I) and La Polar Case, there has been a drive for greater professionalization of members of the board and enhanced disclosure of their corporate governance practices.

There are grounds to view the La Polar case as a backdrop against which General Rule 341 was issued in 2012. Also, there was a "change of mentality" regarding the roles of directors and the board. The role of directors was no longer seen as a privileged position for being close to the controller (in most cases), but increasingly as a professional that demanded knowledge of legal responsibilities and a capacity to challenge the controller and the company's management and require heightened information to carry out their duties.

(e) Public sources:

All retrieved on 14 July 2022

https://www.cmfchile.cl/portal/prensa/615/w3-article-12281.html

https://www.sernac.cl/portal/604/w3-article-3028.html

https://www.latercera.com/noticia/caso-la-polar-svs-impone-multas-por-un-total-de-us56-millones-a-ex-ejecutivos-ex-directores-y-auditora-pwc/

https://www.ciperchile.cl/2012/07/03/la-polar-i-la-red-de-sociedades-y-millonarias-ganancias-que-devela-como-los-gerentes-participaron-del-fraude/

https://www.ciperchile.cl/2012/07/05/la-polar-ii-la-historia-inedita-detras-de-las-ganancias-de-morita-y-sus-gerentes/

https://www.ciperchile.cl/2012/07/09/circulo-verde-la-consultora-que-actuo-como-intermediaria-de-los-dineros-de-la-polar-para-la-sociedad-de-sus-gerentes/

https://www.latercera.com/noticia/caso-la-polar-svs-impone-multas-por-un-total-de-us56-millones-a-ex-ejecutivos-ex-directores-y-auditora-pwc/

https://www.emol.com/noticias/Economia/2018/06/19/910453/Caso-La-Polar-Suprema-confirma-multa-de-860-millones-a-Pablo-Alcalde.html

https://knowledge.wharton.upenn.edu/article/la-polars-accounting-scandal-sends-a-chill-through-chile/

https://www.bbc.com/news/business-13848796
https://www.wsj.com/articles/DJFDBR0020130412e94cekrmt
https://newsbeezer.com/chileeng/la-polar-supreme-court-rules-pwc-and-seeks-compensation-from-afp-capital-and-provida/

3.6 SQM (Cascadas)

Misuse of corporate interest for the benefit of controlling shareholders.

The Sociedad Química y Minera de Chile (*Chemical and Mining Society of Chile*) – SQM is a private mining company engaged in the exploitation, processing and marketing of potassium nitrate and specialty fertilizers, iodine, potassium, and lithium in Chile. SQM was created as a mixed mining company between individuals and the State of Chile (Compañía Salitrera Anglo-Lautaro 62.5% and CORFO 37.5%) in 1968 and was intended to restructure the then weak production of saltpeter, increase investment, and improve exploitation. As a result, SQM acquired the monopoly to exploit and market saltpeter. Soon thereafter, in 1971, through CORFO, the Chilean state acquired 100% of the property and nationalized the exploitation of saltpeter.

Along with over 30 other state-owned enterprises in the period,[15] in 1986 SQM was gradually privatized, ending up controlled by Julio Ponce Lerou, Augusto Pinochet's son-in-law. In that period, nitrate exploitation began in Coya Sur (1986). A potassium nitrate plant was set up in 1993 at the same time as the company began its international development.

(a) What happened:

SQM has a pyramidal corporate structure (also referred as "*Cascadas*" or "waterfall structure", giving the name to the case). The controlling shareholder of SQM used a structure of private investment companies and links with high-profile investment bankers to expropriate minority shareholders by fixing stock market prices and illicitly trading shares of SQM and the other cascades companies.

[15] González, F., Prem, M., Urzúa, F. – The Privatizaion Origins of Political Corporations: Evidence from the Pinochet Regime – The Journal of Economic History, Vol. 80, No. 2 (June 2020).

The modus operandi was for the securities of the listed companies within the corporate group that owned SQM (the principal ones being Norte Grande S.A., Pampa Calichera S.A., Nitratos S.A. y Potasios S.A.) to be sold by each company that held them in a cascade structure at below-market prices to private companies (also related to the controller, under its personal influence or instrumentally for such purposes). Subsequently, these private companies—in most cases after a short lapse of time—sold back the same securities of the cascading companies, at prices higher than the purchase price.

As stated in the SVS investigation, the overprice paid by the cascades and the losses were not the result of bad business judgment, but the result of fictitious and illegal practices that generated earnings for the majority shareholders and/or owners of the private companies. The orchestrated illegal operations went against the social interest of the companies, against public faith and transparency, against the related-party transactions laws and caused severe losses to minority shareholders.

(b) How we found out:
Minority shareholders (primarily the AFPs as institutional investors) requested that the Chilean market regulator investigates irregularities over alleged market manipulation.

(c) The fallout:
The SVS accused the firms of participating in market manipulation through the establishment and use of fraudulent trading schemes using investment companies to create and conduct fictitious trades between 2009 and 2011. The investigation ended with fines of USD70 million on the controller for illegal share trading—the largest single fine it has imposed to date. However, the fine was subsequently reduced by courts. Other SQM executives and partners of Chile's most prominent financial institutions and asset managers that allowed shares auctions and operations without dissemination (BanChile Corredores de Bolsa, Linzor Asset Management, Citigroup Markets and country's leading stockbroker, LarrainVial) were also fined a total of USD164 million. Subsequently, these fines were substantially reduced by the courts.

(d) What we learnt or did subsequently:

The case prompted anti-corruption measures and can be seen as yet another driver of Law No. 21,314, on Transparency and Accountability of Market Agents, enacted in 2021. The new Law also enhanced the powers of the Chilean regulator (formerly SVS, now CMF) granting it enhanced powers to investigate and sanction market abuses.

Finally, the case also triggered a change in market regulation through the SSE, which disallowed direct orders (key in the *Cascadas* case) and increased transparency, boosting competition and liquidity. The new rules included the option of an anonymous market, the redefinition of limits to the amounts and actions via electronic auctions, and a new procedure for competitive offers in a sale auction.

(e) Public sources:

All retrieved on 14 July 2022:

https://www.cmfchile.cl/portal/prensa/615/w3-article-17480.html

https://www.economist.com/news/2014/09/15/nitrate-nightmare

https://www.latercera.com/noticia/caso-cascadas-las-multas-mas-altas-de-la-historia/

https://www.latercera.com/noticia/svs-formula-cargos-a-julio-ponce-por-cinco-infracciones/

https://www.elmostrador.cl/noticias/pais/2012/09/26/como-julio-ponce-lerou-se-quedo-con-soquimich/

3.7 *Lessons from Chile and Open Questions for Further Study*

1. In concentrated markets like Chile and the rest of Latin America, scandals reveal the permanent tension between the controlling shareholder — who in some extreme cases act as the sole proprietors of a company — and the rest of the shareholders, either institutional or retail investors.
2. The involvement of institutional investors in the scandals in Chile, most of the time acting as the ones that discover the problems and alert the authorities and/or pursue charges, goes to show that they can act as an effective controlling mechanism, which may be

enhanced through public policies that allow institutional investors to look for long-term decisions at both a shareholder and board level. Pension Funds, as the most relevant institutional investors in the country, currently have significant restrictions in this regard.

3. The case of La Polar shows that in countries where dispersed ownership is not the norm, then the monitoring mechanisms are as yet insufficiently developed, and frauds may occur.
4. Corporate governing and other financial scandals in Chile tend to occur within the same company. Corporate governing scandals may therefore be symptomatic of deeper corporate problems.
5. Recent corporate governing cases have already served as a catalyst for change and the implementation of new institutional infrastructure to monitor and assess structural corporate governance problems, bringing with them a new institutional framework and better tools to investigate and determine the outcome of future cases. These new tools, together with the push from the general public for greater oversight and transparency will likely change the way companies deal with corporate governance risks.
6. On a positive note, the scandals and regulatory developments outlined above have tended to shape directors' attitudes and awareness of board-level responsibilities. The era when becoming a board member was viewed as a "gift" for a career next to a controlling shareholder are now long gone, and changes have encouraged greater professionalization, where directors must now act independently and weigh up the risks and benefits of joining a company's board.

With new regulation and political turmoil in Chile, there are currently several cases under development and the key areas to prioritize in the future include:

7. The professionalization of the boards brings its own problems of board composition, effectiveness, and accountability of the board members.
8. Given the concentration of the market (even more accentuated than 20 years ago), interlocking issues arise more frequently.
9. The general public is demanding more engagement of companies in public affairs and companies need to design strategies so as

not to be seen as part of the problem, but more as important players in delivering the solutions, engaging increasingly with ESG issues. Therefore, we expect to see a greater focus on transparency, accountability, and non-financial disclosure in the coming years.

4 Colombia

Óscar Armando Pardo Aragón

The Colombian cases of crisis in corporate governing show evidence of different problems that arose in private and public companies and in corporate groups. In the case of private companies, the prime issues arise with the CEOs and management teams, where that their Boards of Directors have proven complacent or lacked diligence in exercising oversight, as will be seen in Interbolsa and Estraval. In these cases, rulings of the State supervisory entities also appear to have come late, such that the damages and impact had already been felt, so bringing these cases of corporate governance failure to the attention of the general public. With regard to corporate groups, there are two cases that have left important lessons. The first case is of the *Cement Cartel*, where a crisis was brought on by an investigation that flagged the importance of conducting risk analyses and measuring their repercussions on market prices. The second case is of the *Diaper Cartel* that shows how practices that are embedded in certain organizational cultures have tended not to be evaluated and controlled at board level; when a scandal arises, the board ends up embroiled through inaction or omissions. It is important to highlight in the cases of the cartels the use of whistleblower and plea bargaining by the regulatory entities that accelerated the investigations and the collection of evidence and alerted the companies to the danger of cartelization.

The cases of Reficar and Saludcoop made the headlines due to the fact that these entities manage public resources and so affected the population at large. In the first case, there were gross deficiencies in board oversight as well as the ramifications that board member decisions took on. The board members involved in these investigations, when found responsible, are liable to respond with their personal assets, which has created

Ó. A. Pardo Aragón
Faculty of Business Administration, Universidad de Los Andes, Bogotá, Colombia
e-mail: oscarapardo@gmail.com

anxiety at the time of being selected as a board member of a state entity. Finally, the case of Saludcoop shows the deficiencies in senior management of public resources in private healthcare benefits and weak controls of the boards of directors, so flagging the relevance of having independent nominee members.

4.1 *InterBolsa*

Speculation and abuse of company powers among Colombia's fast-rising stockbrokers.

In 1991 InterBolsa was a small, Medellin-based firm, found at the bottom of the table of stockbrokers operating, at that time, only on the Antioquia Stock Market. Its founder, Rodrigo Jaramillo, was a well-known local ("*paisa*") businessperson. The trajectory of the company changed overnight when in 1997, Sr. Jaramillo went into partnership with Juan Carlos Ortiz, an economist and a controversial but exceptionally talented stockbroker in Bogota who had been recently expelled from the Bogota Stock Exchange for practices considered not very transparent. With the consolidation of Interbolsa operations, in its six-monthly follow-up in 2006, the certifier BRC Investor Services SA certified its rating as AA, and as 2009 it was upgraded to AA +, as again confirmed in January 2012, when its COP120,000 million (USD58 million) bond issue was also rated AA+.

In the period 2008 to 2011, InterBolsa presented compound growth rates of: 69% in net profits; 42% in equity value; 47% in total assets; and 70% in total liabilities. What's more, InterBolsa represented around 30% of the market, which would have meant a systemic risk, were the regulatory entities not to have acted appropriately and on time, as they did.

(a) What happened:

In 2012, the largest national financial scandal broke concerning millions of dollars that had been diverted by the directors of InterBolsa, the principal stockbroker in Colombia. Initially, the *Premium Capital Appreciation Fund* (*PremiumCAF* - under Interbolsa umbrella), founded by Juan Carlos Ortiz and Tomás Jaramillo (son of the founder) in 2000, was investigated for illegal fundraising by the Financial Superintendency on grounds that InterBolsa appeared to have correspondent relationships with three funds of *Premium Curaçao* by illegally investing Colombian money to make self-loans, specifically Alessandro Corridori (shareholder of Fabricato through InterBolsa's repo[16] practice and family in-law of the Jaramillos) and Víctor Maldonado (an investor in InterBolsa). However, and, at the time, no evidence was found to verify InterBolsa's relationship with the fund, which held most of the investors' money.

Subsequently, the magazine *Semana* published an article in which, according to the Financial Superintendency and Securities and Exchange Commission from the USA, Sr. Carlos Leyton Sinisterra (the firm's broker and cousin of the wife of the InterBolsa executive, César Mendoza) had manipulated bank accounts in that country for amounts that excess of COP12,000 million (USD6 million) from drug trafficking, incurring in the crime of money laundering through a business in Florida, in which false commercial backing had been issued.

However, the primary event that led the company into a public scandal was the acquisition of repos from Fabricato, allowing InterBolsa to inflate the value of the company shares and subsequently sell them at an extraordinary profit. This practice evolved over several years and, according to the calculations of Fabricato itself (a conglomerate that was not aware of InterBolsa's practices), Merryl Lynch and Metropolitan Capital, the share value soon rose from COP30 (USD0.02) to COP120 (USD0.06).

The board of directors of the conglomerate authorized the repo strategy with a ceiling of COP100,000 million (USD54 million) that would have to be captured in the stock market. "The plan was launched at the beginning of 2011 and was so successful that, within a year, shares in Fabricato were the most traded stock on the market, appreciating by 214.1%".

[16] Per Investopedia, a repurchase agreement (repo) is a form of short-term borrowing for dealers in government securities. In the case of a repo, a dealer sells government securities to investors, usually on an overnight basis, and buys them back the following day at a slightly higher price. That small difference in price is the implicit overnight interest rate. Repos are typically used to raise short-term capital. They are also a common tool of central bank open market operations - https://www.investopedia.com/terms/r/repurchaseagreement.asp

In 2012, investors began to question Fabricato's repos when contrasting their "inflated" value with the company's results on paper and by the same strategy announced by the company. In August that year, "the repos with Fabricato shares had flooded the market, making up 20% of the daily operations of this product and had, according to BVC data, COP322,726 million (USD180 million) in circulation. Clearly, the quota that the Board had authorized was exceeded by far".

(b) How we found out:
The scandal came to light following an investigation carried out by the Financial Superintendency and through reporting in the written media, such as *Semana* magazine and national newspapers.

(c) The fall out:
InterBolsa was fined in 2003 by the Securities Superintendency for fraud, massive and habitual collection of public money for illicit investments, conspiracy to commit a crime, manipulation of financial securities, the improper application of funds, and fraudulent accounting practices.

In 2012, these criminal cases led to two members of the board of directors being jailed, along with other people linked to the entity. In addition, the former president of InterBolsa was also sentenced to prison, on top of having to pay a fine of COP7,000 million (USD3.6 million). Moreover, Tomás Jaramillo, son of the president of the holding company was sentenced to five years and nine months in the La Picota prison in Bogota. Juan Carlos Ortiz, received the same sentence, "while Alessandro Corridori was released due to expiration of terms and set in train a series of lawsuits against the State for falsely involving him in the process".

In total the criminal investigation involved 37 people, including executives, members of the boards of directors and legal representatives of InterBolsa, the *PremiumCAF*, and the Corridori Group. Finally, the prosecution filed lawsuits against 25 people who were charged with fraud, manipulation of information, conspiracy to commit a crime, massive and habitual collection of money, failure to reimburse the money collected, aggravated by greed, abuse of investors, and criminal co-participation, among others.

(d) What we learnt or did subsequently:
The main lessons have two spheres:

- The first, the need for regulators to begin supervision of inappropriate practices much earlier, as one of the general conclusions of this case is that the tasks of the supervisors arrived late, when the financial problem was rampant. Although given the size of the company systemic risks to the country's financial sector was contained, it still caused damage to the general public's credibility and trust in the financial markets.
- The second, corporate governance practices need to be authentic and their verification mechanisms with a higher degree of evidence, because even though InterBolsa reported in *Código País* and was a well-qualified entity, this did not guarantee that the corporate governance had been internalized in the company nor did it align itself with ethical and moral principles.

(e) Public sources:
All retrieved on 14 July 2022

Boletín Consultorio Contable. Auditoría Forense: Caso InterBolsa. Universidad Eafit – http://www.eafit.edu.co/escuelas/administracion/consultorio-contable/Documents/A%20Auditoria%20forense,%20caso%20interbolsa.pdf

El Espectador. (2012). Interbolsa, la historia de un desplome – https://www.elespectador.com/economia/interbolsa-la-historia-de-un-desplome-article-385920/

El Tiempo. (2017). ¿Qué viene para los 'cerebros' de InterBolsa enviados a prisión? – https://www.eltiempo.com/justicia/delitos/condenan-a-cerebros-de-caso-interbolsa-73554

Portafolio. (2017). InterBolsa: 5 años de un descalabro que pudo ser peor – https://www.portafolio.co/economia/interbolsa-5-anos-de-un-descalabro-que-pudo-ser-peor-511214

Tautiva, C. (2013). Una Aproximación al Caso InterBolsa. Universidad del Rosario – https://repository.urosario.edu.co/bitstream/handle/10336/4826/TautivaRodriguez-CristianCamilo-2013.pdf?sequence=6

W Radio. (2020). Murió el caso Interbolsa ocho años después del desfalco que dejó más de 1500 víctimas – https://www.wradio.com.co/noticias/actualidad/murio-el-caso-interbolsa-ocho-anos-despues-del-desfalco-que-dejo-mas-de-1500-victimas/20201030/nota/4082229.aspx

4.2 *Estraval*

Unregulated capture of funds and speculation in an up-and-coming financial derivative product.

Estraval was founded in 2000 by two university friends—Juan Carlos Bastidas Aleman and César Fernando Mondragón. The company's operations were categorized in the secondary market (brokerage) in which they bought bundles of *liberanzas*[17] from cooperatives and sold them on to third-party investors. These deals are/were protected by Law 1,527 of 2012, but required the employees' prior authorization and, subsequently these transactions were treated as a portfolio purchase. In just 16 years, Estraval became one of the largest companies in the sector, it is estimated that, together with Elite SA, represented 30% of the *liberanzas* market, with more than 4,600 investors and operations for COP1.1 billion (USD328 millions).

(a) What happened:

For many years, Estraval received money in advance for the purchase of *liberanzas*, having an impact on the illegal capture of money. In addition to selling notes that were past due or selling them on more than one occasion and to more than one investor, offering unrealistic returns far in excess of their economic fundamentals or the financial reasonableness of such a model. "Many clients were made to sign promissory notes up to three times and then resell them, said the Prosecutor's Office".

According to the Colombian Prosecutor's Office Estraval captured, at least COP600,000 million (USD197 million) from investors who saw in the commercialization of promissory notes of debt a business opportunity with dreamed yields of up to 150 percent. However, this *dream* turned into a millionaire scam for over 4,000 people.

Estraval and its subsidiaries Estrategias en Valores, Estradinámicas, Estrategias en Liquidity, and Técnicas Financieras carried out this

[17] A "*liberanza*" (promissory notes of debt) is a special loan through which a debtor employee authorizes his/her employer to make direct payroll deductions from the monthly paycheck to fund the corresponding installment of debt repayments (including fees and interest) directly to the 3rd party—a person or an organization—that had originated the loan.

practice called "twins", where the attractiveness was the interest offered, "they oscillated between 15% and 18% per month, almost three times what a bank would pay for a *Certificate of Term Deposit*, CDT, (currently 6.8% per year)".

> But things didn't stop there. To sustain this business, Estraval and its subsidiaries enlisted the support of a network of cooperatives—many of them only on paper—not only to make loans, but also to raise large sums of money from the general public.

As of 2012, Estraval began to have liquidity problems. That year, the cooperatives stopped approving new drafts, due to the sudden increase in the arrears of payments that employees began to have with them. This had a knock-on effect on the promissory notes, since, without new drafts from the cooperatives, it was impossible for Estraval and the secondary market companies to repackage and resell them. Consequently, Estraval stopped having positive cash flows, which hindered investors from paying.

(b) How we found out:
This corruption scandal first came to light through the sanctions issued by the Superintendency of Companies (in charge of regulating non-bank issuers of securities) and when problems with payments to clients of the entity became evident.

(c) The fall out:
The Superintendency of Companies intervened in Estraval, obliging it to carry out a process of reorganization in May 2016. This led to investor panic and the first complaints from the public.

In 2017, the partners and members of the Estraval board of directors, along with a good part of its management team, were sent to jail for being involved in a multi-million-dollar fraud in financial promissory notes dealings. The criminal investigation concluded that the co-founders and managers had created a "pyramid" scheme. Fernando Joya Rodriguez, COO of the company was captured by the Prosecutor's Office since apparently, he was the one who had given the instruction not to inform his clients of the nature of the financial operations that were being carried out.

"Many of the 4,500 investors who used their money to buy promissory notes to earn fabulous returns are today on the verge of losing all or a good part of their money". At a cost to investors of COP600,000 million (USD197 million), this event is the country's largest financial disaster, surpassing even InterBolsa, which amounted to COP350,000 million (USD115 million).

As of 2020, no one was serving a term in jail for the crimes that were allegedly committed, "803 people had been fully compensated and COP238,000 million (USD65 million) had been recovered, while 4,447 victims were still pending for over COP376,000 million (USD192 million), of which there was no information".

To date (2021), the victims who have been waiting for years to recover at least some of the money invested, "facing the risk of losing the possibility of economic compensation: multi-millionaire losses, now entangled in a corrupt triangle, which, according to one complaint, involves alleged lawyers, civil servants and even a self-styled legal advocate, journalist and rector". Together, this would amount to COP179,000 million (USD49 million) and was agreed with the prosecution by Juan Carlos Bastidas, former director and founder of Estraval, as a preliminary agreement to compensate the victims.

(d) What we learnt or did subsequently:
As in the previous case, the regulators involvement came sometime after the consequences to the users had been felt and were difficult to rectify. In this regard, greater inter-institutional coordination between the supervisory entities is warranted, such as in this case, between the Financial Superintendency and the Superintendency of Companies, so that although they monitor different types of companies, they can share procedures and/or lessons and generate effective and anticipated measures.

On the other hand, corporate governance practices were conspicuous by their absence. The reflection is on what could have been done before the fact in the form of mandatory or voluntary legal proceedings. The answer is that both measures needed to have been taken. Finally, this case flags an evident lack of duty of care and duty of loyalty and invites the conclusion that public interest and that of other stakeholders might have been better protected with a greater participation of independent board members.

(e) Public sources:

All Retrieved on 14 July 2022:

Caracol Radio. (2016). Cómo funciona el negocio de las libranzas en Colombia – https://caracol.com.co/radio/2016/07/26/economia/1469486127_776819.html#:~:text=El%20esquema%20de%20operaci%C3%B3n%20es,pueden%20superar%20f%C3%A1cilmente%20el%2020%25

El País. (2017). Así operaba Estraval, la 'fábrica' de estafas que afectó a casi 300 vallecaucanos – https://www.elpais.com.co/economia/asi-operaba-estraval-la-fabrica-de-estafas-que-afecto-a-casi-300-vallecaucanos.html

Liévano, J.P. (2019). ¿Y de Estraval qué? Superintendencia de Sociedades – https://www.supersociedades.gov.co/Noticias/Paginas/2019/%C2%BFY-de-Estraval-que-%E2%80%93-La-Republica.aspx

Noticias Caracol. (2020).

Semana. (2017). Así cayeron las cabezas de Estraval – https://www.semana.com/nacion/articulo/estraval-capturan-a-los-responsables/513540/

Semana. (2021). El multimillonario "conejo" a víctimas de la pirámide Estraval – https://www.semana.com/nacion/articulo/el-multimillonario-conejo-a-victimas-de-la-piramide-estraval/202100/

4.3 Reficar

The perils of directors' and managers' limits and responsibility on the financial execution of projects involving large investment contracts.

The Cartagena Refinery—Reficar—is today a large industrial and refining complex, vital for the industry and the national economy, the country's energy security and the production of clean fuels. It dates back to 1957 when it was built by Exxon, as a fuel refining complex to supply the demand of the Caribbean coast. Then, in 1974 it was acquired by the Colombian oil company Ecopetrol. At the end of the 1990s, the government warned that the country needed to improve its refining capacity and that the international and national demand for fuels required more efficient and environmentally friendly products.

In 2006, Ecopetrol S.A. decided to sell 51% of its shares to Glencore. However, by February 2009 the Swiss company decided to withdraw from the deal and this led to a process of repurchase of shares by

Ecopetrol. The price agreed to be paid was USD549 million—approximately USD109 million less than the initial price, so as to mitigate any capital losses. From 2008 to 2013, the company showed almost 81% of revenues above annual budget, due primarily to the rise in the price of crude oil. In 2014, the company reduced its income by 45.7%, vis-à-vis the previous year, due to the decrease in exports. Following its acquisition, and to comply with the expansion and modernization process, Reficar recorded annual losses of approximately 17% of the value of sales. The total value of the refinery represents around COP26,000 billion (USD1 billion).

(a) What happened:

In 2019, the most recent scandal that is still in judicial process has been about the alleged irregularities detected in REFICAR's modernization and expansion project of the REFICAR, which belongs to Ecopetrol, the Colombian oil company. These events implied that the Attorney General of the Nation filed an accusation against three former members of the board of directors of Reficar and a former President of Ecopetrol.

Reficar's development was projected to have significant impact on both industrial and national GDP (11% and 6%, respectively). The industrial complex, at the time, was thought to double national refining capacity, process more than 1,000 petroleum derivatives, guarantee the supply of national fuels and the production of cleaner fuels.

The execution of the megaproject involved a contract tender process that involved delays and multi-million losses. The investigations pointed the finger at the US company CB&I in omitting essential documentation following its withdrawal from the country, after delivery of its part in the engineering process to Ecopetrol.

> In total, 2,460 contracts were signed and 18 percent of them registered increases of more than 100 percent –one scaffolding rental alone registered an increase of 370 times. One of the contracts with Foster Wheeler increased 143% - from USD95.2 million to USD231 million. For this reason, Reficar's budget in six years increased 101 percent". […] "Labor costs also impacted the values. The company brought engineers from other countries, especially from Venezuela,

and even welders from the Philippines, because there was not enough qualified labor in Colombia.

(b) How we found out:
The scandal broke with a report by the Comptroller General of The Republic in 2015, which warned of errors made in its execution, which led to large cost overruns of COP4,023 million (USD2 million). This represents a duplication of costs in just five years of development.

(c) The fall out:
In 2021, the Comptroller's Office passed down a fiscal responsibility ruling for COP2,900 million (USD1,57 million) against five former employees of the company, seven members of the board of directors, and four contractors. This decision came after four years of study and mainly involves "the then Presidents of the company as well as the Vice President and the members of the board of directors. It also attributes responsibility to Phillipe Ackerman, Mazu Di Bank, and 6 other representatives of the contractors Downstream Ecopetrol 2008, Grupo Legal Reficar and CB&I.

The fiscal responsibility ruling also shows that the investments and expenses were not related to the modernization process, but that "there was negligence on the part of the officials in promoting low productivity of direct labor, higher expenses in hiring personnel and delays in project-related activities". Additionally, information has come to light in which more than COP450,000 million (USD195 million) was allocated by former REFICAR executives to alcohol and parties with women.

Consequently, the charges brought by the Prosecutor's Office in 2014 for crimes committed by the officials included: undue interest in the drawing up of contracts; embezzlement for appropriation; illicit enrichment; and the falsification of documents.

However, despite the ongoing investigations by the Prosecutor's Office and the Comptroller's Office, the Attorney General's Office decided to close and file the proceedings against several former directors of Reficar (7 members of the board of directors and 3 high-ranking Ecopetrol officials) based on a report from Foster Wheeler in 2009. Additionally, the Attorney General's Office found that no irregular decisions had taken place regarding the approval of changes, since the members of the boards of directors to justifiable decisions in recognizing that the costs were higher than those estimated at the outset and, therefore, it made more sense to continue with the project and finish it rather than assume the expenses for an "unfinished and useless" piece of work.

(d) What we learnt or did subsequently:
This case has regularly figured in the media and has left several lessons. The first is the consequences that board member decisions invariably have significant consequences on their own assets. Second, a decision to convict or exonerate a director depends on what was recorded in the minutes. Several directors have been exonerated in the case because of the evidence of their respective decisions having been recorded in the minutes, reinforcing the counsel that the responsibility of board members and in particular their decisions need to be studied, argued, and appropriately documented. Finally, the absence of controls or emphasis on in-depth analysis of decision-making would suggest that a greater number of independent members with appropriate skills and backgrounds should be invited to join the board.

The scale of public resources involved and the corresponding media exposure in this case has had lasting negative effects on the credibility of corporate governance mechanisms. On the other hand, failures in exercising the duty of care may also be associated with the individual board members not having had appropriate backgrounds, again making the case for better qualified independent directors and advisors with the relevant industry skills.

(e) Public Sources:

All retrieved on 14 July 2022:

Acosta, C. (2021). Contraloría anunció que halló responsabilidad fiscal por COP2,9 billones en el caso Reficar. Asuntos Legales – https://www.asuntoslegales.com.co/actualidad/contraloria-anuncio-que-hallo-responsabilidad-fiscal-por-2-9-billones-en-el-caso-reficar-3159708

La FM. (2019). Corrupción en Reficar: Más de COP450.000 millones se destinaron a alcohol y fiestas con mujeres. – https://www.lafm.com.co/judicial/corrupcion-en-reficar-mas-de-450000-millones-se-destinaron-alcohol-y-fiestas-con-mujeres

Reficar. (2021). Gobierno Corporativo – Biblioteca – https://www.reficar.com.co/en/biblioteca-gobierno

Semana. (2015). La apuesta por la infraestructura energética – https://www.semana.com/economia/articulo/la-apuesta-por-la-infraestructura-energetica/414932-3/
Semana. (2016). Reficar: ¿el escándalo económico del siglo? – https://www.semana.com/economia/articulo/reficar-las-irregularidades-por-sobrecostos/458610/
Semana. (2021). Las razones de la Procuraduría para archivar proceso contra exdirectivos de Reficar – https://www.semana.com/nacion/articulo/las-razones-de-la-procuraduria-para-archivar-proceso-contra-exdirectivos-de-reficar/202153/
Semanario Voz. (2016). Reficar, la máxima corrupción – https://semanariovoz.com/reficar-la-maxima-corrupcion/

4.4 *El Cartel de los Pañales*

The responsibility of directors and managers in ensuring that "old", once-acceptable, business behaviors do not perpetuate in their business culture.

Tecnoquímicas, founded in 1934, and Productos Familia, founded in 1958, are two large domestic pharmaceutical companies established in the Valle del Cauca and Antioquia regions, respectively. They were set up as family businesses that have since grown into regional *Multilatinas* companies.

From 2010 to 2013, Tecnoquímicas recorded a compound growth in sales of 5% and 2% in net profits, during 2013 it registered revenues of COP12,000 million (USD6.3 million) and net profit of COP717 million (USD 384,000). For its part, in the same period, Productos Familia recorded a compound growth in sales of 5% and 6% in net profits, during 2013 it registered revenues of COP39,000 million (USD21 million) and net profit of COP6,562 million (USD3.5 million). Both Tecnoquimicas and Family Products have come to dominate the Colombian diaper market. The only international company to compete in Colombia is the North American company Kimberly Clark.

(a) What happened:

The diaper market in Colombia is an oligopoly where 96% of the market in the last 6 years has been distributed between Tecnoquímicas—Tecnosur (41%), Productos Familia (28%), Kimberly

Clark (21%), and Drypers Andina Sur (6%), with its brands *Winny Ultratrim*, *Pequeñín*, *Huggies*, and *Baby Sec*, respectively.

The Superintendency of Industry and Commerce (SIC), the regulatory body in Colombia, has been alerted to this situation given its role as a guarantor of free competition in the face of market failures arising from acts of collusion and cartels (Law 1340 art. 2). As such, this implies sanctions on the businesses and the managers involved, for which they are liable to the full extent of their assets. In addition, the State, in line with the model of game theory, adopts the *Benefits Program* (Decree 2810/10) by means of which it may partially or totally exonerate participants involved when they inform the authorities of said conduct and collaborate with the delivery of evidence, information and identify others involved.

Physical evidence such as "emails, *WhatsApp* messages, various documents and testimonies from the people involved were collected, which demonstrated the acts of collusion that had been committed for over a decade, which translate into market distribution, pricing, standardization of characteristics of diapers and regulation of marketing and marketing strategies. The modus operandi initially consisted of telephone contacts between senior executives, meetings in private clubs of high national renown, as well as meetings outside the country". According to the SIC, these people were clearly aware that their participation in such acts violated the law since their actions were invariably carried out in a manner not to leave a trace.

The fact that attracted the most attention was the fixing of prices, since it led to the determination of the percentage of increase and the agreement on the discount volume by diaper brand and marketing channel. The agreements also included the prohibition and unification of sampling and advertising. For the SIC, all these events had an impact on reducing innovation and product quality and, therefore, on consumer benefits.

(b) How we found out:

In 2013, an anonymous complaint was filed in which alleged non-competitive commercial practices were reported. As a result, the SIC initiated an investigation into the principal companies that produce and sell baby diapers to establish whether prices had been agreed between them and/or market distribution practices were in place.

(c) The fall out:

The Superintendency of Industry and Commerce accused 16 senior managers (officials and former officials) of the three companies sanctioned for cartelization, for having collaborated, facilitated, authorized, executed, or tolerated the conduct that violated the free economic competition regime.

Through resolution 47,965 of 4th August 2014, the Delegation for the Protection of Competition, formulated a statement of charges against Colombiana Kimberly Colpapel SA, Productos Familia SA, Tecnoquímicas SA, Tecnosur SAS, Drypers Andina SA and 44 natural persons related to said companies (legal representatives, managers, members of the boards of directors, product directors, and channel managers), of which 26 belonged to Kimberly, 6 to Familia, 9 to Tecnoquímicas, and 3 to Drypers.

Although the participation of Drypers in the price agreement was confirmed, such activities could not be verified in its performance after 2006, for which the sanctioning power of the SIC had expired.

Kimberly and Familia were sanctioned under the collaboration benefits program, the former being almost 100% exonerated and the second 50% exonerated.

For its part, Tecnoquímicas was the only one to receive the complete fine "for not being an informer and for having been an active, permanent and leading participant in the investigated business cartel".

The total amount of all the fines was COP208,000 million (USD112 million) and includes individual sanctions against 16 senior managers of the companies in question. The sanctions were reflected in dismissals, fines, public references in the media with their own names, which undermined the reputation of said directors, there have been no cases of jail terms.

(d) What we learnt or did subsequently:

Although apparently the intervention of the board of directors is not clear and evident in this case, and the instructions to collaborate with the regulator were given by the respective boards, the scandal still has consequences on the reputation of the brand and the firm, it is one of the responsibilities of the board and therefore, any decision that attempts to this fact must be dealt with, controlled, and monitored by a board of directors. An important learning in this case is the need to have boards with independent members who care about being attentive to broader interest groups, beyond the information provided by the CEO. In addition, the cases flag the need for independent, strict, and effective audit committees.

Then again, a lack of duty of care is possibly one of the most important lessons from this case, whether through action or omission. On the other hand, it is \ important to highlight the use of mechanisms such as whistleblower and plea bargaining that helped to clarify the investigations, but perhaps more importantly—and positively—they encouraged the companies in this sector and others to avoid cartelization.

(e) Public Sources:

All retrieved on 14 July 2022:

Cano, E. et al. (2015). Núcleo Integrador—Grupo Familia—Papel Higiénico Extrafino Doble Hoja. Universidad Pontificia Bolivariana.

Castro, M. (2018). Análisis de la Cartelización Empresarial desde la Óptica del Control Interno. Universidad Militar Nueva Granada.

Cifuentes, J. Torres, M. (2014). Proceso De Internacionalización De Tecnoquímicas. Universidad ICESI.

Rendón, O. (2014). Consecuencias del "cartel de los pañales". Diario El Mundo – https://www.elmundo.com/portal/noticias/economia/consecuencias_del_cartel_de_los_paniales.php" \l ".YtCAhXZKhD8

SIC. Por cartelización empresarial en pañales para bebé, Superindustria sanciona a 3 empresas y 16 altos directivos – https://www.sic.gov.co/noticias/por-cartelizacion-empresarial-en-panales-para-bebe-superindustria-sanciona-a-3-empresas-y-16-altos-directivo#:~:text=La%20Superintendencia%20de%20Industria%20y%20Comercio%20tambi%C3%A9n%20sancion%C3%B3%20a%2016,de%20la%20libre%20competencia%20econ%C3%B3mica

4.5 *The Cement Cartel*

The responsibility of directors and managers to understand the nature of risks deriving from industrial organizational structures and their effects on market prices.

Three companies in Colombia control 96% of the supply of the cement market. Grupo Argos S.A. has the largest capacity, with 10 production plants; followed by CEMEX Colombia S.A. with 5 plants; and finally, HOLCIM (Colombia) S.A. with a single plant. The remaining 4% of the market is held by Tequendama and San Marcos. All these companies deliver *Portland Cement Type 1* concrete to building sites, primarily in residential housing construction and civil works, and had an aggregate sales volume of COP8,320 billion (USD4,300 billion).

(a) What happened:

The Superintendency of Industry And Commerce (SIC), the regulatory body in Colombia, has been alerted to this situation given its role as a guarantor of free competition in the face of market failures arising from acts of collusion and cartels (Law 1340 article 2). As such, this implies sanctions on the businesses and the managers involved, for which they are liable to the full extent of their assets.

The investigation concluded that there was a price *parallelism* (price inconsistency over time) and found increases of 20% above inflation resulting in exorbitant profits for the producing companies. Additionally, the SIC showed that Argos, CEMEX, and HOLCIM were not participating in a competitive market. On the contrary, they found orderly and coordinated measures had been taken to refrain from engaging in competitive activities. It should be noted that such *parallelism* is not a criminal activity or restrictive practice in Colombia, but it served as evidence of a range of activities that are not characteristic of free-market competition. It also concluded with probative elements on: "[…] (ii) the exchange of detailed and disaggregated information on national gray cement dispatches; (iii) offers made to CEMEX by its competitors in a 'price war' scenario; […] and (v) the existence of concurrent behaviors among the investigated companies, facilitated by exchanges of information, the meetings of the legal representatives and those responsible for the commercial areas and the other facilitating elements that configured as collusion or cartel behaviors between Argos, CEMEX and HOLCIM".

(b) How we found out:

The SIC initiated an administrative investigation on receiving multiple complaints about the rise in the price of gray *Portland Cement Type 1*. The complainants suggested that the country was paying the highest price per ton in the world of its cement, "With an average TRM[18] of COP1,900, the cost in Colombia was around USD250, compared to USD94 from the United States, USD64 from Vietnam, USD230 from Nigeria and USD96 from Germany These compared to other costs in the region with Mexico at USD118, Bolivia USD162, Chile USD113 and, finally, Brazil at USD95".

In addition, they pointed out that regular increases were made every quarter and that the State did not exercise any oversight in this regard, making it sometimes cheaper to import cement. Another denounced fact was that, as there was no control, the large cement companies did not allow new companies to enter the market and "drove to the wall" smaller suppliers.

(c) The fall out:

The penalties delivered by the SIC relate to a corporate cartel in setting the ex-factory prices of gray *Portland Cement Type 1* in the domestic market. In addition to the three companies, the case covers six senior managers of these companies for the individual responsibilities they must assume.

The SIC closed the file on the process against Tequendama and San Marcos, as no elements were found to support their participation in the cartel's price fixing activities.

As to the sanctions on the other companies, SIC ordered that: "Cementos Argos S.A. must pay COP73,771.7 million (USD39 million), CEMEX Colombia S.A. COP73,771.7 million (USD39 million), and HOLCIM (Colombia) S.A. COP54.074.6 million (USD29 million).

All three companies resorted to legal challenges, but finally, through Resolution No. 51694 of 2018, the State Council endorsed the SIC's rulings.

(d) What we learnt or did subsequently:

In this case, most of the companies charged with anti-competitive behavior are multinationals. The main reflection concerns their

[18] TRM (in Spanish *Tasa Representativa del Mercado*) is the official exchange rate calculated by the Superintendencia Financiera de Colombia. It represents the average market price of 1 dollar into Colombian pesos, and it's calculated at the end of every business day using all the transactions of that day.

corporate governance policies at the international level that permeates down to a national level. There is a lack of these corporate policies and a lack of control and monitoring by the boards of directors. In this case, there is participation of international board members because they are subsidiaries or regional headquarters. It also shows the importance of transmitting effective corporate values and principles to its different delegates in countries.

The possible lack of duty of care in this case reaffirms the importance of sharing international practices, more so in the knowledge that reputational risks spread internationally when cartels involve multinationals.

From the government's perspective, there has been no type of exemplary sanctions, such as some type of restriction, expulsion, or prohibition to return to the country or participation in any collegiate body.

(e) Public Sources:

Alzate, S. (2018). Cartel del cemento: Posibles acciones para la defensa de los intereses de los competidores y consumidores afectados por las prácticas anticompetitivas desplegadas por las compañías cementeras. Universidad Eafit.

All retrieved on 14 July 2022:

El Heraldo. (2017). Millonaria multa de SIC al 'cartel' del cemento – https://www.elheraldo.co/economia/millonaria-multa-de-sic-al-cartel-del-cemento-435020

SIC. (2018). Consejo de Estado confirmó sanción por cartel del cemento integrado por CEMEX, ARGOS y HOLCIM – https://www.sic.gov.co/noticias/consejo-de-estado-confirmo-sancion-por-cartel-del-cemento-integrado-por-cemex-argos-y-holcim

4.6 *SaludCoop*

Corruption and controller abuses in the Colombian health system.

SaludCoop EPS[19] was a cooperative body that was the parent company of an economic group, formed under Law 100 of 1993. For fifteen years,

[19] EPS—(in Spanish *Entidades Promotoras de Salud*—public health insurance organizations that are mandatory to provide health care to Colombian residents receiving monthly payroll deductions of 12.5% of gross monthly declared earnings.

SaludCoop was the leading EPS, with a market share of 23.35% of the active population and, during the worst years for the sector, the company grew 176 times, according to its financial statements.

SaludCoop's profits rose from COP3,626 million (USD1.7 million) in 2000 to COP34,236 million (USD15 million) in 2001 and in 2002, SaludCoop grew its top line by 55.6%, to COP53,259 million (USD19 million). In 2003, it was ranked 17 among the 100 largest companies in the country, with sales of $1.3 billion (USD450 million), rising sharply in 2004 to join the top 10 largest companies in Colombia, with sales exceeding $2.4 billion (USD1 billion), a y-o-y growth of nearly 60%.

At the time of its intervention, SaludCoop EPS was made up of 43 separate legal entities. Its size and rapid growth drew the attention of supervisory entities, which found that SaludCoop was using parafiscal and affiliate resources in investments of all kinds, such as biomedical equipment and the formation of companies, some of them abroad such as SaludCoop México that even produced important losses.

(a) What happened:

With the protection of Law 100 of 1993, which regulates and establishes the appearance of *Health Promotion Companies* (EPS) of private origin to assume administrative and financial functions in the provision of health services and guarantee better care of patients, in 1994, a group of more than 10 cooperatives created the EPS SaludCoop. The first meeting of the board of directors, held on 30 November that year, appointed Carlos Gustavo Palacino Antía as Executive President. Its business consisted of promoting membership in remote municipalities and rural areas with a view to subsequently covering the whole country, with a focus on lower-middle-class workers and their families. This growing market allowed the organization to gain a presence in over 800 municipalities, where it built its own clinics and created other EPS—supplementary health services companies. In 2002, it bought the EPS Cruz Blanca, incorporating approximately 560,000 members. The following year, it acquired Cafesalud EPS, adding around 3 million users, which made SaludCoop the largest EPS in the country with over 4 million members and, according to the business ranking of *Semana* magazine, one of the 17 largest companies in Colombia.

The EPS began to present problems in user attention and delays in payments to hospitals and other subcontracted organizations for the provision of services, which also started complaining. Investigations were carried out over 6 years by the Comptroller's Office and the Attorney General's Office and uncovered serious acts of corruption in which a possible cartel was dismantled on the matter of recoveries from the Fosyga (state entity in charge of the administration of the resources of the taxpayers and responsible for financial management to companies or health organizations to guarantee the care of citizens). The guardianships served as a strategy to obtain extra income through the overbilling of medicines, the Minister of Health at the time recognized that the recoveries are "excessively perverse" when going from COP336,000 million (USD143 million) in 2006 to represent COP2.5 billion (USD1,4 billion) in 2010 and that, if it continues like this, "there will be a near collapse in the system" (La Silla Vacia, 2011).

Further acts of corruption were uncovered linked to the president of SaludCoop and members of the boards of directors of companies tied to the group. "They began to create all kinds of companies for medicines, accounting audits, kidney dialysis, software, clothing, surveillance, among others, which mostly depended on the EPS to survive [...] there was money for everything: sponsorship of teams and tournaments of soccer, basketball and golf, construction of schools, purchase of high-end cars, support to build country condominiums, among others. "One of the most controversial trips was made by the eight members of the board of directors to an event in Singapore, on behalf of SaludCoop. There, at the Swiss Hotel the Stamford, Palacino called a meeting where it was decided to acquire tower 3 of the Parallel 108 business center in Bogotá, for COP72,000 million (USD38 million). Something that ended up being done" (La Semana, 2013).

(b) How we found out:

This fact was widely documented by the media since it corresponds to the main case of financial detriment to health that has occurred in Colombia. After the serious complaints and the constant protection presented to companies of the SaludCoop group, the magazine *Semana* documented serious findings of corruption.

(c) The fall out:

The Prosecutor's Office found evidence that the *President* of the board of directors of Cafesalud Medicina Prepagada was the architect of the company that used health money to build "a luxurious Villa Varia golf resort hotel in Meta, hotel and factoring companies, as well as assets related to a school in Bogotá". A renowned educator was also involved, who was also a member of the board of directors of Seguros La Equidad, one of SaludCoop's member cooperatives.

The case had consequences on businesses, professionals, and the legal responsibility of the directors of SaludCoop. Given the irregularities, in November 2013 Carlos Palacino, President and legal representative of SaludCoop, together with 11 other executives, including managers and the board members, were ordered to pay significant fines, disqualified for 18 years from holding public office and working for the State, in addition to being detained in the La Picota prison on charges of misappropriation of public health resources and illicit enrichment. The damages these executives caused is estimated at between COP1.4 billion (USD737 million) and COP2.8 billion (USD1,5 billion).

(d) What we learnt or did subsequently:
Hitherto the misuse of public social security funds had not been a concern, but following the investigations carried out by the Superintendency of Health and the Comptroller's Office, it became clear that health funds cannot be used to make private investments. In this way, private parties entering the market are forewarned of the oversight and strict controls placed on public funds for health care.

The negative effects that affected Colombian society became notorious because there was improper handling of public resources by a private entity in a sector, a sensitive sphere and as public health. Board failures, as seen in dereliction of the duties of loyalty and care were evident in this case. From a corporate governance perspective, this case reflects both the excessive power of an unrestrained CEO and the lack of independent oversight and reporting to the board. This might best be remedied through the appointment of independent directors to constrain the behaviors of the corporate leaders.

(e) Public Sources:

All retrieved on 14 July 2022:

La Silla Vacia. (2011). Robledo and Coronell managed to put SaludCoop against the wall – https://archivo.lasillavacia.com/historia/robledo-y-coronell-lograron-poner-saludcoop-contra-la-pared-24282

Muñoz, S., Ruíz, A. (2016). Recoveries and Financial Crisis of the Health System in Colombia (2008–2014), SaludCoop EPS case study. Universidad Libre – https://repository.unilibre.edu.co/handle/10901/11429

Razón Pública (2018). Carlos Palacino and the embezzlement of SaludCoop – https://razonpublica.com/carlos-palacino-y-el-desfalco-de-saludcoop/

La Semana. (2013). Denuncia - SaludCoop, el desfalco de la historia – https://www.semana.com/nacion/articulo/desfalco-de-salucoop/365644-3/

Rodríguez, M., & Molano, M. (2018). Identification of financial crimes in the case of SaludCoop, under the forensic audit methodology. La Gran Colombia University.

Semana Magazine. (2013). SaludCoop, the embezzlement of history – https://repository.ugc.edu.co/handle/11396/4631

4.7 *Lessons from Colombia and Open Questions for Further Study*

The cases analyzed for Colombia invariably relate to the state of corporate governance practices, as reflected in a many of the following situations and lessons:

1. The negative effects that they leave on society and on the credibility of corporate governing are accentuated when dealing with public resources, the media effect, and the lack of timely results.
2. Regulations and market interventions have tended to arrive late and when those affected most are irreparably hurt. In addition, although there has been progress in the regulation of conflicts of interest, there are still areas to be clarified, not least with regard to the economic groups and the role of independent members.
3. Regulatory entities have made substantive progress learning from international practices and from the particular cases that occur in the national environment. However, oversight is invariably carried

out by a multiplicity of supervisory agencies lacking in coordination or standardized procedures, all of which compounds their silo mentality and unwillingness to share in best practices.

4. Far too often, CEOs are left to their own devices with insufficient oversight/control from the boards of directors that elected them.
5. Instruments such as whistleblower and plea bargaining have proven to be effective elements to avoid antitrust practices and carry out more effective investigations.
6. Fiduciary duty failures, whether by action or omission, may be associated with a lack of effective controls, an absence of adequate profiles in making relevant decisions and/or a lack of independent members with industry skills and analysis to facilitate better decision-making in favor of the company.
7. The role of independent nominee directors remains understated, so weakening a board's oversight of management.
8. International best practices are rarely understood and/or promoted in national agencies.
9. Whether compulsory or voluntary, the regulation of corporate governance practices is an ongoing discussion that still lacks a clear definition.

5 Mexico

Edgar Rogelio Ramírez-Solís

There is a general lack of understanding of Mexico's corruption risk. Moreover, there is also scarce information on the benefits of fighting misbehaviors. Sometimes, crime is even "encouraged" by shareholders and investors, which is reflected in an organization's conduct. Then, there are other cases where the company's problem is generally well-known, but nothing is done.

In 2012, following the US Securities Market Commission and the OECD leadership in implementing anti-fraud reforms, Mexico published the *Federal Anti-Corruption Law for Public Procurement* and the Federal Law for the *Identification and Prevention of Operations with Resources*

E. R. Ramírez-Solís
Tecnológico de Monterrey, Monterrey, Mexico
e-mail: edgar.ramirez@tec.mx

of Illicit Origin. Then, on 27 May 2015, a Constitutional Reform came into force to create a *National Anti-Corruption* system. Then, on 18 July 2016, secondary laws were published in the *Mexican Official Gazette*. So, the problem is not a lack of rules, as will be seen in the selected cases below, but rather that these laws are just not respected. The *National Anti-Corruption* framework has not led to any real change in company behavior.

Corruption cannot be fought without a formal organizational structure to address the problem. Therefore, there must be an appropriate "tone at the top" for corporate governance bodies to function correctly, i.e., a discrete pro-honesty culture. Such a situation would imply the condemnation of misconduct as a way of doing business but also, and more importantly, would create an environment that makes misbehaviors less likely to occur.

This part will review six cases of financial and corporate scandals in Mexico, where the company's first response has been to hide these events hoping that no one will discover them. Nevertheless, unfortunately, such behavior inevitably only postpones the materialization of these risks while at the same time making them more likely to occur.

Companies need to form corporate governance bodies, train their employees in identifying and routing corrupt practices, establish guidelines and procedures to prevent bribery and other misconducts, and develop compliance programs. The following six cases have been selected from a large pool of available events to help identify bad practices and address pending tasks in seeking to consolidate a more robust corporate governance framework.

5.1 Homex

Fraud with international funds in the real estate industry.

Established in Culiacan, Sinaloa, in 1989, Homex began with the development of commercial areas and gradually focused on constructing and commercializing affordable housing. Under this scheme, by the end of 2010, it had developed a presence in 34 cities, located in 21 states of Mexico and three Brazilian cities. In 1999, ZN Mexico Funds acquired a minority stake.

(a) What happened:
Homex appeared to be a model company that got the World Bank, Wall Street investment banks, and US pension funds to invest billions of dollars in the company. Success and profits, however, masked its shortcomings. The housing developments were plagued by infrastructure and building defects, and essential services were not met. As a result, as happened in Querétaro, thousands of residents abandoned their "homes". In 2015, OECD estimated that some 500,000 houses built by Homex (and other developers) between 2006 and 2010 were then empty.

The US Securities and Exchange Commission ("SEC") filed a lawsuit against four former executives of the real estate company. Due to cases like Homex, in 2010, article 17 of the Constitution was amended to establish the concept of collective actions. Subsequently, several laws incorporated the first practical allusions to "Collective Action". In 2011, article 107 of the Constitution was amended to establish the origin of the Amparo lawsuit for collective interests (*Profeco*, 2021).

(b) How we found out:
SEC and mass media.

(c) The fallout:
In 2014, Homex filed for bankruptcy. In 2017, the SEC charged it with "massive fraud", as the company reported the sale of more than 106 thousand houses between 2010 and 2012 that never existed. US authorities revealed that the developer's sales had ballooned by more than USD3 billion.

On 9 October 2014, a "collective action" was initiated against Homex, promoted by 161 affected individuals. The action was resolved by a judicial agreement where MXN31.7 million (about USD2.3 million) was "returned" to those affected by the company's behavior.

Homex continues to generate outrage from residents, and some media, the government, and the Mexican housing industry have turned a blind eye. Executives and the company have avoided any severe sanctions, and there is no evidence that Mexican authorities are investigating a possible criminal offense.

In the meantime, the SEC has been hampered because the four executives named in the complaint have not approved a waiver allowing their representatives, or attorneys, to accept the subpoena on their behalf. The SEC must now organize the delivery of the summons to executives in Mexico, a complex process governed by the *Hague Convention* that may, according to the SEC, take several months. Due to the scandal, the chairman of the board, who holds a controlling stake in Homex, Eustaquio de Nicolás, was replaced as CEO by his brother Gerardo. The latter was separated from the company along with the former CFO.

In a separate SEC case filed against the company in March 2017, Homex settled without admitting or denying wrongdoing and agreed to a five-year ban from the US stock markets. The Mexican National Banking and Securities Commission fined the company USD1.2 million.

Amid mounting public demands for a crackdown on dishonesty and the arrest of some top politicians, legal experts and critics say the impasse, in this case, is a stark illustration of the fact that influential figures in Mexico's business world simply do not have to face the consequences of their actions. This lack of accountability may contribute to Mexico's relatively low foreign investment rating, a warning to investors of the precarious legal recourses.

(d) What we learnt or did subsequently:
Firstly, sufficient capacities are not being generated to guarantee shareholders and employees secure access to information in Mexican companies. Second, the existing mechanisms are not working properly.

(e) Public sources:

All retrieved on 14 July 2022:

El Universal. (2018). Una empresa envuelta en numerosos escándalos: https://www.eluniversalqueretaro.mx/metropoli/17-07-2018/una-empresa-envuelta-en-numerosos-escandaloss

LA Times. (2018). Homex, una empresa constructora de México es acusada de fraude masivo de la SEC, pero el caso se ha estancado: https://www.latimes.com/espanol/mexico/la-es-homex-una-empresa-constructora-de-mexico-es-acusada-de-fraude-masivo-de-la-sec-pero-el-caso-se-ha-es-20180302-story.html

5.2 *Banorte*

When you shouldn't trust your broker.

Banorte was founded in 1899 in Monterrey, where it first started operations as a small regional player. In 1992, Banorte was acquired by a group of entrepreneurs led by Roberto Gonzalez Barrera in the banking privatization process. After the Mexican financial crisis of the mid-1990s, Banorte was able to consolidate its nationwide presence through a series of critical acquisitions. It now operates as a financial group known as Grupo Financiero Banorte (GFNorte), offering universal banking products, a wide array of products and services through its broker-dealer network, annuities and insurance companies, retirement savings funds (AFORE), mutual funds, leasing, and factoring companies, as well as warehousing. As of September 2018, GFNorte had USD147 billion in assets under management (GFNorte, 2021).

(a) What happened:
The National Banking and Securities Commission (CNBV) imposed a fine of MXN5.4 million (about USD300,000) on Orlando Salinas, a former executive of the brokerage house Banorte-Ixe for allegedly having defrauded about a dozen clients in Monterrey of around MXN500 million (USD28.3 million).

The CNBV holds the former Banorte operator responsible for "disposing of the resources received from a client or their securities for purposes other than those ordered or contracted by the latter". The fine is derived from applying the Securities Market Law, and the CNBV considered Salinas's actions seriously. Banorte initiated legal proceedings (Amparo law or "*juicio de Amparo*") to challenge the resolution, and as of 2021, Banorte is still awaiting a solution (*Infobae*, 2019).

The brokerage house has yet to repay damages to the affected parties, and the case remains open. The bank still does not pay and still does not recognize any responsibility.

(b) How we found out:
Mass media.

(c) The fallout:
The sanction was imposed on 29 September 2017, per the CNBV announcement. The fine included the disqualification of Salinas

(who is currently a fugitive) from operating as a financial advisor. After uncovering the alleged fraud, the Banorte-Ixe launched an internal investigation in July 2018 to determine responsibilities. However, the company has not made public its progress or the conclusions of its review.

(d) What we learnt or did subsequently:
From this case can be inferred that, although anti-corruption legislation and legal mechanisms are on the statute books, these measures are complicated to enforce because large corporations can also resort to other legal mechanisms, such as a recourse to constitution protections.[20]

(e) Public sources:

All retrieved on 14 July 2022:

Expansión. (2017). La CNBV anuncia multa a presunto defraudador de Banorte: https://expansion.mx/empresas/2017/10/04/la-cnbv-anuncia-multa-a-presunto-defraudador-de-banorte

GFNorte. (2021). Official website: https://investors.banorte.com/

Infobae. (2019). Pelean en tribunales millonaria multa a las Afore. Retrieved from: https://www.infobae.com/america/mexico/2019/04/30/pelean-en-tribunales-millonaria-multa-a-las-afore/ on 24 March 2022.

[20] In most legal systems of the Spanish-speaking world, the "amparo remedy" or "amparo law" is also called "*recurso de amparo*" or "*juicio de amparo*" and is a remedy for the protection of constitutional rights, found in certain jurisdictions. The remedy is an effective and inexpensive instrument for the protection of individual rights. The "amparo", generally granted by a Supreme or Constitutional Court, serves a dual protective purpose: it protects the citizens and their basic guarantees, and protects the Constitution itself, by ensuring that its principles are not violated by statutes or actions of the State that undermine the basic rights enshrined therein. It resembles, in some respects, constitutional remedies such as the "*tutela*" available in Colombia, the writ of security ("*Mandado de Segurança*") in Brazil and the constitutional complaint (*Verfassungsbeschwerde*) procedure found in Germany.

5.3 *AeroMéxico/Mexichem*

Improper use of privileged information.

AeroMéxico was founded in September 1934 by Antonio Díaz Lombardo and currently operates scheduled airline services to destinations in Mexico; North, South, and Central America; the Caribbean, Europe, and Asia. The Grupo Aero México currently holds the #2 place in the domestic market, behind Volaris, with 24.2%; and was #1 in international market share, with 15.8%, in the 12 months ending March 2020, becoming Mexico's largest international airline group. AeroMéxico is one of the four founding members of the *SkyTeam* airline alliance, together with Air France, Delta Air Lines, and Korean Air.

Mexichem was founded in 1953 with its headquarters in Mexico City and is primarily engaged in transforming chemicals and petrochemicals into products and solutions used in the construction, agriculture, and industrial sectors. Its activities are structured in three production chains: a *Chlorine-Vinyl*; a *Fluorine* division; and an *Integral Solutions* division. In 2018, the Mexichem board of directors appointed Daniel Martínez-Valle as CEO. In 2019, Mexichem was rebranded as Orbia.

(a) What happened:

The National Banking and Securities Commission (CNBV) fined members of the Boards of Directors of the Aeroméxico and Mexichem, among others, for using privileged information, according to government information, which was an unusual of course action to be taken against the interests of large Mexican companies.

According to its database, the CNBV brought indictments against 15 people between August and September to carry out transactions based on insider information in 2012 and 2013. The fines, unusual due to the high profile of the businesspeople, amounted to MXP22.3 million (USD1.18 million).

Under article 362 of the Securities Market Law, privileged information is defined as "*knowledge of relevant events that have not been disclosed to the public by the issuer through the stock exchange on which its securities are listed*". However, it should be noted that the CNBV has only imposed three such fines relating to the use of privileged information since 2015. Moreover, Reuters has been unable to obtain further information on these sanctions (*Reuters*, 2017).

(b) How we found out:
Mass media (*Reuters*).

(c) The fallout:
María Lanzagorta, a spokeswoman for the Commission, told Reuters that all the fines were for the same case involving operations in the same company. However, she did not give further details. The possibilities are administrative not criminal, she said. Among those sanctioned are Ignacio Del Valle Ruiz, member of the board of Mexichem and Rafael Tricio Haro, member of the board of Aeroméxico.

(d) What we learnt or did subsequently:
This case was a rare move against powerful business interests. Therefore, we learnt that the necessary laws already exist; they only need to be applied more frequently and diligently.

(e) Public sources:
All retrieved on 14 July 2022:
El Economista. (2017). CNBV multa a Mexichem y Aeroméxico por utilizar información privilegiada – https://www.eleconomista.com.mx/empresas/CNBV-multa-a-Mexichem-y-Aeromexico-por-utilizar-informacion-privilegiada-20171024-0115.html.
Reuters. (2017). Mexichem, Aeromexico board members fined in Mexico for insider trading – https://www.reuters.com/article/us-mexico-insidertrading-idUSKBN1CT2PK.

5.4 OmniLife

Mixing marital affairs with day-to-day operations makes governing the enterprise more problematic.

The founder of this company was the protagonist of a story that mixed love with the business in a risky way. Grupo Omnilife is a Guadalajara-based multi-level marketing company that distributes dietary supplements. Omnitrion Mexico was officially founded in 11 September 1991 by Jorge Vergara and some partners. Vergara's associates later sold him the rights for Omnitrion Mexico; its name was changed in 2000 to Omnilife. Omnilife owns many cash-and-carry distribution centers throughout Mexico and is active in other countries— - chiefly in Latin America, Canada, the United States, Spain, and Russia. Grupo Omnilife has over 3,500 employees and is also the holding company for several other enterprises, some engaged in such high-profile areas as movies, magazines, live shows, and soccer. The corporation is currently owned by the founder's son: Amaury Vergara.

Amaury is the second son of the first marriage of the founder. Jorge Vergara married four times. Jorge had three children with his first wife, Maricruz Zataraín; the first child was Yelena, and the third was Kenya, a company member. The second marriage was with Rossana Lerdo de Tejada; this union produced a daughter: Uma. The third wife was Angélica Fuentes. Jorge met Angélica when he invited her to be the CEO of Omnilife in 2007. Angélica restructured the company and made it more profitable. A year later, she married Jorge in 2008. By 2010, she acquired 43% of the total shares of Omnilife and founded *Angelíssima*, a beauty and cosmetics brand. With Angélica, Jorge had another two daughters: Valentina and María Ignacia. In 2015, Angelica was accused of mismanaging resources and wanting to use the sales network to benefit the *Angelíssima* business unit. When the couple split up in the same year, Jorge returned to Rossana Lerdo and remarried her in 2017. The third wife was the most problematic for the company.

(a) What happened:

A home-grown, multinational company lacked effective corporate governing processes to prevent a series of anomalies within the company. It all started when Jorge found out that his then-wife Angélica Fuentes and CEO had mismanaged it. The "love story" between the two became a scandal that fueled the business, sports, and gossip pages of the jet-set when, on 3 April 2015, Jorge Vergara dismissed Angélica Fuentes as CEO of Grupo Omnilife-Angelissima-Chivas.

Since Jorge Vergara's death on 15 November 2019, his son—Amaury—has implemented a strategy to bring the business back to profitability following the financial debacle. In an interview with *Forbes* magazine, Amaury stated "*We have made an effort to institutionalize the company, to implement true corporate governance and to be very clear about our directions and responsibilities in the countries*" (*Forbes*, 2020).

(b) How we found out:

Mexicanos Contra la Corrupción y la Impunidad (MCCI) and El País.

(c) The fallout:

After seven years of marriage, Jorge Vergara and Angélica Fuentes separated in 2015, which is when the legal battle for the Chivas soccer team and Grupo Omnilife began. Jorge Vergara won the court case in 2016; Angélica was charged with illicit enrichment at Vergara's expense, as the judge ruled that Angélica had bought shares in the group's companies with Vergara's money. Then, in 2020, Angélica Fuentes began several legal proceedings against Vergara's succession in family and civil matters in the city of Guadalajara and this situation will surely test Amaury Vergara's leadership.

(d) What we learnt or did subsequently:

This case confirms that a solid corporate governance framework is essential. In more mature economies than Mexico, 36% of the family businesses surveyed by KPMG are now considering appointing a non-family CEO as a strategic move for the next 12 months. In this task, having a robust family and corporate governance protocols may make the difference between success and failure.

Family businesses in Mexico are currently the principal engines of the national economy, but they face great challenges in ensuring their long-term survival.

By strengthening corporate governance practices, family businesses can capitalize on their competitive advantages, garnering greater vision and balance in their decision-making processes, thus facilitating their long-term growth and development (KPMG, 2019).

(e) Public sources:

All retrieved on 14 July 2022:

https://contralacorrupcion.mx/la-fgr-detecta-5-millones-de-dolares-de-ohl-en-cuenta-de-lozoya/

Forbes (2020). Grupo Omnilife-Chivas: la jugada de Amaury Vergara para recuperar el imperio. Retrieved from: https://www.forbes.com.mx/revista-impresa-grupo-omnilife-chivas-la-jugada-de-amaury-vergara-para-recuperar-el-imperio/ on 24 March 2022.

https://expansion.mx/empresas/2016/12/02/12-uvas-12-escandalos-empresariales-en-mexico-que-marcaron-2016

KPMG (2019). La importancia del gobierno corporativo en las empresas familiares. Retrieved from: https://www.delineandoestrategias.com.mx/blog-de/la-importancia-del-gobierno-corporativo-en-las-empresas-familiares#:~:text=El%20gobierno%20corporativo%20es%20una,en%20el%20desarrollo%20del%20negocio on 24 March 2022.

5.5 *OHL México*

Corruption in highway construction.

OHL México is a wholly owned subsidiary of OHL, a Spanish multinational construction and civil engineering company. The parent is involved in infrastructure and commercial property construction, homebuilding and the operation of toll roads, and other transport concessions. In the latter, the Group is particularly active in Mexico. The company's roots stretch back to May 1911, with the foundation of Sociedad General de Obras y Construcciones Obrascón, S.A. in Bilbao, whose first project was the construction of two wharfs in the Port of Lisbon. Following the scandal, OHL México now operates under the name Aleática.

(a) What happened:
OHL México faced a number of accusations of corruption with the main one pointing to Emilio Lozoya, a former director of Pemex (the state-owned oil company). The controversy arose in May 2015, after a series of leaked telephone conversations. One included a chat between a senior OHL executive and Mexico's transport minister after the top brass of the Spanish parent apparently held a private meeting with Mr. Peña Nieto (former Mexican President [2012–2018]). The telephone recordings were posted on YouTube and included chats between OHL executives apparently discussing, among other things, ways to inflate the toll road's rates and to pay for the holidays of government officials. OHL said the recordings of its executives were done illegally and were edited to mislead listeners. OHL is involved in a project that had an original budget of MXP5.637 billion (about USD345 million), an amount that then grew to MXP18.628 billion (USD1, 131 million), an amount the

company later pleaded, falsely, to MXP23.376 billion (USD1400 billion). With those fake numbers, the government modified the concession so OHL could make more money by increasing tolls by 50% (until the year 2051). Not only that, but the government also later rejected the installation of an independent verification system to assess the exact traffic flows, the toll collections and the effective services work carried out at the site. That system concluded that OHL had already recovered its investment on the project and so the concession should come to an end.

In July 2021, in carrying out a recapitalization plan the Amodio brothers became the principal shareholders of the Spanish construction company OHL, gaining control of 25.96%. With that, Luis Amodio was voted in as Chairman of the Board of OHL Worldwide in June 2020.

Following the corruption scandals in Mexico, the company is now adhering to the *Global Compact* of the United Nations and its *2030 Agenda*, following the *Guiding Principles on Business and Human Rights* (*Reporte Indigo*, 2021).

(b) How we found out:

Mexicanos Contra la Corrupción y la Impunidad (MCCI) and the newspaper EL PAÍS.

(c) The fallout:

The file that the Attorney General's Office (FGR) drafted by Emilio Lozoya includes indications of possible new bribes, now from companies linked to OHL, a construction company of Spanish origin that was benefited with multimillion-dollar contracts and concessions by the Government of Enrique Peña Nieto, according to documents to which *Mexicanos Contra La Corrupción y la Impunidad* (MCCI) and EL PAÍS had access.

(d) What we learnt or did subsequently:

The main problem in Mexico is impunity. Deep and widespread impunity is at the center of national problems such as insecurity, unequal access to justice, violence, corruption, and the violation of Human Rights.

In a context characterized by widespread impunity, a firm's owners may be tempted to alter the data or under-report in those cases where the information reveals irregularities. Faced with this problem, it is necessary to guarantee an agencies' autonomy in generating public information to avoid arbitrary modifications and promote corporate governance mechanisms to facilitate information auditing.

(e) **Public sources:**

All retrieved on 14 July 2022:

El País. (2017). Caso OHL México. Retrieved from: https://elpais.com/noticias/caso-ohl-mexico/ on 24 March 2022.

Expansión. (2016). 12 uvas... 12 escándalos empresariales en México que marcaron 2016. Retrieved from: https://expansion.mx/empresas/2016/12/02/12-uvas-12-escandalos-empresariales-en-mexico-que-marcaron-2016 on 24 March 2022.

Mexicanos contra la corrupción. (2021). La FGR indaga posibles nuevos sobornos a Lozoya de una trama de empresas investigadas por su relación con OHL. Retrieved from: https://contralacorrupcion.mx/la-fgr-detecta-5-millones-de-dolares-de-ohl-en-cuenta-de-lozoya/ on 24 March 2022.

5.6 *Exportadora De Sal (ESSA)*

A marriage of convenience between the government and international companies.

The Mexican government set up Exportadora de Sal, S.A. (ESSA) in April 1954. Over the rest of that decade, it slowly developed new areas of salt production based on evaporation by the sun of seawater over an area of around 90 Km^2, with an annual output of 80 kilotons of salt and an operational infrastructure able to annually produce, transport, and ship over 7 million tons p.a. ESSA currently owns 281 Km^2 of evaporation ponds or concentration areas. ESSA entered the Japanese market in 1960 and subsequently expanded its operating capacity, production, and commercialization, including developing a new port facility and the "Chaparrito" salt washing plant on the island of Cedros in the state of Baja California. The company is currently owned by the Mexican government (51%) and the Japanese corporation Mitsubishi (49%).

(a) **What happened:**

The Financial Intelligence Unit (UIF) filed four complaints of acts of fraud with the Attorney General's Office (FGR), against the former head of ESSA, Jorge Humberto López Portillo Basave, and other officials of the Ministry of Economy, during the administration of Ildefonso Guajardo in the government of former President Enrique Peña Nieto.

(b) How we found out:
Mass media.

(c) The fallout:
ESSA is jointly owned by the Mexican State and the Japanese multinational Mitsubishi and has received various observations from the Superior Auditor of the Federation since the middle of the Peña Nieto administration.

(d) What we learnt or did subsequently:
The high levels of impunity in Mexico are not limited to federal institutions, but tend to be replicated in the states, which share similar degrees and conditions of impunity.

Impunity feeds back and multiplies the consequences of phenomena such as insecurity, violence, unequal access to justice, corruption, or the violation of Human Rights. International reports coincide in pointing to the magnitude and consequences of these phenomena (*Le Clercq*, 2021).

There are no easy ways out, and the way is to generate more capacities for justice and accountability institutions, both in government and companies. The big question is whether Mexico can reform itself or whether it necessarily requires some kind of international mechanism against impunity and corruption.

(e) Public sources:

All retrieved on 14 July 2022

Le Clercq, J. A. (2021). México en la medición de la impunidad del Índice Global de Impunidad 2020. Retrieved from – https://theglobalamericans.org/2021/01/mexico-en-la-medicion-de-la-impunidad-del-indice-global-de-impunidad-2020/ on March 27th, 2022.

Milenio. (2021). UIF denuncia a ex funcionarios de Exportadora de Sal por actos de corrupción. Retrieved from – https://www.milenio.com/politica/uif-denuncia-funcionarios-exportadora-sal-corrupcion on 27 March 2022.

5.7 *Lessons from Mexico and Open Questions for Further Study*

1. In a country like Mexico, with a long history of corruption both in the private sector and in the government, we must deal with specific cases (such as Homex) to adapt the legislation to new ways of committing fraud.
2. Impunity in Mexico is as severe as it is dishonest. A serious obstacle to applying the law is constituted by the "Amparo Trial" (for example, Banorte). This legal mechanism, designed to prevent abuses of authority, must be reformed in order to avoid white-collar criminals from evading justice.
3. The use of privileged information should have stronger sanctions than other countries to discourage this ingrained practice among large Mexican companies (for example, Aeroméxico and Mexichem).
4. Corruption in private companies (OHL México) and mixed capital companies (Exportadora de Sal) is an issue that must be dealt with thoroughly since, when thinking about misconduct, most citizens believe that it only occurs in the Government. Individuals and the Government must be equally monitored and sanctioned by a more robust set of laws.
5. Strong corporate governing has proven to be an effective tool to avoid problems, especially in family businesses (for example, Omnilife). We still have a long way to go in establishing mechanisms that promote transparency, justice, and equity among the different stakeholders of Mexican companies.

6 Peru

Enrique Díaz Ortega

Good corporate governing has been on the retina of the Peruvian stock market for a little over two decades, in the expectation that it will contribute to the development and strength of the local market. The SMV (formerly CONASEV) and the Lima Stock Exchange have actively sought to guide companies on the path to good governance practices.

E. Díaz Ortega
Cornell University, Ithaca, NY, USA
e-mail: ediaz@mcifperu.com

However, the final decision, and corresponding responsibility, rests with the companies themselves.

The Peruvian stock market is clearly imperfect and shallow, which is no surprise given the country's weak institutional and legal framework. This context has only served to limit deeper and more sustained advances in best governance practices. A host of notorious situations confirm this reality and serve as proof of the shortcomings revealed in the corporate governing of companies.

The cases described here are not intended to be the only ones of relevance, but more an attempt to represent flagrant misbehaviors that, we hope, will explain the concepts of good governing, all of which have received wide public attention in the media. Likewise, looking at these cases, they throw into relief the diversity of questionable practices from the perspective of governing, even when they had been covered with legality. Among them, the most notorious are the limited exercise of transparency, infringements of investor property rights, violations of internal controls, and poor risk management, to name but a few.

6.1 Credicorp

Fallout from Presidential campaign contributions.

Credicorp Ltd. (with the New York Stock Exchange (NYSE) and Bolsa de Valores de Lima (BVL) trading code: BAP) is an *exempted* company set up in Bermuda on 17 August 1995, pursuant to the Bermuda Companies Act of 1981, as Credicorp's holding company, to coordinate the policy and management of its subsidiaries, which included BCP (Peru's largest bank) as a standalone company, BCP Bolivia (the bank's subsidiary in Bolivia), MiBanco (a financial institution focused on microfinance), Grupo Pacifico (a composite insurance company), Prima AFP (a pension fund manager), Credicorp Capital (an investment bank) and ASB (and offshore investment company).

(a) What happened:
In the Peruvian presidential elections of 2011, two candidates, with radically different profiles, contested the electoral second round run-off. On the one hand, Keiko Fujimori, representing *libertarian* economic ideas (the "right") and on the other hand, Ollanta Humala, representing more *socialist* ideas (the "left"). At the time,

the latter candidate was closely associated with former President of Venezuela, Hugo Chávez, and was accused of promoting a *Chavista* ideology, that it was argued might seriously harm the country's economic growth.

Dionisio Romero Paoletti, at the time Chairman of Credicorp, donated USD3.6 million to Keiko Fujimori's election campaign. This money was paid in cash and was not reported to the National Office of Electoral Processes (ONPE), the body in charge of overseeing national elections. It was subsequently confirmed that these contributions came from both the Credicorp holding company and the Romero family.

(b) How it was made public:
In November 2019, during investigations into the Fuerza Popular party (led by Ms Fujimori), the Office of the Prosecutor, looking into allegation of money laundering, asked Dionisio Romero Paoletti to provide a statement confirming the existence of contributions that might not have been declared. The (by then former) Chairman of Credicorp, stated that he had given the money to Keiko Fujimori's campaign in 2011, as well as having contributed to other campaigns in subsequent years. This news was quickly circulated by the press and international media. In addition, the information was shared widely on social media and led to criticisms from all sectors.

(c) The outcome:
Credicorp suffered a serious reputational blow. Various media outlets and opinions reported and criticized Sr. Romero Paoletti's behavior and Credicorp and its subsidiaries' apparent lack of transparency in its political lobbying activities. Although those involved argued that no crime had been committed in paying these contributions, the alarm triggered a reputational crisis in the company, as verified by its initial reaction in running a social media campaign and publishing an open letter in the press with the message that everything had been done for the good of the country and that no illicit act had been committed. In a letter addressed to the staff and employees, Sr. Romero Paoletti assured that "making these contributions to Fuerza 2011 was the responsible decision to face down the threats to Peruvians posed by *Chavismo*".

Weeks after the dissemination of the campaign, Dionisio Romero Paoletti resigned from the *Corporate Governance Committee* of

Credicorp Ltd., of which he had been President. Then, a couple of months later in April 2020, Romero Paoletti was not nominated for re-election as a director while, simultaneously, Credicorp appointed four new independent directors.

Subsequently, the Superintendency of the Securities Market (SMV) gave notice to Credicorp Ltd. that it was opening an investigation with a view to fining the company. This was published on the SMV website as an *hecho importante*, stating that this procedure occurs "as a consequence of not having taken steps to disclose to the market the contributions made to political campaigns in 2011 and 2016". In March 2021, the SMV decided to apply a penalty of 300 *Unidades Impositivas Tributarias*, equivalent to PEN1,080,000 (around USD300 thousand) for contributions to the political party Fuerza Popular in 2011.

(d) What we learnt or did later:

Credicorp did not publicly acknowledge having committed any wrongdoing in making these contributions to a presidential candidate. However, the company was making change in decisions at the Board level, possibly to lessen the reputational exposure that linked it more to Mr. Romero Paoletti, as Chairman of the company.

The main government action occurred through the SMV, which ended up fining the company for lack of timely disclosure of contributions to the Keiko Fujimori campaign.

In Peru, these types of decisions are not mandatory for others that are subject to similar problems (jurisprudence). Nor have there been regulatory amendments related to the case.

(e) Public references:

All retrieved on 14 July 2022:

https://www.larepublica.co/globoeconomia/revuelo-en-peru-porque-credicorp-reconocio-aporte-a-keiko-fujimori-2934485

https://gestion.pe/peru/politica/dionisio-romero-paoletti-reconoce-aporte-de-us-365-millones-a-campana-de-keiko-fujimori-durante-el-ano-2011-noticia/

https://elcomercio.pe/politica/dionisio-romero-paoletti-revela-que-credicorp-dono-us36-millones-a-campana-de-keiko-fujimori-el-2011-noticia/

https://cnnespanol.cnn.com/2019/11/20/alerta-peru-presidente-de-credicorp-afirma-que-entrego-us-365-millones-a-keiko-fujimori-para-su-campana-electoral/
https://credicorp.gcs-web.com/

6.2 *Graña y Montero*

Illegal payments in a consortium to obtain bids for public works projects.

Graña y Montero is a Peruvian construction company based in Lima. It was established in 1933 as a construction company specializing in buildings, but has subsequently expanded its business to larger works, such as railways and roads. It also expanded its operations across Latin America. Its share was traded on the Lima Stock Exchange and on the NYSE (as an ADR).

(a) What happened:

In 2005, the CONIRSA consortium, made up of the large construction consortia Odebrecht, Graña y Montero, ICCGSA, and "JJC Contractors General", paid bribes to the government of former President Alejandro Toledo [2001–2006] to win tenders for sections 2 and 3 of the Interoceanica Sur highways.

Then, during the second government of former President Alan García [2006–2011], Graña y Montero participated as a consortium, again with Odebrecht in the construction of sections 1 and 2 of the Lima Metro. According to the confession of a former Odebrecht official, Graña y Montero collaborated with the payment of bribes to the authorities to win the Lima Metro tender.

(b) How it was made public:

In the midst of the investigations of the *Lava Jato* case on bribes paid by the Brazilian company Odebrecht, Jorge Barata, a collaborator of the Office of the Prosecutor revealed in February 2017 that Graña y Montero knew of the bribes paid to former President Alejandro Toledo for the *Interoceanic Highway* project in 2005.

Later, the same former Odebrecht official pointed out that Graña y Montero also had knowledge of the bribes paid for the construction of the Lima Metro in Alan García's second government.

(c) The outcome:
At the end of February 2017, the value of the company on the Lima Stock Exchange (BVL) suffered two sharp falls, which amounted to a loss of over 60% following Jorge Barata's statements. The stock on the New York and Lima stock exchanges entered a spiral of volatility, falling to USD2.18 on the New York Stock Exchange in March 2017, compared to USD8.63 in August of 2016.

In May 2017, the Ad Hoc Office criminally denounced Graña y Montero for alleged irregularities in the Interoceanica Sur tender. The complaint included José Graña Miro Quesada, former President of the Graña y Montero board; Fernando Camet Piccone, from the company JJC Contractors Generales S.A.; and Fernando Castillo Dibos, from ICCGSA.

The company took a series of measures to safeguard financial stability in an attempt to convince the market that it had already begun a transformation process. New investors were invited to make capital injections of USD130 million, executives implicated in the corruption allegations were removed from their positions and from the board, and new directors were appointed to make up a new board, all of which was carried out by the end of 2020.

On 2 November 2020, the General Shareholders' Meeting of Graña y Montero S.A.A. approved the modification of its corporate name to Aenza S.A.A. ("Shame"). In an *Hecho de Importancia* published on the Superintendency of the Securities Market (SMV) website, Aenza's Corporate General Manager, Luis Díaz Olivero, reported that, together with the board of directors, a substantial transformation had taken nearly four years to recover from the company's deep crisis.

In May 2021, the reformed construction company Aenza (ex Graña y Montero) signed a preparatory agreement for effective collaboration with the Special Team of the Prosecutor's Office and the Ad Hoc Office of the *Lava Jato* Case, after acknowledging that, together with its subsidiaries Graań y Montero S.A. and Concar S.A. had committed crimes of corruption in 16 infrastructure projects that had been developed in Peru between the years 2003 to 2016; and also that they simulated competition in the public tenders called for another 48 projects.

(d) What we learnt or did later:

The company apologized "for the mistakes that were made by the previous management" and promised to comply with the highest standards of corporate governance and ethical behavior. For its part, at the beginning of October 2017, Congress approved Bill No. 1410 that modifies Emergency Decree No. 003, through which the assets of both corrupt companies and their partners and consortia may be retained. Likewise, they will not be able to continue doing business with the State and will have to pay civil damages in favor of the State.

(e) References:

All retrieved on 14 July 2022:

https://gestion.pe/peru/politica/grana-y-montero-pago-us-38-millones-a-odebrecht-para-ser-parte-del-gasoducto-noticia/

https://rpp.pe/economia/economia/los-7-golpes-que-sufrio-grana-y-montero-por-el-caso-odebrecht-noticia-1092474

https://www.laoyconsultores.com/caso-odebrech-grana-montero-las-demas-consorciadas/

https://www.americaeconomia.com/aenza-ex-grana-y-montero-la-carrera-de-la-mayor-constructora-de-peru-por-sobrevivir-su-fuerte-crisis

https://www.esan.edu.pe/conexion/actualidad/2018/12/10/como-funciona-la-corrupcion-en-el-peru-analisis-del-caso-odebrecht/

https://ojo-publico.com/2722/lava-jato-ex-grana-montero-confeso-corrupcion-en-16-obras

6.3 *Alicorp*

Financial losses caused by irregular trading of derivatives.

Alicorp is a mass-consumption company, founded in 1956, and is a leader in the Peruvian market, with industrial operations in six Latin American countries: Argentina, Brazil, Chile, Colombia, Ecuador, and Peru, where it has its main headquarters. It exports to more than 23 countries and is the second largest mass-consumption company in the Andes region. Its shares are listed on the Lima Stock Exchange.

(a) What happened:
In March 2013, Alicorp issued a bond for USD450 million, primarily to finance its acquisitions of companies, such as the case of Global Alimentos (purchase completed in April 2014). All the Peruvian Pension Funds (AFPs) acquired this new bond. At that time, the issue was highlighted by the market: the rate of 3.88% obtained was considered the lowest rate for a corporate bond in Peruvian history and the economic situation at that time offered positive perspectives for the growth of the company.

However, in addition to the debt and the growing needs to finance working capital expenditures, there was an additional problem — the rise in the dollar, driven by expectations for a rise in the United States Federal Reserve interest rate. As a result, in 2013 the company recorded an exchange rate loss of PEN122 million (USD44.9 million).

In 2014, despite an 8% increase in revenues, the company's year-on-year net profits fell 96.3%: from PEN331 million (USD122.6 million) in 2013 to PEN12 million (USD4.4 million) in 2014. It should be noted that this figure was adjusted in the audited financial statements since the unaudited financial statements had reported a net profit of PEN19 million (USD7.0 million).

The company explained that a non-monetary loss had been recorded due to variations in trading in derivatives, amounting to PEN257 million (USD4.2 million), of which PEN207 million (USD76.7 million) corresponded to positions of raw materials affected by the price fluctuations in international agricultural commodities.

The poor results in 2014 were produced by losses related to very broad *collars* in their derivative hedges, together with the sale of *puts*, which had a negative impact due to the fall in the prices of agricultural commodities towards the end of that year. These negotiations were related to an alleged speculation on the part of those in charge of dealing in the derivatives.

(b) How it was made public:
Given the dissemination of the poor results for 2014, Alicorp publicly reported that these were mainly due to financial losses related to derivatives trading. The company said in a statement that it lost PEN228 million (USD93.3 million) due to derivatives and

another PEN35 million (USD12.3 million) from the depreciation of the *Nuevo Sol* (PEN).

(c) The outcome:
The company announced that the Finance Manager would be leaving the company in May 2015. Likewise, weeks later, it was announced that the General Manager, a family member of the controlling business group, would also be stepping down.

In May 2015, the risk rating agency Moody's downgraded the credit rating of Alicorp's international bonds from Baa2 to Baa3, with a stable outlook. This cut was due to the high debt ratio that the company held throughout 2014 (greater than 2.5 times debt/EBITDA). In addition, Fitch maintained Alicorp's credit rating at BBB, but changed its outlook from *stable* to *negative*. This downgrade affected the value of the bonds, and therefore the equity of their holders, as was the case of the AFPs, which also made known their concern about these high-risk financial operations by the company, which were also little understood, denoting limited transparency and insufficient risk management, despite being listed on the Lima Stock Exchange.

(d) What we learnt or did later:
In addition to administrative changes in management, Alicorp announced that it would take measures to improve its results, focusing on improving operating margins, reducing the level of working capital, cutting its exposures to exchange rate volatility, and improving the company's leverage, in addition to using simpler hedge derivatives.

For its part, no government body has issued any provision or standards relating to the events that occurred in this case.

(e) References:
All retrieved on 14 July 2022:

https://elcomercio.pe/economia/peru/razones-habrian-impulsado-salida-sacchi-alicorp-189615-noticia/

https://elcomercio.pe/economia/negocios/utilidad-alicorp-cayo-94-3-2014-pese-aumento-ventas-334943-noticia/

https://www.peru-retail.com/estudio-investigacion/alicorp-enfrenta-un-duro-panorama-ante-los-cambios-en-el-mercado/

6.4 *Arca Continental | Lindley*

Irregular negotiations in the purchase of shares.

Corporación Lindley S.A. is a Peruvian company founded in 1910, dedicated to the manufacture and distribution of beverages. It is mainly known for the creation of the *Inca Kola* soft drink, but since 1999 it has also been the exclusive *Coca-Cola* distributor in Peru (both soft drinks are the most consumed in Peru, with over 50% market share each). The common shares and investment shares of the company are listed on the Lima Stock Exchange.

EMBOTELLADORA ARCA was a Mexican multinational company that was formed in 2001 following the mergers of the three largest bottling companies—ARGOS, ARMA, and PROCOR in the north of the country, so becoming the second largest Coca-Cola bottler in Mexico. The merger with GRUPO CONTINENTAL in 2011 created EMBOTELLADORAS ARCA CONTINENTAL so consolidating its national deal with Coca-Cola. Following acquisitions in Ecuador and Argentina, ARCA CONTINENTAL is the largest bottler in Latin America and, together with Coca-Cola, has since expanded into southwestern states in the USA, making it the second largest Coca-Cola bottler in the Americas.

(a) What happened:

The Lindley Corporation sold 47.52% of its total shares to Arca Continental in September 2015, for USD760 million. In this way, the Mexican company became the controlling shareholder. The family was also paid a further USD150 million to refrain from competing in the same business, i.e., to permanently withdraw from the bottling industry in Peru. In turn, in February 2016, Lindley completed the purchase of 64.5 million shares of the Mexican company.

There were several questions about this transaction, especially from the holders of *investment shares* (securities without voting rights that are also listed on the Lima Stock Market, as dictated in law). They argued that the principles of investor protection, fair and equitable treatment, as well as transparency had all been violated. The holders of these *investment shares* invited the regulatory authority to review their case given the suggestion that throughout the sale-purchase process, there had been abuses and violations of market transparency relating to the way the negotiations had been communicated as they developed. This position had two components: firstly, only a *notional* value had been assigned to *investment shares*, flagging a 300% differential between *investment* and *common* share prices; and secondly, that Lindley did not disclose information in a timely manner regarding the nature of its negotiations with Arca Continental.

(b) How it was made public:
Initially, the holders of *investment* shares publicly petitioned the regulatory body to review the sales-purchase transaction given the perceived irregularities and violation to their rights.

Then, in November 2015, the Superintendency of the Securities Market (SMV) reported, as an *Hecho de Importancia* that it would be opening an Administrative Sanctions Process to look at possible claims against Lindley.

(c) The outcome:
The SVM initiated the process Administrative Sanctions Process by issuing letter No. 5157-2015-SMV/11.2 and this process subsequently resolved that the Peruvian corporation had committed seven significant regulatory violations during the sales-purchase process.

Four of the infractions are considered "very serious" and defined as "presenting to the SMV, the stock market, the investor, and any other market subject inaccurate, false, or biased information; or disclose said information in the market".

The three remaining offenses are "serious", according to the regulations, for "not communicating important facts that have a significant impact on the market".

The sanction consisted of a fine amounting to 200 *Unidades Impositivas Tributarias* (UIT), equivalent to PEN790,000 (around USD240,000). Through a statement, the company accepted the sanction and informed that it will not appeal the SMV's decision, thus concluding this Administrative Process.

(d) What we learnt or did later:
In Peru, there has been a controversy about whether *investment shares* are effectively stocks. They are similar to non-voting shares (they do not have voting rights), but they are not part of the company's capital, although they are part of the equity. The facts seem to indicate that the negotiations focused on the controlling

shareholders who were informed of the transaction; and therefore, the same level of information had not been provided to holders of *investment shares*. This was finally sanctioned by the SMV.

As a result of this case, no law or regulation was modified to prevent this type of irregularity. The sanction is intended to serve as a dissuasive measure so that similar events do not occur again.

(e) References:

All retrieved on 14 July 2022:

https://www.arcacontal.com/

https://en.wikipedia.org/wiki/Corporaci%C3%B3n_Lindley_S.A

https://en.wikipedia.org/wiki/Arca_Continental

https://rpp.pe/economia/economia/smv-sanciono-a-corporacion-lindley-por-venta-a-arca-continental-noticia-981364

https://economica.pe/smv-sanciono-a-lindley-por-venta-a-arca-con-s-790-000/

https://gestion.pe/economia/empresas/lindley-responde-inicio-proceso-sancionador-colaboraremos-smv-105917-noticia/

https://www.arcacontinentallindley.pe/detalle-noticia.php?id_noticia=000001784

https://www.americaeconomia.com/negocios-industrias/multilatinas/arca-continental-concreta-alianza-con-lindley-por-us760-millones-y-#:~:text=La%20mexicana%20Arca%20Continental%20(AC,del%20sistema%20global%20de%20Coca%2D

6.5 Milpo

Irregularities in the delisting process of a mining company that generated discrepancies with minority shareholders.

Compañía Minera Milpo is a Peruvian mining company headquartered in Lima and listed on the Lima Stock Exchange. The company was founded in 1949 and is owned by the Brazilian conglomerate Grupo Votorantim. It is engaged in the exploration and exploitation of mining claims, as well as in the extraction, concentration, and sale of zinc, copper, lead, silver, and gold. It operates four mining units: the El Porvenir mine, located in Pasco; the Chapi mine, located in Moquegua; and the Cerro Lindo mine, located in Ica; and the IVAN mine and refinery, located in Antofagasta, Chile.

(a) What happened:

In 2017, Milpo requested that the Superintendency of the Securities Market (SMV) to delist its common shares delisted from the securities registry of the Lima Stock Exchange (BVL). In March of that same year, the SMV approved the petition on condition that it launched a *Public Purchase Offer* (or OPC, for its Spanish acronyms) beforehand in which the minimum price would be determined by an independent valuation entity. At the end of that same month, a request for proposals (RFP) was made to select the valuing entity—Summa Asesores Financieros subsequently being chosen.

The SMV gave Summa approximately 90 days to submit its valuation report on Milpo. However, Summa asked for extensions on two occasions. Summa finally delivered their valuation report 17 days late. This report assessed the value of common shares at PEN4.16 per share, while the share closed that same day on the BVL at PEN4.60 on the BVL.

On release of the valuation report was released, the following day the stock fell by 12%, to PEN4.05 the following day. This drop was related to the fact that the consensus of analysts was for a base value per share of PEN4.40. In the subsequent days Summa presented the SMV with an update of its valuation report to the SMV, indicating a price of PEN3.97—13.7% lower than their original valuation. However, the SMV refused to accept the change given it fell outside the delivery date set for deliver the report, as well as in consideration that it had already had an affected the market.

At the end of May, Milpo gave its opinion on Summa's valuation report and reported a relevant fact ("*Hecho de Importancia*"), that was published by the SMV. First, it declared that it had found material errors in the valuation report that had an adverse impact on the value of its shares. The company argued that certain tax contributions, such as the *Special Mining Tax*, had not been included in the projected future cash flows. According to Milpo, this omission alone had a USD69.6 million impact, so reducing the common share price by PEN0.19. In other words, the price per common share should have been PEN3.97. Therefore, it invited Summa to make the a correction. However, again, this was not accepted by the SMV.

Secondly, Milpo then indicated that the OPC would not be launched based on a price reflecting these material errors and they would therefore not proceed with the offer. The SMV ruled on this and indicated that it would not accept the change in the price referred to in the original Summa report.

It should also be noted that hitherto Milpo had been part of several BVL indices, and in particular the *Good Corporate Governance Index*. However, following these events, Milpo subsequently ceased to be part of that index, suffering a loss in trade frequency and market interest in its shares.

(b) How it was made public:

The case first came to light on the publication of Summa's valuation report. Subsequently, through an official letter published by the SMV, its surprise at Summa's request to update the report, which immediately raised doubts in the market and among minority shareholders. Finally, following the publication of Milpo's *Hecho de Importancia* on the SMV website, in which the company confirmed its disagreement with the estimates for the OPC.

(c) The outcome:

The OPC did not take place and Milpo was unable to carry out its plans to delist from the BVL. The minority shareholders pointed out the irregularities in the valuation of the company and argued that the controllers of Milpo had sought to manipulate the information and so lower the price. This tension between minorities and the company was exacerbated by the marked difference between Summa's estimates and those of the brokerage firms.

(d) What we learnt or did later:

The truncated delisting process made it clear that the interests of a listed company may differ markedly from the interests of other investors in the market. In turn, the existing regulations allowed the company to suspend the process when the price set was not as expected. The regulations ended up being part of the problem in so far as they generated rigidities that were insurmountable. That said, there have subsequently been no regulatory changes to correct this.

According to specialists in corporate law, there is a lack of coordination between the *Securities Market Law* (LMV) and the *General Companies Law* (LGS) regarding public limited companies (SAA for its acronym in Spanish). This lack of coordination results in a legal vacuum in Peruvian legislation that does not contemplate the concept of a "squeeze out", in the process where a listed company is taken private. However, as indicated, no initiatives have been taken to address this legal vacuum.

(e) References:
All retrieved on 14 July 2022:

https://semanaeconomica.com/economia-finanzas/banca/207582-deslistado-de-milpo-por-que-los-accionistas-minoritarios-no-quieren-vender

https://elcomercio.pe/economia/negocios/milpo-laberinto-secuelas-lecciones-fallido-deslistado-428509-noticia/?ref=ecr

https://semanaeconomica.com/economia-finanzas/mercado-de-valores/229351-milpo-por-que-se-cayo-su-deslistado-en-la-bvl

http://www.latinomineria.cl/blog/2017/06/05/milpo-laberinto-secuelas-lecciones-fallido-deslistado/

6.6 *BAYER/Aventis*

A merger in peru leading to claims for damages to investment shareholders[21]

Bayer Perú S. A is a subsidiary of its Leverkusen-based, German multinational parent Bayer A. G and was established and incorporated in Peru to develop activities relating to the commercialization of a range of industrial and consumer products in the agriculture, environmental, human health, animal health, and textiles sectors, among others. For its part, Aventis Cropscience Perú S.A. was a Peruvian division of the Paris-based French multinational pharmaceutical and healthcare company Sanofi S.A. Following Aventis Cropscience GMBH, sale in May 2002 to Bayer A. G in Germany, management of the respective Peruvian divisions immediately began talks to merge the local companies.

Bayer was an issuer of *investment shares*, a type of security unique to the Peruvian market. *Investment shares* (an *acción de inversión*, formerly known as an *acción de trabajo*) derive from the *Industrial Communities* established in 1970 under the *General Law of Industries*, which fostered worker participation in the profits, ownership, and management of a company.

[21] Over the years, there have been several situations where it has been considered that the rights of investment shares have been harmed. We have chosen one of them, which also prompted a resolution of the regulatory body in favor of investor protection.

Although *investment shares* use the name "shares", they do not represent joint-stock units of a company's capital, thus differing from equity, as they are recorded in an "Investment Shares Account" in a company's financial statements. That said, this type of security has also—from time-to-time—been listed on the Lima Stock Exchange.

The Investment Shares Law grants economic rights to their holders, namely: to participate in the distribution of dividends and maintain a constant ratio between the Investment Shares Account and the capital account.

(a) What happened:

Through a session of the General Shareholders' Meeting on 14th October 2002, Bayer Perú S. A approved a project to merge with Aventis Aventis Cropscience Perú S.A., through which Bayer would absorb all Aventis' equity.

The *merger by absorption* between Bayer and Aventis was to be based on the financial situation of both companies as of 30 June 2002.

The capital and equity situations of the two companies, as well as the new merged company, are provided in the Table 1 below.

As can be seen, Aventis had no *investment shares* and also had negative equity.

Aventis shareholders received one Bayer share for every 9 Aventis shares.

What stands out is that *investment shares* were not considered in the exchange, and thus the proportional relationship between capital

Table 1 Bayer & Aventis Capital and Investments Share Statements on 31 June 2002 (PEN)

Accounts	*Bayer*	*Aventis*	*Bayer (merged)*
Capital	9,153,000	11,187,422	20,340,422
Investment shares	3,462,000	0	3,462,000
Legal reserve	1,831,000	385,361	2,216,361
Other reserves	23,306,000	0	23,306,000
Accumulated profit (loss)	5,677,000	(19,742,597)	(14,065,597)
Net worth	43,429,000	(8,169,813)	35,259,186

and *investment shares* was modified to the detriment of the holders of the latter.

(b) How it was made public:
Bayer's *investment shareholders* and minority shareholders complained to the securities market regulator (CONASEV), arguing that they had not received equitable treatment and that their rights had been affected. This led CONASEV to open an investigation into the operation.

(c) The outcome:
In November 2002, CONASEV issued a Resolution with the following reasoning:

> As a result of the merger, the holders of investment shares will see their participation diluted, affecting their right to maintain the proportion with respect to the capital stock account. The merger is being financed out of resources from Bayer's reserves and retained earnings accounts, over which investment shareholders also have rights. The merger agreement does not violate the General Companies Law or the Investment Stock Law, but this agreement and its consequences are harmful to investment shareholders in generating unequal treatment regarding common shareholders.

In this way, CONASEV ordered the exclusion of Bayer's *investment shares* from the RPMV (this entails delisting from the stock market), based on the cause of serious risk for adequate investor protection. With this, Bayer was required to make a Public Offering to purchase the *investment shares*, giving its holders the opportunity to sell their securities at a price set by an independent valuation entity.

(d) What we learnt or did later:
Investment shares are not really shares, because they do not constitute part of a company's capital. However, they do proffer economic rights similar to those of common shares. As indicated, they were created specifically as an employee incentive compensation instrument and not as a regular, tradable security. However, they ended up being traded on the stock market. Those who acquired them understood that their economic rights would be respected and, in particular, that their relevance within the equity of the company would <u>not</u> be diluted with capital increases.

The legal framework contains gaps and imperfections that have created investment risks, such as those outlined in this case. Investor protection is thus exposed and requires timely and decisive action by the stock market regulator and/or the stock market itself. Legal uncertainty for these types of security have always been latent in the Peruvian market.

Precisely with an aim to reduce such vulnerabilities, in 2006 a law was subsequently enacted to encourage the exchange of these *investment shares* for common shares, or, alternatively for a company to grant investment shareholder redemption rights. In practice, the exchange has never occurred and, similarly, their redemption rights largely have not been applied either.

(e) References:
All retrieved on 14 July 2022:

https://agnitio.pe/articulo/caso-lindley-y-caso-bayer-acciones-de-inversion-vs-acciones-con-o-sin-derecho-a-voto/

http://revistas.pucp.edu.pe/index.php/iusetveritas/article/download/12294/12858/

https://pirhua.udep.edu.pe/bitstream/handle/11042/2446/DER-L_003.pdf;sequence=1

6.7 *Lessons from Peru and Open Questions for Further Study*

1. The Stock Market is known as a bastion to promote good corporate behavior. Listed companies are expected to adhere to the best standards of corporate governance. However, as can be seen, holding true to these practices is put to the test in extreme situations and Peruvian companies have come up short in many of these cases, despite having promoted themselves as being at the vanguard of high standards of corporate governance. The formal (compliance on paper) would be overvalued with respect to the factual (actual execution).
2. One of the central objectives of good governance is to contribute to the protection of investors in general, and more so when it comes to minority shareholders' interests. The cases analyzed serve to show that directors have tended to flaunt this aim in not insisting on their duty of care, especially with regard to board members of listed companies on the stock market.

3. Important strategic and business decisions have been shown to be made by small groups of people linked to the controlling or majority shareholder; leaving out other members of the board or minority shareholders; thus, breaching essential accountability mechanisms that good governance demand.
4. Listed companies take on a commitment to enhanced transparency vis-à-vis the market, and even more so towards their investors, who entrust the financial resources to the company. In particular, investors should be alerted to substantive events that may affect the value of their investments. Several of the selected cases serve to confirm that companies (and/or their principal executives) are selective and tardy in sharing relevant information, so putting their investors' assets at risk.
5. Corruption will inevitably find fertile ground in companies with weak corporate governance programs. Peruvian companies have been no exception and unbridled ambition to earn more money has led to the complete destruction of companies (Graña y Montero).
6. Stock market regulators, even when they have taken measures to promote good governing, have still been caught out, subsequently having to react, as seen in the cases. Even still, the sanctions imposed have not had the effect of correcting the distortions described here. It is worth evaluating whether such misbehaviors might better be corrected by granting greater legal powers to the regulator, or, in addition, by insisting that they implement and apply more effective monitoring mechanisms.
7. The *investment shares* represent a special challenge for the Peruvian capital market, and this will likely constrain its development. The legislation that created and protects them is outdated and is largely inconsistent with the rest of the stock market's prevailing legislation. This has encouraged businesses to take advantage of the gaps, and although they are covered with legality, they have shown little interest in good governing, when it is the latter that must prevail if the market is to develop effectively. At the end of the day, for the development of strong capital markets in Peru, a decision is needed whether to maintain *investment shares*, or seek to replace them with securities that provide better protection to their holders.

7 Conclusions on the Impact of Scandals on Corporate Governing Development in Latin America

Jonathan Callund and Gonzalo Jiménez-Seminario

The country authors in the chapter faced a number of challenges in preparing the thumbnails of their "top six" cases; firstly, in determining which of the many cases in their local jurisdiction to consider and those to leave out, and then the process of selection of those most "relevant", in terms of their impact on the promotion of better corporate governance regulations and practices.

7.1 First Cut Review of the "Top 6" Scandals in Each Country

Having selected and researched their cases, it is clear that at a local and regional level, there are some similarities among them. Consequentially, in preparing these conclusions, we have opted first to assess each case following general criteria:

1. The nature of the entities involved, whether: a state-owned enterprise, a traded public company on the local or international stock exchange or a private, closely held company.

   The companies involved state-controlled are ESSA and OHL/Pemex from Mexico and Petrobras in Brazil. The majority of the cases involve corporations *traded* on the local and/or international stock exchanges, predominantly in Chile and Brazil. The other cases are *privately held* companies — mostly in Colombia, but with none in Chile or Brazil. However, the national government or state regulatory agencies might be part of the problem through their action or inaction, as in the cases of Bayer Peru and the regulator's long-lasting ambiguity regarding the economic standing

J. Callund
Callund y Compañía Ltda, Santiago, Chile
e-mail: jonathan.callund@callund.cl

G. Jiménez-Seminario
Pontificia Universidad Católica de Chile, Santiago, Chile
e-mail: gjimenez@proteus.cl

of *investment shares*; likewise, the corruption of state officers by Graña y Montero. In Colombia, the SaludCoop case involved the misuse of public funds and State-participated company EcoPetrol (Refinería de Cartagena case) of mixed private-public capital, or of civil servants in the Estraval case.

2. As to the reach of the scandals, this has been assessed as *International* when a non-Latin American corporation or entity is involved—for example the SEC, NYSE, or a Swedish multinational. Likewise, they are deemed *Regional* when the parties affected extend beyond the national frontier. And *Local* when they only affect their home market.

   It will be noted that half of the cases in Brazil and Peru and two of the six cases in the other countries involved international parties. None of the cases could be termed Regional, as despite the impact of Odebrecht on all six countries, it also had international ramifications.

3. Rather than media sources and the general public as the initiator, whether *whistleblowers* or *plea-bargaining* instances were involved in bring the case to light, revealing key information and, ultimately, favoring some of the parties with discounted fines—for example in Colombia, in the *El Cartel de los Pañales* case, the parties who "came clean" paid 50% of the fine. The same was the case with FASA in Chile.

   Given the relevance and knock-on effects of the Odebrecht and *Operation Car Wash* cases, other cases in the region came to light as a result of plea bargaining, the dominance of Brazil (Petrobras, Odebrecht, JBS, Grupo EBX, and IRB) can also be spilled over into Colombia (*El Cartel de los Pañales* and *The Cement Cartel*), Peru (Graña y Montero), but less conspicuous in Argentina (Benito Roggio and Skanska) and Chile (FASA).

4. How the regulatory authorities and/or courts dealt with the cases, isolating where the cases involved:

   a. *Fines!* - monetary penalties or compensatory payments for diffuse damages or settlement agreements either on the individuals (executives and/or board members) and/or the legal entities;

      Two-thirds of all cases involved fines and/or compensatory payments, predominantly in Brazil, Chile, and Colombia in five of the six cases, but less predominant in Argentina, Mexico, and Peru, where only half of the cases involved financial penalties.

b. Effective *Jail time!* served, whether while awaiting trial or following sentencing.

Overall, there were only eight cases here the cases led to real jail time, these were in Brazil in two-thirds of the cases (Petrobras, Odebrecht, JBS, and Grupo EBX) and Colombia in half the case (InterBolsa, Estraval, and SaludCoop) involved management and directors serving time. The only other case was in Chile (La Polar). None of the cases in the other three countries involved jail time.

c. The parties *Rectifying the situation!* through mitigating measures, such as apologies, firing directors and managers, changing internal codes/procedures, to atone for the misdeeds.

5. As with the case of fines, 22s of the 36 cases (61%), led the parties to carry out overhauls in their internal procedures and changes in their leadership teams at both board and management levels. This was predominant in Peru, in five of the six cases, the most emblematic being in Graña y Montero, Credicorp and Alicorp, and Argentina, most notably in Benito Roggio e Hijos SA and Tecnoquímicas/Tecnosur and Productos Familia in Colombia, where it was the result in four of the top six cases. In Chile this happened in the cases of LA POLAR, PEHUENCHE, and SQM.
6. The broad themes, uncovered in the review include:

a. political motivation; influence peddling;

One-third of the cases involved domestic and regional politics, with five of the six cases in Brazil (Petrobras and Odebrecht being the most relevant) and two-thirds of the six cases in Argentina (most notably YPF and Vicentin). It figured in two cases in Peru (e.g., Graña y Montero), one in Colombia (Reficar) and Mexico (ESSA) and none in Chile.

b. the forming of cartels/antitrust behaviors

There were two cases in Brazil (Petrobras and Odebrecht) and likewise two big cases of cartels in Colombia (cement and diapers) and one in Chile (retail pharmacy). These were not the subject matter for the cases in Argentina, Mexico, and Peru.

c. management fraud and/or abuse

This was the second most important and generalized theme, underlying 17 of the 36 "top six" cases (47%), with four in Argentina (DACSA, Skanska, Vicentin, and TGLT, three apiece in Chile (ENDESA, La Polar, and SQM), Colombia (InterBolsa, Estraval and SaludCoop), and Mexico (Homex, Banorte, Aeroméxico/Mexichem) and two in Brazil (Petrobras and Odebrecht) and Peru Credicorp and Graña y Montero.

d. bribery

Again, Brazil tops the list with four cases (Petrobras, Odebrecht, JBS, and Grupo EBX) and then there were two apiece in Argentina (Benito Roggio and Skanska), Mexico (OHL México and ESSA), and Peru (Credicorp and Graña y Montero). None in Chile or Colombia.

e. self-dealing

This came through in 15 of the 36 cases (42%), predominantly in Colombia, where all but once case involved self-dealing. This was present in half the cases in Brazil and Chile. It featured in two cases in Mexico and one apiece in Argentina and Peru.

f. abuse of dominant position

This was the basis for all the cases in Chile. It was present in five cases in Colombia, four in Brazil, three in Mexico, and one in Peru. This was not found in the Argentine cases.

g. abuse of minority shareholders

Likewise, this was essential to almost all the cases in Chile. It was present in 2 cases in Argentina, Brazil and Peru but not a theme in Colombia or Mexico.

6. Although the focus on these cases was more on their impact on the development of local and regional regulations and corporate governing practice, the cases also reveal the breakdowns in behaviors of individuals and boards, and how they upheld their fiduciary responsibilities.

   a. duty of care

   In assessing the cases, it was found that 31 of the 36 (81%), involved breaches in directors' duties of care. This was found in all the cases in Argentina, Chile, and Colombia, five cases in Brazil, and four cases in Mexico and Peru.

b. duty of loyalty, including the mismanagement of conflicts of interest

Although less prevalent, still 26 of the 36 cases (72%) were found to have involved non-fulfillment of director's duty of loyalty to the shareholders and, more to the other blockholders. This was found in all but one of the cases in Argentina, Brazil, and Chile, two-thirds of the cases in Colombia and Mexico, and half the cases in Peru.

7. The authors have concluded assessing the overall impact on corporate governing development—whether *positive*, *mixed*, or *negative* in each territory, not so much taking a long-term outlook, but more relating to how the public perceived each case's impact in terms of "justice was done and seen to be done", "no one got away with murder", whether it "led to better rules", "greater powers/teeth" for the regulators and/or local stock exchange, "moved the dial" in terms of explaining the "importance of corporate governance" in the eyes of the financial community and general public, reinforced the need for non-executive independent directors/professional board members.

a. Positive

The most positive impact was seen in the cases in **Chile**, <u>all</u> of which led directly to statutory and regulatory changes:

- Enersis was a key driver for the OPA (Public Tender Offer) law and sharing the premium for control between blockholders and regular shareholders;
- ENDESA, strengthened the position of minority interests and institutional transparency;
- FASA, added further protections for minority shareholders through enhanced transparency standards and mechanisms to address the (ab)use of privileged information, while with the tenor of negotiations with the FNE

and SVS, was also a precursor to the soon-to-be implemented and novel *delación compensada*[22] mechanism in Chile;

- Pehuenche, helped in defining and regulating Related-Party Transactions;
- La Polar, promoted the creation of the financial consumer protection agency, raising external audit standards, and helping formalize the roles of directors — reinforcing the roles for independent directors — and the board as a whole, while strengthening the importance of internal control systems. Another positive spillover was in making board members individually legally liable for not being aware of what was going on in the company, thus establishing not only board member rights, but also their entitlement to being informed of company dealings; and
- SQM, helped enhance the powers of the regulator to investigate and sanction, introducing further measures to enhance transparency and regulate market agent behaviors and encourage new stock exchange trading rules.

In **Colombia**, three cases stand out as having had positive effects; Estraval, *El Cartel de los Pañales*, and *The Cement Cartel*, all of which brought home the need to improve coordination among the many regulators, enhance their technical competencies and speed of response in the investigation and resolution of these cases. Likewise, half of the cases in **Peru** were also deemed to be constructive, namely: Credicorp — for the speed and transparency of the SMV's handling of a delicate situation with sensitive political repercussions;

Graña y Montero — in terms of the SMV's coordination, oversight and validation of the 4-year management transition and reorganization in to the renamed Aenza S.A.A.; and

Bayer/Aventis — for CONASEV's role in reversing *investment share* component of the operation, as well as clarifying

[22] "leniency" in English common law. A figure of compensation through reduced penalties for information, which allows those who present precise, true, and verifiable information to the prosecution regarding an act of collusion - https://alessandri.legal/en/antitrust-update-chile/

the economic and status of such *sui generis* financial instruments available in an important number of Peruvian listed companies, while overseeing the implementation of the new PO conditions.

b. Mixed

The most mixed impact of the cases is found in **Brazil**, where despite being seen as examples where the legislators have taken note by introducing reforms and the regulators having fulfilled their role of oversight and execution of remedies in each case of malfeasance, in five cases (Petrobras, JBS, Grupo EBX, IRB, and AmBev) they have also been found wanting as regards the remedies and improvement proposals to the prospective corporate government environment.

There were three cases, in **Argentina** (YPF, Vicentin, and TGLT) and **Colombia** (InterBolsa, Reficar, and SaludCoop) where, weighing the balance, the regulators have been found deficient and the general public has not been in receipt of the protections nor recompenses, so falling short of the mark, and that despite real jail time having been served in InterBolsa and SaludCoop in Colombia. There are no cases of jail time in Argentina.

c. Negative

In terms of promoting better corporate governing, the worst situations were found in **Mexico** (Homex, OHL México, and ESSA) and **Peru** (AliCorp, Arca Continental, and Milpro), where half of the cases were deemed to have had negative effects on their environment, while also leading to heightened mistrust of the financial markets in general reinforcing the sense of impunity for white collar crime.

7.2 As an Emerging Market, Why Latin America Might Offer Different Lessons

The six-point framework in Table 2 brings together and analyzes the common threads arising in the 36 cases provided by the country authors and their scandal cases, with an eye to identifying and reflecting on the distinctive aspects of corporate governing scandals in Latin America. The analysis may help in connecting the dots and explain in greater detail some key features of the Latin American context:

Table 2 Reflections on Corporate Boards in Latin America

*Country/*Criteria	*Argentina*	*Brazil*	*Chile*	*Colombia*	*Mexico*	*Peru*
(a) Family Connections	• BENITO ROGGIO •TGLT	•AMBEV •ODEBRECHT	•FASA •SQM	•PAÑALES	•OMNILIFE	•ALICORP •ARCA •GRAÑA Y MONTERO •CREDICORP
(b) Political Connections	•YPF • Benito Roggio •SKANSKA •Vicentin	•ODEBRECHT •IRB •JBS •PETROBRAS • EBX	•SQM	•REFICAR	•ESSA •OHL	•GRAÑA Y MONTERO •CREDICORP
(c) Institutional Void	•DACSA •YPF • BENITO ROGGIO • VICENTIN	•EBX	• ENDESA •PEHUENCHE •SQM	•SALUDCOOP • CEMENTO •ESTRAVAL • PAÑALES	•ESSA •OHL •HOMEX	•ARCA •MILPO •BAYER
(d) Managers Agency	• DACSA •SKANSKA	•IRB	•LA POLAR	•SALUDCOOP •REFICAR •INTERBOLSA	• BANORTE	• ALICORP
(e) Business Group Agency	•TGLT •YPF	•AMBEV •EBX	•PEHUENCHE •SQM	• CEMENTO •PAÑALES •SALUDCOOP •REFICAR •INTERBOLSA	•AEROMÉXICO-MEXICHEM • OMNILIFE	•MILPO •ARCA •CREDICORP •ALICORP
(f) Multinational Agency	•SKANSKA	•JBS	•ENERSIS	• CEMENTO •PAÑALES	•ESSA •OHL	

Source Authors assessments based on six criteria outlined below

(a) Family Connection:

Argentina	*Brazil*	*Chile*	*Colombia*	*Mexico*	*Peru*
• BENITO ROGGIO •TGLT	•AMBEV •ODEBRECHT	• FASA •SQM	•PAÑALES	•OMNILIFE	•ALICORP •ARCA •GRAÑA Y MONTERO •CREDICORP

While families are the predominant type of ownership around the world (Chua et al., 2003), the family connection in corporate governing scandals is manifest and broadly on display in the principal Latin American cases selected. One third, i.e., 12 of the 36 of the cases selected, involve family business groups and, what is more telling, not one of the six countries studied fails to reveal at least one family business scandal. And, while Colombia and Mexico had just one such connection, Argentina, Chile, and Brazil had two cases and there were four in Peru. The most frequent cases combined both family connections with political corruption (five in total: one in Argentina, Brazil and Chile, and two in Peru), and two with cartels (one in Chile and one in Colombia). There were also four Family *blockholder* abuses, with one in each country — Brazil, Peru, Chile, and in Argentina. Then, there was the case of misclassification of derivative operations in Peru and a quasi-couple/family falling apart in Mexico, to complete the picture.

(b) Political Connections:

Argentina	*Brazil*	*Chile*	*Colombia*	*Mexico*	*Peru*
•YPF • BENITO ROGGIO •SKANSKA •VICENTIN	•ODEBRECHT •IRB •JBS •PETROBRAS • EBX	•SQM	•REFICAR	•ESSA •OHL	•GRAÑA Y MONTERO •CREDICORP

The internationally praised public-private partnership (Healy, 2014) may carry a dark side in Latin America. Only slightly more important than family influence is the undue political influences between business and state (or more precisely, government) connections as sources of corporate scandals: 15 out of the 36 cases highlight the importance of negative public-private partnerships: Brazil tops the list with five cases; Argentina with four; Peru and Mexico exhibit two each, while Chile and Colombia had just one such case. Thus, state capture appears to constitute a highly relevant contributor to bad corporate practices in Latin America. And this is particularly relevant in the two countries with sustained traditions of state intervention.

***(c) Institutional Voids*[23]:**

Argentina	*Brazil*	*Chile*	*Colombia*	*Mexico*	*Peru*
•DACSA •YPF • BENITO ROGGIO • VICENTIN	•EBX	• ENDESA •PEHUENCHE •SQM	• SALUDCOOP • CEMENTO •ESTRAVAL	•ESSA •OHL •HOMEX	•ARCA •MILPO •BAYER

Khanna and colleagues (Khanna & Palepu, 2010; Khanna & Yafeh, 2007; Khanna & Rivkin, 2006) have been arguing since late 1990s that institutional voids are a source of market incompleteness in emerging markets. Consistently, 17 of the 36 cases point to the impact of incomplete and/or inconsistent institutional and regulatory arrangements as having contributed to corporate problems. Four in Argentina; three in each of the others; except the one case in Brazil, all of which can be associated with weak regulatory frameworks and institutions.

The problems identified include: passive gatekeepers, especially in Argentina; a lack of regulatory coordination, as seen in Colombia and Peru; missing key rules and definitions in Colombia, Mexico, and Peru; deficient regulatory enforcement in Chile and Mexico, where a lack of specialized regulatory teams was especially important, as was the cases in Chile and Brazil.

[23] *Institutional Voids* include uncertainty and ambiguity in the regulatory frameworks, government bureaucracy, inefficient rule and law enforcement mechanisms, improper factor markets, excessive red tape, and poor property rights protection. See Khanna and colleagues' references at the end of the chapter.

(d) Management Agency:

Argentina	*Brazil*	*Chile*	*Colombia*	*Mexico*	*Peru*
• DACSA • SKANSKA	• IRB	• LA POLAR	• SALUDCOOP • REFICAR • INTERBOLSA	• BANORTE	• ALICORP

This "typical" Anglo-Saxon type of corporate scandal is not as prevalent in the region and appeared in only nine cases, with greater frequency in Argentina and Colombia. Chile, while having one of the most developed capital markets (along with Brazil) in the region, presents fewer cases, which might be explained by the practices for its traded companies to have consolidated, controlling blockholder groups, with few powerful counterparts (Lefort & Walker, 2000).

(e) Business Group Agency:

Argentina	*Brazil*	*Chile*	*Colombia*	*Mexico*	*Peru*
• TGLT • YPF	• AMBEV • EBX	• PEHUENCHE • SQM	• CEMENTO • PAÑALES • SALUDCOOP • REFICAR • INTERBOLSA	• AEROMÉXICO-MEXICHEM • OMNILIFE	• MILPO • ARCA • CREDICORP • ALICORP

Although the above cited literature (see Khanna & Palepu, 1997) stresses, the value of business groups as *marker completers*, the cases show that one-third of the regulatory frameworks were incomplete, giving rises to loopholes that were taken advantage of by business groups.[24] There are 17 such cases of business groups involved in scandals, five in Colombia, four in Peru and two in each of the other countries. The presence of business groups, most of them family controlled, is another well-established characteristic of Latin America markets.

[24] Despite its popularity in academic literature, the concept of institutional voids has been criticized as colonialist and western-centric, anchored around a single, correct and orderly institutional model, assuming a teleological convergence. For a critique, see Bothello, J., Nason, R. S., & Schnyder, G. (2019). However, given the evolutionary perspective of corporate governing taken in this book, it represents a convenient way to capture the common phenomenon of incompleteness of both markets and regulatory rules.

(f) Multinational Agency:

Argentina	*Brazil*	*Chile*	*Colombia*	*Mexico*	*Peru*
•SKANSKA	•JBS	•ENERSIS	• CEMENTO •PAÑALES	•ESSA •OHL	

Latin America has long been a backyard market for American, British, German and Spanish multinationals (MNCs). However their presence in corporate scandals is not only conspicuous, but more surprising. This fits with the current debate about the interaction between home and host countries' corporate governance practices, with special application to their effect on emerging markets (Aguilera et al., 2019a, 2019b; Bhaumik et al., 2019). Seven of the 36 scandals involved multinational companies, providing support to some theories, suggesting that multinationals may adjust their corporate behavior to their local institutional settings. Here, the case data shows that, in some cases, multinationals might even have been the sources of corporate bad practices in their host countries and therefore these MNCs might be advised to review their foreign practices and align them with home countries' more stringent standards.

8 Conclusions

These cases raise a series of corporate governing challenges for Latin America that can be classified into four fronts:

- The first relates to the need to strengthen regulatory frameworks and supervisory entities (beyond the financial sector), to have effective governmental measures to prevent or better address corporate scandals. Regulatory bodies' priorities need to be focused on robust risk management systems, detection and management of conflicts of interest, and related-party transactions guidelines.
- The second front, and probably one of the most important elements in this discussion, is the recognition that good corporate governing goes beyond the mere compliance with regulatory requirements or filling out corporate governance documents. It is far more about the interiorization, within each company, of a corporate culture based

on accountability, ethics, and transparency. Only an entrepreneurial approach to corporate governing will create a healthy business environment that promotes professional boards of directors as the first and the most adequate gatekeepers and checks and balances for companies.

- A third front is the lack of transparency found in most Latin American markets as regards just who a company's beneficial owners are. This is standard practice in most developed economies and financial centers, ensuring potential and real conflicts of interests are flagged, so providing stakeholders and watchdogs with appropriate information for their decisions and enforcement respectively. A recent proposition by Wolfersdorff (2022) argues that formal and mandatory disclaimers of final beneficial ownership might be an effective measure and a step in the right direction.
- As seen in various countries, a committee of independent directors has been established by law and has been instrumental in avoiding potential expropriations to minority shareholders by the controlling blockholder as shown in one of the cases. However, its scope and attributions are limited to: (i) flagging potential conflicts of interests among related-party transactions with the company; (ii) proposing and interacting with the external auditors in providing an independent opinion to shareholders about the accuracy of the financial statements; and (iii) examining the compensation systems of the top management team—CEO and direct reports. Consequently, empowering and expanding the functions and rights of the corresponding Director's Committee to oversee the quality of board practices, taking the initiative in drafting a first cut at the "Comply-or-Explain" questionnaire to be approved by the board, contracting external consultants to enhance their knowledge and insights into the company's operations and business, and even providing an independent public opinion about the corporate governing might be of great help to institute change at the board level.

Then again, strengthening boards with the incorporation of professional directors with a higher level of independence, knowledge, commitment, and ethical criteria is to be advocated as an antidote to the opportunistic behaviors shown in this section.

We also anticipate the benchmarks across the six selected countries covered in this book to be of value to the nations concerned—as well as their Latin American peers—and also to emerging and transitioning markets around the world.

As a final reflection, we can celebrate the transparency and positive social reactions of modern-day society in flagging the human condition—individual and small-group "bad behaviors"—and the positive reactions to scandals that have increasingly come to light, so instituting processes to promote ways of tackling the issues and reinforcing better practices.

References

Aldrighi, Dante Mendes. (2011). Risks of wrongdoing in public companies and ways to cope with them. In Susan Rose-Ackerman and Tina Søreide (Ed.), *International handbook on the economics of corruption* (Vol. 2, chapter 8). Edward Elgar Publishing.

Aguilera, R. V., Crespí-Cladera, R., & de Castro, L. R. K. (2019a). Corporate governance in Latin America: Towards shareholder democracy. *AIB Insights, 19*(2), 13–17.

Aguilera, R. V., Marano, V., & Haxhi, I. (2019b). International corporate governance: A review and opportunities for future research. *Journal of International Business Studies, 50*(4), 457–498.

Alzate, S. (2018). Cartel del cemento: posibles acciones para la defensa de los intereses de los competidores y consumidores afectados por las prácticas anticompetitivas desplegadas por las compañías cementeras. Universidad Eafit.

Becker, G. (1968). Crime and punishment: An economic approach. *Journal of Political Economy, 76*(2): 169–217.

Bevir, M. (2009). The construction of governance. *International Journal of Organization Theory & Behavior.*

Bhaumik, S., Driffield, N., Gaur, A., Mickiewicz, T., & Vaaler, P. (2019). Corporate governance and MNE strategies in emerging economies. *Journal of World Business, 54*(4), 234–243.

Bothello, J., Nason, R. S., & Schnyder, G. (2019). Institutional voids and organization studies: Towards an epistemological rupture. *Organization Studies, 40* (10), 1499–1512.

Briozzo, A. (2011), "Valuación de oferta pública inicial PYME: el caso de DACSA". Presented at the XXXI Financial Management National Conference. See public sources for the document.

Brooks, R. (2018). Bean counters: the triumph of the accountants and how they broke capitalism. London: Atlantic Books.

Campos, N., Engel, E., Fischer, R. D., & Galetovic, A. (2021). The ways of corruption in infrastructure: Lessons from the Odebrecht case. *Journal of Economic Perspectives 35*(2): 171–90.

Cano, E. et. al. (2015). *Núcleo integrador—grupo familia—papel higiénico extrafino doble hoja*. Universidad Pontificia Bolivariana.
Castro, M. (2018). *Análisis de la cartelización empresarial desde la óptica del control interno*. Universidad Militar Nueva Granada.
Chua, J. H., Chrisman, J. J., & Steier, L. P. (2003). Extending the theoretical horizons of family business research. *Entrepreneurship Theory and Practice, 27*(4), 331–338.
Cifuentes, J., & Torres, M. (2014). *Proceso de Internacionalización de Tecnoquímicas*. Universidad ICESI.
da Costa, A. P. P. (2017). Corporate governance and fraud: Evolution and considerations. *Corporate Governance and Strategic Decision Making, 23*.
Eisenhardt, K. M. (1989). Agency theory: An assessment and review. *Academy of Management Review, 14*(1), 57–74.
Gao, C., Zuzul, T., Jones, G., & Khanna, T. (2017). Overcoming institutional voids: A reputation-based view of long-run survival. *Strategic Management Journal, 38*(11), 2147–2167.
Garner, Bryan A., ed. (2000). *Black's law dictionary* (7th ed.). St. Paul, Minn.: West Group. p. 1173. ISBN 978-0-314-24077-4.
González, F., Prem, M., & Urzúa, F. (2020, June). The privatization origins of political corporations: Evidence from the pinochet regime. *The Journal of Economic History, 80*(2).
Gaspar, Malu. (2020). *A organização: A odebrecht e o esquema de corrupção que chocou o mundo*. Companhia das Letras.
Healy, R. (2014). Corporate political behavior: Why corporations do what they do in politics. Routledge.
Janis, I. L. (2008). Groupthink. *IEEE Engineering Management Review, 36*(1), 36.
Kashwan, P., MacLean, L. M., & García-López, G. A. (2019). Rethinking power and institutions in the shadows of neoliberalism: (An introduction to a special issue of World Development). *World Development, 120*, 133–146.
Khanna, T., & Rivkin, J. W. (2006). Interorganizational ties and business group boundaries: Evidence from an emerging economy. *Organization Science, 17*(3), 333–352.
Khanna, T., & Yafeh, Y. (2007). Business groups in emerging markets: Paragons or parasites? *Journal of Economic literature, 45*(2), 331–372.
Khanna, T., & Palepu, K. (1997). Why focused strategies. *Harvard Business Review, 75*(4), 41–51.
Klimczak, K. M., Sison, A. J. G., Prats, M., & Torres, M. B. (2021). How to deter financial misconduct if crime pays? *Journal of Business Ethics*. Advance online publication. https://doi.org/10.1007/s10551-021-04817-0
La Semana. (2013). *Denuncia—SaludCoop, el desfalco de la historia*. https://www.semana.com/nacion/articulo/desfalco-de-salucoop/365644-3/

La Silla Vacia. (2011). *Robledo and Coronell managed to put SALUD-COOP against the wall.* https://archivo.lasillavacia.com/historia/robledo-y-coronell-lograron-poner-saludcoop-contra-la-pared-24282

Lefort, F., & Walker, E. (2000). Corporate governance: Challenges for Latin America. *Abante, 2*(2), 99–111.

Miller, B., & Uriegas F. (2019). Anti-Corruption Watch—Latin America's Biggest Corruption Cases: A Retrospective - From Mexico to Argentina, iconic scandals have reshaped politics. AQ examines their origins—and fallout.

Muñoz, S., & Ruíz, A. (2016). *Recoveries and financial crisis of the health system in Colombia (2008–2014), SALUDCOOP EPS case study*. Universidad Libre.

Rodríguez, M., & Molano, M. (2018). *Identification of financial crimes in the case of SALUDCOOP, under the forensic audit methodology*. La Gran Colombia University.

Rose-Ackerman, S. & Søreide, T. (ed.). (2011). *International handbook on the economics of corruption* (Vol. 2_). Edward Elgar Publishing.

Schneider, B. R. (2013). *Hierarchical capitalism in Latin America.* Cambridge University Press.

Tricker, R. (2012). The evolution of corporate governance. *The SAGE handbook of corporate governance*, 39–61.

Sontag, R. (2019). Para uma história da delação premiada no Brasil. *Revista Brasileira de Direito Processual Penal,* 5(1): 441–468.

von Wolfersdorff, J. (2022). Capitalismo, Taurus, Santiago, Chile.

CHAPTER 4

The Latin American Corporate Governing Landscape—Its Past, Present, and Future

Andrés Bernal, Catalina Rojas, and Michelle Mora

Talking about ENRON in a corporate governance paper might seem a cliché. However, this case brought the corporate governing discussion into the world's spotlight, considering that it proved that failures in different dimensions (including interactions between ownership, board of directors, risk management, control environment, ethics, and information disclosure) could significantly impact a company's sustainability. It was 20 years ago (when the ENRON case first came to light) that

A. Bernal (✉) · C. Rojas · M. Mora
Governance Consultants, Bogotá, Colombia
e-mail: andresbernal@gcsa.co

C. Rojas
e-mail: crojas@governanceconsultants.com

M. Mora
e-mail: mmora@governanceconsultants.com

A. Bernal
iDirectores, Bogotá, Colombia

J. Callund et al. (eds.), *Corporate Governing in Latin America*,
https://doi.org/10.1007/978-3-030-85780-6_4

the world realized that corporate governance is much more than regulation, best practices, and global standards; it is also social awareness, robust institutional frameworks, and a corporate culture based on transparency, accountability, and good decision-making. Taking into consideration all these elements, the main purpose of this chapter is to provide the reader with a general overview of the corporate governing evolution in Latin America over the last two decades,[1] which is the approximate timeframe where the corporate governing conversation began to appear in the business environment. This chapter considers not only regulatory aspects but also the institutional developments that have shaped the corporate governing framework within six major Latin American economies.[2] It has a descriptive approach and does not attempt to measure or analyze the degree of implementation of corporate governance regimes in Latin American countries or their impact.

This document is based upon three main perspectives: (i) a description of how regulation, self-regulation, and investors' standards are setting the requirements companies and issuers need to fulfill to shape their corporate governance systems; (ii) three milestones on the evolution of corporate governing in Latin America; and (iii) finally, some thoughts about future trends that we understand might have a relevant influence on corporate governance conversations over the coming years.

1 A Brief Reference to Regulation, Self-Regulation Initiatives, and Investor Perspectives

In Latin America, corporate governance rules and guidelines have their origin mainly in three sources:

a) Each country's compulsory regulation;
b) Voluntary standards contained in the country codes of each jurisdiction; and

[1] Needless to say, CG should not be presented in Latin America, nor in any other region in the world, as a subject created 20 years ago. Nevertheless, the classical corporate agency problem has been present for a long time and has been addressed through Corporate Law via the board's fiduciary duties.

[2] Argentina, Brasil, Chile, Colombia, México, and Perú.

c) More recently, in the practices promoted by institutional investors, particularly, those with a worldwide reach, such as BlackRock. By exercising their voting rights in the companies in which they invest, they contribute to implementing governance standards in accordance with their investment policies.

In several countries in the region, the corporate governance discussion has also incorporated regulation and voluntary corporate governance standard codes promoted by private initiatives, particularly, from international organizations such as the Inter-American Development Bank (IADB), and its global initiative of Development Financial Institutions (DFIs) committed to including corporate governance analysis in its investments.

In addition, the initiatives from international organizations have contributed to amplifying the scope of companies that could be recipients of the principles and best practices of corporate governance, including non-listed companies, mainly family businesses and small and medium-sized enterprises (SMEs). Such is the case of the CAF, Banco de Desarrollo de América Latina, and the Center for International Enterprise (CIPE), who were among the first institutions to promote corporate governance for companies beyond listed corporations. Similarly, private business associations, business schools, chambers of commerce, and DFIs became corporate governance activists, expanding the reach of corporate governance standards to SMEs, SOEs and family businesses. In several countries, including Argentina, Colombia, Peru, and Mexico, private initiatives cooperate with regulators and stock exchanges to promote corporate governance standards, helping build self-regulatory recommendations.

1.1 The Compulsory Corporate Governance Regulation

Over the last 20 years, several countries in the region started a trend to update their securities laws with the aim of developing their public markets or supporting specific public policies. These changes in the regulatory frameworks are explained in more detail in the different chapters of this book. As the reader might find throughout the different chapters, each of the countries promoted legislative and/or regulatory changes to define new rules for board structure, responsibilities, and independence criteria, as well as provisions to improve the control environment of issuers.

The corporate governance discussion was mainly focused on the following topics:

a) Adequate number of independent directors on the board of directors;
b) Independent director definition (from whom should a director need to be independent from);
c) Separation of CEO—Chairman positions, i.e., the executives from the Board members;
d) Requirement for a board audit committee; and
e) Shareholders' rights, including practices to increase the level of participation of minority stockholders in annual general meetings (AGMs).

Latin American countries have gone through various social and political processes in the last 20 years, which have influenced the adoption of specific corporate governance reforms. However, it is worth mentioning that in most of them, there has been a greater emphasis on strengthening and expanding the regulation of listed companies to promote greater dynamism on those who want to seek other forms of financing, as well as investors that want to provide capital to new forms of investment.

In that order, the main regulatory provisions on corporate governance in Latin America are contained in each country's corporate and securities market legislation, with specific provisions associated with the composition and responsibilities of the board of directors, some measures to protect shareholder rights, and their responsibilities in the exercise of their ownership. Likewise, the compulsory regulatory framework includes some provisions relating to control architecture, particularly on how the external auditor is appointed, its potential conflicts of interest, and to whom it should report within the company (the board of directors, a directors committee—were one to exist, or the shareholders). Finally, there are provisions relating to greater disclosure requirements for companies, clarification of the responsibilities of the board of directors in matters such as risk and control, the role of the audit committees, and special measures to protect minority shareholders.

Table 1 provides the main regulatory measures that each country has adopted in terms of corporate governance.

1.2 The Voluntary Standards: The "Comply or Explain" Model

In the late 1990s, following the global trend, Latin America began adopting corporate governance codes. After Brazil enacted its first code in 1999, other countries in the region followed the idea of promoting good governance practices through Guidelines as a supplement to their respective legislative frameworks (Santos et al., 2020). In recent years, several countries have sought to reform their corporate governance practices by updating their voluntary corporate governance Codes, based on the work of the Organization for Economic Co-operation and Development (OECD) and CAF (World Bank, 2014). These codes have also responded to specific changes in the national contexts.

Latin American codes have predominantly been established under the English "comply or explain" model, or its variation "comply or not and explain" (OECD, 2016), allowing companies enough flexibility to adapt the provisions that best suit their specific context. The "comply or explain" models, or their variants, aim to contribute to value creation by establishing an information scheme that allows key stakeholders and the market in general to have sufficient information to evaluate the state and quality of companies' corporate governing systems.

Nonetheless, in some cases, the model has raised issues regarding the degree of commitment made by companies to comply with corporate governance best practices.[3] Moreover, the ultimate responsibility for verifying compliance or explanations sits with investors and the regulators, which has proven to be difficult and burdensome. (Keay, 2014). Additionally, in most cases, investors prefer to build their own information requirements, since those contained in "comply or explain reports" do not necessarily match their needs or expectations. Therefore, these

[3] As there is no legal obligation to adopt the code's Guidelines, in the "comply or explain" system, companies may choose to implement the recommended practices, but it is mandatory to disclose the Guidelines adopted and explain why the remaining Guidelines were not adopted. Similarly, the "comply or not and explain" system seeks to strengthen the compliance dimension by requiring companies to explain both the Guidelines not adopted and those adopted.

Table 1 Main Corporate Governance Regulation in Latin American Countries[4]

General overview	*Regulatory definition*	*Regulatory reference*
Argentina The regulations that apply to companies are related to corporate, bankruptcy, labor, tax, and criminal law. In particular, the Corporate Law regulates aspects concerning who is responsible for a company's activity. In 2017, the SUPERINTENDENCY OF BANKING AND INSURANCE (SBS) also issued a regulation on *Good Corporate Governance* (BGC) and *Comprehensive Risk Management* for all financial entities and insurance companies, with special emphasis on the board of directors, risk controls and management issues. In 2018, the Head of the Cabinet of Ministers enacted Decision 85 dictating *Good Governance Guidelines for Companies* for corporations with majority state participation	Board of directors: • Public companies must have a board of directors composed of at least three members. The size of the board of directors, quorum requirements, and voting standards are outlined in each company's bylaws • They are required to establish an Audit Committee composed of three or more members of the board of directors, the majority of whom must be independent, according to the criteria established by the NATIONAL SECURITIES COMMISSION (CNV). Companies may also have a Supervisory Committee, composed of three members who must be lawyers or accountants. Their responsibilities include supervising the company's management, attending all general or extraordinary shareholders' meetings, and, in general, supervising the company from a legal point of view. All members of the *Supervisory Committee* must be independent. The *Audit Committee* may absorb the responsibilities of the *Supervisory Committee*, should this be approved in an *Extraordinary General Shareholders' Meeting*	"The company law" in its articles 59, 266, 269, 270 and 274 The National Decree 677/2001 Regulation RG No. 516 Resolution No. 606 Administrative Decision 85/2018

[4] For further information, the reader is referred to the country-specific chapters, from which this information has been extracted.

General overview	Regulatory definition	Regulatory reference
Argentine regulation has a series of corporate governance principles, standards, recommendations, and best practices for State-owned enterprises. For example, Decree 677/2001 of the NATIONAL SECURITIES COMMISSION regulated corporate governance practices to ensure "transparency" and "trust." Through Regulation RG No. 516, the NATIONAL SECURITIES COMMISSION defined the list of the minimum content of the *Corporate Governance Code* (CGS). This Resolution was subsequently amended in 2012 by Resolution No. 606. It required companies to incorporate the *Corporate Governance Code*, including in their reports an analysis of the financial statements, together with a self-assessment of corporate governance and the degree of compliance with the rules proposed by the NATIONAL SECURITIES COMMISSION. Companies were asked to explain the reasons in case of non-compliance	• The maximum amount of directors' remuneration, including salaries, and other benefits, may not exceed 5% of the profits for the year if the company does not distribute dividends and may be increased proportionally up to 25% of the profits for the year if the company distributes dividends. In accordance with the Companies Law and CNV regulations, these limits may be exceeded if the resulting amount of remuneration is insufficient to cover the fees of directors performing specific functions, provided this has been expressly approved in a shareholders meeting. Information on aggregate remunerations paid to directors, statutory supervisors, and senior executives must be disclosed in the relevant offering memorandum being securities are being issued Ownership: • The members of the board of directors, the audit committee, and the supervisory committee are appointed at the *Ordinary Shareholders' Meeting* • Minimum quorum and voting requirements are established by law, and the company's bylaws may establish stricter requirements	

(continued)

Table 1 (continued)

General overview	*Regulatory definition*	*Regulatory reference*
	• Any shareholder has the right to nominate directors during an *Ordinary Shareholders' Meeting* provided that the candidates comply with the CNV's independence requirements • Information and documents to be considered during the shareholders' meeting must be submitted at least 15 business days before the meeting day • To attend meetings, shareholders must be registered in the *Shareholders' Meeting Attendance Record Book*. In addition, shareholders must present their certificate of ownership duly issued by the depositary agent at least three business days before the meeting date • If shareholders wish to vote at the meeting, they must attend it in person or through a previously appointed proxy. Directors, statutory supervisors, managers, and other company employees are not permitted to act as proxies for independent shareholders • Increases in capital stock (through the issuance of new shares) must be approved by the shareholders' meeting, as well as the distribution of dividends. In addition, 5% of profits earned each fiscal year must be allocated to a legal reserve until it reaches 20% of capital stock • Any investor wishing to obtain control of a publicly traded company must launch a public tender offer at a fair price for a prescribed period and subject to the procedures stipulated by CNV regulations	

General overview	Regulatory definition	Regulatory reference
Brazil In 1976, the Brazilian Corporate Law (Law No. 6,404) was enacted, as well as the law creating and disciplining the *Comissão de Valores Mobiliários*—CVM (Law No. 6,385) In 1997, Law No. 9,457 amended the Corporations Law, eliminating the label provision previously established In 2007, there was a new reform of the Corporations Law, which made disclosure of financial statements mandatory for public companies in accordance with *International Financial Reporting Standards* (Law No. 11,638) As for the Securities Law, a reform was introduced in 2002 that granted CVM greater statutory autonomy at the administrative, operational, financial, and budgetary levels	Board of Directors: • The board of directors requires a minimum of three directors. According to the BRAZILIAN NATIONAL SECURITIES COMMISSION, the recommended standard is a range of five to nine directors, with a minimum of two directors with finance and accounting experience. If the company is also listed on the *Novo Mercado*, two of the members, or at least 20% of the board of directors (whichever is greater), must qualify as independent • Under *Novo Mercado* rules, the Chief Executive Officer (CEO) may not be appointed Chairman of the board of directors • In addition to the board of directors, the law requires that there be an Audit Committee (or fiscal council) charged with overseeing the audit functions of the board. Companies may also create a Supervisory Board, which has primary responsibility for overseeing the actions and decisions of management and the board of directors. Given this structure, neither executives nor directors may serve on the Supervisory Board	Law No. 6,404/1976 Law No. 6,385/1976 Law No. 10,303/2001 Law No. 11,638/2007

(continued)

Table 1 (continued)

General overview	*Regulatory definition*	*Regulatory reference*
	Ownership: • Minority and different classes of shareholders may attend shareholders' meetings so that each of them may appoint a member to represent them on the board of directors • In the case of mergers, the acquiring company must appoint companies to assess the risks and analyze the company's equity to be acquired. The approval of the statutory report does not exclude the shareholders' right to oppose it • Shareholders have a preferential right to acquire new shares, regardless of the type of shares (capital structure, mergers, sale of assets, and other special operations)	

General overview	*Regulatory definition*	*Regulatory reference*
Chile The main sources of corporate governance rules applicable to listed corporations in Chile are the Corporations Law (Law No. 18,046) and the Securities Market Law (Law No. 18,045), both enacted in 1981 and amended several times since then Other important legal bodies are the Regulation of Corporations (Supreme Decree No. 702/2011 of the MINISTRY OF FINANCE), the General Rules issued by the COMISIÓN PARA EL MERCADO FINANCIERO (CMF), and the special rules on corporate governance issued by the SUPERINTENDENCY OF PENSIONS applicable to private Pension Fund Administrators (AFPs) To build a robust corporate governance regime and improve capital markets, Congress introduced Law No. 19,768 and No. 19,769 of 2001 (also known as the "Capital Markets Law I") and Law No. 20,190 of 2007 (also known as the "Capital Markets Law II"). Subsequently, to comply with the OECD Principles of Corporate Governance, Chile enacted Law No. 20.382 (also called "Corporate Governance Law")	<u>Board of Directors:</u> • A listed company is required to appoint at least one independent director. Shareholders representing at least 1% of the company's shares may nominate the independent director • A listed company is obliged to establish a Board Committee when its market capitalization reaches 1.5 million *Unidades de Fomento* (approx. USD60m), and at least 12.5% of its voting shares are held by shareholders that control or hold less than 10% of its shares • This *Board Committee* must be chaired by one of the independent directors and is charged to monitor related-party transactions, all dealings with external auditors, as well as overseeing the company's compensation policy <u>Ownership:</u> • Chilean companies are allowed to create multiple classes of stock with different voting rights for each class • There are provisions imposing supermajority vote approval, such as mergers, reorganizations, capital reductions, dissolutions, transfers of substantial assets, and the granting of collateral or personal guarantees to secure third-party obligations (exceeding specific amounts) • Shareholders with at least 10% of the company's share capital can call a *Special Shareholders' Meeting*	Law No. 20,382 Law No. 19,768 Law No. 19,769 of 2001 and Law No. 20,190 of 2007 Law No. 18,046 and Law No. 18,045. Supreme Decree No. 702/2011 of the MINISTRY OF FINANCE

(continued)

Table 1 (continued)

	General overview	*Regulatory definition*	*Regulatory reference*
	Colombia The 1995, Colombian Commercial Law dictates the regulations on corporate governance. They include provisions regarding shareholders' rights, information disclosure, creditors' rights, and the duties of the board of directors and executive officers In 1998, new regulations granted rights and protection mechanisms to minority shareholders In 2002, Resolutions 116 and 157 introduced regulatory initiatives regarding shareholder rights and regulating inappropriate practices in securities trading, Law N°964/2005 established mandatory rules for public companies regarding investor protection and information disclosure	<u>Board of Directors:</u> • Listed Companies' Boards of Directors must have a minimum of five directors and a maximum of ten; 25% of the directors must be independent • There is a mandatory separation of Chairman and legal representative positions • The Audit Committee is mandatory and must have at least three directors, including all the independent directors. The chair must also be independent <u>Ownership:</u> • Share classes with multiple voting rights are not allowed, although share classes carrying no votes are permitted in the capital structure • Shareholder approval is required for share issuances without preemption • Shareholders with at least 20% of the company's share capital can call a special meeting	*Código de Comercio*, Law 222 - 1995 and Law 446 - 1998 Resolutions 116 and 157, and Law N°964 2004
Mexico	The Company Law (enacted in 1934 and amended in 1996) and the Securities Market Law (1975) are the main legal sources of corporate governance. The Securities Market Law has special regulations for public Companies. In addition, many requirements that promote more transparency in financial reporting have been made legally enforceable through amendments to this later Law	<u>Board of Directors:</u> • The board must not have more than 21 members. At least 25% of the board must be independent, and any shareholder who owns 10% of voting shares is entitled to appoint at least one board member. • Board committees cannot have fewer than three directors. The shareholders must appoint the Chair of these committees. • The independence standard in Mexican Public Companies should be no less than 40% of the board.	General Law of Mercantile Corporations and Securities Market Law

	General overview	Regulatory definition	Regulatory reference
	These amendments were designed to improve the quality of information presented in annual reports to investors through better definitions of the structure and duties of the board of directors and audit committee, establishing guidelines for the protection of the rights of minority shareholders, and the implementation of procedures related to the independence of external auditors, as well as internal control provisions	• Companies are required to establish an Audit Committee and a Corporate Governance Committee, composed of independent directors • Shareholders are not asked to approve the compensation of executives. Ownership: • Shareholders with at least 10% of the company's share capital can call a special meeting • Mexican companies are allowed to create multiple classes of stock with special rights. Non-voting or restricted voting shares may be issued, representing up to 25% of the company's paid capital stock • The board must present financial results and directors and auditor reports to shareholders for approval at the *Annual Shareholders' Meeting*	
Peru	The Companies Law from the mid-1990s has specific references to corporate governance, whereas the Securities Market Law makes no such references. The Securities Law has since been partially modified concerning the responsibilities of the board members of the companies regarding money laundering and corruption issues In 2017, the BANK, INSURANCE & PENSIONS SUPERINTENDENCY (SBS) also issued a *Rule on Good Corporate Governance* (GCG) *and Comprehensive Risk Management*, which applies to all financial institutions and insurance companies. The provisions are focused on the board and control and risk management matters	Board of Directors: • Listed companies are not required to elect independent directors, establish committees, or disclose substantial information. • Directors may appoint "substitute" or "alternate" directors • Controlled companies require at least 30% of the board of directors to be independent and 40% for non-controlled companies Ownership: • Director compensation is usually presented to shareholders after the annual meeting as an aggregated report	Companies Law and Securities Market Law

mechanisms alone do not guarantee the promotion of a better corporate governing culture.

A survey conducted for the 2016 LATIN AMERICAN CORPORATE GOVERNANCE ROUNDTABLE showed a prevalent perception in several companies in the region that codes function as a list of requirements that increase costs and efforts. This notion negatively affects companies' commitment to the practices recommended by the codes. For this reason, regulators and corporate governance authorities in the region face significant challenges in defining better and more effective reporting schemes. Reporting schemes are expected to allow comparability between companies, the creation of tools to measure the effectiveness of the codes, and, most importantly, to encourage companies to identify the benefits of adopting good governance practices and the opportunities for improvement in this area for their organization (OECD, 2016) (Table 2). Table 5 provides a summary of Corporate Governance Codes adopted in the six countries under review.

1.3 The New Corporate Governing "Influencers": Institutional Investors

Institutional ownership in the world's listed companies has significantly increased over the last few years. Institutional investors represent the largest investor category at a global aggregate level by holding 43% of world market capitalization, followed by private corporations holding 11%, the public sector holding 10%, and strategic individuals owning 9%.[5] Institutional investors, as managers of third-party funds, usually demand greater security in investments by analyzing factors such as the existence of independent directors, investment and financing policies, conflicts of interest policies, and other corporate governance practices (Núñez & Oneto, 2012).

In that sense, worldwide, institutional investors have adopted a more active role in requiring higher corporate governance standards, driven by their duty of care to act diligently with respect to the investments they participate in. As a result, their voting policies have become a reference for better corporate governance standards, making institutional investors

[5] 2021 OECD *Corporate Governance Factbook.*

Table 2 Summary of Corporate Governance Codes Adopted in the Region[6]

Code	*Year of creation*	*Objective*	*Scope*	*System of compliance*	*Regulatory supervisor*	*List of contents*
Argentinian code (*Código de Gobierno Societario*)	2007 (last update—2019)	To be an instrument to protect the rights of investors, creditors, and the public in general. Seeks to avoid or limit the possibility of dissemination of asymmetric information	Mandatory for all listed companies	Disclosure—Comply or not and explain	National Securities Commission of Argentina (*Comisión Nacional de Valores – CNV*)	• Shareholders and annual general meeting • Board of directors. • Control environment • Transparency and disclosure • Remuneration • Responsible relationships with the community • Ethics.
Brazilian IBGC code (*Código das Melhores Prácticas de Governança Corporativa -IBGC*)	1999 (last update—2015)	To be a reference in corporate governance, contributing to the sustainable performance of organizations and influencing the agents of the society toward greater transparency, justice, and responsibility	Voluntary	Voluntary	There is no compliance monitor for the code	• Shareholders and annual general meeting • Board of directors • Management • Risk management • Conflicts of interests • Control environment • Transparency and disclosure • Ethics.

(continued)

[6] Source: OECD - Strengthening corporate governance codes in Latin America (2016).

Table 2 (continued)

Code	*Year of creation*	*Objective*	*Scope*	*System of compliance*	*Regulatory supervisor*	*List of contents*
Brazilian inter-agent code (*Código Brasileiro de Governança Corporativa*)	2016	To make public the corporate governance practices adopted by listed companies so that interested parties can decide on their relevance, considering the code's recommendations, the company's stage of development, and the explanations provided	Mandatory for all listed companies	Disclosure—Comply or explain	Brazilian Securities and Exchange Commission (*Comissão de Valores Mobiliários – CVM*)	• Shareholders • Annual general meeting • Board of directors. • Management • Risk management • Control environment • Conflicts of interest • Ethics.
Chilean code (*Norma de Caracter General No. 385*)	2012 (last update—2015)	To be a tool for investors to have enough information to make the right investment decisions	Mandatory for all listed companies	Disclosure—Comply or not and explain	The Financial Markets Commission (Comisión para el Mercado Financiero -CMF)[7]	• Shareholders and annual general meeting • Board of directors • Risk management • Conflicts of interest • Control environment • Transparency and disclosure • Evaluation by a third party

[7] In 2017, the Comisión del Mercado Financiero (CMF) replaced the Superintendency of Securities and Insurance (Superintendencia de Valores y Seguros -SVS) as the regulatory entity of securities, insurance, and banking industries.

Code	*Year of creation*	*Objective*	*Scope*	*System of compliance*	*Regulatory supervisor*	*List of contents*
Colombian code (*Código País*)	2007 (last update—2014)	To guide the best corporate practices that are expected to be adopted and implemented by issuers seeking to raise their corporate governance standards	Mandatory for all listed companies	Disclosure—Comply or explain (with comply or not and explain characteristics)	FINANCIAL SUPERINTENDENCY OF COLOMBIA (*SUPERINTENDENCIA FINANCIERA DE COLOMBIA – SFC*)	• Shareholders and annual general meeting • Board of directors. • Management • Risk management • Conflicts of interests • Control environment • Transparency and disclosure
Mexican code (*Código de mejores prácticas de Gobierno Corporativo – CCE*)	1999 (last update—2018)	To help companies in the process of institutionalization; transparency of their operations; adequate disclosure; to be competitive in a global context; to be able to access financing on favorable terms; to have a stable succession process; and to be permanent over time for the benefit of their shareholders and third parties	Mandatory for all listed companies	Disclosure—Comply or not and explain	THE MEXICAN STOCK EXCHANGE, but the regulator (*COMISIÓN NACIONAL BANCARIA Y DE VALORES*)	• Shareholders and annual general meeting • Board of directors. • Control environment • Evaluation and remuneration • Financial and planning function
Peruvian code (*Código de Buen Gobierno Corporativo para las Sociedades Peruanas*)	2002 (last update - 2013)	To help create an authentic corporate governance culture in Peru, which improves the perception of companies by investors, promotes business development, and contributes to creating value in the Peruvian economy	Mandatory for all listed companies	Disclosure—Comply or explain	SUPERINTENDENCY OF THE SECURITIES MARKET (*SUPERINTENDENCIA DEL MERCADO DE VALORES – SMV*)	• Shareholders and annual general meeting • Board of directors • Management • Risk management • Transparency and disclosure

vehicles for strengthening the governance systems of the companies in which they invest (Dasgupta et al., 2020).

Considering that Latin America is characterized by ownership concentration and that pension fund managers have become the predominant institutional investors in the region's markets, they acquire a relevant role given their ability to positively influence the interests of minority shareholders (Blume & Alonso, 2007). The Chilean case is a good example of the positive influence of Pension Fund Administrators (AFPs) on the corporate governance discussion. Chilean regulation does not allow AFPs to hold more than 7% of the capital of a single issuer, which reduces their individual influence on governance. That said, the AFPs have been able to coordinate their votes and achieve representative percentage to allows them to elect board members and so exert a direct influence over the corporate governance of their investments (Mendes, Sousa & Silva, 2015). For more information on the impact of AFPs and minority shareholder protections in Chile, see the Chile chapter in this book.

Despite the persistence of legal barriers[8] and market shortcomings,[9] the corporate governance activism of the region's institutional investors can be seen primarily through the way they exercise of their roles as owners: voting at shareholder meetings, nominating (usually independent) board members, alerting the markets when harmful corporate governance practices are identified, disclosing their governance policies, and requiring the companies in which they invest to develop their codes of good governance (Blume & Alonso, 2007).

More recently, global investors such as BlackRock are promoting and taking the corporate governance conversation in the region to new frontiers by establishing higher standards than those displayed in local regulations or in the country codes themselves. Considering this context, some initiatives are underway in the region to align the regulators and investors' visions regarding what is expected from issuers in terms of corporate governance, particularly what they should report to the market.

At the time of writing this chapter, the CAF Latin American Development Bank is conducting a study with regulators and the most

[8] Limits on investments and lack of proxy voting mechanisms.

[9] Short-term investments horizons, free-rider problems, ownership patterns prevalent in the market, conflict of interests, institutional investors' internal governance problems.

influential investors within the Pacific Alliance.[10] The project has shown preliminary evidence of an evolution of governance standards toward *Environmental, Social, and Governance*—ESG aspects, the recognition of the need to refine corporate governance reports for the benefit of investors and issuers, and the importance of corporate governance practices to be implemented in differentiated weightings or to identify new practices for alternative investment vehicles. In any case, there is a general acknowledgment of the accountability that issuers must have with respect to the information they disclose.

For 2021, Table 3 summarizes the main topics institutional investors are focused on regarding corporate governance standards.

2 Three Milestones of Corporate Governing Evolution in Latin America

2.1 Where Does the Regional Corporate Governance Conversation Converge?

Latin American countries do not have a homogeneous approach to their corporate governance regulation or orientation. Since the region has had, for more than two centuries, different colonization and migration processes, it harbored Spanish, Portuguese, French, German, British, and North American influences. As a result, and as the reader might find in the other chapters of this book, each country in the region has adopted its own corporate governance framework, emphasis, and rules that companies need to implement. Nonetheless, a common denominator for corporate governance in Latin America is the work and influence of the OECD.

The OECD has had a significant impact on the work of regulators, stock exchanges, investors, academics, and corporations within the region . One example is how the Latin American Corporate Governance Roundtable (LACGRT),[11] organized by the OECD and International Finance Corporation (IFC)/World Bank Group, has been an effective scenario to promote a regional dialogue among regulators, experts, and policymakers that have strengthened the development of corporate governance standards.

[10] Chile, Colombia, Peru, and Mexico.

[11] After 2010, the Regional Roundtable is held every 2 years.

Table 3 Recommended standards from institutional investors[12]

Board of directors	• Directors must attend at least 75% of the meetings • Directors are considered overcommitted if they participate in more than 5 Boards of Directors, or in the case of a CEO or member of Senior Management participates in more than 3 Boards of Directors. Overcommitted Directors shall not be considered when identifying potential Board candidates • In terms of diversity, all personal factors, such as gender, ethnicity, race, and age, as well as professional characteristics, such as industry, area of expertise, and geographic location of the director, should be considered when identifying potential board member candidates • Boards are expected to monitor human capital management • Companies are encouraged to have at least two women on their boards • In the Board renewal processes, periodic performance reviews and evaluations of Board members are encouraged to ensure the sufficient and adequate existence of competencies, perspectives, skills, and experiences, • Boards are expected to have a good mix of short, mid, and long-term directors, • It is recommended that individual directors, members of a committee, or the entire board not be re-elected due to: Material failures in governance, stewardship, risk oversight (including, but not limited to, environmental, social, and climate change issues), or fiduciary responsibilities at the company; or egregious actions related to a director's performance on other boards that raise substantial doubt about their ability to oversee management effectively and serve the interests of shareholders at any company, • A remuneration structure that incentivizes and rewards executives appropriately and is aligned with shareholders' interests, particularly with the generation of long-term sustainable value, must be ensured
Shareholders	• Shareholders must be guaranteed the right to vote individually for each nominee for the board of directors • The economic and strategic rationale behind proposed mergers, acquisitions, asset sales, or other special transactions should be clearly explained to shareholders • Shareholders are expected to have a meaningful opportunity to participate in the annual meeting and interact with the board and management in virtual settings; companies should facilitate open dialogue and allow shareholders to voice their concerns and provide uncensored information • Shareholders should not have companies voting power on matters they have not been allowed to review and understand

(continued)

[12] Source: BLACKROCK—*Pautas de votación para valores de América Latina* (2021); ISS—America's proxy voting Guidelines updates for 2021. Benchmark Policy Changes for US, Canada, and Latin America (2020).

Table 3 (continued)

Control Environment	• The auditor is expected to be free from any impediment to act as an effective check on management • It is recommended that companies have independent audit committees with at least one financial expert • Audit committees should have a procedure for annually assessing the auditor's independence. • The audit committee is expected to certify the content of financial/audit reports
Environmental, Social, and Governance (ESG)	• Companies should disclose employee demographics, such as gender, race, and ethnicity, along with the steps taken to promote diversity, equity, and inclusion • Companies should disclose compensation data by gender, race/ethnicity, or report on their policies and goals to reduce any gender or race/ethnicity pay gap • Companies are expected to articulate how they align with a global warming scenario and the global aspiration to achieve net greenhouse gas (GHG) emissions by 2050 • Companies are expected to disclose how they are considering environmental challenges, along with opportunities for innovation, within their emissions reduction strategy and efforts • Companies are expected to effectively monitor and mitigate environmental risks with appropriate due diligence processes and board oversight • Robust disclosure is essential for investors to evaluate companies' business practices and strategic planning regarding environmental risks and opportunities effectively

The Roundtable was launched in 2000 to convene regulators, policymakers, and market participants from both Latin American and OECD countries, to raise awareness and promote the implementation of the recommendations of the OECD's principles, first issued in 1998 (OECD et al., 2010).[13]

One of the main purposes of the LARTCG has been to facilitate the dialogue between the public and private sectors, to encourage Good Corporate Governance policies and practices among companies, considering each country's local circumstances. By these means, The

[13] As the Roundtable's manager, Daniel Blume, noted, "By meeting annually either in plenary form or through Task Forces focused on specific issues, the Roundtable has helped the region's regulators and market participants to understand the latest trends in global markets and to continue to adapt their national frameworks to ensure that they are consistent with global corporate governance standards including the G20/OECD Principles of Corporate Governance as last revised in 2015.".

ROUNDTABLE has since become a valued forum for analyses and research on corporate governance and a launching platform for initiatives and projects on the subject, as well as an effective mechanism to promote corporate governance standards in different countries in LATAM. To that end, the LARTCG has contributed to building an agenda according to the region's main challenges, such as the need to develop capital markets and the best standards for conglomerates (business groups)[14] and State-owned enterprises[15] governance.

The ROUNDTABLE has gathered representatives from Latin American countries such as Argentina, Bolivia, Brazil, Canada, Chile, Costa Rica, Colombia, Dominican Republic, Ecuador, Mexico, Panama, Peru, Uruguay, and Venezuela, and other OECD members such as Spain, Sweden, Turkey, the United Kingdom, and the United States.

Many of the initiatives supported by the LARTCG have had significant impacts on the development of corporate governance standards, such as the *Novo Mercado* in Brazil, and the governance framework for state-owned enterprises, as will be explained below.

2.2 *The Brazilian Experience:* Novo Mercado

Latin American stock markets are among the smallest and least active markets in the world (Chong & López, 2007). In recent decades, the region has been unsuccessful in developing its capital markets[16] due to some specific features considered deterrents to sustained inflows and consolidation of foreign direct investment (FDI). Among these are a high-ownership concentration, the dominant presence of business groups, the availability of other sources of funding, in some cases under subsidized terms, and a dual role of banks acting as both direct lenders and

[14] See the OECD report on Corporate Governance of Company Groups in Latin America (2015).

[15] Due to the importance of State-owned enterprises for the region CAF and OECD created a specific type of Network only for State-owned Enterprises and governments acting as owners.

[16] "The years following the 2008 global financial crisis saw a global shift in capital from US and European markets toward emerging markets in Asia. The Latin American and Caribbean (LAC) region has not benefited from this shift. Domestic markets in the region have struggled to attract new companies to go public, which means that these markets have remained highly concentrated around a relatively low number of listed companies largely dominated by company groups" (OECD, 2019).

underwriters of bonds and equity (OECD, 2019). Stock exchanges and securities regulators have tried several strategies to promote *Initial Public Offerings* (IPOs) as well as the interest from the "buy-and-sell-sides" to attain less concentrated ownership in companies and diversify the number of listed companies. However, these attempts have but produced small concrete results; and the number of listed companies is still relatively scarce, when compared to other regions in the world.

Nonetheless, it is worth mentioning that *Novo Mercado* (NM) in Brazil, as a special segmentation of the Sao Paulo stock exchange,[17] has helped promote corporate governance enhancement of securities issuers within Brazilian capital markets. It was created in 2000 following a democratic process with market participants, where they discussed alternatives and solutions to the lack of dynamism and relevance of Brazil's equity market (Santana et al., 2008). *Novo Mercado* encouraged listed companies to improve their governance standards beyond the practices required by law, providing certification of corporate commitments to higher governance standards verifiable by the market players.

Companies wishing to participate in the NM segment would have to comply with requirements such as having a share capital composed exclusively of common shares (without the possibility of creating a multiple share class structure), adopt measures to expand shareholder rights, and ensure greater transparency, and more comprehensive information disclosure (Black et al., 2010). Later, to offer companies easier conditions to enter the Brazilian market, two additional intermediate segments were created, Level 1 and Level 2 (Santana et al., 2008). This self-regulatory arrangement has continued to evolve, including *Bovespa Mais* and *Bovespa Mais* Level 2 to facilitate the gradual entry of small and medium-sized companies onto the exchange, while encouraging high standards of governance (B3, s.f.a.).

With time, the NM showed outstanding results. By mid-2008, the market capitalization of B3 companies had increased by more than 700%, and international investors became 37% of the total value, compared to 26% in 2002 (Chávez & Silva, 2009). As for the special segments, NM initially had 15 companies in 2001; today, there are more than 200 listed companies.[18] Additionally, different studies have demonstrated that

[17] Currently known as "B3.".

[18] Per information available on the B3 website, last consulted on 14th October 2021.

companies listed in NM and having higher levels of governance practices had a positive impact on abnormal stock returns (Chávez & Silva, 2009; Moura & Norden, 2018; Ganz et al., 2020); presented increases in the value and liquidity of their shares and a reduction in volatility (Chávez & Silva, 2009; Carvahal & Quental, 2008); and adopted a stronger culture of information disclosure (Mendes-Da-Silva & Onusic, 2012).

NM has become an example for countries where corporate governance legislation is not sufficiently developed and has demonstrated that securities markets can play a crucial role in helping companies to adopt higher governance standards, become market players and optimize their chances for growth and sustainability. Finally, NM presented a strong case on how self-regulation and private incentives could create positive dynamics to attract foreign investment, develop capital markets, and strengthen the local business sectors based on corporate governance standards. For that reason, NM has set an example for other countries in LATAM, such as Argentina, Colombia, Costa Rica, México, and Peru, to structure similar initiatives.

2.3 Governing Challenges for Latin American State-owned Enterprises

Another dimension where LATAM benefited from institutional initiatives to face corporate governing challenges relates to state-owned enterprises. In Latin America, the state plays a preponderant role in the region's economies, being the owner of several companies that provide services and carry out business activities in different sectors (Musacchio et al., 2015). Across Latin American, state-owned enterprises are key players in each country's economy, contributing significantly to GDP and supplying essential goods and services (oil, energy, financial services, telecommunications, among others) (World Bank, 2014). Moreover, in some cases, these companies have active participation in the local capital markets, either through the issuance of debt or shares listed on the stock exchange. Nonetheless, the performance of these state-owned and run business has not always been satisfactory, considering that these companies are subject to the burden of their bureaucracy, and in many cases, corruption and misspending of resources (Andrés et al., 2011). From a corporate governance perspective, it has been a significant challenge for the region to establish the parameters for the performance of the state as a shareholder,

Table 4 Comparative Listing of B3 Segments

	Bovespa Mais	Bovespa Mais Nível 2	*Level 1*	*Level 2*	*Novo Mercado*
Share Capital	Only common shares	Multiple share class structure	Multiple share class structure (as per legislation)	Multiple share class structure (with additional rights)	Only common shares
Minimum percentage of free float	25% until the 7th year of listing	25% until the 7th year of listing	25%	25%	25% or 15%, if the Average Daily Trading Volume is above BRL 25 million
Public offering of shares	-	-	Share dispersion efforts	Share dispersion efforts	Share dispersion efforts
Composition of the board of directors	Minimum of 3 members (according to law), with a unified term of up to 2 years	Minimum of 3 members (according to law), with a unified term of up to 2 years	Minimum of 3 members (according to law), with a unified term of up to 2 years	Minimum of 5 members, of which at least 20% must be independent, with a unified term of up to 2 years	Minimum of 3 members, of which at least 2 or 20% (whichever is greater) must be independent, with a unified term of up to 2 years
Disclosure in English and Portuguese	-	-	-	Financial statements	Material Information or Benefit distribution information and results press releases

(continued)

Table 4 (continued)

	Bovespa Mais	Bovespa Mais Nível 2	*Level 1*	*Level 2*	*Novo Mercado*
Disclosure of additional information	Securities trading policy	Securities trading policy	Securities negotiation policy and code of conduct	Securities negotiation policy and code of conduct	Internal regulations of the Board of directors and its Advisory Committees; Code of Conduct; Nomination Policy; Risk Management Policy; Related-party Transaction Policy; Securities Trading Policy; Annual report of the statutory audit committee; Quarterly minutes of the Board of director' meetings.
Annual public meeting	Optional	Optional	Mandatory	Mandatory	A public meeting must be hold until five business days after the disclosure of the quarterly and annual financial statements about the information disclosed
Tag-along rights	For all common shares	For all share classes	For 80% of common shares	For all share classes	For all common shares
Audit	Optional	Optional	Optional	Optional	Mandatory
Internal Auditing	Optional	Optional	Optional	Optional	Mandatory

Source B3 Listing **Committee** segments (s. f.)

as well as the standards of good governing based on the best practices in this area.

Over the past 20 years, institutional efforts have been made to define a series of practices and standards, to strengthen state-owned enterprises governance. In that sense, the CAF Latin American Development Bank issued, in 2010, the Guidelines for State-owned Enterprises Good Corporate Governance (*Lineamientos para el Buen Gobierno Corporativo de las Empresas del Estado*), updated in 2021. These guidelines have the purpose of being a framework that orientates public policies, as well as management decisions, to consolidate the State-owned enterprise's corporate governance and, therefore, improve their performance and transparency (Ibarguen et al., 2021). These guidelines have been used to implement reforms in corporate governance practices in Latin American state-owned enterprises, with the support of CAF, and contributing to the effective promotion and strengthening of corporate governance in the region (Ibarguen et al., 2021). The new 2021 version of the Guidelines is focused on the revision of the dynamics and operations of the board of directors' committees to ensure they adequately comply with their functions; the introduction of a new chapter on control and risk management; and the inclusion of new corporate governance practices throughout the different areas.

On the other hand, Latin America has harbored other institutional initiatives to promote corporate governance for state-owned enterprises. For example, since 2011, the Latin American Network on Corporate Governance of State-owned Enterprises jointly organized by OECD and the CAF Latin American Development Bank has been an active scenario for the exchange of practices and knowledge on State-owned enterprises' governing policies and practices based upon the OECD *Guidelines on Corporate Governance of State-owned Enterprises* (OECD, s.f. a). The Network has gathered senior policymakers and State-owned enterprises executives from Argentina, Brazil, Chile, Colombia, Ecuador, Mexico, Paraguay, Peru, and Uruguay. The activities from this Network are part of the Latin American Roundtable on Corporate Governance.

The Network's priorities include:

a) Raising awareness of all concerned constituencies on the importance and challenges related to the good corporate governance of state-owned enterprises;

b) Evaluating the current state-owned enterprises corporate governance policy frameworks and practices and benchmark these compared to international best practices as described in the Guidelines;
c) Influencing policymaking by providing a forum where policymakers, practitioners, and experts can share knowledge and experience among peers;
d) Supporting viable and effective reforms by discussing and analyzing policy options, developing relevant recommendations, and agreeing on priorities for reforms; and
e) Promoting implementation of the OECD Guidelines on Anti-Corruption and Integrity for State-owned enterprises.

3 What's Next? Some Guessing and Predictions

As the reader might have seen in this chapter, the Latin American corporate governance landscape has been influenced by global regulatory trends and shaped by public–private initiatives of stock exchanges, local regulators, and international financial institutions. However, social, economic, and political events have also had an impact on the conversation in the last 20 years. During this period, the region has benefited from good economic conditions vis-a-vis solid commodity prices (Ocampo, 2017), the boom of the Chinese economy as a recipient of Latin American products (Jenkins, 2017), and pro-business governments.[19]

However, the evolution of the economic and political landscape in the last 4 to 5 years makes it complicated to portray its future. Currently, the region is battling against the socio-economic crisis derived from the pandemic,[20] and several countries, such as Brazil, Chile, Colombia, and Peru are experiencing unusual levels of social turmoil and violence. Moreover, worldwide one of the main consequences of the pandemic is the

[19] Under the current circumstances, we understand this statement may be seen as controversial; however, making an overall analysis of the last two decades, we consider that in the countries analyzed in this study (Argentina, Brazil, Chile, Colombia, Mexico, Peru), the general tendency has been for national governments to be "pro," or at least, neutral to business development.

[20] At the time of writing, the region is facing a profound crisis primarily relating to the consequences of the COVID-19 pandemic.

growth in the power of the state in most countries.[21] For that reason, corporate governance developments for, say, the next 20 years (2042) will be highly influenced by the handling of the post-pandemic effects and the political dynamics in the region. Having warned the reader about the difficulty to predict what will happen in an unstable region; surrounded by a volatile world, and in which political events will determine its outcomes substantially, here are some of the authors' ideas about the future of corporate governance in Latin America for the next two decades.

From our perspective, there are three main driving forces to the future of corporate governance in Latin America:

a) The global commitment and interest among international investors, local regulators, regional companies, and stakeholders for a strong ESG orientation in the post-COVID world;
b) An entrepreneurial mindset leveraged by technological developments to enable financing alternatives, expand alliances, and facilitate the compliance of partners' agreements; and
c) The transformation of boards of directors as a source of knowledge[22] based on effective dynamics and diversity.

The ESG factor is already shaping the future of corporate governance in the world. In Latin America, this may have some specific traits, including the importance for companies in improving the dialogue with local communities, employees,[23] and governments in terms of sustainable development and companies' shared value. On the other hand, all this interest in sustainability and the need to improve social conditions and create social welfare will make society more aware of the importance of governing for not-for-profit organizations (NFPOs). Moreover, NFPOs are key players regarding strategic topics for the region's development, including health, education, and recreation. For these reasons, we

[21] Nicholas Christakis on the three shifts of the world after the pandemic (The Economist, 2021).

[22] Please note that we are using wisdom and not knowledge to emphasize the integral contribution that a board of directors can make to a business or a non-for-profit organization.

[23] Mainly generation Z and millennials that will be the main percentage of the workforce in these years.

believe that a stronger focus on best practices and governance standards for NFPOs will be a sensible move to consider in the coming years.

Secondly, it is expected that the Latin American corporate landscape may not change dramatically in the next two decades. The scale of *multilatina* corporations and the level of synergies created within companies' conglomerates in a context of volatile political environment and complex business regulations reduce the interest of global players for strong stakes in the region. For that reason, we are expecting to see mostly the same corporate players during the next two decades. In that context, entrepreneurs will become a strong force for business evolution. Furthermore, Latin American entrepreneurs will benefit from crowdfunding initiatives, private-equity industry sophistication, and technological cost reductions to build companies and do business. This new realities will likely require a fundamental rethink of certain corporate governance practices to account for and appropriately respond to these entrepreneurs' emerging environments and requirements.[24]

The governing challenge in Latin America and, likely, the rest of the world, will be less dependent on the principal-agent theory associated with dispersed ownership of listed companies and institutional investors[25]; and more related to managing expectations among controlling—minority shareholders, general—limited partners in venture capital contexts, and shareholders agreements to assure a long-term understanding among partners regarding their contributions in ideas, capital, networks, and specific knowledge. This situation will require reformulations of what we currently consider to be best corporate governance practices. Thus, for example, the emphasis on the definitions of independent directors will be less on their independence and more on professionalization and the expertise that external directors can bring to the company. Shareholder agreements will be more important than corporate governance codes (because internal agreements will be key for business developments

[24] Few local initiatives are already incorporating this new governance landscape, such as the Corporate Governance Guidelines for private enterprises (*Guia de Buenas Prácticas de Gobierno Corporativo para Empresas Competitivas, Productivas y Perdurables*—2020) from the Bogotá–Colombia Chamber of Commerce, structured with the technical advice from Governance Consultants.

[25] As we are seeing, the capital markets are suffering a global delisting problem associated with several causes.

and stability), and business control practices will be more focused on risk management rather than on assuring financial information to third parties.

Finally, the third driving force is the transformation of regional boards of directors. Our understanding is that one of the main consequences of COVID for corporate governing is the effect on boards, especially on the need for a more diverse composition, higher expectations about their contribution, and a more virtual environment through remote meetings. Latin American boards of directors are experiencing increased expectations from shareholders, stakeholders, and regulators about their strategic insights and long-term contributions to business organizations. This new context may create an incentive for better and more contributing boards, which will lead shareholders to progressively look and demand better directors. On the other hand, individual directors will feel the pressure to update their knowledge, assume a more committed role, and become more involved in the company's strategic decisions, as well as developing new skills to enable such better decision-making processes. This situation will increase the need for directors' training programs, knowledge-sharing communities specifically focused on directors, and learning process continuity.

Furthermore, with the broader acceptance of virtual meetings for boards and committees, the quality of candidates will be more demanding, benefiting international, and sub-regional directors' integration. We expect companies to notice that having a diverse board will improve their decision-making processes through its value creation. From our perspective, a diverse board will consider three main dimensions: more women, younger generations, and foreign directors. Based on these three aspects of diversity and the pressure of different stakeholders to improve, Latin American boards will likely transform their modus operandi and increase their contribution through better decision-making.

These three main forces will confront immediate governing challenges derived from the new business reality after COVID, including the fast evolution of fixed-income financing strategies, governance practices within insolvency procedures, and the continuous evolution of multinational corporate groups.

In this framework, discussions on governing may well become a good reference point for a dialogue between governments, society, media, academia, and business on improving corporate transparency, ethics, accountability, and better decision-making to create value and development for Latin America (Table 4).

References

Andrés, L. A., Guasch, J. L., & Azumendi, S. L. (2011). Governance in State-owned enterprises revisited: the cases of water and electricity in Latin America and the Caribbean. *World Bank Policy Research Working Paper*, (5747).

B3. (s. f. a). Listing segments | B3. http://www.b3.com.br/en_us/products-and-services/solutions-for-issuers/listing-segments/bovespa-mais/

B3. (s. f. b). Empresas Listadas | B3. https://www.b3.com.br/pt_br/produtos-e-servicos/negociacao/renda-variavel/empresas-listadas.htm

Black, B. S., De Carvalho, A. G., & Gorga, E. (2010). Corporate governance in Brazil. *Emerging Markets Review*, *11*(1), 21–38.

BlackRock. (2021). *Pautas de votación para valores de América Latina*. BlackRock Investment Stewardship. https://www.blackrock.com/corporate/literature/fact-sheet/blk-responsible-investment-guidelines-latam-spanish.pdf

Blume, D., & Alonso, F. (2007). Institutional investors and corporate governance in Latin America: Challenges, promising practices, and recommendations. *Financial Market Trends, 2*, 93–131.

Cámara de Comercio de Bogotá, Confecámaras, & Superintendencia Sociedades. (2020). *Guía de Buenas Prácticas de Gobierno Corporativo para Empresas Competitivas, Productivas y Perdurables*. http://hdl.handle.net/11520/25983

Chávez, G. A., & Silva, A. C. (2009). Brazil's Experiment with Corporate Governance. *Journal of Applied Corporate Finance, 21*(1), 34–44. https://doi.org/10.1111/j.1745-6622.2009.00214.x

Chong, A. E. & López—de—Silanes, F. (2007). Corporate Governance in Latin America. *Inter-American Development Bank*.

Dasgupta, A., Fos, V., & Sautner, Z. (2020). Institutional investors and corporate governance. *Foundations and Trends in Finance, forthcoming, European Corporate Governance Institute*—Finance Working Paper 700/2020, Available at SSRN: https://ssrn.com/abstract=3682800 or https://doi.org/10.2139/ssrn.3682800

Ganz, A. C. S., Schlotefeldt, J. O., & Rodríguez Junior, M. M. (2020). Corporate governance and capital asset pricing models. *Revista de Administração Mackenzie*, 21(2). https://doi.org/10.1590/1678-6971/eramf200010

Ibarguen, A., Oneto, A., & Gómez-Zorrilla, J. (2021). Lineamientos para el buen gobierno corporativo de las empresas del Estado. *CAF*

ISS. (2020). *Americas proxy voting guidelines updates 2021. Benchmark Policy Changes for U.S., Canada, and Latin America*. https://www.issgovernance.com/file/policy/active/updates/Americas-Policy-Updates.pdf

Jenkins, R. (2017). *China and Latin America* (pp. 182–197). Routledge.

Keay, A. (2014). Comply or explain in corporate governance codes: In need of greater regulatory oversight? *Legal Studies, 34*(2), 279–304.

Mendes-Da-Silva, W., & Onusic, L. M. (2012). Corporate e-disclosure determinants: Evidence from the Brazilian market. *International Journal of Disclosure and Governance, 11*(1), 54–73. https://doi.org/10.1057/jdg.2012.14

Mendes de Paula, G., Sousa Ribeiro, K. C. D., & Silva de Almeida, N. (2015). Corporate governance and corporate debt issuance in Latin America: Institutional investors, investment banks, rating agencies and new empirical evidence. *Corporate governance in Brazil, Chile, Colombia, Mexico and Peru: The determinants of risk in corporate debt issuance.* Santiago: ECLAC/CAF/IDB/OECD, 2015. *LC/W., 654*, 63–83.

Moura, L., & Norden, L. (2018). Does good corporate governance pay off in the long run? Evidence from stock market segment switches in Brazil. *Revista Brasileira De Finanças, 17*(3), 1–25.

Musacchio, A., Ayerbe, E. I. P., & García, G. (2015). Stateo-owned Enterprise Reform in Latin America. *Inter-American Development Bank.*

Nuñez, G. & Oneto, A. (coords.) (2012). *Gobernanza corporativa en el Brasil, Colombia y México. La determinación del riesgo en la emisión de instrumentos de deuda corporative.* Santiago: Economic Commission for Latin America and the Caribbean (ECLAC)/CAF-Development Bank of Latin America/Inter-American Development Bank (IDB)

OECD, International finance corporation, Global corporate governance forum, & gobierno de España. (2010). *Mesa Redonda Latinoamericana de Gobierno Corporativo. Capitalizando sobre una década de progreso.* https://www.oecd.org/daf/ca/corporategovernanceprinciples/47103859.pdf

OECD, (2003). *White paper on corporate governance in Latin America.* https://www.oecd.org/daf/ca/corporategovernanceprinciples/18976210.pdf

OECD. (2015). *Corporate governance of company groups in Latin America.* OECD Publishing.

OECD. (2016). *Strengthening corporate governance codes in Latin America.* The 2016 Meeting of the Latin American corporate governance roundtable. https://www.oecd.org/daf/ca/LART-2016-Strengthening-Corporate-Governance-Codes-Latin-America.pdf

OECD. (2017). *Background Issues Note on Equity Market Development in Latin America.* Latin American Corporate Governance Roundtable Task Force on Equity Market Development. https://www.oecd.org/daf/ca/2017-Task-Force-Latin-American-Equity-Market-Development-Issues-Note.pdf

OECD. (2019). *Equity market development in Latin America: Enhancing access to corporate finance.* https://www.oecd.org/corporate/ca/Latin-American-Equity-Markets-2019.pdf

OECD (2021), *OECD Corporate governance factbook 2021*, https://www.oecd.org/corporate/corporategovernance-factbook.htm.

OECD. (s.f. a). *Latin American network on corporate governance of state-owned enterprises—OECD*. https://www.oecd.org/daf/ca/latinamericannetworkoncorporategovernanceofstate-ownedenterprises.htm

OECD. (s.f. b). *OECD-Latin American roundtable on corporate governance—OECD*. https://www.oecd.org/daf/ca/latinamericanroundtableoncorporategovernance.htm

Ocampo, J. A. (2017). Commodity-led development in Latin America. *Alternative pathways to sustainable development: Lessons from Latin America* (pp. 51–76). Brill Nijhoff.

Reyes, F. (2007). Corporate governance in Latin America: A functional análisis. *U. Miami Inter-Am. l. Rev., 39*, 207.

Santana, M. H., Ararat, M., Alexandru, P., Yurtoglu, B. B., & da Cunha, M. R. (2008). Novo Mercado and its followers: Case studies in corporate governance reform. In Global Corporate Governance Forum and International Finance Corporation.

Santos, A. A., Crispim, S. F., Oliva, E. C. & Dornelles, M. (2020). Codes of corporate governance of Latin American countries: Analysis of UN practices. *RAM. Revista de Administração Mackenzie*, 21.

The Economist. (2021). *The long goodbye to covid-19*. https://www.economist.com/leaders/2021/07/03/the-long-goodbye-to-covid-19

World Bank. (2014). *Corporate governance of state-owned enterprises in Latin America: Current trends and country cases*. World Bank Group.

CHAPTER 5

The Institutional Construction of Corporate Governing in Latin America

Magdalena Díaz Le-Fort, Gonzalo Jiménez-Seminario, and Jonathan Callund

1 Latin American History

Broadly speaking, the history of the social and economic development of Latin America since independence in the early 1800s has taken the countries through similar historical processes. Throughout the nineteenth

M. Díaz Le-Fort
Universidad del Desarrollo (UDD), Santiago, Chile
e-mail: manedlefort@gmail.com

Chilean-Indian Chamber of Commerce, Vitacura, Chile

G. Jiménez-Seminario
Pontificia Universidad Católica de Chile, Santiago, Chile
e-mail: gjimenez@proteus.cl

Proteus Management, Governance & Effectuation, Santiago, Chile

J. Callund (✉)
Callund y Compañía Ltda, Santiago, Chile
e-mail: jonathan.callund@callund.cl

J. Callund et al. (eds.), *Corporate Governing in Latin America*,
https://doi.org/10.1007/978-3-030-85780-6_5

century the primary focus was on nation building and the transition to independence, as reflected in the territorial struggles to draw each new country's national borders, largely along similar political lines to those left by the Spanish and Portuguese empires, and the swings of the political between the liberal groups and more conservative and authoritarian governments (Bethell, 1992). But all the countries opted to set themselves up with new constitutions as republics. Regardless of the timing and depth of individual country divergence, as a subcontinent, their economies and business focus were homogeneous, with largely *traditional* agrarian economic structures dominated by extractive mining and fishing industries and the gradual development of business centers that would show the way to modernity in certain sectors, controlled primarily by foreign capital from London and New York. This is notably the case with English foreign direct investment (FDI) in mining and the railways. The key economic driver for development was extraction of raw materials under an export-oriented classical liberalism model (Bulmer-Thomas, 2017).

At the beginning of the twentieth century, these guidelines began to be questioned given the arrival of left-wing ideas coming, above all, from the triumph of the Russian Revolution. In the case of Chile, it is characteristic, since it was the first country in Latin America where a POS (*Partido Obrero Socialista*) emerged, which later evolved into the PC (Communist Party) in 1921—the work of Emilio Recabarren (Salazar, 2012). On the other hand, the crisis of 1929, which had a very negative effect on these export-led economies, brought on yet another conception—the advent of *economic nationalism*. Just as most of the "world closed," Latin America did too, but its economy was (and remains) weak in industrial capacity, with its pockets of industry still foreign owned. With the dramatic collapse of Latin American economies and their slow recovery in the 1930s and 1940s, an alternative vision emerged, namely the promotion of national industry and autarky.[1]

Thus, by the middle of the twentieth century, most of the countries in Latin American had opted for a model of *Import Substitution Industrialization* (ISI), as developed, and promoted by ECLAC (Economic Commission for Latin America and the Caribbean),

[1] According to Deardorff's Glossary of International Economics, "Autarky" is *the characteristic of self-sufficiency, usually applied to societies, communities, states, and their economic systems.*

which emerged under the umbrella of the post-war United Nations. Its second Executive Secretary, the Argentine economist Raúl Prebisch (1950 to 1963), through the publication of the report "*The economic development of Latin America and its principal problems*" pushed the Latin American economies to industrialize with the aim of developing the whole continent and eliminating—or reducing—its structural problems of poverty, low-added value of its economic production, stagnant growth and a dependence on foreign markets, and foreign demand and persistent low levels of productivity. This encouraged the development of new, home-grown companies, many of which were State funded and owned (ENAP, ENDESA and CAP are key examples in Chile; Compañía Vale do Rio Doce (CVRD) and Petrobras from Brazil; Gas del Estado, Agua y Energía Eléctrica and Aerolíneas Argentinas in Argentina; Empresa Colombiana de Petróleos S.A. or SATENA in Colombia, Cemex, and Pemex in Mexico y Petroperú and Banco de la Nación in Perú) (Zanatti et al., 2021), all were established following the guidelines of the ISI model. Despite resulting in several successful cases, in terms of promoting national industry (as seen in the case of Chile, with the three *Radical* governments 1938–1952), the balance of payments soon entered a crisis due to excessive levels of external national debt (Correa-Sutil, 2001).

On the political spectrum, the 1960's in Latin America were characterized by their left-wing and revolutionary factions, triggered largely by the "success" of the Cuban Revolution in 1959. The "traditional left" became radicalized and numerous guerrilla groups emerged (*Montoneros* in Argentina, *Tupamaros* in Uruguay, *Sendero Luminoso* in Peru, *MIR* and *VOP* in Chile, *Comando de Libertação Nacional* in Brazil, among others). Such was the political polarization and the division of society that practically every Latin American country, between the 1970's and 1980's, fell into military dictatorships, sworn to eradicate the "Marxist cancer." Many were supported by the United States. Particularly Brazil and the *Southern Cone* (Argentina, Chile, and Uruguay) saw the emergence of what political scientist Guillermo O'Donnell (1988) called *Bureaucratic-Authoritarian States*, characterized by a suspension of pre-existing political and democratic institutions with an aim to restore social order.

With the failure of socialism, many military-run countries that experienced this political upheaval attempted to introduce a liberal economic order, their economies remained stagnant. But there was one clear exception—Chile, which ditched the ISI model for free-market policies, also known as the emergence of ***neoliberalism*** (Taylor, 2006). This was a first in the region and anywhere in the world—a whole decade before even the United Kingdom and United States of America. These policies were carried out during a military government that lasted 16 years (1973–1990). The manual or template known as "*El Ladrillo*" (De Castro, 1992)[2] sets out the bases of the economic policy of the Pinochet government with the economic and political decomposition of the Salvador Allende short-lived socialist regime. The Chicago University professor and free-market thinker, Milton Friedman was a mentor of the neoliberal students who returned from Harvard, Chicago, and MIT to lead the implementation of new and radical policies to open up the Chilean economy to competition and FDI. The economic team is known as the "Chicago Boys."

However, the Latin American trajectory—apparently—was destined to suffer new economic crises.

The so-called **Debt Crisis** that broke out in Mexico in 1982 and that affected all the countries of the region has been associated with several interrelated causes: the aggressive placement of funds from petrodollars, surpluses from the OPEC countries on the part of international banking that were eagerly taken by the Latin American countries to finance their development model generating an excess of external debt, and the rapid rise in interest rates by the FED to control North American inflation, catalyzed by the announcement of Mexico of that it could not meet its financial commitments (Toussaint, 2006).

The Debt Crisis ended up shaking the economy of all the countries in the region, drastically increasing unemployment and poverty. This last

[2] *El Ladrillo*—"the brick" in Spanish—is considered by many to be the basis of the economic policy of Chile's military government. The paper sets out an alternative economic program in response to the process of economic decomposition that Chile was experiencing in the early years of the 1970's, based on its diagnosis of the economy of the time, being characterized as closed, with regulated prices, high inflationary tendencies, and severe imbalances in its balance of payments. Rather, the authors set out the need to free up domestic prices, radically reduce the size of the public sector, finance the fiscal sector and public companies, establish a realistic exchange rate, lower external tariffs, create a capital market, modernize the agriculture, open up the land market and establish a decentralized commercial, monetary, fiscal and tax policies, as well as social security and healthcare reforms. De Castro, S. (1992). El ladrillo: bases de la política económica del gobierno militar chileno.

element continues to be one of the most urgent burdens to improve. Such was the disaster that the United States created the "*Washington Consensus*" in order to "save" the economies of the subcontinent. The term Washington Consensus was coined in 1989 by economist John Williamson, who proposed ten conditions as a "standard package" to get Latin American countries out of the financial crisis:

1. Fiscal policy discipline, with avoidance of large fiscal deficits relative to GDP;
2. Redirection of public spending from subsidies ("especially indiscriminate subsidies") toward broad-based provision of key pro-growth, pro-poor services, like primary education, primary health-care and infrastructure investment;
3. Tax reform, broadening the tax base and adopting moderate marginal tax rates;
4. Interest rates that are market determined and positive (but moderate) in real terms;
5. Competitive exchange rates;
6. Trade liberalization: liberalization of imports, with particular emphasis on elimination of quantitative restrictions (licensing, etc.); any trade protection to be provided by low and relatively uniform tariffs;
7. Liberalization of inward foreign direct investment;
8. Privatization of state enterprises;
9. Deregulation: abolition of regulations that impede market entry or restrict competition, except for those justified on safety, environmental and consumer protection grounds, and prudential oversight of financial institutions; and
10. Legal security for property rights.

These measures were supported by the International Monetary Fund (IMF), the World Bank, and the US Treasury Department. The formulas encompassed policies that fostered macroeconomic stabilization, liberalization, state downsizing, financial deregulation, and the expansion of market forces within the domestic economy. Despite the efforts of the economic policies protected by the Washington Consensus, aggregate economic growth in Latin America did not achieve satisfactory figures and was transformed into what ECLAC called the "lost decade" (the 1990's) (Bértola, L., & Ocampo, A., 2012).

During the mid- and late- 1980's, Latin American countries struggled to reinstate and strengthen their democracies and institutional framework that had led to a deep rift in their societies. Complex transitions to democracy took place. Chile was the last country to recover its democracy (in March 1990), but these delays came with the benefits of financial and economic solvency (e.g., low and controlled inflation and strong economic and export-led growth since 1985). As a whole, Latin American countries all refocused their efforts on growth by opening up and developing relationships with international markets under the liberal model, aware of the failures of international socialism and the collapse of the USSR in 1991. Latin America quickly consolidated itself as the leading raw materials export market. Only Brazil, the most industrialized country in the region, was able to—temporarily—avoid this dynamic.

The ***Asian Crisis*** ushered in the twenty-first century, which, although it affected Latin America, does not compare with the magnitude of the Debt Crisis. Although during the present century Latin American politics have tended to stabilize, the protests for greater social justice are felt with increasing force and persistence. Some countries have been involved in significant institutional crises (in particular, Bolivia and Ecuador) and others have promoted the nationalization of their raw materials and a fight against "North American imperialism" (Ecuador, Bolivia, and especially Venezuela). Elsewhere, former guerrilla leaders were elected as President (Brazil, Nicaragua, and Uruguay).

Several countries have strengthened their relations with the United States through the signing of Free Trade Agreements, **FTA**s (Chile, Mexico, Colombia and Peru). Finally, some have tried to imitate the European model of regional integration, as is the case of MERCOSUR (Argentina, Brazil, Uruguay and Paraguay), although, despite its aspirations, this has fallen far short of the levels of commercial and political integration of the EUROPEAN UNION.

The **Subprime Crisis** mainly affected the rich countries, while Latin America was somewhat removed from the dramatic effects subsequently seen in Europe. This was largely due to the dynamism of the high Chinese demand for commodities generated in the region that brought about rapid and sustained growth in the period 2000 to 2014 (Bértola, L., & Ocampo, A., 2012).

However, despite the economic progress achieved, the social crisis in the region worsened substantially. This social crisis combined with indigenous (mainly Bolivia, Chile, Ecuador, and Mexico), racial (Brazil), political-ideological (Ecuador and Venezuela), internal warfare (Colombia), and social (Argentina and Chile) disturbances, as well as the growth in institutional corruption (Argentina, Brazil, Peru, and Venezuela).

All this occurred in a context of fragile democracies throughout the region, the rise of drug trafficking (Colombia and Mexico), violence, truncated welfare states (Argentina), violence (Colombia and Mexico), among many other structural ills.

There have been extended periods of continuous social unrest throughout most of the countries in Latin America, culminating in 2019 with what has become known as the *estallido social*—literally "social explosion"—as seen in Chile, Colombia and Peru, Ecuador, and Haiti.

We conclude this section with the evidence that Latin American history is relatively homogeneous, and that it has been following similar patterns in which political, economic, and social elements are intertwined, demonstrating a shared institutional weakness. As we will see below, this has an important correlation with the development of corporate governing.

Despite the gloomy picture cast by the previous historical analysis, it does not consider important factors to be more optimistic for the future. These include the strong development of *multilatinas*,[3] MNCs of Latin American origin, a growing number of unicorns made in LA, (Mercado Libre, Despegar, Betterfly, Cornershop, Notco), strong investment in venture capital, incubators and accelerators that are changing the face of the region. Additionally, social entrepreneurship reaches new peaks every day, creating a more ecological awareness, a greater sense of social and corporate responsibility (including the exemplary work carried out by the Association of Corporate Secretaries, ASCLA based in Peru, led by one of our co-authors), as well as important collaboration between large corporations and startups, which are changing the face of the company in the region, putting on a more friendly face, closer and committed to social reality.

Another vital factor of change, in which Chile also stands out, has been the promotion of entrepreneurship through the government agency

[3] https://www.bcg.com/publications/2018/why-multilatinas-hold-key-latin-america-economic-future.

STARTUP CHILE as well as the creation of dynamic associations of entrepreneurs (such as ASECH), initiatives that have subsequently spread throughout the region, giving a sense of mission, identity and belonging to small entrepreneurs in Latin America.

Family businesses—and the business families that are behind them—are of themselves a force for progress, development, and bearers of hope for greater equity and social commitment. Several of the authors of the chapters in this book are witnesses to the work of these institutions, so the jury is still out of the room when it comes to the socioeconomic future of Latin America.

We highlight the case of Chile not only as a pioneer in the adoption of free-market policies, but also because it has achieved significant economic progress, while simultaneously becoming a symbol of the region's social unrest.

2 CHILE AS A CORPORATE GOVERNING TRENDSETTER

An important inspiration and source of insights for this book is Jiménez-Seminario (2018)'s doctoral dissertation at the UNIVERSITY OF LIVERPOOL. In this work, informed by *Grounded Theory* (Glasser & Strauss, 1967), he developed an analysis of the evolution of corporate governing in Chile, proposing a conceptual framework to understand corporate scandals as both the results and catalysts for the evolution of how organizations have been governed over the previous forty years. Given Chile's precociousness in the region (and the world?) as a role-model for the road to implementing economic freedoms, preceding Ronald Reagan and Margaret Thatcher's "revolutions" by many years, this research provides both conceptual and empirical lenses to map the evolution of corporate governance practices and regulation in the six countries under study.

Figure 1 sets out the purported paradigms in economic and social liberalization and the corresponding insights they provide, as they evolve through three sequential and coexisting institutional logics, namely:

- <u>As of 1973:</u> A predominantly ***economic institutional*** **logic** implemented and perfected by the so-called *Chicago Boys*, a group of young Chilean economists primarily trained at the UNIVERSITY OF CHICAGO, who, working during Augusto Pinochet's military government, established and consolidated a comprehensive and

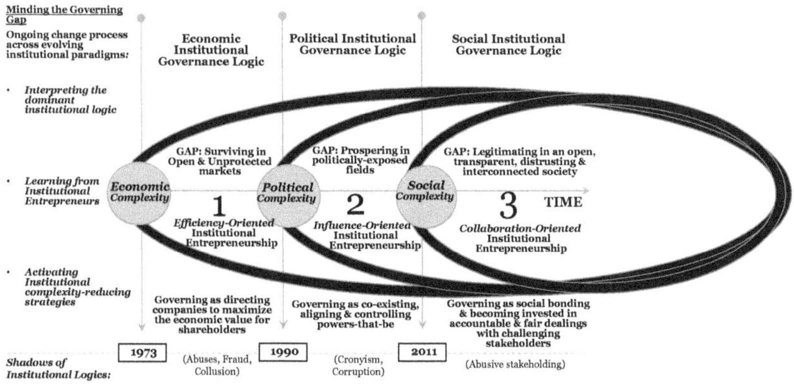

Fig. 1 Paradigms in the Evolution of Corporate Governing (*Source* Jiménez-Seminario 2018)

successful free-market economic model as of the mid-1970s, which has largely remained in place for the last fifty years. As explained above, this was a reaction to decades of protectionism and failed attempts to promote economic growth and reduce poverty by applying the ISI Model proposed by the ECONOMIC COMMISSION FOR LATIN AMERICA AND THE CARIBBEAN, ECLAC, that broadly inspired the autarkic and protectionist economic policies implemented throughout the region. Businesses promptly hired young professionals familiar with the "new" economic theories and began the learning process of playing by the new rules. The overarching governance imperative of the time is (and was) seen to have been *to maximize the economic value and the powerbase of controlling shareholders in a context of lax regulation—and even weaker enforcement.* Values and ethics were seen more as personal issues and separated from business matters (Jiménez, 2018). This led to material increases in efficiency, but unfortunately also opened the door to permissive behaviors, such as collusion, cartels, fraud, and insider trading. In a mindset of better to apologize than ask for permission, any rational cost–benefit assessment, at the time, showed that paying the financial penalties—if/when caught—would systematically be more convenient vis-à-vis the economic payback of such bad practices.[4]

- As of 1990: A ***political institutional*** **logic** derived from the return to democracy in March 1990 and the expansion of the business community, after 16 years of authoritarian military government, with its strong ties to the business sector. This new order of things was perceived as critical for regulated sectors, such as pensions, energy, telecoms, banking, and other financial services, and attracted multinationals—several of them being State-controlled companies from Spain. Those new foreign investors moved quickly and incorporated political figures—many close to the *Concertación* (a wide alliance of center and left-wing parties governing Chile without interruption, from 1990 to 2010)—as board members. Such links were assured to "smoothen" the relationships between business and the political establishment, and this *coziness* continues to date (2022). The governing imperative in this period led to a coexistence with the powers-that-be (known as "*poderes fácticos*" in Chilean jargon), but subsequently evolved into attempts to gain control of the political forces, through the financing of individual politicians and whole political parties, taking advantage of loopholes in the legislation.
- As of 2011: A ***social institutional*** **logic** which first came to light in 2011 with the transversal environmental protests against HydroAysén, a substantial hydro-electric plant in the "virginal" Chilean Patagonia. This was followed by university student demonstrations, which in turn sparked regular mass middle-class rallies against for-profit, poor-quality education that burdened parents and students alike with heavy debts, combined with the restricted access to graduates from "new" universities to the better-paying jobs. Regional and environmental protests, opposition to the private pension funds, the emerging feminists and LGTB movements, were among the leading themes for marches that have since become routine. These propelled a step-by-step drive toward the mother of all rebellions, which occurred in October 2019, when extremely violent riots ensued across the whole country for weeks and a mass protests brought over a million people together to express their frustration at the pace of development of improved social rights,

[4] Gary Becker "Crime and Punishment: an economic approach" JPE Vol. 76, No.2 (Mar-Apr 1968) pp. 169–217.

as well as the continuing inequalities and privileges. This combination of violence and public demonstrations obliged the government to negotiate with the opposition to propose in November 2018 the drafting of a new Constitution—a world precursory democratic, popular, bottom-up, gender-equal and ethnic-respectful process approved by nearly 80% of the voters that is due to approve or reject a proposal for a new *Carta Magna* in September 2022. This ongoing social institutional logic is still underway and corporate boards are trying to cope with its expectations and demands. Gender equality, sustainability, minimum pay levels, business impact in the local community and even worker-representation on company boards are some of the aspects that have been tabled and many ongoing controversies have persuaded the main corporate actors that it is hardly going to be business as usual. Thus, legitimacy and consideration of stakeholders are now high among current priorities.

Interestingly, and even more challenging, is the fact that the different institutional logics have not been replaced or merged, thus leading to significant increases in the degrees of complexity in carrying out the governance function. Hence, the need for a framework—see Table 1 to assist in mapping and calibrating the emerging matrix of evolving institutional logics to gain a greater understanding of the multiple themes that are shaping the evolution of corporate governance practices, using the tools of *Grounded Theory*, proposed by Barney Glasser (1992).

We will now use this framework to assess the parallels, differences, and evolution vis-à-vis the Chilean process to gain a greater understanding of the various contexts found in the other five countries under review.

3 Latin American Corporate Governing Evolution

The following table summarizes the application of the previous template to Argentina, Brazil, Colombia, Mexico, and Peru. In it we provide a few broad-brush attempts at tracing an analogy of the evolution of corporate governing in the rest of Latin America (excepting Chile).

Again, three subsequent paradigms can be identified: a mainly political institutional logic, a dominant economic institutional and a social institutional logic (Table 2).

Table 1 6Cs—Drivers in evolution of corporate governing in Chile

6Cs	*Phase I* Conceptualized	*Phase II* Conceptualized	*Phase III* Conceptualized
Context	**Economic** Institutional Governing logic.	**Political** Institutional Governing logic	**Social** Institutional Governing logic
Condition	Traditional industrial and family businesses	Business Groups, *Chicago Boys*	Business Groups, *Chicago Boys*, Political actors
Causes	Institutional entrepreneurs by Chicago Boys	Institutional entrepreneurs by Spanish State-owned enterprises and political actors	Institutional entrepreneurs by social actors
Covariance	Pro-business regulation, deriving from Milton Friedman theories.	Pro-business regulation, deriving from OECD and Globalization	Activist regulation, deriving from new laws and social sensibilities
Contingencies	Collusions, frauds, Stakeholder abuses, Environmental damage	Crony capitalism, corruption, bribery.	Increased exposure to stakeholder demands, complaints and abuses
Consequences	*Governing gap*: Survival, achieving efficiency, growth, maximizing shareholder value	*Governing gap*: Coopting, controlling, aligning with powers-that-be, exerting influence	Legitimacy vis-à-vis an open, transparent, distrusting, open, and interconnected society

Source Jiménez-Seminario (2018) based on Glaser, B. (1992)

Although they differ in the ultimate reasons, both neoclassical and structuralist economists agree that the ECLAC model of *Industrialization by Import Substitution*—strongly influenced by the Argentinean economist, Raúl Prebisch—was not as successful in Latin America as it has been in Asia, given that the former never evolved into a successful export-oriented development strategy as happened in the later region. The most accepted description is one by the historian Victor Bulmer (2007) who traced the influence of the ISI model in most of the region from 1929 to 1989; proposing as the end-date, the year of the Latin American Debt Crisis and *The Washington Consensus*. This was a period where Latin American countries became primarily internally focused, with the State playing a predominant role and a large degree of protectionism. Bustelo (1992) has described the protectionism of Asian countries as an *incubator* of competitive export companies, while calling the Latin American equivalent a *greenhouse*, offering a shield to inefficient and non-competitive

Table 2 6Cs—Drivers in evolution of corporate governing in Latin America

6Cs—Sociological Family Capturing the ongoing basic social process in LA	*AUTARKY 1938—1989 ISI Model Crisis, Military Dictatorships, Political intervention of Economy and Society*	*LIBERALIZATION 1990 - > onwards Washington Consensus "Lost Decade" 1989–2000, Democracy recovered, Privatization-Marketization, Commodities Boom 2000–14*	*SOCIAL UNREST 2011 - onwards, peaking in 2019 Immigrations 2015–21, Middle Income Trap, End of tolerance of Corruption, Discrimination, and Inequality*
Context: Emerging Institutional Logic	**Political** Governing Logic	**Economic** Governing Logic	**Social** Governing Logic
Condition: Dominant actors, political and economic elites	Charismatic leaders, dominant political parties (PRI, Peronism, etc.), military dictator rule; traditional elites	Business groups, Spanish State-owned enterprises, *Multilatinas*, politicians' favorites, high profile financiers, bankers	Business groups, Political actors, traditional elites, Unicorn entrepreneurs (MercadoLibre, etc.)
Causes: Institutional entrepreneurs promoting and/or imposing an emerging new institutional logic	ECLAC, Raúl Prebisch (father of the ISI Model)	Washington Consensus: FMI, World Bank, US Treasury's recommendations for structural reforms and economic liberation	Social Actors begin to dominate the scene and some few businessmen adopt pro-social and pro-environmental policies
Covariance: Concurrent forces occurring in the period along the basic social process	National industry Protective regulation—protectionism, state intervention, populism	Pro-Market regulation—derived from FMI and influenced by globalization and Chilean successful experience	Activist regulation—new laws and social sensibilities distinctions between legality & legitimacy
Contingencies: Categories of corporate scandals incubated by the dominant logic	Crony Capitalism, corruption, bribery of state officials and capture of political parties	Collusions, frauds, stakeholders abused, insider trading, environmental damage, Controlling shareholders abuses Economic growth derived from rally of commodities (1998–2014)	Increased exposure to stakeholders' demands, complaints and extorsions Mass protests

(continued)

Table 2 (continued)

6Cs—Sociological Family Capturing the ongoing basic social process in LA	*AUTARKY 1938—1989 ISI Model Crisis, Military Dictatorships, Political intervention of Economy and Society*	*LIBERALIZATION 1990 - > onwards Washington Consensus "Lost Decade" 1989–2000, Democracy recovered, Privatization-Marketization, Commodities Boom 2000–14*	*SOCIAL UNREST 2011 - onwards, peaking in 2019 Immigrations 2015–21, Middle Income Trap, End of tolerance of Corruption, Discrimination, and Inequality*
Consequences: Key governing gap faced by main governing actors	Coopting, controlling, and aligning the powers-that-be affecting business	Surviving, efficiency, growing, and maximizing value for shareholders	Business Legitimacy vis-à-vis a transparent, distrusting and interconnected society, political sophistication

Source Jiménez-Seminario/Díaz Le-Fort

industries. Therefore, this period can be characterized as intensely political, with dirigiste States and often accompanied by military governments or strong charismatic leaders, intervening directly in economic and social affairs. Therefore, this suggests that a political logic was predominant in a somewhat autarkic period up until 1982. The consequences of crony capitalism, of governments picking winners, bribery, and the corporate capture of political parties, were natural consequences of such a state of things. Until, that is, things could go no further, given the massive crisis of the Debt in 1982, which required strong structural adjustments.

The Argentinian and Brazilian scandals profiled in this book show a clear lineage or genealogy inherited from the ISI times, with government officers intervening in favor of their protégés or bending the rules to provide state-guaranteed rents. This also stresses the relevance of State-owned enterprises as both a source of state influence and strongholds of the powers-that-be. Therefore, in this period *governance* becomes associated with *Resource-Dependence Theories* (Pfeffer, XX), by which companies protect their turf or capture State protection. This is mainly done through public–private deal-making and the presence of conspicuous former political actors on the boards of directors.

3.1 *Economic Institutional Logic (1989—onwards)*

Just as the experience of Korea, Taiwan, Hong-Kong, and Singapore provided a strong enhancement to sustain the ISI model in the 1970's (Bustelo, 1992), the economic success of the Chilean "*neoliberal* experiment," followed by the conservative revolution by Reagan and Thatcher in the 1980's, combined with the Debt Crisis, propelled the push forward to experiment with this new economic model. This new economic viewpoint was associated with the *Washington Consensus* decalogue, uniting the IMF, the WORLD BANK, as well as the US TREASURY conditions to help Latin American countries in restructuring their economies after the Debt Crisis.

The *Washington Consensus* proposed by British economist John Williamson in 1989, brought together the fiscal discipline, export-orientation, capital market liberalization, privatization, and deregulation required by the global financial sheriffs to help Latin America get back on a square footing.

Thus, the progressive opening up of Latin American economies came as soon as 1990. Argentina was the first to open its economy under President Carlos Menem, quickly followed by Mexico in 1991, Peru in 1992, Colombia in 1994, and finally Brazil in 1998. A ready reckoner to establish the liberalization of each national economy is the year of the privatization of the State-owned energy and telecoms enterprises, as well as each country's privatized pension programs (with the exception of Brazil).

Pro-market economic policies were put in place and the globalization process propelled a drive for increasing competitiveness and efficiency. Thus, *governance* became surviving, maximizing profits, and growing by any and all means.

The key players in this period are both traditional and new business groups, who committed to the the privatization processes carried out across the region, *multilatina* corporations, financiers, and bankers, some of them close to governing political parties. However, in different countries there were also diverse active catalyzers. For instance, in Brazil, SAO PAULO STOCK EXCHANGE (BOVESPA) and the local equivalent to the American SEC (CMV), played major roles as institutional entrepreneurs.[5]

[5] See Chapter VII Brazil

In addition, this stage had a powerful external catalyst in the rally in commodity prices, propelled by the economic growth of China, creating a huge wave for Latin American exporters of raw materials and minerals to surf between 1998 and 2014.

Naturally, some of the drawbacks of these important market-focused policies and the ensuing processes of accelerated growth encouraged the emergence of cases of collusion, insider trading, environmental damage, and stakeholder abuses, so setting the stage to move on to a third wave of *governing* gaps.

3.2 Social Institutional Logic (2011—onwards, Peaking in 2019)

In 2011, the world experienced unheard of social explosions that took it by storm—from Brazil to Bolivia, Mexico to Morocco and much of the Middle East. In Latin America the root causes are still not completely understood, but centuries-old inequality, poverty, discrimination, political scandals, corporate abuses, racism, indigenous rebellions are seen as primary contributors to this social upheaval. All of this exacerbated through the emerging, better educated, demanding, and challenging younger generations.

The peak of this process occurred in 2019, when multiple social groups took to the streets, dominated the news, and began putting pressures on political players to make change happen. Since then, mitigated partially by the COVID pandemic, the jury is still out on how and what changes will be implemented. However, the social agenda has become a major part of the challenge of organizational *governing* and a new "*governing gap*" needs to be understood to begin taking appropriate action.

Thus, the key current players are social movements, and business is struggling for its legitimacy vis-à-vis a demanding, challenging, and unforgiving society with the power to act, the determination to make itself heard and significant levels of mistrust.

Just like in the Chilean case, the three waves are not replacing each other, but are merging or sometimes dominating others, but always in a combined fashion, increasing exponentially the complexity of *governing*. Thus, boards of directors need to be critically aware of the three institutional pillars to be considered in their performance and conforming activities, namely, meeting their fiduciary responsibilities (finding out what the problem is); their strategic role (establishing what their action plan should be); and, even more critically, designing their generative role (asking themselves what questions they need to ask as governing bodies).

Therefore, we can confidently state that Latin America is constantly ***minding its governing gap*** and will most likely remain in such a mode for some time to come.

4 Conclusions and Perspective of Latin American Corporate Governing Evolution

Having presented three superimposed paradigms, synthesizing the evolution of corporate governing evolution in Latin America, it is as well to consider where the Sub-continent is heading. As such, what might be the next wave affecting corporate governing in the region, which takes us into prospective analysis, where some evidence is already in place.

The COVID-19 pandemic has not only shown just how interconnected we are globally, but it has also brought an acceleration of remote communications, making this a "smaller" world. Thus, corporate governing is facing a new institutional logic associated with globalization—a 4th paradigm—building out of the earlier three.

Figure 2 summarizes the regional history and provides an outlook for the future, including a snapshot of the potential beneficial effects of the UN's *Sustainable Development Goals*. The ESG implications promise to have a positive influence in the quality of corporate governing in the region.

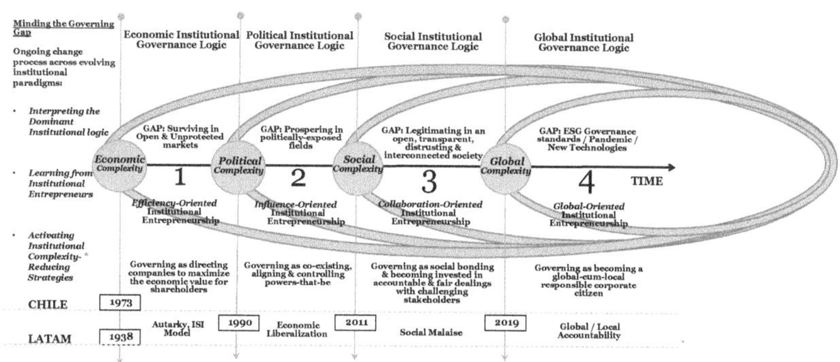

Fig. 2 Paradigms in LATAM Corporate Governing Evolution (*Source* Díaz Le-Fort & Jiménez-Seminario, adapted from Jiménez, 2018)

As seen, the next emerging paradigm might well be ***Global Institutional Logic***, where ÷ candidates may be threefold:

- the endemic pandemic, which may stay for a very long time that has accelerated the globalization through digitalization and makes global trends travel faster, facilitating corporate governing convergences
- the ESG global standards, increasingly required by influential impact investors, whose ideas are even penetrating the largest investment funds of the world, although they have become contested recently and may derive into another kind of sustainability metrics and consistent expectations (place footnote: The Economist, 2022, https://www.economist.com/weeklyedition/2022-07-23 accessed August, 9th, 2022);
- the increasing comparability of corporate governing practices and the potencial emergence of eventual globally accepted principles; and. (next bullet) the challenges posed by new AI technology, which are introducing an increasing level of transparency, facilitating accountability

Social issues such as inequality, climate change and overpopulation, as well as the burning challenges posed by uncontrolled immigration, are other key difficulties challenging the basis of individualism and neoliberalism.

The conclusion seems to be that global problems require global solutions. And corporate governing cannot avoid them. Again this calls for global corporate governing principles (footnote/reference: OCDE (2016), Principios de Gobierno Corporativo de la OCDE y del G20, Éditions OCDE, Paris.https://doi.org/10.1787/9789264259171

The previous and next chapters show the measures being developed in the six countries under study as well as the particular gaps, institutional entrepreneurs, and advances to date.

As a final point, and to conclude on a more optimistic note, in spite of the difficulties, we can still affirm that scandals remain a wake-up call to act, as they pressure for improved regulations and, in baby steps, better practices, up-dated mindsets, and push big business to become more responsible corporate citizens, so contributing to society as a whole.

References

Azcona, J. M., & Sierra, J. R. (2019). Historia de las guerrillas en América Latina. Los Libros de La Catarata.

Baer, W. (1972). Import substitution and industrialization in Latin America: Experiences and interpretations. *Latin American Research Review, 7*(1), 95–122. https://www.bcg.com/publications/2018/why-multilatinas-hold-key-latin-america-economic-future

Becker, G. "Crime and Punishment: an economic approach" JPE Vol. 76, No.2 (Mar-Apr 1968) pp. 169–217.

Bértola, L., & Ocampo, A. (2012). Latin America's debt crisis and "lost decade".

Bethell, L. (1992). Historia de América Latina, Vol. 6 y 7, Barcelona. Crítica, Cambridge University Press.

Bulmer-Thomas, V. (2017). La historia económica de América Latina desde la independencia. Fondo de cultura económica.

Bustelo, Pablo (1992). "The Misconceptions of «Development Economics", *Finance and Development*, Vol. 22, No. 2, June 1985.

CEPAL, N. (2004). Una década de desarrollo social en América Latina, 1990–1999.

Chait, R. P., Ryan, W. P., & Taylor, B. E. (2011). *Governance as leadership: Reframing the work of nonprofit boards*. John Wiley & Sons.

Ciclos, A7io]], Vol.]], No. 2, ler. semestre de 1992 La industria en periodos de transición. La industrialización en América Latina y el Este de Asia: una comparación entre Brasil y Taiwan, 1930–1980 Pablo Bustelo.

Correa Sutil, S., Figueroa Garavagno, M. C., Jocelyn-Holt Letelier, A., Rolle Cruz, C., & Vicuña Urrutia, M. (2001). Historia del siglo XX chileno: balance paradojal.

De Castro, S. (1992). El ladrillo: bases de la política económica del gobierno militar chileno.

Economic Commission for Latin America and the Caribbean, strongly influenced by the Argentinean economist, Raúl Prebisch.

Glaser, B. G., & Strauss, A. L. (1967). *The discovery of Grounded theory: Strategies for qualitative research*. Aldine Publishing Company.

Glaser, B. (1992). *Basics of grounded theory analysis*. Sociology Press.

Jiménez, G. (2018). *Minding the corporate governing gap: The instititional construction of corporate governance in Chile*, doctoral dissertation, University of Liverpool.

Lal, D. "The poverty of development economics" (London, 1983)

Linz, J. J., & de la fé, T. G. (1990). Transiciones a la democracia. Reis, 7–33.

O'Donnell, G. (1988). *Bureaucratic authoritarianism*. University of California Press.

Ranis, G. "Contra Deardorff's glossary of international economics in the political economy of development policy change", in G. Gereffi & D. L. Wyman (eds.),

"Manufacturing Mir Deardorff's Glossary of International Economics acles. Paths of Industrialization in Latin America and East Asia" (Princeton, 1990), pp. 207–230.
Ranis, G. "Employment, income distribution and growth in the East Asian Context: A comparative analysis", en V. Corbo, A. O. Krueger y F. Ossa (eds.), "Export Oriented Development Strategies. The Success of Newly Industrializing Countries" (Boulder, Co., 1985), pp. 249·274
Ranis, G. y Orrock, L. "Latin America and East Asian NICs: Development strategies compared", in E. Durán (ed.), *Latin America and the World Recession* (Cambridge, 1985), pp. 48.66.
Ocampo, J. A. (2009). Latin America and the global financial crisis. *Cambridge Journal of Economics, 33*(4), 703–724.
Ocampo, J. A. (2017). Commodity-led development in Latin America. In *Alternative pathways to sustainable development: Lessons from Latin America* (pp. 51–76). Brill Nijhoff.
Ponce, A. F. (2006). Openness and foreign direct investment: The role of free trade agreements in Latin America.
Prebisch, R. (1949). El desarrollo económico de la América Latina y algunos de sus principales problemas= The economic development of Latin America and its principal problems.
Salazar, G. (2012). Movimientos sociales en Chile: Trayectoria histórica y proyección política (Vol. 3). Uqbar.
Taylor, M. (2006). *From Pinochet to the Third Way: Neoliberalism and social transformation in Chile*. Pluto Press.
Toussaint, E. (2006). La crisis de la deuda mexicana y el Banco Mundial. Comité para la Abolición de la Deuda del Tercer Mundo, 1–6.
Williamson, J. (1990). The Washington Consensus. Washington, DC.
Zanatti, M. M., Bucheli, M., & Lluch, A. (Eds.), (2021). Historia Empresarial en América Latina: temas, debates y problemas. Universidad del Pacífico.

PART II

Country Chapters

CHAPTER 6

Argentina

Hugo Gaggiotti, María de los Ángeles Lucero Bringas, and Ismail Adelopo

1 Introduction

The objective of this chapter is to provide a critical account of the evolution of corporate governance in Argentina. Corporate governance has remained a popular issue given the increasing global awareness about corporate misbehaviors of alarming proportions, including but not limited to the cases of ENRON, WorldCom, and Parmalat. The speed of their occurrence, implications, and the multi-layered dimensions of responses,

H. Gaggiotti (✉) · I. Adelopo
Faculty of Business and Law, University of the West of England, Bristol, UK
e-mail: hugo.gaggiotti@uwe.ac.uk

I. Adelopo
e-mail: ismail.adelopo@uwe.ac.uk

M. de los Ángeles Lucero Bringas
Faculty of Business and Economics, Universidad Católica de Córdoba, Córdoba, Argentina
e-mail: angeleslucerobringas@gmail.com

J. Callund et al. (eds.), *Corporate Governing in Latin America*,
https://doi.org/10.1007/978-3-030-85780-6_6

arguably are some of the reasons that have made corporate governance discourse relevant, poignant, and enduring. If we narrow the meaning of corporate governance to the suggestion that it is simply the "way corporations are run", then the predominant considerations around shareholder's primacy and the fundamental debates about the principal-agent dichotomy may be relevant and sufficient. While the development of the discourse on corporate governance seems to emerge from the misdemeanor of the corporate world, its implications are beyond the corporate precincts. In fact, its antecedents, as we would argue in this chapter, seem grounded in the institutional fabrics of the context, in our case, the Argentinian case. Allowing a minimalist view of corporate governance will no doubt leave many governance issues unaddressed. Such perspectives will not only be limiting, but it may also be misleading. Even in Anglo-Saxon contexts, it is now realized that corporations are constituents of multiple competing objectives and interests, and cultural and management traditions play a crucial role in how corporations are managed. This means that the days of the single bottom-line, i.e., supreme focus on profitability, seem numbered, given the ascendance of the *triple bottom-line* discourses, at least in spirit if not yet in action. Thus, shareholder supremacy, as frequently espoused in agency theory, is rightly, giving way to stakeholder theoretical perspectives.

Yet, as corporations assume global prominence and expand their influences into diverse jurisdictions due to globalization and the impact of technology, the Anglo-Saxon conceptualization of corporate governance is vigorously challenged, becoming apparently inadequate, giving way to broader and context specific ideas of how corporations are, and should be run. In this sense, there are emerging discourses around country—based and institutionalized constructions of corporate governance. Directly related to this is the role of ethics, values, culture, political, and economic institutional arrangements that are context specific and dynamic. The argument being that these institutional arrangements are crucial. They shape the nature of corporate governance architecture in places and provide the foundation for the effectiveness or otherwise of laws and regulations. In other words, corporate failures are symptomatic of broader institutional and political failures.

This suggests that a better approach would be to consider corporate governance as part of the mechanisms within the broader institutional and organizational settings (Adelopo & Rufai, 2018). In this way, corporate governance discourse reflects the wider concerns in a context. Although risky, this allows a holistic approach to governance and a reflection of the organizational reality in a context. It is in this way that the root causes of corporate failures will enjoy proper attention rather than superficial treatment. This institutional and organizational construction of corporate governing is missing in the vast amount of corporate governance literature. This literature has given far too much prominence to the positivist and deductive-quantitative analytical approaches to corporate governance to the detriment of the other methods of enquiry in the field.

This study addresses part of these gaps by approaching corporate governance in a unique context: Argentina. Argentina is a noteworthy case for the study of corporate governance because of its paradoxical and extreme circumstances (Gaggiotti, 2012). It was one of the world's ten wealthiest nations between 1880 and 1930; and represented a fully integrated economy in the global market of commodities for almost 200 years. Based on GDP, it is currently the third-largest economy in Latin America and has ranked among the top 30 economies of the world for the past decade (World Bank, 2010; IMF, 2010). Argentina was the preferred destination for foreign investment and corporate expansion by many MNCs between 1989 and 2002. However, this unrestricted access partly accounts for the collapse of over 82,000 local SMEs in the country. The economic prognosis of the country at the turn of the 21st century was precarious with a 21% unemployment rate and more than 11 million people below the poverty line (Cortés Conde, 2003). Nowadays, Argentina has one of the least developed stock markets in Latin America, approximately 200 companies are registered on the Argentina Stock Exchange, 0.01% of the firms registered.

Corporate Argentina mirrors the political and economic situation in the country. Corporate governance practices are largely non-existent and at best really, emergent. Until 1991, there was almost a monopoly of family-owned companies in Argentina (between more than 80% of SMEs and 100% of MNCs, following the Inter-American Development Bank). This characteristic gave a particular local meaning to words like "governance," "trust," and "ethics". However, Apreda (2001) observed a rapid increase in foreign ownership of most big family companies in the early 1990s. Foreign groups and investment funds expanded their ownership imposing their own corporate governance practices, in a clear indication of mistrust in the local practices of corporate governance. Following a similar pattern in other Latin American economies, Argentina was ambivalent when adopting corporate governance practices developed internationally, particularly in Anglo-Saxon countries. Argentina initiated its own corporate governance reforms, sometimes following international codes sometimes not, either because of internally promoted reforms inspired by nationalistic ideologies or in response to international demands (Briano Turrent & Saavedra García, 2015). The absence of a national corporate governance guidance in the country seems to aggravate the tensions in many corporations with significant foreign ownership as they attempt to harmonize their home country corporate governance systems with the Argentinian corporate structures dominated by family businesses.

The effects of this collision of dual practices that are alternatively implemented—a very local South American / Rioplatense / Argentinian one, based on SMEs, Argentinian politics, and customary practices of corporate governance, and a global, standardized Euro/Asian/American, based on MNCs and international standards—are still unknown. Argentina is indeed an under-researched context within the corporate governance literature, despite being a unique historical case from which to study how governance practices could be implemented and ignored periodically.

Exploring the ways in which ethical organizational ambivalence, as a social phenomenon with wider implications in other spheres of life, is contriving to shape the evolution of corporate governance in the Argentinian context could be illuminating to understand other cases in Latin America and abroad. Our intention in this chapter is to bring the Argentinian society into the spotlight in terms of its cultural and institutional arrangements, their functionality, and the multiple forces that shape corporations and how these forces affect corporate governing and development.

2 Organizational Roots of Corporate Management

A way of approaching the status of corporate governance in Argentina is to analyze the corporate antecedents of the country (Briozzo et al., 2008). The Argentinian corporate arena is dominated by family businesses managed by closely knit family members, friends, and allies. Trust is a central part of this management arrangement. Consequently, management by non-family members or independent outsiders is very rare due to mistrust. Even large multinational corporations such as ARCOR still maintain their family presence on the board.[1]

Mainstream literature (Gutierrez & Marcos, 2018; Kraakman, 2017; Suess-Reyes, 2017) suggests that implementing active governance bodies based on family links contributes to trust, much more than considering the continuity of the family business in which family bonds, relations, and networking are based solely on trust. However, it is not clear that applying the basic principles of governance and management will favor transparency in decision-making and control in Argentina's organizations. It could indeed be that the recurrent Argentinian crises could be explained by the fact of the impossibility to apply mainstream corporate governance approaches, instead of making "trust" the main ethos of governing outside of the family business. The case of Argentina has been described by Colazingari and Rose-Ackerman (1998) as a "paternalistic democracy," where family social ethos ("father," "mother," and even "family" became concepts to explain the social and the organizational) underpins any other organizational practices; management and governing even transcend government policies and legal practices. Etcheverry and Manóvil (2013) suggested that mistrust and uncertainty is common in Argentina because there is no unique legal or regulatory framework that provides a consistent definition of corporate governance.

It is true that, as Adnan and Ahmed (2019) argued, there is no single corporate governance model. Shen and Gentry (2014) pointed out that governance depends on strategic management models. Among the two widely acknowledged corporate governance approaches, i.e., the Anglo-American model and the central European model. The former is oriented toward the management practices of shareholders or the market, while the latter focuses on the management practices of parties or relationships (Ahmad & Omar, 2016). The central European model emphasizes the relationships between the firm and controlling shareholders, with financing being less dependent on the capital market than on banks. It is

[1] The number one company in Argentina, the multinational ARCOR, tried for years to recruit an external CEO. The third generation of founders (the company was founded in 1951 but its origins date from 1924) are still in charge of the daily management of the company even though an alliance with COCA-COLA was signed in 2010. This similarly happened with TECHINT, now a global MNCs, founded in 1945, where a fourth generation of managers of the same family still run the company. In both cases, the origins of the corporations were constructed as ancient stories of Italian founders. Mistrust in non-family ties was a common practice when governance these corporations.

possible to situate the corporate governance practices in Argentina within a permanent tension between the two or within ad-hoc local models based on ideological and political contexts.

Another aspect to highlight to evaluate the applicability of a corporate governance model in a particular case is to consider the degree of development of the market in which it is immersed. In this sense, Argentina is usually considered an emerging economy with a developed non-consolidated market, in permanent fluctuation and change. Usually, emerging economies have tried to adopt the legal system of developed countries, particularly the Anglo-Saxon system, either due to internally promoted reforms or in response to international demands. However, Argentina has oscillated between implementing alternative models or justify the no implementation of any model based on local circumstances.

Unlike developed markets where the share capital is atomized, the quality of the investors is institutional, and there is asymmetry between the investor and the management, this is characterized by transparency, accountability, and abundant information. In (still) developing non-consolidated markets such as Argentina's, capital ownership is concentrated, companies are characterized by being family-controlled and closed, the control agents are clearly defined, the owners and management are exercised by the same network of people, the information is scarce and there is low protection to minority shareholders.

3 The Legal Framework for Corporate Governance

The first article of Argentina's National Constitution defines the country as a representative, republican, and federal state. A Federal Government and 24-districts coexist, the latter made up of 23-provinces plus the Autonomous City of Buenos Aires, which is also the Capital of the Nation.

As in most federal republics, Argentina has a presidential system of government with a division of powers between the National Executive, the Legislative and the Judiciary arms of the government. The judiciary administers justice and adjudicates in the spirit and letter of the constitution. The legislative arm of government makes law for the smooth running of the country. Argentina maintains a bicameral legislative house—made up of a Chamber of Deputies and another of Senators. The Regulations applying to companies relate to corporate, bankruptcy, labor, tax, and criminal law. The specific regulations, that regulate who is responsible for the activity of a company, are found in what is called "the company law," in its articles 59, 266, 269, 270, and 274. The legal narrative of these articles is not unlike the provisions found in other Latin American countries. Even when the statutory provision may be made for the existence, for example, of an executive committee made up of the same directors for the management of common businesses, or when general or special managers are appointed, the responsibility of the management body—the board of directors—remains unaltered or unchanged.

4 A Chronological Account of Corporate Governance

The emergence of corporate governance gathered pace in the 1990s, following a raft of corporate failures around the globe (Morck, 2007). Argentina was not excluded from these discussions or for seeking an international standard to define the implementation of corporate governance. As in many other countries, the implementation of the emerging standards and market regulation was through the creation of independent national bodies and through implementing or modifying regulations based on individual cases, such as listed companies, but not on all Argentine companies. The National Securities Commission (Comisión Nacional de Valores, CNV) was founded as the official body to oversee the promotion, supervision, and control of the Argentine securities markets. Although an independent entity, it depends on the Secretary of Finance of the Argentine Ministry of Finance. Hence, political power always permeates CNV practices. As declared in its founding declaration, the intention of the CNV is "*to **protect** investors and promote the development of a **transparent**, inclusive, and sustainable capital market that contributes to the economic and social progress of the country*" (emphasis added). That said, it was not until 70 years after its foundation that the National Securities Commission (Comisión Nacional de Valores, CNV, see Table 1) first attempted to regulate the practice of corporate governance, as it did through a national decree (677/2001).

The decree had its origins in the analysis of corporate governance practices in Latin America, carried out by investment banks in the United States. The study was motivated by knowing what the latest reforms in these countries had been in relation to the election of their directors,

Table 1 Argentine National Securities Commission (CNV)

1937	The National Securities Commission was established, dependent on the Central Bank of the Argentine Republic and with functions of an advisory nature
1946	It is ratified by Law No. 13,894. Decree No. 15,353 creates the National Securities Commission, made up of representatives of the Central Bank
1968	Through Law No. 17,811, of a federal nature, the National Securities Commission was created as an organized state division, as a national independent entity of a technical nature, with jurisdiction over the entire territory of the Nation
1969	As of January 1, Law No. 17,811 comes into force, regulating in its entirety the securities market, covering the public offering, the organization and operation of the stock exchange institutions and the actions of stockbrokers and other people dedicated to trading securities
2001	National Decree 677/2001 was promulgated. The main intention was to guarantee "transparency" and "trust"
2012	On November 29, Law No. 26,831 on the Capital Market was enacted, repealing the two previous basic regulations, Law No. 17,811, and Decree No. 677/01, as well as other secondary provisions. The purpose of Law 26,831 was the development of the Capital Market in an equitable, efficient, and transparent manner, protecting the interests of the investing public, minimizing systemic risk, and promoting healthy and free competition
2018	On May 9, the Productive Financing Law No. 27,440 was enacted, which modernizes and completes the regulatory framework of the Argentinian capital market, providing it with instruments with a direct impact on the real economy, such as financial trusts for mortgage loans, common funds of closed investment and new instruments for SMEs

Source www.cnv.org

governance, and regulation for the public offering of listed companies. Trust and confidence were part of the core discourse of the decree:

> That it is necessary to ensure the full validity of the rights enshrined in article 42 of the national constitution, establishing a statute of the rights of the "financial consumer", fundamentally addressing the aspects of transparency in the field of Public Offering, and advancing in the establishment of an adequate legal framework that increases the level of protection of the saver in the capital market.
>
> That the natural objectives of financial markets are to promote their own development, favor their liquidity, stability, solvency, and transparency, and create mechanisms that allow guaranteeing the efficient allocation of savings to investment.

> That said purposes derive from the main objective of creating the "confidence" and "security" necessary to lower the cost of capital and increase the financing of companies.
>
> That in recent years there have been phenomena such as the greater relative importance of the private sector in the creation of wealth, the emergence of the so-called "institutional investors" as main agents in the channeling of savings and the dissociation of the ownership of companies regarding your address.
>
> That in this context, awareness has been promoted worldwide about the importance of having adequate corporate governance practices and a regulatory framework that legally enshrines principles such as "full information" "transparency", "efficiency", "protection of the investing public", equal treatment between investors and the protection and the stability of financial entities and intermediaries".
>
> That, in this sense, the legal uncertainty created by non-transparent regimes or systems where the legal framework or its applicability are deficient, causes a distortion in the savings and investment decisions of economic agents, affecting their choice in favor of liquid assets with less risk.
>
> In this way, inadequate levels of protection "weaken" financial systems, driving savers towards safer markets. (Decree 677/2001)

Decree 677/2001 inspired other legal initiatives, such as, in 2004, the Argentine Institute for the Government of Organizations (IAGO), a body created jointly by the Business Foundation for Quality and Excellence (FUNDECE) and the Institute for Business Development (IDEA), that developed the *Code of Best Corporate Governance Practices* for the Argentine Republic (IAGO, 2004). This Code provided guidelines for better administration and control of companies with the aim to increase their market value. They were a set of rules aimed at generating transparency, facilitating access to the capital market, improving business management and risks, reducing transaction costs, and allowing the identification and resolution of conflicts of interest. Although the original intention of the code was to be applied to companies with a public offering, its implementation was recommended to any kind of business organization.

Despite numerous attempts to standardize governance practices, it was not until 2007 that the CNV approved, through the Regulation RG No. 516, a list with the minimum contents of the *Corporate Governance Code* (CGS). The CGS covers the critical issues regarding transparency and governing that companies must include to take their shares public. Among the most notable points were those relating to the board of directors in general and its degree of independence, the relationship with shareholders and the community in general.

In 2012, the CNV, in its resolution No. 606, modified the Regulation RG No. 516 and required companies to incorporate the *Code of Corporate Governance*, including in their reports financial statement analysis, together with self-evaluations of corporate governance and the degree of compliance with the standards proposed by the CNV. Companies were asked to explain the reasons in case of non-compliance.

Resolution No. 606 sets out the following principles:

1. Make transparent the relationship between the issuer, the economic group that is part of it and its related parties.
2. Lay the foundations for the solid administration and supervision of the issuer.
3. Endorse an effective policy for the identification, measurement, administration, and disclosure of business risk.
4. Safeguard the integrity of financial information with independent audits.
5. Respect the rights of shareholders.
6. Maintain a direct and responsible link with the community.
7. Remunerate fairly and responsibly.
8. Promote business ethics.
9. Deepen the scope of the code.

The main intention of resolution No 606 was to increase transparency of both the company and the market, with the assumption that transparency promotes healthy competition. Private consultancies started to operate in Argentina developing indices rating the "degree of good governance" of companies (Corzo, 2016). In particular, the Center for Financial Stability (CEF) developed the *Transparency and Dissemination Index* (ITD) measuring quantitatively the evolution of corporate governance for each of the Argentine companies who decided to adhere to the resolution.

The initiative had an impact in the following years in a broad spectrum of Argentine organizations and management bodies. At the end of 2016, the first meeting of the CORPORATE GOVERNANCE WORKING GROUP (GTGT) took place in Argentina, led by the director of the CNV. The main objective of the meeting was to coordinate different interest groups and the implementation and strengthening of the Corporate Principles of the OECD and the Group of Twenty (G20). Among those who participated in the meeting were the Undersecretary Representative of the OECD and members of the INSTITUTE OF BUSINESS AND PUBLIC GOVERNANCE (IGEP), the ARGENTINE INSTITUTE FOR THE GOVERNMENT OF ORGANIZATIONS (IAGO) and the INSTITUTE FOR BUSINESS DEVELOPMENT OF ARGENTINA (IDEA). Private consultancy firms and business research institutes were also active participants. Among others were the Business Foundation for Quality and Excellence (FUNDECE), the CHAMBER OF STOCK COMPANIES, CAPITAL MARKET ACADEMY, the PwC Chair of Governance of Organizations of the IAE BUSINESS SCHOOL, the ETHICS AND COMPLIANCE ASSOCIATION and FOUNDATION FOR LEADERSHIP AND RESPONSIBLE ORGANIZATIONS (FLOR).[2]

At the end of 2016, Argentina became an associate member within the *Corporate Governance Committee* of the OECD (OECD, 2020). Under this framework, the Director of the CNV followed the economic political agenda of President Macri: to use corporate governing as an economic discourse to improve the performance and development of Argentine companies and to encourage national and foreign investment in the country. The economic agenda was dominated by the integration of Argentina into the global markets and economy and to join the OECD. In President Macri's speech, he stressed that Corporate Governance was synonymous with leadership and good management practices that ultimately rely on good decision-making. Demonstrable good decision-making, following President Macri's line of thinking (who was a businessman before having been elected president) would improve the capacity of Argentina for foreign investment.

At the beginning of 2017, the CORPORATE GOVERNANCE WORKING GROUP had a second meeting looking at the following issues:

1. To create a culture of corporate governance and transmit its advantages and value.

[2] https://www.flor.org.ar/en/2017.

2. To disseminate the principles of the OECD and other references of good international practices.
3. To update the standards according to international practices, adapting them to the Argentine reality.
4. To generate training mechanisms for directors, managers, executives, external, and internal auditors.
5. To increase diversity on the boards and attract local, and foreign investors.

The same year, the Minister of Finance presented to the Secretary General of the OECD, Argentina's Plan of Action during a bilateral meeting during the G20 meeting in Buenos Aires. The plan included a series of actions with active participation of OECD experts and Argentine officials to strengthen public policies and efforts to implement reforms on corporate governing, transparency, and anti-corruption policies. The main points of the reform relate to economic policies, statistics, competition, investment, federalism, public governing and modernization of the state, regional development and multilevel governing, the fight against corruption, education and skills, and digital education. In 2018, Argentina received active support from the OECD in its vision of "Building consensus for equitable and sustainable development" and the corporate governance agenda looked firmly established as a government policy.

5 Argentina as an Emerging Country for Emerging Corporate Governance

We must not lose sight of the fact that corporations and companies compete with other institutions for the allocation, ownership, and use of the social resources of a community. The environment in which they operate is an essential component. The context in which companies operate in emerging countries is central to understanding their reality.

Argentina does not escape these characterizations as an emerging country. In Argentina, there is no important development on this issue—not in academia nor in the industry. The underdeveloped market (a capital market that is not significant in terms of traded volumes) and stocks as relevant investment alternatives mean that good corporate governance practices and their recommendations are not considered important. Some internal codes or standards are observed in multinational corporations with a presence in the country mainly in keeping with the expectations of their home countries.

An approximation of the difference in contexts between developed and an emerging market such as Argentina can be gleaned from five important indicators identified below:

a. *Shareholder interests*: In emerging countries, there is a concentration of shareholdings, generally in families or family groups where compared to developed markets where shareholding is dispersed and there are sophisticated investors including institutional investors. Therefore, the key differentiating factor is the concentration of ownership.
b. *Independence*: The boards of directors as governing bodies are closed and internal and only represent the interests of shareholders to groups in emerging countries. Open and non-executive boards characterize corporations from core countries where the interests they represent are varied and broad belonging to different classes of investors. The key characteristic of this criterion is the dependence on management and control of share ownership.
c. *Capital Markets*: The development of capital markets shows great differences between countries and the context regarding investments and access to capital. In emerging countries, there is poor development of these markets and few takeovers, as well as little active IPOs. In fact, when companies with potential appear in these countries, they quickly carry out their IPOs in markets such as Wall Street or Nasdaq to obtain funds for their development. The defining characteristic of this criterion is the ease of access to capital.
d. *Transparency*: This is a key aspect for the relationship of corporations with their environment. The dissemination of information in the developed economies is wide and easily accessible by individuals. The key aspect is information management.
e. *Responsibility*: The protection of minority holdings is a differential between developed and emerging countries. In the latter, there is a manifest lack of protection of minority holdings. Legal certainty is the aspect that defines this criterion.

5.1 Corporate Governance and the Private Sector

Unlike in the developed countries, there are no recognized codes of good practice in Argentina. The norms arise from the regulations, basically in the legal framework and in terms of the government and its organs, the laws address issues related to shareholders and their assemblies, as well as the board of directors and directors. There is no legislation governing a CEO and management.

As was said, the capital market is underdeveloped and the MVA (the basic indicator of a country's level of industrialization adjusted for the size of the economy)/GDP (Gross Domestic Product) ratio in comparison with those of developed countries of little relevance. These issues are aggravated by currency instability and periodic devaluations that cause the value of companies to fluctuate constantly so making difficult the comparison of trends and patterns.

Closely held companies are characterized by the lack of disclosure of their financial statements and information regarding their evolution and performance. These shortcomings arise from a lack of any need to go to financial markets to raise funds, where knowledge of that information is essential and mandated. At the same time, the election of board members is limited to a small circle, generally made up of trusted family members or employees.

Publicly listed companies are regulated by the National Securities Commission, which is the body that controls and regulates the local capital market and, consequently, the activities of the companies that make their shares public in terms of information, transparency, control, audits, etc. Control is carried out based on the regulatory framework established for this class of companies. The integration of the governing bodies is more open to people of diverse origins. Majorities and minorities in the shareholders' meeting are respected, as well as shareholdings of different classes. The boards include minority representatives.

The control bodies in Argentina are represented by the appointment of a sindicato (trustee)—a figure that oversees the interests of the shareholders or by the shareholders themselves, depending on criteria in the legislation. For large companies, the sindicato is replaced by a collegiate body or Supervisory Commission, as established in the company law. There are no mandatory commissions within the boards relating to the control of financial statements and auditing carried out by of independent directors as there are under the Sarbanes Oxley Act in the United States.

5.2 *Corporate Governing and the Public Sector*

In Argentina, there are companies wholly or partially owned by the state. In a brief classification, companies called Sociedades Estatales (state corporations), which operate as true joint-stock companies in which the total share ownership belongs to the Argentine state. There are also sociedades de economía mixta (Mixed economic corporations) that are made up of state entities and private entities, their operation is regulated by special laws. Interstate, binational companies or companies that are in a process of liquidation overseen by a state intervenor can also be included in this classification.

Some companies with a majority State participation, which are true public limited companies, are listed on the stock market (such as YPF or HIPOTECARIO BANK), have private participation in the composition of the shareholder. As for capital, it is that the property and the votes correspond to the majority of 51% to be able to form the social will. As of 2018, there were 41 of these companies, in that year Administrative Decision 85/2018 of the Chief of the Cabinet of Ministers was promulgated, which is called *Good Governance Guidelines for Companies with Majority State Participation*, and established a set of recommended good practices for this class of companies.[3] This fact is a milestone because good practices include those developed by the so-called listed companies where the public is associated with the private in terms of parameters of efficiency, transparency, information, etc.

As for the governing bodies in the companies indicated above, they operate through representatives of the state in the case of the shareholder meetings. In turn, directors are appointed by the corresponding state agencies and are considered public officials whose conduct is judged by public ethics laws.

5.3 *The Organizational Limits of Corporate Governance in Argentina*

In Argentina the capital market is small, as in many of the developing countries. The use of corporate governance concepts, usually based on the implementation for listed companies, has always been associated with

[3] BO/14-2-2018.

companies from developed countries. However, the use and encouragement of private and SMEs to implement corporate governance practices is growing. Many of the initiatives that emerge from the business sector are those that see benefits in their implementation.

Corporate governing practices in companies arise as a response to providing transparency and trust to management and control groups, who on occasions would have been accused in Argentina of abuse of power to the detriment of the rest of the investors and impeding sustained development. There is a growing perception in Argentina that by implanting corporate governance practices, not only will the performance of the companies themselves be optimized, but also the abuses of those who run them restricted. Corporate governance practices in Argentina are usually associated with the potential reduction of inter and intra organizational corruption.

5.4 *Corporate Governance Practices in Argentina: Non-political Mediated Initiatives*

According to Andrea Grobocopatel, a member of the family business Grobocopatel Hermanos SA. founded in 1967 and devoted to the commercialization and collection of cereals and oilseeds, the main motivations to follow the path of Corporate Governance practices lie in the possibility of accessing capital or reducing its cost, achieving better operating results, giving an accurate response to market pressures, achieving a correct risk analysis through efficient supervision and control, balancing the divergent interests of shareholders (a factor of great relevance especially in family businesses) and to fundamentally contribute to the sustainable development of companies, institutions, and countries (Grobocopatel, 2010).

This testimony shows how management was aligned with the adoption of Corporate Governance practices such as the "Public Offering Transparency Regime" sanctioned by the Executive Power through Decree 677/2001. A direct consequence was the creation of multiple formal and informal institutions devoted to measuring corporate governance in Argentinian organizations. An example was MERCO and IAGO (Argentine Institute for the Government of Organizations), that was created to "spread the principles of corporate governance at the request of the Presidents and Directors of the institutions, IDEA and the Business Foundation for Quality and Excellence (FUNDECE)".

In September 2019, and for the eighth consecutive year "Los grobo" (GROBOCOPATEL HNOS SA) again held first place as the company with the best corporate reputation and image in its sector awarded by MERCO (BUSINESS REPUTATION MONITOR CORPORATE). MERCO is a reputational assessment instrument that has become a benchmark monitor throughout the world. It was launched in 2000 and is based on a multi-stakeholder methodology made up of six evaluations and twenty-five sources of information. It has a presence in twelve countries: Spain, Colombia, Argentina, Chile, Ecuador, Bolivia, Brazil, Mexico, Peru, Costa Rica, Panama, and in process in Portugal. It is the first audited monitor in the world, since the monitoring and verification of its production process and results is subject to an independent review by KPMG, according to the ISAE 3000 standard, which publishes its opinion for each edition. All the weighting criteria are public and, like the results of each edition, can be consulted on this website.

In the company category, for the eighth consecutive year, the multinational family company ARCOR SA ranked first in the MERCO ranking in relation to social responsibility and corporate governance. ARCOR SA is the most important food company in Argentina. Through sustainable management, it develops leading brands that reach people in more than 100 countries. It has commercial offices in America, Europe, and Asia and more than 40 plants in Latin America.

For MERCO, a responsible company with appropriate corporate governance is one that has:

- *Ethical Behavior*: become attached to handle issues related to ethics and written anti-corruption policies;
- *Transparency and governance*: implementation of transparency and corporate governance policies while controlling corporate governance risk;
- *Responsibility toward employees*: promoting talent management programs and managing diversity and equal opportunities for company employees;
- *Commitment to the environment and climate change*: through the measurement and management of environmental impact, the responsible purchase of raw materials and with a clear position against the phenomena associated with climate change; and
- *Contribution to the Community*: It is achieved through evaluation systems of the social impact and the social requirements necessary

for the supply chain, as well as the development of programs with the environment.

MERCO standards for corporate governance are defined to draw up a provisional ranking of companies. First, it looks at members of a board of directors of companies with a turnover of more than USD40 million and proceeds to provisionally rank the ten most responsible companies with the best corporate governance, except for their own. The second part of the process is carried out by professional managers with corporate governance experience who then value each of the companies in the provisional ranking from 0 to 100 regarding a set of standard criteria. This panel includes experts in *Corporate Social Responsibility*, financial analysts, academics, economic journalists, government, NGOs, unions, consumer associations, influencers, and social media managers, among others. This panel assessment is followed by the *Evaluation of Merits* by MERCO technicians who analyze the 50 main indicators of the companies in the provisional ranking. Together, this data is crossed with the information from MERCO Consumption, constituted by a sample of the population of consumers that assesses the commercial reputation of the companies ranked based on four criteria:

- *Ethics*: it is an organization that does not deceive its customers.
- *Ecological*: protect the environment.
- *Social*: is committed to social challenges.
- *Job attractiveness*: it is a company to work with.

Thus, with the cross-checking of all these variables, the Global Ranking of Companies with the Best Responsibility and Corporate Governance is elaborated.

Another initiative, replicating the successful experience of the IBGC (Brazilian Institute of Corporate Governance), the most important institute of Corporate Governance in the region, is IAGO certification for directors who have satisfied the requirements relevant training and performance.

These efforts to raise awareness and disseminate corporate governance practices, beyond interference from political powers or for a few listed companies, are the result of an increased awareness of the importance of corporate governance practices. Today, a large part of the Argentine business community is aware of and makes use of corporate governance, not only for better management, but also to contribute to their development and growth. Indeed, there is a consensus that good corporate governance practices aim for companies to be able, in addition to maximizing their profits, to exercise their functions responsibly and in compliance with rules; favoring growth and sustainable development through a set of principles that regulate the transparent behavior of companies.

Initiatives like MERCO and IAGO are however not independent from the political and ideological context that permeate most of the formal and informal organizational practices in Argentina. Recent cases such as the entry into bankruptcy of the family business VINCENTIN SAIC are unknown in respect to corporate governance practices. Cases like VINCENTIN SAIC show the opaque practice of corporate governance and the damage that occurs when corporate governance is not openly practiced. The law, regulations, and recommendations for good governance practices exist but are not necessarily followed. They are in force, indeed, and they do not differ too much from the rest of the Latin American countries, but their implementation is aleatory.

6 Analysis of Corporate Governing in Argentina: An Expert's Word

Recognized Argentine experts on the subject define corporate governance as a relationship between stakeholders and the company to determine and control the strategic direction and performance of organizations. In this relationship, the government imposes guidelines to establish the necessary order of relationships between the shareholders and the highest levels of leadership. Based on these reflections, corporate governing has a well-defined space, which is part of a triangle of relationships between the so-called stakeholders (including shareholders), the governing bodies and the management of the organization (Meléndez, 2020).

Melendez has analyzed how different organizational roles interplayed when corporate governance practices took place in Argentina.

a. The CEO usually is the delegate of the board of directors and runs and operates the organization based on their own definition of governing. Their work is made up of governing and management characteristics at the same time. It is considered the most powerful individual in the organization for managing resources and the levers that mobilize the administration.

b. The board in turn is the one who manages the governing structure to impose and manage power.
c. The shareholders' meeting brings together the capital holdings and voting possibilities, it operates according to the characteristics of the shareholders.

7 Conclusion

The previous analysis has brought the characteristics of Argentinian society in terms of its cultural, institutional arrangements, their functionality, the multiple forces that shaped companies and corporations and how these forces have affected the meaning and implementation of corporate governance in the country. We suggest that decades of entrenched organizational practices of trust and mistrust could be one of the reasons why the successful implementation of corporate governance in Argentina is still under construction.

The ambivalent and oscillating development of corporate governance in Argentina has the potential to underline the difficulties of any country, which embarks on recurrent changes and crises. Despite being a unique historical case from which to study how governance practices could be alternatively implemented or ignored, we claim that Argentina has been an under-researched context within the corporate governance literature.

Indeed, a critical account of the evolution of corporate governance in Argentina illuminates quite interesting organisational practices that help to understand the impact of economic, political, and social vicissitudes on corporate governance: a constant change of rules, sporadic decision-making, unstable political and legal frameworks, and local-global tensions when alternating in following paradigms. All combined has the power to jeopardize the successful implementation of corporate governance at a national level let alone for corporations.

References

Adelopo, I., & Rufai, I. (2018). Trust deficit and anti-corruption initiatives. *Journal of Business Ethics, 163*, 429–449.

Adnan, A., & Ahmed, N. (2019). The transformation of the corporate governance model: A literature review. *Copernican Journal of Finance & Accounting, 8*(3), 7–47.

Ahmad, S., & Omar, R. (2016). Basic corporate governance models: A systematic review. *International Journal of Law and Management, 58*(1), 73–107.

Apreda, R. (2001). Corporate governance in Argentina: The outcome of economic freedom (1991–2000). *Corporate Governance: An International Review, 9*(4), 298–310.

Briano Turrent, G., & Saavedra García, M. (2015). The composition of the board of directors and the shareholding structure as explanatory factors of transparency in corporate governance in Latin America: Evidence in listed companies in Argentina, Brazil, Chile and Mexico. *Management Studies, 31*(136), 275–286.

Briozzo, A., Pesce, G., & Reimer, G. (2008). *Corporate governance in Argentina*. XXVIII Conference on Financial Administration. National University of the South, Argentina.

Colazingari, S., & Rose-Ackerman, S. (1998). Corruption in a paternalistic democracy: Lessons from Italy for Latin America. *Political Science Quarterly, 113*(3), 447–470.

Cortés Conde, R. (2003). The Argentine crisis of 2001–2002. *Latin American Journal of Economics, 40*(121), 762–767.

Corzo José, L. (2016). Practices for good corporate governance in Argentine companies. *Accounting and Administration Writings, 7*, 49–74.

Decree 677/2001. *Regime of transparency of the public offer*. Ministry of Justice and Human Rights. http://servicios.infoleg.gob.ar/infolegInternet/anexos/65000-69999/67128/norma.htm. Accessed 15 August 2022.

Etcheverry, R., & Manóvil, R. (2013). Argentina. In A. Fleckner & K. Hopt (Eds.), *Comparative corporate governance: A functional and international analysis*. International Corporate Law and Financial Market Regulation (pp. 958–1012). Cambridge University Press.

Gaggiotti, H. (2012). Giving sense to global careers: Exploration of the structural, cultural and contextual difficulties in Argentina. In Y. Baruch & C. Reis (Eds.), *Careers without borders: Critical perspectives* (pp 107–134). Routledge.

Grobocopatel, A. (2010). *Why talk about corporate governance*. Rosario Stock Exchange Magazine. https://bcr.com.ar/sites/default/files/gob%2520corporativo.pdf. Accessed 15 August 2022.

Gutierrez, O., & Marcos, D. (2018). *Corporate governance: Measurement in listed companies in Argentina*. 38th National Conference on Financial Administration. Buenos Aires' University, Argentina, pp. 225–251.

IAGO. (2004). Argentine Institute of Corporate Governance. *Code of best governance practices of organizations for the Argentine Republic*. Argentina.

IMF. (2010). *2010 International Monetary Fund. Gross domestic product*. http://www.imf.org/external/pubs/ft/weo/2010/02/weodata/index.aspx. Accessed 15 August 2022.

Kraakman, R. H. (2017). *The anatomy of corporate law: A comparative and functional approach* (3rd ed.). Oxford University Press.

Meléndez, H. (2020). *"Interview" with María de los Ángeles Lucero Bringas*. Universidad Católica de Córdoba.

Morck, R. (2007). *A history of corporate governance around the world: Family business groups to professional managers*. University of Chicago Press.

OECD. (2020). *Evaluation process to Argentina 2019–2020*. http://www.oecd.org/env/country-reviews/EPR-Argentina-RPB-SPANISH-FINAL-web.pdf. Accessed 15 August 2022.

Shen, W., & Gentry, R. J. (2014). A cyclical view of the relationship between corporate governance and strategic management. *Journal of Management and Governance, 18*(4), 959–973.

Suess-Reyes, J. (2017). Understanding the transgenerational orientation of family businesses: The role of family governance and business family identity. *Zeitschrift für Betriebswirtschaft, 87*(6), 749–777.

World Bank. (2010). *Gross domestic product 2010*. Retrieved from http://siteresources.worldbank.org/DATASTATISTICS/Resources/GDP.pdf. Accessed 15 August 2022.

CHAPTER 7

Brazil

Dante Mendes Aldrighi and Luiz Ricardo Kabbach de Castro

1 Introduction

In the 1990s, the corporate governance debate gained momentum both inside and outside academia, reflecting the overwhelming understanding among capital markets' practitioners and scholars that the ruthless pursuit of shareholder value should be touted. This debate reached Brazil when its publicly traded companies were managed with a noticeable bias in favor of controlling shareholders. Poor legal protection, the weak enforcement power of the Brazilian securities and exchange commission (*Comissão de Valores Mobiliários*, henceforth CVM) and the highly concentrated ownership and control, generally by families or the state through control-enhancing mechanisms, rendered minority shareholders vulnerable to expropriation (Leal & da Silva, 2007).

D. Mendes Aldrighi
Department of Economics, Universidade de São Paulo, São Paulo, Brazil
e-mail: aldrighi@usp.br

L. R. Kabbach de Castro (✉)
School of Economics and Business, Universidad de Navarra, Pamplona, Spain
e-mail: lkabbach@unav.es

J. Callund et al. (eds.), *Corporate Governing in Latin America*,
https://doi.org/10.1007/978-3-030-85780-6_7

In 1997, the lower chamber of Congress began to discuss a bill to amend the corporate law with a view to reducing the imbalance of corporate power among shareholders. Enacted four years later (Law N°10,303/2001), the amended corporate law was a diluted version of the original bill, due mostly to the active lobbying of the controlling shareholders' association (ABRASCA). Nonetheless, it represented a significant improvement in outside investors' protection. In 2002, the securities law was also amended, enlarging CVM's administrative, operating, and financial autonomy, including mandated stability for its board members.

Besides these critical yet modest legal steps toward reducing Brazil's corporate governance gap, the SÃO PAULO STOCK EXCHANGE (then BOVESPA, now B3) promoted a major institutional breakthrough. At the end of the 1990s, macroeconomic turmoil and the incidence of a new tax on every financial transaction are seen as principal causes for the stagnation of Brazil's the equity market shrinking stock trading and stock market capitalization, escalating delistings, and diversion of trading to foreign stock exchanges (e.g., through *American Depositary Receipts*—ADRs of the major companies' shares).

In this context and inspired by the DEUTSCHE BORSE's *Neuer Markt* launched in 1997, B3 created the special listing segments ("*Nível 1*," "*Nível 2*," and "*Novo Mercado*"), which require firms' commitment to stricter governance standards than those of corporate law. By voluntarily deciding to list their shares on these special listing segments, firms can signal their commitment to sound governance practices, mitigating investors' information asymmetry. The B3 institutional innovation that created the three-tiered special listing segments, and the corporate and securities law amendments paved the way to attracting domestic and foreign investors, facilitating the long-expected expansion of the equity market, and fueling initial public offerings (IPOs) between 2004 and 2007.

In the following years, the CVM and B3 took other initiatives to improve both the regulatory framework and its enforcement to enhance minority shareholder protections, corporate transparency, and disclosure requirements. For example, in 2008, the CVM launched the *Enforcement Office*, while the B3 started a discussion to amend its bylaws governing membership to the premium listing segments. After that, B3 carried out two other revisions of their listing requirements, each of them through a process comprising public hearings with companies and investors and voting by the listed companies.

By accelerating the cross-border flows of information, trade, and finance, globalization has made consumers and investors increasingly aware of corporate governing issues, including environmental, social, and ethical dimensions. However, recent cases of corporate misbehavior show that overlooking governing has far-reaching adverse repercussions. First, "*Mensalão*," a corruption scheme by which some politicians of the then ruling party bribed congressmen between 2005 and 2006 to guarantee their votes for the approval of government bills. This corruption scheme embezzled money from a telecommunication business group privatized in 1998, which had the state-owned enterprises and pension funds among their controlling shareholders.

Second, the collapses in 2015 and 2019 of two tailing dams owned by VALE, one of the world's largest mining companies, laid bare how egregious myopic approaches to costs and profits could engender catastrophic social and environmental consequences, with dramatic economic and reputation losses. VALE's indifference to non-financial stakeholders' interests resulted in fatal casualties (more than 300 people died in both incidents) and irreversible environmental damages over an extensive area.

Third, beginning in March 2014, the "*Lava Jato*" (Operation Car Wash) case uncovered that PETROBRAS, an oil company controlled by the Brazilian government, was a central player in a corruption scheme. The investigation revealed that PETROBRAS's high executives and politicians from the ruling coalition parties received bribes from the company's prominent suppliers (e.g., ODEBRECHT, MENDES JÚNIOR, CAMARGO CORRÊA, and OAS). Had the *Anti-Corruption Act* (Law N°12,846/2013) not been in effect in 2014, this scheme might never have come to light. The new law established civil and administrative liability concerning acts of corruption on legal entities, including severe economic sanctions, loss of assets or rights, compulsory dissolution, and leniency agreements. As of January 2021, the "*Lava Jato*" case had 79 operational phases with more than 200 arrests, 174 convictions, 17 leniency agreements, and BRL14.7 billion (USD2.8 billion) in expected recoveries to public funds, among other sanctions. This anti-corruption operation represents a watershed in the relationships between government and privately-run companies, historically marked by non-investigated suspicions of favoritism and lack of commitment to combat corporate misbehavior.

The FEDERAL GOVERNMENT and its agencies have been critical protagonists in Brazil's corporate governing scene, whether as a controlling or a minority shareholder of major publicly traded companies. Until the 1990s, it directly controlled companies accounting for the majority of B3 market capitalization. However, the privatization of state-owned enterprises throughout that decade—including VALE, EMBRAER, CSN, USIMINAS, and TELEBRAS—sharply reduced government equity participation (Aldrighi, 2011).[1] Despite that, the government managed to retain political influence over privatized firms through equity investments by the pension funds of BRAZILIAN NATIONAL DEVELOPMENT BANK (BNDES) and State-owned enterprises and subsidized loans from the BNDES (Lazzarini, 2011; Mussachio & Lazzarini, 2014).

This chapter provides an overview of Brazil's leading protagonists of corporate governing over the last two decades. Besides this introduction, Sect. 2 describes the most relevant changes in the Brazilian economy and the institutional framework, emphasizing some legal and regulatory developments. In Sect. 3, we also describe Brazilian publicly listed firms' ownership to show the dominance of family and state-led business groups, highlighting the implications of the concentration of control and ownership to the board of directors, the market for corporate control, and the public–private political connections. Section 4 focuses on institutional players that have contributed to shaping the Brazilian corporate governing environment and practices: CVM, B3, domestic and foreign institutional investors, and associations representing the minority shareholders and the controlling shareholders. Finally, Sect. 5 concludes by pointing out the current corporate governing challenges in Brazil.

2 THE ECONOMIC AND INSTITUTIONAL CONTEXT

The Brazilian economic and institutional setting has undergone profound transformations since the 1990s. At the macroeconomic level, two pivotal policy shifts provided credibility and economic stability: the "Plano Real," launched in 1994, which managed to control the longstanding high-inflation; and the government commitment to the "macroeconomic tripod"—inflation target, floating exchange rates, and law-enforced fiscal responsibility. In addition, there were significant reforms toward a more

[1] The share of state-owned companies in B3 market capitalization plummeted from 61.2% in June 1997 to 22.3% in March 2007.

competitive economic environment at the microeconomic level. Notably in trade liberalization, deregulation in several industries, and privatization of state-owned companies in the telecommunications, steel, mining, and petrochemical industries.

However, the country's largest stock exchange, B3, continued to lose importance, with shrinking initial public offerings (IPOs) and seasoned equity offerings, the predominance of domestic institutional investors, and declining total stock market capitalization and stock trading. A combination of factors accounts for B3's underperformance. First, in the 1990s, the corporate law (Law N°6,404/1976) and the law creating and disciplining CVM (Law N°6,385/1976), both enacted in 1976, provided weak legal protections to minority shareholders, with CVM hardly ever exercising its monitoring and enforcement assignments. As a result, punishment of market manipulation and corporate wrongdoings were rare. In 1997, the Federal Government, aiming at increasing the proceeds of the ongoing privatization in the telecommunications sector, passed a new law (Law N°9,457/1997). This law eliminated the tag-along provision from the corporate law, whereby the acquirer of a company's controlling block could launch a public tender offer for all outstanding shareholders at the same price paid for it. Discussions in Congress on the corporate law amendment to improve minority shareholder rights faced strong opposition from the controlling shareholders. Second, besides the potential risk of expropriation, equity investments appeared unattractive to investors due to the competition of government bonds, which offered a combination of low risk, high returns, and liquidity. Furthermore, high transaction costs from brokerage fees and a tax on financial transactions also inhibited stock trading.

In December 2003, acknowledging that weak investor protections were impairing the equity market and that political economic factors obstructed legal changes to attract outside investors, B3 launched the special listing segments ("Nível 1," "Nível 2," and "Novo Mercado"). The new listing segments required companies to comply with stricter governance standards than those under corporate law. However, some firms opted not to list in the special segments and remained in the "Traditional" segment, so a regulatory dualism emerged (Gilson et al., 2011).

"Novo Mercado" presents the most stringent admission rules, followed by "Nível 2" and "Nível 1." Besides the requirements of corporate law, companies listing on "Nível 1" have since been required to comply with more detailed disclosure of financial information, insiders' securities ownership and trading, and related-party transactions; a minimum free float of 25% of the shares outstanding; and share dispersion in public offerings. Similarly, listing under the "Nível 2" segment imposed full tag-along rights to control transfers of common shares and 80% in the case of preferred shares; a compulsory public tender offer for at least the economic value in case of delisting or exit of the segment; private arbitration to solve corporate disputes; disclosure of financial statements in accordance with international standards; a minimum of five members on the board of directors with at least 20% independent directors; and voting rights to preferred shareholders in case of mergers and spin-offs. On top of "Nível 2" requirements, companies listed on the "Novo Mercado" may only issue ordinary shares. In 2004, B3 launched "Bovespa Mais," a listing segment dedicated to small and medium-sized firms (SMEs).

Amendments to both the corporate and securities laws further helped to mitigate the imbalance favoring controlling shareholders. In 2001, a new Corporate Law (Law N°10,303/2001) brought essential changes to the corporate governance regulation: a minimum of 80% tag-along rights for minority shareholders; the right for minority shareholders to nominate one director if their stocks account for at least 15% of the company's total equity; and the right for owners of non-voting shares to receive dividends. It also reduced the upper limit to issue non-voting shares from 66.6% to 50.0% of the companies' total capital (binding only for new issues) and categorized insider trading and market manipulations as "crimes against capital markets." In 2002, the Securities Law reform (Law N°10,411/2002) empowered CVM with greater statutory autonomy at the administrative, operating, financial, and budgetary levels. Finally, in 2007, a new amendment to the corporate law obliged public companies to disclose financial statements according to the *International Financial Reporting Standards* guidelines—IFRS (Law N°11,638).

In the 2000s, the Brazilian economy appeared sound and favorable to businesses, despite the economic and political turmoil caused by the 2001 presidential election campaign—which led the leftist candidate to power—and the global financial crisis in 2007. Foreign direct investment inflows and the massive shock to the terms of trade—which increased by more than 48% from December 2002 to October 2011 due to China's high demand for commodities—allowed Brazil to accumulate substantial foreign exchange reserves.

Even with the Workers' Party administration's counter-cyclical spending policies over the international financial crisis, the public sector yielded primary fiscal surpluses, contributing to the decline of public debt until 2014. Furthermore, the country's GDP grew on average by more than 4% p.a. over 2004–2013, despite a slight decline in 2009. As a result, inflation was stabilized at low levels, although slightly above its target rate in a few years. However, the commodities boom combined with the high domestic interest rates led to an appreciation of the Brazilian Reais (BRL) until 2011, harming the competitiveness of the manufacturing industries.

The relatively successful strategy for coping with the global crisis boosted the Federal Government's confidence to embark on ambitious public investment policies and fiscal stimuli to encourage private investment. Accordingly, on top of tax benefits for select sectors, the government transferred significant funds to capitalize the BNDES, the disbursements of which jumped from BRL64.9 billion in 2007 to BRL168.4 billion in 2010 and BRL190.4 billion (USD81 billion) in 2013. Consequently, the primary fiscal balance started deteriorating in 2011 and turned to deficits in 2014, which continued to increase until 2016, spreading uncertainty and contributing to the GDP's plummeting in 2015 and 2016.

The worsening in macroeconomic conditions led to a political crisis that culminated in President Rousseff's impeachment. The subsequent administrations of Presidents Temer and Bolsonaro shifted policies toward a more market-oriented approach and advanced several economic reforms to address the fiscal imbalances. As a result, in the three years preceding the COVID-19 pandemic, the primary fiscal deficit shrank somewhat, but economic growth remained sluggish (averaging 1.4% a year from 2017 to 2019). And, the BNDES had to reduce its balance sheet and repay its debt to the Treasury.

Regarding the legal framework, a watershed change was the introduction of plea bargaining into civil and criminal laws in 2013 and 2017, respectively. In the criminal sphere, Law N°12,850/2013 allows public prosecutors and courts to engage in plea agreements that can reduce the penalty for defendants who voluntarily and materially cooperate with the investigation or criminal procedure. This new legal provision was pivotal for *Operation Car Wash*, which investigated corruption schemes in Petrobras involving high-level politicians and some of the main Brazilian business groups. In the civil sphere, Law N°13,506/2017 defined the oversight rules for offenses in capital markets and securities issuance, assigning to the Central Bank and the CVM the enforcement authority over financial institutions and the securities market, respectively.

Overall, the institutional and policy changes introduced by Congress and government agencies (including the CVM), the implementation of B3's special governance listing segments, and initiatives led by other private institutions and companies have contributed to enhancing corporate governing in Brazil over the last two decades. Therefore, the following section discusses the ownership structure of publicly listed firms and the implication thereof on the corporate governing environment in Brazil.

3 The Ownership Structure of Brazilian Public Companies

Notwithstanding the important changes in the institutional framework regulating corporate governance in Brazil, ownership and control structures in publicly traded companies remains highly concentrated. The largest ultimate shareholder (LUS) held, on average, at least 66% of the voting rights and 46% of the cash-flow rights in every year in the period 2003–2013 (Aldrighi, 2020). Taking a 50% voting-right cutoff as a control definition, almost 78% of the sample companies had a controlling shareholder in 2013, against 83% in 2003. Even for *Novo Mercado*-listed companies, where the one-share-one-vote rule is obligatory, the LUS voting-right concentration was still high—averaging 46%.

High discrepancies between controlling shareholders' voting and cash-flow rights stem from dual-class shares, pyramidal ownership, and shareholder agreements. Before the 2000s, most Brazilian listed companies had a significant fraction of their equity capital issued as non-voting shares (PN shares). For example, in 2003, 53% of the sample companies had issued at least 50% of the equity capital as PN shares and 18% up to the then legal upper limit of 2/3 of the company's capital. However, the 2001 corporate law reform prevented listed companies from issuing additional non-voting shares exceeding 50% of their capital. In addition, the *Novo Mercado* impediment of dual-class shares reduced the importance of PN shares in subsequent years: the mean (median) fell from 42% (50%) in 2003 to 23% (0%) in 2013, when 27% of the companies had issued at least 50% of the total capital as PN shares, and 11% of the companies reached the limit of 66%.

Families prevailed among the LUS (46% in 2013), followed by shareholders' agreements, which grew in importance over the period from 16 to 24%. Shareholder agreements for companies listed on the *Novo Mercado* accounted for an even higher percentage (30%). Regardless of the LUS type, most companies are indirectly owned—almost 73% in 2013. Part of them rely on pyramidal structures (18% of the publicly listed companies), with some comprising at least five intermediate companies.

Controlling shareholders also enhance corporate control through their boards of directors. In 2013, they nominated at least 50% of the board to more than 85% of the companies (the average was 74% of the board), suggesting that directors were bound to merely rubber-stamp the controlling shareholders' decisions. The CEO was also a director or the Chairman in 51% and 16% of the listed companies, respectively (60% and 29% in 2003). The fall in the percentage of joint CEO/Chairman positions is probably due to B3's new regulation banning companies listed on *Nível 1*, *Nível 2*, and *Novo Mercado* from CEO-duality as of May 2014.

It is worth noting that most of the largest companies in Brazil belong to business groups (BGs), whereby a single entity, generally a family or the state, controls the main decisions of several legally independent firms. Brazilian BGs display some idiosyncrasies. First, the Federal, State, and Municipal governments have historically controlled the larger publicly listed companies, the majority of which are organized as BGs, such as PETROBRAS and ELETROBRAS and the now privatized companies VALE, TELEBRAS, CSN, and USIMINAS. The state-owned development bank, BNDES, has played a pivotal role in supporting large state-controlled and privately-run companies. On top of being the leading domestic provider of long-term credit, it has held substantial equity stakes in many of the largest BGs' companies.[2]

During and in the aftermath of the global financial crisis, under President Lula da Silva and President Roussef, the FEDERAL GOVERNMENT strengthened BNDES lending capacity, tripling the bank's disbursement between 2007 and 2013 and converting it into the primary vehicle to implement industrial policies. Most of the bank's subsidized loans

[2] In 2014, BNDESPar owned, among other equity stakes, 30% of the capital of FIBRIA, a company then affiliated to the VOTORANTIM business group, 25% of JBS, 20% of MARFRIG, 12% of VALE and 10% of its controlling company (VALEPAR), 13% of TELEMAR's ordinary shares and 100% of its preferred shares, 12% of SUZANO, 7% of CPFL ENERGIA, 6% of GERDAU, and 5% of EMBRAER.

were allocated to the largest BGs, some of which were targeted as "national champions." Even after the policy shift in 2016 that reduced its balance sheet and adjusted lending rates to market levels, BNDES and BNDESPAR—the investment arm of BNDES—have retained relevant stakes in Brazilian BGs' key companies.[3]

Along with some state-controlled companies' pension funds, BNDES' below-market rate loans and equity stakes allowed some BGs to embark upon bold expansion and internationalization strategies without relinquishing their families' control—as was the case with JBS, ODEBRECHT, and MARFRIG.

The second feature of Brazilian BGs derives from the way privatization was carried out in the 1990s. To achieve its purpose of maximizing privatization revenues in the telecommunication, electric power, and mining companies, the Federal Government auctioned its controlling blocks of shares instead of selling the shares through dispersed public offerings, as was done in the United Kingdom and South Korea. To attract domestic and foreign bidders to the auctions, the government mobilized BNDES, and pension funds sponsored by state-controlled companies to provide funds. Consequently, the winning bidders were usually consortia comprising privately-owned domestic and foreign BGs, BNDES, and pension funds.

VALE is a good example of this type of ownership arrangement. The winning consortium of VALE's privatization in 1997, VALEPAR S.A., was a holding company comprising BRADESPAR S.A. (a holding company of the bank-centered business group BRADESCO), the Japanese trading company MITSUI & CO. LTD, BNDESPAR, and LITEL PARTICIPAÇÕES S.A., owned by the government-related pension funds PREVI, FUNCEF, and PETROS. A shareholder agreement among leading shareholders defined Vale's corporate control. The agreement was signed in 1997 with a 20-years tenure.

In 2013, VALEPAR S.A. held 52.7% of VALE's common shares and was owned by LITEL (with a 51.3% stake in its total voting capital), BRADESPAR (17.3%), MITSUI (15.3%), and BNDESPAR (9.8%). Having an 80.6% stake in LITEL, PREVI, and BNDESPAR controlled more than

[3] In 2018, BNDES or BNDESPAR held equity capital participation in, for example, the state-controlled companies PETROBRAS and ELETROBRAS (10% and 20%, respectively), and the privately-run JBS (21%), MARFRIG (34%), SUZANO (11%), VALE (6%), and EMBRAER (5%).

61% of VALEPAR's equity capital, implying that VALE, purportedly a privatized company, continued to be de facto controlled by the government. To join the *Novo Mercado*, VALE converted its preferred shares into ordinary shares in 2017. Following the expiration of the shareholders' agreement in November 2020, it now has less concentrated ownership, with no defined controlling shareholder: LITEL now holds 11.6% of the shares, BRADESPAR, 5.7%, MITSUI, 5.6%, and BNDESPAR, 3.7%.

Third, families tend to control most of the BGs. According to an annual survey conducted by the Brazilian economic newspaper *Valor Econômico* (*Valor Grandes Grupos*), in 2018 families controlled 17 of the 30 largest Brazilian BGs in revenues, national or subnational governments controlled six groups, and the others had no defined controlling shareholder. In the case of JBS and MARFRIG, families retain control through shareholders' agreements with BNDES, even holding stakes in their BG's key companies lower than those the bank owns.

Families tend to reach and retain control of BGs through dual-class shares and complex pyramidal structures. COSAN S.A. is a telling illustration of such a strategy. Listed on the *Novo Mercado* since its IPO in 2005, it appears both as a key investor and investee in an intricate BG ownership structure, comprising a series of long, indirect, and pyramidal chains. To achieve control over COSAN S.A., the Ometto Family led its shareholders in 2007 to exchange their shares for those of a Bermuda-registered holding company, COSAN LIMITED, which issued two classes of common shares following its IPO on the NYSE: class A shares, entitling their holders to one vote per share, and class B shares in two series, each worth ten votes per share. While class A shares are freely transferable and not convertible, class B shares are convertible to class A shares at the holder's option. In 2018, COSAN LIMITED held 59.0% of COSAN S.A. shares and had three companies controlled by Rubens Ometto as its main direct shareholder, ensuring him a 42.8% stake and given the tenfold voting power of class B shares, its control. In 2019, the Ometto family owned all the class B shares, which are not listed on any stock exchange, and 14.5% of class A shares, amounting to 49.0% of its total shares.

Fourth, the largest Brazilian BGs usually have a controlling shareholder, although the number of those that do not have a controlling shareholder has increased slightly over the last few years. Among the 30 largest BGs in 2018, seven had no defined controlling shareholder, including VALE, BRF, OI, and EMBRAER. For example, BRF was constituted in 2009 due to the merger between two family-controlled food

BGs. As a result, BRF had two major shareholders in November 2020—the pension funds PETROS (11.41%) and PREVI (9.24%), with no shareholder agreement among them. Similarly, EMBRAER'S largest shareholders were an investment company (BRANDES INVESTMENTS PARTNERS), 15.1% holding, and BNDESPAR (5.4%). At the same time, the BRAZILIAN FEDERAL GOVERNMENT holds a golden share, entitling it to veto powers on matters concerning military programs, controlling interest, and public offerings.

4 INSTITUTIONAL PLAYERS

4.1 Brazil's Securities and Exchange Commission (CVM)

As of 2002, the CVM has followed a more *proactive* approach, leading important regulatory and enforcement initiatives. Besides creating a dedicated division to detect and probe into suspicions of irregularities and illicit behavior involving public companies and the issuance and trading of securities, CVM defined two critical measures in 2009. The first was Instruction N°480,[4] which requires public companies to complete and publish a standard form (*Formulário de Referência*—FR) containing comprehensive information about the issue of securities, including ownership structure and managerial and director remuneration. The second measure was Instruction N°481, which made meeting the requirements for proxy voting at general shareholder meetings and dissident shareholders' initiatives less burdensome.

In 2010, the BRAZILIAN INSTITUTE OF FINANCE EXECUTIVES (IBEF—*INSTITUTO BRASILEIRO DE EXECUTIVOS DE FINANÇAS*)[5] sued the CVM alleging that the compensation disclosure guidelines placed the executives' personal security at risk and violated their rights to intimacy and privacy warranted under the Federal Constitution. The IBEF obtained a preliminary injunction that allowed firms not to comply with the guidelines. In 2018, the court ruled that "[...] the Normative Instruction in question does so following the supervisory powers attributed

[4] CVM regularly reviews the regulatory framework by issuing either "Instructions," norms regarding specific corporate issues such as securities offerings or information transparency and disclosure, or "Deliberations," pronouncements that clarify any ambiguity underlying legal or normative aspects.

[5] IBEF is the association that represents private and publicly listed firms' top level financial officers.

to the CVM, there being no conflict between it and current legislation (the Federal Constitution)," so obliging publicly listed firms to disclose management and director's aggregate remuneration.[6]

In 2017, the CVM edited Instruction N° 586, whereby listed companies should submit a mandatory report on their compliance with the "Brazilian Code of Corporate Governance." Following the British "comply-or-explain" approach, firms should comply with a series of corporate governance recommendations or explain the non-compliance. In addition, this new Instruction amended the rules regarding transparency and securities trading defined in Instruction N°480.

Finally, on the enforcement front, a law that became effective in 2017 (Law N°13,506/2007) allows the CVM to negotiate with corporate and securities law offenders through a plea bargain or settlement agreement and extends its enforcement power to apply both pecuniary and non-pecuniary sanctions. As a result, the number of warning notes alerting market players that their acts might lead to administrative sanctioning rulings rose from 290 in 2017 to 488 in 2019, a period over which the CVM initiated 345 investigation proceedings, dissued 327 administrative sanctioning rulings, and applied over BRL1.5 billion (USD288 million) in fines. For example, in 2019, the CVM imposed a fine on the São Paulo State Government, as the controlling shareholder of Empresa Metropolitana de Águas e Energia (EMAE), for the alleged use, free of charge, of flood control services provided by the company and an infringement of the duty of loyalty. In another case, the CVM applied a more than BRL20 million (USD104,000) fine to OSX Brasil SA's controlling shareholder and Chairman for insider trading.

4.2 B3

B3, the Brazilian Stock Exchange, has been a leading institutional promoter of better corporate governance practices. Unequivocally, its most innovative initiative was the creation in December 2000 of the three-tiered listing segments, which enhanced governance standards on transparency, disclosure, shareholder rights, and free floats. Gilson and

[6] A recent study analyzed the listed firms that did not comply with Instruction n° 480 during the injunction relief period and concluded that non-compliance behavior is associated with poor governance practices, finding no evidence that compensation disclosure incites acts of violence (crime rates) (Barros et al., 2020).

colleagues (Gilson et al., 2011) labeled this as a regulatory dualism experiment that allows for the coexistence of *traditional* companies that submit to the corporate law and *new entrants* or already listed companies that adhere to the new listing segments' higher governance standards and the corporate law. This privately led institutional innovation was a reaction to investors' weak legal protections, the Brazilian stock exchange's shrinking size and liquidity,[7] and the resistance of the largest listed companies' controlling shareholders to adopting higher governance standards.

B3 has reviewed these listing segments' rules on three occasions to keep pace with the best international governance practices. The first review discussions began in 2005 and came into force in February 2006, enhancing the independence of the board of directors, including an arbitration clause in the corporate statutes. Among other domestic and international factors, the second review was motivated by the global financial crisis and the increasing demand for tighter corporate governance, the new CVM regulation (Normative Instruction N°480/2009), and the corporate law amendment (Law N°11,638/07), which aligned Brazilian accounting standards to IFRS. Market players participated actively in the discussions surrounding B3 in 2009 and 2010, including representatives of companies in the special listing segments. The new rules came into force in May 2011, except for the prohibition of CEO/Chairman duality, which only became effective in May 2014.

In 2015, discussions on the third review focused on the "*Novo Mercado*" and "*Nível 2*" and included a public consultation, a public hearing, a second round of public hearings, and restricted hearings. B3 disclosed the information collected from market participants and academics to support further discussions and organizing proposed amendments. Even though publicly listed firms from the special listing segments voted against the proposals arising from the public hearings, the Board of the CVM decided to go ahead and adopt them. The CVM also defined different timeframes for implementing each proposal—some were enforced in January 2018, and others took effect as of April 2021. New

[7] According to CVM, initial public offerings (IPOs) between 1995 and 1999 raised USD550 million in Brazil and more than USD320 billion in the United States. In the late 1990s, Brazilian companies increasingly used the New York Stock Exchange to reach more liquidity. In 2000, the *American Depository Receipts* of 28 out of the 495 companies listed on the Brazilian stock exchange accounted for more than one-third of the entire Brazilian stock market trading volume (Santana et al., 2008).

companies that listed their shares on the "*Novo Mercado*" by December 2017 were allowed to delay compliance with these new requirements until 2021.

In 2005, B3 created the *Corporate Sustainability Index* (ISE B3) as one of the governing initiatives to encourage publicly listed companies to introduce more sustainable practices. In September 2020, B3 got together with S&P Dow Jones' efforts to launch the *S&P-B3 Brazil ESG Index*. The new index covers 96 most engaged companies in environmental, social, and governance (ESG) issues, such as Lojas Renner, Banco do Brasil, Itaúsa, Itaú Unibanco, Bradesco, Klabin, and Natura.

4.3 Institutional Investors

The importance of individual investors in B3 has been rapidly growing in the last few years. There were 620 thousand in 2017, 1.6 million in 2019, and 3.1 million in November 2020. Nonetheless, individual investors are unlikely to play a proactive governing role, given the high coordination costs for carrying out collective actions. In this regard, institutional investors (such as pension funds, insurance companies, banks, asset management firms, mutual funds, and investment companies) seem to have enough incentive and power to exert their voice and monitor firms. While institutional investors may help to restrain the moral hazard of management or controlling shareholders', they also create an additional layer of agency, such as self-interested decision-making with other people's money.

In Brazil, pension funds from the major state-owned enterprises—Previ (Banco do Brasil), Petros (Petrobras), and Funcef (*Caixa Econômica Federal*) —have stood out in the corporate scene. Previ, Petros, and Funcef hold significant equity stakes in several Brazilian companies and participated as a member of the controlling blocks in some of them. The significant ownership of these funds is primarily due to the scale of their investment portfolios—with equity holdings exceeding BRL365 billion (USD70 billion) in September 2020—and their intense participation in the privatization process in the 1990s—generally through consortia embracing BNDESPar and domestic business groups.

The State-owned enterprise's pension funds were also involved in corporate governance cases, either as a plaintiff or a defendant. For example, in 2008, Previ filed a formal complaint with the CVM against

AMBEV's controlling shareholders for the acquisition, in 2004, of LABATT, a Canadian brewery holding company owned by INTERBREW (also a controlling shareholder of AMBEV). PREVI accused AMBEV's controlling shareholders of breaching their duty of care, neglecting the duty of diligence, making decisions pervaded with conflicts of interest, and releasing incomplete information. In 2009, a CVM committee accepted the defendant's proposal of payment to settle the case (*Processo Administrativo Sancionador* CVM N°09/2008).

Another example of investor activism was a reparation claim that PREVI and PETROS submitted to the BRAZILIAN ARBITRATION CHAMBER in 2017 against PETROBRAS for losses related to the company's stock price plunge in the aftermath of the "*Operação Lava Jato*" (*Operation Car Wash*). Even though the arbitration chamber ruled in favor of the plaintiff in May 2020, concluding that Petrobras disclosed incomplete and false information to the market, the courts reversed the decision in November 2020.[8] Unlike the U.S. investors, to whom PETROBRAS agreed to pay BRL3 billion (USD580 million) in reparations, its shareholders in Brazil were not compensated as Brazilian corporate law has no clause rendering companies liable for controlling shareholders' or management's illicit behavior. Moreover, in 2018 PREVI and PETROS contested BRF's economic underperformance and forced changes in the company's board of directors. However, there are also episodes where those pension funds might have acted against their beneficiaries' interests. For example, in 2020, public prosecutors charged PETROS, FUNCEF, PREVI, and VALIA's former executives with wasteful investments in SETE BRASIL, a PETROBRAS' drilling rig supplier for pre-salt oil fields.[9]

After President Rousseff's impeachment (August 2016), PREVI seems to be shifting its investment strategy from holding controlling stakes to increasing diversification, reducing the board of directors' participation,[10] and campaigning to implement ESG principles on market participants. Indeed, in 2016, PREVI, PETROS, and FUNCEF joined AMEC's "stewardship" code, committing to monitor the investee companies actively and

[8] *Valor Econômico*, 29 October 2020, https://valor.globo.com/impresso/20201029/.

[9] *Valor Econômico*, 9 January 2020, https://valor.globo.com/politica/noticia/2020/01/09/gestores-de-fundos-de-pensao-sao-denunciados-por-aportes-na-sete-brasil.ghtml.

[10] *Valor Econômico*, 9 January 2020, https://valor.globo.com/politica/noticia/2020/01/09/gestores-de-fundos-de-pensao-sao-denunciados-por-aportes-na-sete-brasil.ghtml.

improve their governance.[11] More recently, PREVI applied for a seat on the *Principles for Responsible Investments' board*.[12]

Foreign and domestic investors and mutual funds also own significant equity stakes in Brazilian publicly listed companies,[13] part of which trade as ADRs on the NEW YORK STOCK EXCHANGE. For example, ADRs account for 49% of EMBRAER's shares, almost 38% for VALE, and 30% for PETROBRAS shares other than the 36.7% stake owned by the FEDERAL GOVERNMENT. Although these institutional investors are prone to short-termism and thus more willing to exit than monitor the companies, there is anecdotal evidence of effective initiatives against corporate self-dealing and bad governing. For example, in 2009, the coordinated action of three institutional investors prevented the chairman of DASA, a clinical laboratory chain, from being reelected. Although not the controlling shareholder, DASA's founder and chairman abusively used his privileged position to contract services from firms of his relatives (Aldrighi, 2011).

Another remarkable case refers to an asset management firm, SQUADRA, that in February 2020 denounced fraudulent behavior in the INSTITUTO DE RESSEGUROS DO BRASIL—IRB, a reinsurance company privatized in 2013. SQUADRA, which held and disclosed a short-selling position in IRB, issued a report casting doubt on the company's regular above-average performance and pointed out inconsistencies in their financial reports. As a result, IRB's share price plummeted from BRL39.89 on 2nd January to BRL10.00 on 31st March to BRL9.07 on 24th April.

The IRB's executives also spread rumors that Berkshire Hathaway was investing in the company. However, BERKSHIRE publicly refuted that it owned or intended to own IRB's shares. Afterward, IRB's CEO and CFO resigned. The new management team hired an independent auditing firm to investigate the case. The probe showed that the

[11] AMEC is the acronym for the ASSOCIATION OF CAPITAL MARKET INVESTORS.

[12] *Valor Econômico*, 26 November 2020, https://valor.globo.com/financas/noticia/2020/11/26/previ-busca-engajar-investidores-de-paises-emergentes.ghtml.

[13] For example, BRANDES INVESTMENT PARTNERS holds 15.1% of EMBRAER's voting capital; BLACKROCK owns a 5% stake in ULTRAPAR PARTICIPAÇÕES, 2% in KLABIN and 5.2% in VALE, where CAPITAL RESEARCH GLOBAL INVESTORS has a 5.11% stake; KAPITALO INVESTIMENTOS holds 5% of BRF's capital, while PETROS and PREVI have 11.4% and 9.2%, respectively; CAPITAL INTERNATIONAL INVESTORS and DYNAMO, 10% and 3.5% in GERDAU S.A.; and GOLDENTREE FUNDO DE INVESTIMENTO EM AÇÕES and XP GESTÃO DE RECURSOS, 9.9% and 7.1% in VIA VAREJO.

former management had manipulated the balance sheet and other financial statements, omitting BRL1.3 billion (USD250 million in 2020) in liabilities and consequently inflating profits, escalating share prices, and leading to undue bonus payments of BRL60 million (USD11.6 million). The company shared the results of the internal investigation with the Prosecutor's Office and CVM.[14]

Ironically, in 2019, three firms—specialized in financial analysis services, finance education, and financial data, respectively—had awarded IRB the prize of "company of the year." This award is a recognition to "companies that had gone public in the three previous years and excelled at profitability, share performance, and corporate governance." Indeed, the reported return on net worth in 2018 was 32%, while the average among the reinsurance companies was 5.9%.[15]

4.4 *Association of Capital Market Investors and Brazilian Association of Public Companies*

The Association of Capital Market Investors (AMEC) represents the interests of investors, notably institutional investors, and asset management firms. At the same time, the Brazilian Association of Public Companies (ABRASCA) brings together the largest public companies. ABRASCA has traditionally opposed changes in the regulatory framework status quo, biased toward controlling shareholder interests—as it did in the discussion of the 1997 bill to reform the corporate law.

Examining AMEC and ABRASCA's practices and positions in recent debates on corporate governance issues, we can better highlight their motivations and priorities. First, ABRASCA supported the elimination of the mandatory disclosure of quarterly companies' earnings, arguing that it would reduce compliance and disclosure costs. Contrary, AMEC claimed that quarterly earnings' disclosure was necessary due to the high market volatility and information asymmetries in Brazil's capital markets.[16]

[14] *Econômico*, 21 September 2020, https://valor.globo.com/financas/noticia/2020/09/21/irb-poderia-nao-ter-sobrevivido-a-fraudes.ghtml.

[15] https://www.infomoney.com.br/negocios/irb-brasil-re-a-ex-estatal-que-triplicou-de-valor/.

[16] *Valor Econômico*, 17 August 2018, https://valor.globo.com/empresas/noticia/2018/08/17/fim-do-balanco-trimestral-volta-a-cena-com-trump-e-reforca-debate.ghtml.

Understanding that regulation is excessive and troublesome, ABRASCA and THE BAKERY, a global consulting firm on corporate innovation, developed a proposal for streamlining listed companies' paperwork and processes, reducing their securities issuance and compliance costs, and fostering transparency and efficiency.[17] Since 2018, ABRASCA and B3, supported by the CVM, have been working on ways to reduce paperwork duplication from the multiple mandatory reports and make investors more long-term oriented.[18]

Second, AMEC, ABRASCA, and other organizations joined the *Capital Market's Initiative* (IMK) to discuss the implementation of super-voting shares ("*voto plural*") in the corporate law.[19] The bill proposing the super-voting shares has been pending in Congress since 2018 (Bill N°10,736/2018). The main alleged objective of the super-voting shares is to enhance entrepreneurs' voting power and thus provide incentives for small firms to go public. IMK designed a task force, with the CVM's coordination, to formulate a proposal. AMEC opposed the super-voting shares, arguing that, unless safeguards to protect minority shareholders' rights are provided, they will strengthen the controlling shareholders' power.

For those defending the super-voting shares for startup companies, founders and entrepreneurs add value to the business. Therefore, allowing them to retain control of: their" company, shortly after an IPO should reinforce outside investor confidence in its financial sustainability. Moreover, keeping control over their companies would make it less attractive for founders to list on the U.S. stock exchanges, which allow other controlling enhancing mechanisms.[20]

The last version of the IMK's proposal regarding the super-voting shares includes some of the safeguards suggested by AMEC, such as

[17] *Valor Econômico*, 18 December 2020, https://valor.globo.com/empresas/noticia/2020/12/18/companhias-abertas-terao-programa-de-inovacao.ghtml.

[18] *Valor Econômico*, 20 August 2018, https://valor.globo.com/financas/noticia/2018/08/20/ideia-reforca-debate-sobre-engajamento-e-longo-prazo.ghtml.

[19] IMK is a forum created by the MINISTRY OF ECONOMY in June 2019 to discuss and propose public policies to develop the Brazilian capital markets. This forum put together representatives from the CENTRAL BANK, CVM, the Economic Planning Secretary, the Treasury Special Office, the NATIONAL TREASURY, and private sector institutions, including AMEC, IBGC, ABRASCA, and ANBIMA.

[20] The founders of XP INVESTIMENTOS, PAGSEGURO, and STONE launched the IPOs in the NYSE using a dual-class share structure to avoid losing control of their companies.

restricting the super-voting shares only to private firms going public, as in the United States; limiting the validity of that type of shares to seven years (a sunset clause), with the possibility of a three-year extension under minority shareholder consent; and ensuring exit rights to the shareholders with reimbursement at the economic value.[21] ABRASCA criticized the proposal, arguing that the details on the super-voting shares should be defined in a company's statutes rather than in law.

Third, opposing views between AMEC and ABRASCA also appear in a provision of the bill designed to regulate startups submitted to Congress by the Secretary of Economy (*Marco Legal das Startups*, Bill N°146/2019). The bill proposed that the CVM can "waive or modulate" the obligation for a board of directors and a fiscal committee for publicly listed companies with annual revenues below BRL500 million—which make up over 1/3 of the firms listed the B3. Also, it recommends a minimal number of Directors from two to one and makes non-mandatory the disclosure of financial statements, dividend payouts, and securities public offerings through financial institutions. AMEC fought the proposed bill, emphasizing that Boards of Directors provide critical advisory and governance services.[22] Nevertheless, Congress approved the initiative in Law No.182 in May 2021, after several amendments, including retaining the requirement for a board of directors and fiscal committee.

Fourth, ABRASCA contested B3's authority to rule on preferred shareholders' rights after the stock exchange had determined, in April 2020, that shareholders of both common and preferred shares are entitled to vote on the proposal of ENEVA, an energy company, to acquire AES TIETÊ, controlled by AES. By owning 61% of the voting shares (amounting to 24% of the total capital), this U.S. company considered that it could block the deal even if approved by the shareholders'

[21] *O Estado de São Paulo*, 3 November 2020, https://economia.estadao.com.br/noticias/governanca,proposta-de-voto-plural-limita-super-ordinaria-a-empresas-estreantes-na-bolsa,70003498682.

[22] *Valor Econômico*, 8 December 2020, https://valorinveste.globo.com/mercados/renda-variavel/empresas/noticia/2020/12/08/governo-pode-acabar-com-exigencia-de-conselho-para-empresa-listada-em-bolsa.ghtml.

assembly. ABRASCA claimed that an Arbitration Chamber was the appropriate forum to resolve controversies on statutory rules.[23]

4.5 *The Brazilian Corporate Governance Institute (IBGC)*

Founded in November 1995, the Brazilian Corporate Governance Institute (IBGC) is a private institution promoting the best corporate governance practices. In 2016, IBGC and another ten institutions established a task force that produced the "*Brazilian Corporate Governance Code*" (BCGC), which adopted the "comply-or-explain" approach, whereby companies should either comply with the code's recommendation or explain why they do not. In 2017, the CVM, through Instruction N°586/2017, made mandatory the disclosure of corporate governance practices according to the BCGC. More recently, the IBGC launched the "*Agenda Positiva de Governança*" (Positive *Governance Agenda*), proposing several guidelines to foster corporate governance practices along six pillars: (a) ethics and integrity; (b) diversity and inclusion; (c) social and environmental issues; (d) innovation and transformation; (e) transparency and accountability; and (f) the future of boards.

The IBGC has also supported the Secretary for the State-owned Enterprises' Coordination and Governance, subordinated to the Ministry of Economy, to develop a governance framework for state-owned enterprises, to be based on the OECD best governance practices. These companies are expected to adopt that framework following their respective shareholders' approvals. Among other provisions, the framework includes the alignment between state-owned enterprises' strategic planning and governance, the regulation compliance procedures (Law N°13,303/2016), and transparency practices.

5 Conclusion and Future Directions

This chapter reviewed the key institutional features and actors that have shaped corporate governing in Brazil. After describing the institutional

[23] Out of the nine complainers, only two companies had controlling shareholders with the majority of the total capital and thus could complete mergers or acquisitions without preferred shareholders' approval. *Valor Econômico*, 25 May 2020, https://valor.globo.com/financas/noticia/2020/05/25/direito-de-preferencialistas-no-nivel-2-gera-debate.ghtml.

and economic context over the past two decades, we discussed the protagonists and their roles in the Brazilian corporate governing landscape, such as the FEDERAL GOVERNMENT, publicly listed companies and their business groups, institutional investors, CVM, B3, IBGC, ABRASCA, and AMEC.

We have shown that corporate governing in Brazil has changed significantly, with companies, the regulatory and enforcement authorities, and institutional investors increasingly acknowledging the importance of governance to company's value creation and accommodating different stakeholders interests. Moreover, market players' broad recognition of better corporate governance practices has driven several institutional developments at both the legal and self-regulatory levels, reinforcing better corporate practices and regulatory enforcement.

Reflecting on the international trend, most of the corporate governance actors in Brazil have been increasingly attentive to environmental and social issues. First, global warming concerns have intensified the pressure over how companies manage their supply chains. For instance, given Brazil's prominence in the global provision of goods and inputs intensive in natural resources, consumers and investors have put high pressure on producers to follow environmentally sustainable practices. Also, the collapse of Vale's tailing dams served as a warning call to managers and controlling shareholders for the importance of balancing profitability and environmental requirements. To encourage publicly listed companies to adopt sustainable practices, B3 created in 2005 the *Corporate Sustainability Index* (ISE B3), and in 2020 they joined efforts with S&P Dow Jones to launch the S&P-B3 Brazil ESG Index.

Second, companies have increasingly pursued diversity in gender, race, disability, sexual orientation, and national origins. Openness to different social, cultural, and behavioral backgrounds has been perceived as conducive to innovative outcomes. More specifically, recent corporate governance guidelines have emphasized the participation of women on boards and the hiring and promotion policies committed to guaranteeing diversity within the corporations.

Third, corporate governance is now more attentive to corporate compliance with ethical tenets, behavior integrity, accountability, transparency, and a fair balance of power among the different stakeholders. In this regard, IBGC's recent initiative, the "Positive Governance Agenda," endorsed by several private organizations (including ABRASCA, AMEC, and B3), attempts to enhance the governance agenda by creating and sharing social-economic value.

Indeed, recently, the BRAZILIAN CONGRESS had to define the legal setting for disciplining entrepreneurs and creditors' rights and duties: a bill passed in the Congress to adjust corporate governance rules and practices to contemplate startup firms and to foster innovation and entrepreneurship, and a proposal for reforming bankruptcy law proposal to protect suppliers of capital.[24]

Finally, being inherently dynamic, corporate governing should persist in promoting corporate practices and initiatives directed at creating shareholder value while balancing the rights and duties of all stakeholders. Nonetheless, several challenges remain. For example, how are companies that have shifted to more dispersed ownership making appropriate adjustments to their governance practices? In addition, what is the role of the board of directors in companies with a controlling shareholder? And, how to accommodate the diverse and conflicting interests of the multiple groups of stakeholders or to be loyal to the controlling shareholder, who probably nominated its members? (Gelman et al., 2015).

In summary, initiatives of the major players and changes in the institutional, economic, and business environment have improved corporate governing in Brazil over the last twenty years. However, several challenges remain to be addressed, and new ones are emerging. The private sector, lawmakers, and the overall society seem to be aware of their duty to enhance corporate governing. The quest for the right balance among the different stakeholders' diverse and often conflicting interests should be guided by the common goal of sustainable economic development.

REFERENCES

Aldrighi, D. (2011). Especulações sobre a evolução recente do mercado de capitais no brasil. In P. G. Duarte, S. D. Silber, & J. J. M. Guilhoto (Eds.), *Brasil e a Ciência Econômica em Debate: O Estado da Arte em Economia*. São Paulo.

[24] In May 2021, Congress approved the "*Marco Legal das Startups*" Bill N°146/2019, while Bill N°4458/2020) aiming to provide the judicial and extrajudicial framework to reorganize the bankruptcy procedures, including cross-border insolvency and cooperation between national and foreign courts, the possibility of suspension of liens during the judicial recovery, the inclusion of labor credits in extrajudicial recovery, the payment of debts with the FEDERAL GOVERNMENT, and the inclusion of the negotiation processes during a period of public calamity.

Aldrighi, D. (2020). *Revisiting the link between ownership concentration and financial performance: Evidence from Brazilian publicly traded companies.* European Financial Management Association Meeting.

Barros, L. A. B. d. C., da Silveira, A. D. M., Bortolon, P. M., & Leal, R. P. C. (2020). Facing the regulators: Noncompliance with detailed mandatory compensation disclosure. *Emerging Markets Finance & Trade, 51*, S47–S61.

Gelman, M., Kabbach-de-Castro, L. R., & Seidler, V. (2015). Efeitos da vinculação de conselheiros ao acordo de acionistas no valor da firma. *Revista de Administração de Empresas—RAE, 55*(3), 345–358.

Gilson, R., Hasmann, H., & Pargendler, M. (2011). Regulatory dualism as a development strategy: Corporate reform in brazil, the United States, and the European Union. *Stanford Law Review, 63*(3), 475–537.

Lazzarini, S. G. (2011). *Capitalismo de Laços: Os Donos do Brasil e Suas Conexões.* Rio de Janeiro.

Leal, R. P. C., & da Silva, A. L. C. (2007). Corporate governance and value in Brazil (and in Chile). In A. Chong & F. L. de Silanes (Eds.), *Investor protection and corporate governance: Firm-level evidence across Latin America* (Chapter 3, pp. 213–288). Stanford University Press.

Mussachio, A., & Lazzarini, S. G. (2014). *Reinventing state capitalism: Leviathan in business, Brazil, and beyond.* The Harvard University Press.

Santana, M. H., Ararat, M., Alexandru, P., Yurtoglu, B. B., & da Cunha, M. R. (2008). *Novo Mercado* and its followers: Case studies in corporate governance reform. *Global Corporate Governance Forum—IFC, 5*, 1–77.

CHAPTER 8

Chile

Matias Zegers Ruíz-Tagle and Carla Meza Morales

1 Introduction

Corporate governance as an evolving concept and as an explicit purpose of the regulation has been present in Chile for well over 30 years. This chapter aims to present the evolution and current state of corporate governance regulation, the practices, and future challenges in related topics.

The analysis draws on a revision of the public information available on the Chilean market and its regulatory evolution. The chapter is structured as follows. Following this short introduction, the first section briefly analyzes the background of corporate governance regulations in Chile, the main attributes of the capital markets, and their evolution over the last 20 years. The second section then examines the evolution of corporate governance in Chile, looking at some of the cases that preceded legal

M. Zegers Ruíz-Tagle (✉) · C. Meza Morales
Pontificia Universidad Católica de Chile, Santiago, Chile
e-mail: mzegers@baz.cl

C. Meza Morales
e-mail: cbmeza@uc.cl

J. Callund et al. (eds.), *Corporate Governing in Latin America*,
https://doi.org/10.1007/978-3-030-85780-6_8

reforms, the political aspects involved, the strategy pursued to promote reforms in corporate governance, and the current status. The key amendments that shaped current corporate governance practices and regulation include (i) the Tender Offers and Corporate Governance Law, the direct consequence of a capital market scandal—the *Chispas* case, which led to the strengthening of minority shareholder rights in 2000; (ii) several amendments were made to the law to ensure Chile's accession to the OECD in 2010; (iii) the introduction of a particular type of Corporate Governance Code (regulatory requirement for disclosure that the Chilean regulator considers to work similarly to a code), and finally, (iv) the transformation process in the regulator to improve its own governing and strengthen its powers of oversight of the financial system as a whole. This section provides all the elements needed to understand the current state of corporate governance regulation and practices in Chile.

The third section details the country's current corporate governing framework, explaining that most of the regulation of corporate governing is contained in law (primarily in the prescriptive Corporation Act and Securities Market Act, both enacted in 1981, although amended several times since). This section also outlines the principal points of the current Chilean Corporate Governance Code. Finally, a fourth section concludes by referring to the ongoing and prospective challenges of corporate governing in Chile.

2 Main Characteristics of the Chilean Capital Market

Chile has an open, market-oriented economy characterized by a high level of foreign trade, a good reputation for solid financial institutions, and a strong macroeconomic framework, with well-recognized features that sustain resilience and encourage investment (OECD, 2021c). Per capita income has more than doubled over the past 20 years and is now the highest in Latin America.

The Chilean capital market is considered among the strongest in Latin America, with the largest levels of market capitalization as a share of GDP in 2019 (OECD, 2019a, 2019b). Stock market capitalization amounted to USD294,7 billion at the end of 2017 comprising 212 domestic companies in the same year, the average market capitalization of a Chilean public company was USD1.3 billion, when compared to an average of USD200 million in 1997. Regarding the number of listed companies per inhabitants, in 2017 Chile topped this indicator in Latin America with 12.4 public companies per million of inhabitants (OECD, 2019a).

Major features of Chile's corporate governing landscape are its concentrated ownership structures and the limited liquidity in its capital market, with most firms controlled by conglomerates or business groups that are also small (OECD, 2011a). These characteristics shape domestic corporate governance regulation, by putting a focus on minority shareholder protections,[1] as will be explored in the next two sections. The principal characteristics affecting the corporate governing framework are discussed below.

2.1 Concentrated Ownership

Like the rest of Latin America, the Chilean equity market features a high degree of defined control and the presence of companies identified with a relatively small number of entrepreneurial individuals and groups (Lefort & Urzúa, 2008). Companies belong to large conglomerates, which in turn tend to have interests in multiple sectors of the economy, including the financial sector.

Conglomerates tend to structure holdings through pyramidal structures (or multi-layered), which are used to obtain funding from minority shareholders without losing control (Lefort, 2010). In other cases, conglomerates use stock series with preferential voting rights. Chilean large economic groups have ties with most directors on the boards of listed companies, creating an interlocking phenomenon that has been described in Chile.[2]

Company Groups have existed in Chile for well over a hundred years, but more recent historical and political processes have shaped the way in which they are organized today. In the decade of 1980, a privatization process was implemented partly with the purpose of achieving dispersed

[1] According to the OECD Corporate Governance Chilean revision, the predominance of company groups, high ownership concentration, and low liquidity in Chilean markets are characteristics that tend to weaken the effectiveness of market mechanisms, leading to the Chilean authorities' own conclusion that "*the central corporate governance challenge in Chile is the risk of minority shareholder expropriation at the hands of controlling shareholders*" (OECD, 2011a).

[2] See Salvaj and Couyoumdjian (2016) and Cárdenas (2016).

firm ownership and developing the local capital markets. However, Chilean business groups rapidly took over most newly privatized firms, sometimes in association with foreign companies (Lefort, 2010).

While the ownership concentration phenomenon was highly described and studied in the decade of 2000,[3] there has been less comprehensive academic research on ownership concentration in recent years, probably because there has been little significant change over the past decades, despite advancements in shareholder protection regulation, not reflecting the anticipated "property de-concentration" consequence of raising shareholder protection.[4] The latest OECD research over most listed companies in Chile shows that, for 2020, almost 80% of the companies' largest shareholders hold more than 50% of the equity (OECD, 2021a, 2021b).

Regardless of concentration, pyramidal structures, and interlocking of board members, Chilean companies tend to perform well in rankings of transparency and shareholder protection in relation to other Latin American countries (however, they do not perform well regarding other developing economies). While there is a strong institutional framework factor, the performance also relates to the numerous changes in different legal bodies to strengthen minority shareholders, the international expansion of Chilean firms through the issuance of ADRs (Lefort & González, 2008) or engagement in foreign direct investment (FDI) giving rise to the Multilatinas.[5]

2.2 *Limited Liquidity*

The Chilean stock market is relatively illiquid, by traditional measures such as turnover and bid-ask spreads, when compared to other comparable economies. According to an IMF report, this trait has led to an increase in the cost of equity in Chile by as much as 3.5% per year (IMF, 2016).

The IMF concludes that global factors (such as changes in global risk appetite) seem to be more important than domestic macroeconomic factors (such as inflation or economic activity) in explaining the variation

[3] See Lefort and Walker (2000), Lefort and Urzúa (2008), and Salvaj and Couyoumdjian (2016).

[4] Thesis developed by La Porta et al. (1999).

[5] For an in-depth analysis, see Losada-Otálora and Andonova (2017).

of stock market liquidity in Chile where it is seen that a few institutional characteristics of Chile's corporate governing framework, such as the relatively poor protections of minority shareholders, play a more relevant role. This report suggested that strengthening corporate governing in Chile may also enhance stock market liquidity. However, the report does not go into much depth on the evolution of Chilean regulations in strengthening minority shareholder protections, nor does it suggest which other measures to take to reach a desirable level of protection and therefore enhance liquidity.

2.3 *Pension Funds as Minority Shareholders*

The principal domestic institutional investors are the country's six pension fund managers (*Administradores de Fondos de Pensiones*—or AFP, per its Spanish acronym) that manage Chile's mandatory pension savings. They invest locally and abroad. Other institutional investors in the market are foreign investors, insurance companies, and the mutual fund industry. These actors comprise the main minority shareholder group in the industry.

Pension funds have strongly influenced corporate governing in Chile by performing a monitoring role and by actively defending minority shareholder rights in several cases, including in the case of takeover attempts to ensure fair prices are offered to minority shareholders (the "*Chispas* Case" discussed in the next section), and defending fairness in related-party transactions (the "Enersis Case"[6]). Also, they have historically pressured for more disclosure requirements. Due to their importance, pension funds generally elect at least one board member in large, listed corporations, so being able to influence boards and, in recent years, these efforts have tended to be coordinated across the AFPs.

Existing regulations require pension funds to disclose their overall corporate governance voting policies. They are obliged to attend shareholder meetings and exercise their voting rights in cases where they hold

[6] Although not analyzed in this chapter, this is a good example of AFP activism. In 2011 Endesa Spain sought to bring about a capital increase in Enersis Chile under terms that would not be favorable to all its shareholders. Through AFP activism, the Chilean regulator deemed the capital increase to be a transaction among related parties that require stricter regulation and granting better terms for minority shareholders. The terms of the agreement were subsequently discussed in 2015 in a new restructuration process and, again, the AFPs played a vital role in reinforcing to respect minority shareholder rights.

more than 1% of a corporation's equity. They must announce their votes publicly at the shareholders' meeting, as well as report their votes to the Pension Fund Superintendency. However, under a specific AFP regulation, once a board candidate is elected, the AFPs may not communicate with "its" board member, so denying them the possibility to exercise a level of direct shareholder activism, other than by exercising its standard shareholders rights. It is worth noting that, as in many other jurisdictions, fiduciary duties apply to board members, regardless of whether a board member is deemed *independent* or not, as described by the Chilean Corporations Act.

2.4 A Small State-Owned Enterprise Sector

After a wave of privatizations in the mid-1980's, today, the state-owned enterprise sector is relatively small in comparison to the overall economy, but it includes companies that play a major and strategic role in the economy, such as Codelco (the world's largest copper producer and a major source of government revenue) and Banco Estado (the only Chilean state-owned bank).

The Public Enterprise System ("SEP", per its Spanish acronym) is a technical advisory body of the state, created in 2001, the purpose of which is to bring together and coordinate the decisions and representation that the state is responsible for as owner in state-owned enterprises. It acts as a quasi-holding structure, coordinating state's ownership function for most State-owned enterprises (20 out of 32), but separate legal and institutional arrangements are in place for many of the larger or more prominent state-owned enterprises (such as Codelco and Banco Estado referred to above).

The Transparency Act, enacted in April 2009, requires all State-owned enterprises to disclose the same information and comply with the same accounting standards as private enterprises. Regarding corporate governance, Chile has been taking important steps to make supervisory arrangements more uniform, by establishing a new SEP *Code of Conduct* (which includes policies on internal management and board obligations, CEO role, internal and external audit, risk management, and supervision) and new procedures for the appointment of independent directors in the state-owned enterprises under its supervision. This process of implementing corporate governance improvements has been an incentive to professionalize the boards in state-owned enterprises.

3 The Evolution of Corporate Governing in Chile

The legal and regulatory framework for capital markets, company law, and corporate governing has been revised repeatedly over the past 20 years in response to domestic and international events. We can identify at least four defining moments for the evolution of the corporate governing framework we explore in this section. First, the "*Chispas*"—meaning *little sparks* in Spanish—case, that triggered a first legal reform to specifically protect minority shareholders and changed the *mentality* toward corporate governing in Chile, as well as other significant cases. Second, Chile's accession process to the OECD, which prompted several legal and regulatory reforms. Third, the introduction of a corporate governance code. And fourth, which can be seen as an aftermath of the commitments Chile assumed on joining the OECD, the reform to the Chilean market regulatory body.

3.1 Chispas and Other Notable Cases

Chispas[7]

The controversial case of *Chispas* marked the beginning of a new stage in financial regulation regarding the protection of minority shareholders. The case was the catalyst for Law No. 19,705 in 2000—still (mostly) in force today—that includes public offerings of mandatory shares in the event of changes in control, better corporate governing in the form of obligatory implementation of Directors' Committees, the regulation of related-party transactions and the rights of ADR holders.

Prior to Law No. 19,705 in 2000, there were no rules regarding tender offers and the transfer of any shareholding, such that transfers of controlling stakes of any size could be carried out as a private transaction to the detriment of minority shareholders. The principle of non-discrimination was absent, making it possibile (and, then, legal) to direct public tender offerings to some shareholders, to the exclusion others. The payment of differentiated prices for different share packages was also not prohibited. Moreover, the earlier legislation did not consider it a duty to inform the public of a party's intention to make a bid in a tender or ensure the

[7] "*Chispas*" in Spanish means "sparks", as in electrical sparks, in English.

minimum information that should be made available. Finally, no references was made to the role of directors and managers during a tender process.

Although complex, the *Chispas* case can be summarized as follows. In 1997, Enersis—the largest Chilean holding company operating in the electrical utility sector—as a result of the privatization of Chilectra—was acquired by Endesa España. The voids in the law of the time allowed Enersis' controllers to obtain disproportionate benefits, obtaining the entire control premium at a price substantially above the prevailing market level. The sale conditions were possible due to the existence of two classes of shares: A and B. While Class A shares had the right to higher dividends, they had no voting rights. Enersis was effectively controlled by Class B shareholders, who owned 0.06% of the company, but had voting rights that allowed them to elect much of the board. Class B shares were held through a series of corporate structures grouped together into what became known as the "*Chispas*" companies, because of their names.[8] In addition to being shareholders of Class B shares, the controllers held positions on the board of Enersis or were C level executives.

Endesa España negotiated the terms of the sale directly with the controllers of Enersis (also, board members and/or senior executives), who held the Series B, which resulted in a public tender offer for Class A and B shares but offered to pay a price 840 times higher for Class B shares. In addition, Endesa España gave Class B shareholders the option of buying at a preferential price up to 5% of its own shares and assured them that they would be retained as managers of Enersis for a period of at least 5 years.

Pension funds that had the non-voting shares opposed the deal, and the initial terms of the public offering (IPO or OPA in Spanish) were eventually struck down by the market regulator, a decision that was subsequently upheld by the Supreme Court. The Chilean authorities pressed charges against the controllers, arguing primarily on grounds of breaches in their duty of loyalty as board members.

Due to the flaws in the legal framework exposed by the *Chispas* case, Public Tender Offers (OPAs) and Corporate Governance Law

[8] The so called "*Chispas*" companies were: "Compañía de Inversiones Chispa Uno S.A.", "Compañía de Inversiones Chispa Dos S.A.", "Compañía de Inversiones Luz S.A.", "Compañía de Inversiones Luz y Fuerza S.A.", and "Compañía de Inversiones Los Almendros S.A.".

were enacted in December 2000. The new Law introduced the concept of a "tender offer" into Chilean legislation, establishing the current market information requirement and pro-rata public bidding procedures. It made compulsory tender offers obligatory under certain circumstances (including where share transfers lead to a change in a company's control, or if the transfer allows a single person to hold more than two-thirds of the company) and new triggering events for withdrawal rights (among them, high levels of concentration of ownership or the sale of a large proportion of assets). Law No. 19,705 also imposed stricter rules regarding the use of privileged information and insider-trading.

More importantly for this chapter, the Law introduced significant corporate governance reforms. Firstly, it set higher requirements to avoid damages as results of transactions in which any of the directors has an interest: a strict transparency principle prevails, operations must be previously approved by the board, and must be carried out under arm's length conditions (an independent opinion may be needed if such conditions are not easily determined). Secondly, it introduces the obligation to name a "Directors' Committee" (comparable to an Audit Committee) in listed companies of a certain size (measured in terms of its market cap) to ensure adequate supervision of the company, particularly in cases of related-party transactions. The Committee must comprise three directors, the majority of which must be independent of the company's controller. Thirdly, it recognizes voting rights for holders of ADRs. Finally, it introduces, for the first time, the concept of a *Derivative Action,* which allows shareholders (holding at least 5% of the company) and directors, to claim in the name of and on behalf of the corporation, a compensation for losses caused by third parties.

The *Chispas* Case was the first to openly challenge corporate governing principles in Chile, ending in a much-commented legal reform. However, as Clarke (2009) highlights "*perhaps the most important development was the cultural change that came with the new regulations. The reformers helped to generate concern for the rights of investors. The reform also strengthened the general public's perception that securities market regulations are enforced for the abuses of both small participants and those of economic agents exercising major influence over the market*".

In the following years, in an effort to build a more robust corporate governance regime and to enhance capital markets, Congress enacted a series of further legal reforms, introduced by Law No. 19,768 and Law No. 19,769 of 2001 (also known as the "*Capital Market I Law*") and Law No. 20,190 of 2007 (also known as the "*Capital Market II Law*"), which perfected the control tools and sanction powers of the Superintendency of Securities and Insurance ("SVS").[9]

To date no other case or scandal has had the critical legal implications that the *Chispas* Case had. However, some other cases have shaped the corporate governing landscape in recent years.

Farmacias Ahumada S.A.

In 2009 the SVS fined all the directors of Farmacias Ahumada S.A. (also known as "FASA"), one of the major drugstore/pharmacy retailers in Chile, for breaching their duty monitor and to be informed about certain antitrust violations committed by some of its employees.

The case was full of corporate governance mistakes made by the majority shareholder of the company, who held the title of Chairman of the board and was also the company founder (among them, misinformation, nepotism, and the dismissal of minority shareholders such as the AFPs, who also played an important role in this case, pushing corporate governing reforms within the company). The FASA case highlighted the importance of not only the rights of board members of being informed, but also their duty to exercise such rights.

This case was also a background for the Corporate Governance Law that will be analyzed in the following section. The case had enormous press repercussions and, as an aftermath, many companies started to introduce codes of conduct or internal corporate governance regulation.

[9] Other Laws were subsequently issued making up what is considered as a "*Capital Market Bicentenary Reform Agenda*"—a collaborative process that allowed the private sector to contribute with initiatives. Part of this reform process is contained in the regulations:

- Law 20,522 of 2011, that modernizes and promotes the competition of the financial system;
- Law 20,544 of 2011, relating to derivatives taxation;
- Law 20,667 of 2012, relating to the insurance contract;
- Law 20,715 of 2013, on protection of credit debtors;
- Law 20,712 of 2014, also known as Single Funds Act ("LUF" as per its Spanish acronym); and.
- Law 20,789 of 2014, which gives legal recognition to the Financial Stability Board (already created by decree in 2011).

La Polar

In 2011 a major credit fraud and accounting practice scandal shook the country. La Polar was one the biggest retailers in the country. It was acquired by a private equity firm which, in turn, listed the company on the Santiago Stock Exchange, so becoming one of the very few cases where there was no single shareholder controlling the company.

The case revealed that non-concentrated firms were subject to oversight problems that had hitherto not been seen in a traditionally concentrated market like Chile's.

The case exploded in 2011, after the Chile's national consumer protection service (SERNAC) had received many complaints from La Polar's customers about the company's store credit card management program. As was later found out, La Polar's executives had unilateral renegotiated (rolled over) the overdue debts without its customers' knowledge or consent. This fraudulent practice, together with fraudulent accounts, served to keep it reported delinquency rates low while artificially swelling the size of its loan portfolio and collections of fees and interest surcharges.

The case quickly garnered broad press coverage. La Polar subsequently admitted to the fraudulent practices and the company's market value fell (by some estimates) by over 95%, dragging down the Chilean stock market and causing enormous losses for the pension funds managed by the AFPs.

The company had to compensate its clients. The main senior executives were successfully prosecuted. The SVS, also fined all the board of directors, several senior executives and ex-executives and the external auditors for breaching their fiduciary duties, triggering litigation for damages that took over 10 years to resolve.

Cascadas

More recently, the cases of *Cascades*—the word for "cascades" in Spanish—deserve to be highlighted because of the pyramidal corporate structure—in this case taken to an extreme—that business groups were able to use in Chile.

In the *Cascades* case, the controlling shareholder of the listed company SQM S.A. (a nitrate and lithium group) used a structure of private investment companies to expropriate minority shareholders by fixing stock market prices and illicitly trading shares of SQM and companies linked to SQM. The securities were sold at below-market prices to companies related to the controller and subsequently resold, after a short lapse of time, and in most cases, back to the same cascading companies, at prices higher than the original purchase prices.

The case has been called the largest legal case regarding the stock market in Chile and the SVS imposed what was the highest historical fine on the Chairman and (then) controller for market manipulation. This fine was, however, subsequently reduced by the courts.

The regulator also fined other SQM executives and partners in Chile's most prominent financial institutions and asset managers that had allowed share auctions and operations without the required dissemination (fines that in the case of the latter were also later reversed by the Court of Appeals).

This case prompted anti-corruption measures and can be seen as a background of Law No. 21,314, enacted in 2021 and several aspects of which are commented on further in below.

3.2 *Chile's Accession to the OECD*

The OECD Council agreed to open accession discussions with Chile on 16 May 2007, setting the terms, conditions, and process for accession. In this context, the OECD Corporate Governance Committee was invited to examine Chile's position regarding its core corporate governing features and to provide a formal opinion on Chile's ability and willingness to submit and implement the recommendations laid down in the OECD Principles of Corporate Governance and the OECD Guidelines on Corporate Governance for state-owned enterprises. In May 2010, Chile officially became an OECD Member on its successful completion of these and other procedures. The OECD Corporate Governance Committee published its conclusions in 2011.

To comply with the OECD, Chile enacted Law No. 20,382 which improves corporate governance in private companies (also called "Corporate Governance Law"). The Law was approved by Congress in September 2009 and published on 1 January 2010, in time to be considered in a review by the same OECD Corporate Governance Committee.

As reported by the OECD at the time, Law No. 20,382 establishes new protections for minority shareholders through enhanced transparency standards and mechanisms to address the use of privileged information, related-party transactions, conflicts of interest, and provisions to improve the definition of independent directors and strengthen their role in reviewing sensitive issues. In addition, the law strengthened the governance of Chile's largest state-owned enterprise, the copper mining company Codelco (OECD, 2011a).

The most important changes introduced by Corporate Governance Law—most of which are in force today as discussed in Sect. 3—included:

Independence in the Boardroom

The law established that companies with a higher market capitalization and certain percentages of shareholders control must have a board of directors with no less than 7 members that oversee the corporation, at least one of them being independent. This independent director must also be a member of the *Directors' Committee* (as stated above, equivalent to an *Audit Committee*).

The Law also improved the conditions and criteria that independent directors are required to fulfill, mainly relating to economic criteria (i.e., incentives), rather than the previous definition which focused on who elected the director.

The definition of "independence" changed. Prior to Law 20,382, a director was considered independent if he/she had been elected as a director at a Shareholders Meeting after having excluded the votes of any controlling shareholder or any party related to the controlling shareholder. With the Law under analysis and beginning 1 January 2010, directors are considered independent if they have not fallen into any of the following categories during the 18 month prior to his/her election: (i) had a relationship, interest or relevant dependency on the company, its subsidiaries, controlling shareholders, principal officers or occupied a senior position in any of the foregoing; (ii) had a close family relationship with any person mentioned under paragraph (i); (iii) had worked for a not-for-profit organization which received significant funds from individuals referred to in paragraph (i); (iv) had been partners or shareholders (with a direct or indirect participation of more than 10%) in, or held a senior position in a company that has provided significant services to persons specified in paragraph (i); (v) had been a partner or shareholder (with a direct or indirect participation of more than 10%) in, or held a senior position with company's main competitors, suppliers or customers. Subsequently. Law 21,314 added that anyone who had been appointed as a board member in a subsidiary within the same timeframe is also not deemed independent.

Improvements of the Regulation on Related-Party Transactions ("RPT")
To better address related companies within pyramid structures of company groups, and conflicts of interest, the Corporate Governance Law introduced a new chapter to the Corporation Act on listed company RPTs. RPTs are defined as transactions between the company and one or more individuals or entities related to the company (e.g., directors, managers, or senior executives of the company or their relatives, legal entities in which any of the foregoing individuals own, directly or indirectly, at least 10% of the shares or equity rights of the legal entity, among others).

Improvements in Information Disclosure
It improved the handling of information with the Chilean regulator at the time ("SVS", today "CMF") and black-out period policies. Also, it improves investment portfolio disclosure requirements on managers' and majority shareholders.

Shareholders Voting Process
The law also regulates the details of assets held in custody (proxy voting and custodian voting).

External Audit Services
The law regulates conflicts of interest by determining that a company's external auditors must be independent from the firms that they audit, and that revenues from one client may not exceed 15% of the auditing firm's total revenues.

3.3 The Road to Enacting a Chilean Corporate Governance Code

While there had been unsuccessful attempts in the past, after Corporate Governance Law, there was a genuine "push" to create a Corporate Governance Code with significant impact and a high degree of adherence. This idea was developed jointly by the SVS and the Instituto Chileno de Administración Racional de Empresas ("ICARE"). The first step in creating the code was an event to raise awareness of the need to create a culture of self-regulation through a code of corporate governance among key market representatives.

ICARE was originally tasked with drafting the code, but this arrangement failed and ICARE was never able to issue a draft. The regulator regained control of the initiative and presented a first draft of the Code at a second big event to raise awareness. The proposal was communicated to the market and was subject to a public consultation, which presented the opportunity for professionals, directors, and experts to analyze the draft and provide comments. During the period of public consultation, the regulator received many more suggestions than similar processes conducted in the past.

In 2011, the SVS issued General Rule No. 341, mandating listed companies to answer an annual questionnaire—which was made public on the regulator's website—covering 19 specific practices of corporate governance that companies must implement or else explain why particular practices have not been implemented, following a "*comply or explain*" *approach.*[10] The questionnaire comprises questions in four sections: (i) Operations and composition of the board of directors; (ii) Relationship between the company, its shareholders, and the public in general; (iii) Management and risk control; (iv) Evaluation by a third party.

The declared objective of the capital market authority regarding the Code was *to provide the market with better and more reliable information relating to whether the listed companies are complying with certain corporate governance practices*. While the authority's declared purpose of the tool is not to achieve a high percentage of adoption of practices, compliance with the code does raise some issues of concern, especially regarding the usefulness of the discussion and the information provided for companies, shareholders, potential investors, and other stakeholders.

In the early stages of adoption of the Code, the *Corporate Governance Centre* at Pontificia Universidad Católica de Chile reported that companies complied with the code in a formal, standardized way, because they "*had to*" (fear of reprisals for non-compliance) rather than because they genuinely "*wanted to*". Given that some players pushed for a "ranking" of corporate governance practices, the Centre stated that it would actually be counterproductive to carry out an analysis of the state of corporate governance practices in Chile based on compliance reports submitted by companies, mainly because, even in the first year, it was treated as a mere

[10] Later, consequence of the commentaries of the market authority to the first disclosure process in 2015, it was clear that the approach was rather a "*comply or not, and explain*" approach, where an explanation was required irrespective of the answer given.

formality to comply with the Code. Three years after implementation of the Code, comprehensive research carried out by the Centre has shown that 60% of General Rule No. 341 had been adopted before the rule—i.e., showing little impact—and information contained in the answers seems to have become standardized and scarce, suggesting a mere compliance or "box-ticking" exercise (Godoy et al., 2018).

After a revision and reform process started in 2014, the SVS repealed General Rule No. 341 and issued a revised version of the Chilean Code through General Rule No. 385 which deepened the sections already contained in General Rule No. 341. According to the regulator, Rule's No. 385 main aim is *to generate debate within companies on matters of corporate governance practices and to improve the information reported by corporations in the local market and so generate incentives for investors to make their investment decisions privileged those companies in which their interests are best protected.*

General Rule No. 385 contains board of director related practices, and also compels listed companies to provide information on the existence of internal audit committees, corporate social responsibility programs, policies concerning social responsibility and sustainable development, and whistleblower reporting channels, among others. Rule No. 385 broadens the scope of the original sections and 19 practices by disaggregating the original practices into 99 sub-practices, aiming "*to better capture the different reality of each entity*". Today, reported implementation only reaches an overall level of around 30%. Again, while reaching a high implementation percentage is still not the final objective as declared by the authority, the rule has been criticized by the market actors, who do not feel represented by the instrument, and feel therefore driven to issue formal answers because of the way that practices are presented (i.e., too specific to leave room for alternatives) and the time-consuming exercise of revising 99 detailed practices.

Along with General Rule No. 385, SVS enacted General Rule No. 386 to enhance transparency standards and, for the first time, introduce corporate social responsibility practices by promoting, among other things, management diversity (e.g., in relation to gender, nationality, age, and length of tenure for board members and high-level executives).

Content of General Rules No. 385 and No. 386 will be further explained below, and a new reform process will be addressed in the final section.

3.4 *Strengthening of the Chilean Securities Regulator*

In 2011, in the accession process, the *Corporate Governance Committee* pointed out that the authority at the time, the head of the SVS, was directly appointed and removable by the President without cause, which raised issues of independence. The Committee recommended providing adequate checks and balances to protect against the risk of political intervention in enforcement decisions (OECD, 2011a).

In February 2017, after many years of discussion in Congress, Law No. 21,000 replaced the Securities and Insurance Superintendency with the Financial Market Commission (hereinafter, CMF for its Spanish acronym), which began operations on December 14, 2017. Law No 21,000, in connection with Law No. 20,130, also contemplated the integration between CMF and the Banking Regulator (previously, the Superintendency of Banks and Financial Institutions). This came about in June 2019.

The role of the CMF is far broader than its predecessor the SVS, and it includes oversight of the whole market and financial sector under a *twin peaks* structure. Also, for the first time, the Law explicitly provides that the market regulator has a broader mandate to promote sound functioning of the financial system, market development, and oversee financial stability and systemic risk. In this sense, the CMF is called on to secure the proper functioning, development, and stability of the financial market, facilitating the participation of market agents and promoting duly standards.

The new regulatory body has an improved governance structure (under a new collegiate supervision scheme of technical nature with 5 *Commissioners*), more independence from political cycles,[11] new and enhanced attributions, and improved specific administrative sanctioning regimes. Additionally, enforcement procedure and due process guarantees are substantially enhanced through the appointment of a *Special Prosecutor* who oversees the *Enforcement Unit*, handling the investigation and enforcement proceedings and granted independence from the CMF Board (previously, the functions of investigation and sanctioning were not separated, and hither to the Superintendent was "*judge and jury*" in any dispute at the same time).

[11] The Chair is appointed for the same term as the President of the Republic (4 years); the commissioners are appointed to staggered terms by the President and ratified by the Senate, holding office for 6 years and replaced in pairs every three years, as applicable.

Law No. 21,000 stresses the fact that market participants should self-regulate in corporate governing matters, business ethics, transparency, and fair competition. The obligation to self-regulate may be fulfilled in the following ways: (i) by being part of the Financial Self-Regulation Committee that may be constituted or (ii) the entities may establish their own rules and codes of conduct in the matters, for subsequent approval by the CMF, without being obliged to be members of the *Financial Self-Regulation Committee* that may exist. The *Financial Self-Regulation Committee*, not constituted by the private sector to date, must ensure effective compliance with the good practices enacted and resolve conflicts that occur between market players.

4 Corporate Governing Today

To date, Chile's approach in addressing corporate governance has been largely based on "*hard law*", especially when compared to other countries in the region. Private sector initiatives, such as self-regulation and voluntary codes, have played less of a role than they have in other countries in the region (OECD, 2016).

The principal sources of corporate governance rules applicable to listed corporations in Chile are contained in the Corporations Act (Law No. 18,046) and the Securities Market Act (Law No. 18,045), both enacted in 1981 and amended several times since. As mentioned before, other important legal bodies are the Corporations Regulation (Supreme Decree No. 702/2011 of the Ministry of Finance), the General Rules issued by the CMF, and the special rules regarding corporate governing issued by the Superintendency of Pensions applicable to Private Pension Fund Administrators.

General rules on corporate governance are applicable to listed corporations and closed corporations, but other arrangements exist for partnerships limited by shares or special norms for other types of legal entities.

The listed company regime is enforced mainly by the CMF, which has the authority to issue instructions and orders to apply and allow compliance of relevant laws and rules, to solve inquiries and petitions, and to investigate claims made by shareholders, investors, or other legitimate interested parties. Other enforcement bodies include the Superintendency of Pensions, the Central Bank, and Courts of Justice when compliance problems arise. The Ministry of Finance promotes changes in regulation and plays a policy coordinating role, including hosting monthly coordinating meetings for a prudential risk overview.

4.1 *Legal Provisions*

Listing Requirements

The listing process is mostly governed by law. Public limited companies must first register with the CMF and be added to the Securities Registry. With that, the company can then—if it chooses—list on the stock exchanges. Only then, with these requirements met, can trading begin in their shares. The stock exchanges may not deny a company's right to be listed in the Securities Registry, nor impose additional requirements to those required by law on companies that have decided to be listed. The stock exchanges, however, can suspend the transactions of a share if there are indications of the existence of relevant information not disclosed to the market, or if the market price undergoes significant fluctuations without apparent cause.

Corporate Governing Structures

The board of directors oversees the management of a company and represents it judicially and extrajudicially in compliance with its purpose, being vested with all the managing authorities that neither the law nor the by-laws vest in the shareholders acting in shareholders meeting.

Corporate boards in Chile are single-tier boards—two-tier structures are not considered in the Corporations Act.

The composition of boards varies according to the type and size of a company. Closed corporations shall have at least three directors. Listed companies must have at least five board members. Under certain size circumstances,[12] listed companies are required to have at least seven board members, which must include one independent director and a *Board Committee*. The upper number of board seats, the term of appointments,

[12] When listed companies reach a market capitalization of 1.5 million *Unidades de Fomento* (USD60 million approximately) and at least 12.5% of the company's voting shares are held by shareholders that control or possess less than 10% of all the company's shares, an independent director must be appointed, and a *Board Committee* must be established.

and the existence of alternate directors may be contained in the Company by-laws.

Directors are appointed and removed by shareholders acting in shareholder meetings. The following persons cannot be appointed as board members: minors (under 18 years of age); directors who have been revoked owing to the rejection of the balance sheet by a shareholder meeting; individuals with certain criminal records (including bankruptcy crimes); and authorities regarding entities that they supervise or control. There are other restrictions to being a director of listed corporations or their affiliates, such as being a Senator, Congressman, State Minister, CMF officer, or stockbroker. Except for independence in certain cases, there are no required criteria that individual directors or the board must fulfill, such as age, gender, nationality, diversity, or expertise.[13]

The independence concept was amended by Law No. 20,382, as explained in the previous section. Before the reform, a director was independent if he or she had been elected without controlling shareholders' votes. Currently, a person shall not be considered "independent" if, at any moment during the last 18 months:

1. they have held any economic, professional, credit or commercial connection, interest or dependency of relevant volume and nature, with the company, the other companies from the same group, its controller, the senior management of any of them, or have been a director, CEO, manager, senior executive, or their consultants;
2. they possess certain family relationships with the above-mentioned persons;
3. they have been director, CEO, manager, or senior executive of a non-profit organization that has received contributions or donations from the persons indicated in (1);
4. they have been a partner or shareholder who has owned or controlled, directly or indirectly, 10% or more of the capital;
5. they have been a director, CEO, manager, or senior executive of an entity that has rendered legal or consultant services, for relevant amounts, or an external auditor of the persons indicated in (1); or

[13] As per General Rule No. 386, the annual report shall contain information about diversity in the board of directors, reporting on the number of directors by gender, nationality, age-range, and years as director. It shall also include information about the professions or occupations of directors appointed during the last two years.

6. they have been a partner or shareholder who owned or controlled, directly or indirectly, 10% or more of the capital, directors, CEO, managers or senior executives of the main company's competitors, suppliers, or clients.

Recently, in April 2021, Law 21,314 added that anyone that has been appointed as a board member in any subsidiary within the same timeframe is not independent. Also, the Law grants the CMF the authority to determine the requirements that a director must satisfy in order to be considered independent.

The board meetings must be chaired by the chairman of the board. Unless otherwise provided for in the Company by-laws, board resolutions must be approved by the majority of board members with voting rights at a meeting and the chairman has a casting vote.

The boards of directors of listed companies shall hold ordinary meetings at least once a month. A company's by-laws may establish a higher frequency or other specific requirements.

The Corporations Act states that the position of CEO is incompatible with that of the board Chairman. Similarly, an auditor or company accountant may not be Chairman of the company, and, in listed corporations, these functions are also incompatible with being a board member. This prohibition leads to a strict separation between the board and senior officers of the company, eliminating some potential conflicts of interest that may arise when the Chairman and the CEO are the same person.

4.2 Directors' Duties and Liabilities

The Corporations Act contains fiduciary duties regulation. Directors owe both a duty of care and duty of loyalty to all shareholders. This duty of loyalty implies that board members must abstain from acting in the event of a conflict of interest and must not appropriate corporate business opportunities for their own benefit or for any shareholder or group of shareholders, including those who elected them. There are also other duties, such as confidentiality, information—configured as a right, rather than a duty—and rendering of accounts.

Directors must always act with the care and diligence that people ordinarily employ in their own businesses (ordinary standard of care—*culpa leve*—as defined in Chilean civil law) and they are jointly and severally liable for damages caused to the company, the shareholders, or third parties. Managers have the same duties and liability as directors.

Directors appointed by a shareholders' group have the same duties toward the company and other shareholders as the remaining directors, i.e., not being able to waive their duty to them in defending the interest of the shareholders' group that elected them. Moreover, they cannot approve by-law amendments, issue securities, approve policies, or make decisions that would move away from benefiting the company in its entirety.

Director's liability can be civil, criminal,[14] or administrative and any provision in the corporate by-laws and any agreement adopted by the shareholders that tends to release or limit the directors' liability is void. If a director does not wish to assume any responsibility for an act or agreement of the board of directors, his or her dissent shall be recorded in the minutes of the relevant directors' meeting and shall be informed to shareholders in the next ordinary shareholders' meeting.

4.3 Board and Management Compensation

The company's by-laws must determine if directors shall be remunerated or not. If remunerated, board compensation must be annually approved at the regular shareholders' meeting. The annual report to shareholders' meeting must detail all payments made to the board members annually, including any payments that do not relate to their functions as members of the board of directors. The members of the directors' committee shall be remunerated. The remuneration shall be fixed, every year, by the ordinary shareholders' meeting. The remuneration of any director´s committee member shall not be less than the remuneration that any regular board member receives, increased by one-third.

Shareholders do not have a "say on pay" regarding executive remuneration; it is determined by the board of directors or by the senior

[14] Law No. 21,121, enacted in late 2018, incorporated "Disloyal Management" to the Chilean criminal system. This new criminal offense penalizes any person's mismanagement of third-party assets, resulting in a loss, when performed through or with an abuse of his/her authorities or other actions or omissions that are manifestly contrary to the asset owner's interests. Law provides that this criminal offense aims at managers and directors of listed companies and certain regulated corporations.

management. However, the shareholders are the ones that set the board's compensation, as explained above.

Having said all that, companies are not required to disclose the pay ratio between the CEO's compensation or Directors and other workers.

4.4 *Shareholder Rights*

Most shares are issued based on "one share, one vote". Shares with multiple votes are banned by the Corporations Act. However, shares with limited or no voting rights are allowed. In a limited number of cases, dual class shares with restrictive or preferential rights are permitted. Preferred shares must be approved by two-thirds of the voting shares and permitted by the company's by-laws. Corporations Law prohibits cross-shareholdings.

The Corporations Act expressly provides for certain matters to be reserved for shareholders and which are to be decided either in ordinary or extraordinary shareholders' meetings. Ordinary meetings are held once a year, as provided for in the by-laws of the company, and decide on matters that expressly relate to approving the company's financial statements, dividend distributions, election or revocation of the board members, and the appointment of external auditors.

Extraordinary shareholders' meetings are held at any time where it is necessary to decide on material matters, including by-law amendments, a company's dissolution, corporate conversions, mergers and spin-offs, the sale of relevant assets, bond issuances, among others.

There is a 10-day minimum public notice period for shareholder meetings and requirements for sending notification to all shareholders.[15]

Shareholders that own more than 10% of outstanding shares with voting rights may request the board of directors to convene an ordinary or extraordinary shareholders' meeting, expressing in their request the matters to be discussed at the meeting.

Shareholders who own more than 10% of voting shares may formulate comments and propositions relating to the company's business and to require their inclusion in the annual report; and related to the matters

[15] This minimum notification period in advance for notifying shareholders of any kind of meeting—including the annual general meeting—was recently amended by Law N°21.314 published on 13 April 2021, previously, it was 20-days).

put up for vote by the board in shareholders' meetings and to include them in the information to be sent to shareholders.

Dissenting shareholders enjoy appraisal rights to demand from the company a buyout for their shares at market value if they vote against certain fundamental matters. Dissenting shareholders comprises shareholders who oppose in the same meeting the agreement reached by the shareholders or, who being absent at that meeting informs the company about his or her disagreement within 30 days as of the meeting's date. Appraisal rights must be exercised within 30 days after the shareholders' meeting that gave rise to the dissenting shareholders' appraisal right. The market value for shares that are traded on stock exchanges will be the weighted average of the stock market transactions of the shares during a period of 60 trading days between the ninetieth and thirtieth day prior to the shareholders' meeting that gave rise to the dissenting shareholders' appraisal right.

4.5 *Shareholder Actions*

A derivative action is available to any shareholder or group of shareholders representing at least 5% of the voting shares, or any board member, that may bring on behalf of the company against anyone who may prove to be liable for damages arising from, or losses incurred by the company as a result of, a breach of applicable laws and regulations, or of the company's by-laws. The shareholder or board member must be pursuing a corporate right (as opposed to an individual right) to procure a court judgment in the company's favor.

Perhaps because of the length and cost of court processes, shareholders do not normally use the courts to pursue private rights of action but tend to use the CMF as the vehicle for submitting complaints when they believe their rights have been violated. While private arbitration is legally an option to ensure quicker resolution of disputes, it is not typically used (OECD, 2011a).

4.6 *Mandatory Dividend Policy*

The Corporations Act establishes a minimum dividend requirement, by which publicly listed companies are required to pay out a minimum 30% of the previous year distributable earnings, after taxes, as dividends on common stock, unless otherwise agreed by the unanimous consent of the shareholders. Dividends are paid once they are approved at the shareholders annual meeting.

Excess dividends may be paid on a voluntary basis and as agreed in the shareholder meeting.

4.7 *Related-Party Transactions (RPTs)*

As explained above, RPTs are defined as transactions between the company and one or more individuals or entities related to the company (directors, managers, or senior executives of the company or their relatives, legal entities in which any of the foregoing individuals own, directly or indirectly, at least 10% of the shares or equity rights of the legal entity, among others). Listed companies may enter into related-party transactions provided that they are intended to contribute to the corporate interest, the transaction is at arms' length as to the market price, terms, and conditions, and the transaction complies with the related-party transaction procedure detailed in the Corporations Act.

Pursuant to the related-party transaction procedure, individuals who have a personal interest in the transaction must immediately report the situation to the board of directors. Before the company enters into the corresponding transaction, it must be approved by the company assets, the furnishing of collateral or personal guarantees to secure third-party obligations (except in the case of subsidiaries, in which case the board's approval will suffice), the dissolution of the company and other similarly relevant matters.

Corporations Law requires the disclosure of all related-party transactions in the next general meeting, except for those considered of non-relevant amount, the ones involving a subsidiary whose equity is controlled by 95% or more, and those considered ordinary according to the "usual operations" policy approved by the board.

Law 21,314 recently enacted,[16] strengthened the level of protection to minority shareholders when the company approves RPTs, as the Directors Committee must issue a formal opinion, a special policy about habitual operations has to be in place and they have to be reported to the market. The Law also includes a new presumption of liability of directors in the event that they approve RTPs contravening rules set by the law and a new

[16] Enacted on April 13, 2021.

locking period of 30 days prior to the disclosure of its financial statements in which directors, main executives, and their related parties cannot carry out transactions in securities issued by the company.

4.8 *Audit Provisions*

Chile's Corporations Law stipulates that an external auditor must be independent of the firm it audits, and that revenues from one client may not exceed 15% of the auditor's total revenues (however, this percentage may be waived on a vote of approval by two-thirds of the shareholders). There are no provisions mandating a change in audit firms, but partners in an audit firm are deemed to lose their "independence" after 5 years of having conducted audit services for a listed company (that said, an external audit company may continue carrying out the work, but a different partner will need to be named to perform the process). Audit companies are also now supervised by the CMF.

4.9 *Corporate Governance Code*

In June 2015, the SVS issued General Rules No. 385 and No. 386 to improve and expand the information to be published by publicly traded companies regarding their corporate governance, corporate social responsibility, and sustainable development. These rules are known today as the "*Chilean Corporate Governance Code*".

Under General Rule No. 385, all listed companies are instructed to provide the CMF on an annual basis, with answers to a survey on a "*comply or not and explain*" basis, on 99 detailed practices in four main areas. The authority did not issue a guide on how it is expected to answer for each practice and information made available by companies most of the time is restricted to the minimum. The information is publicly available through the authority's web page.

General Rule No. 385 contains corporate governance practices regarding:

1. *The board's functions and composition*. This section is the longest and more detailed of the document. It includes the disclosure of 51 practices within 11 sub-topics. The main practices are the following:

a. The board of directors has a procedure or mechanism for the induction of each new board member, which aims to facilitate the process of obtaining information regarding several aspects of the company;
b. The board of directors has a procedure or ongoing training mechanism of the board of directors for updating knowledge;
c. The board of directors has a policy for contracting experts that advise it on accounting, tax, financial, legal, or other matters;
d.–g. The board of directors meets at least quarterly with the external auditing company in charge of auditing the financial statements; company's risk management unit or equivalent responsible party; internal auditing unit, compliance officer or equivalent responsible party; unit of Social Responsibility, Sustainable Development, or responsible party with an equivalent function;
h. The board of directors performs, each year, site visits to the different offices and facilities of the company;
i. Of the meetings referred above, at least one meeting for each point is held without the presence of the company's CEO.
j. The board of directors has a formal procedure in place for ongoing improvement; and
k. The board of directors has a system to keep information available to each board member.

2. *Relationships between the company, shareholders, and the public in general.* The section starts by referring to board member election practices. Regarding shareholder rights, it gathers information about mechanism, system, or procedure that permits the shareholders to participate and exercise their right to vote remotely. It also asks if the following information is available to the public: social responsibility and sustainable development policies, identification of the relevant stakeholders, company's relevant risks, including sustainability risks, indicators measured by the company in terms of social responsibility and sustainable development, the existence of goals and developments made by sustainability indicators. Finally, it inquires if the company has a unit for relations with shareholders, investors, and press, and if the company has an updated easy-accessible website.

3. *Risk management and internal control.* This section compels companies to disclose if the board of directors has implemented a formal Risk Management and Control process and a whistleblower channel. It also requires disclosing formal procedures to identify the diversity of skills, conditions, experiences, and visions that its senior executives should possess and if there are organizational, social, or cultural barriers that could be inhibiting the skills, conditions, experiences, and visions. Furthermore, the section addresses succession plans. Finally, regarding salary structures and compensation policies of the CEO and other senior executives, the section asks if there is a revision policy in place (and whether if it is performed assessed by a third party), a dissemination policy on the website of the company and if salary structures and policies are subject to shareholder's approval.
4. *Third-party assessment.* This section is the least complied with in terms of yes/no answers. It contains 4 practices referring to whether the adoption of practices described above has been reviewed and validated by a third-party external to the company.

General Rule No. 386 mandates companies to include information in the annual report concerning: Diversity of gender, nationality, age, and length of tenure of directors, senior managers, and other executives reporting directly to the board, and in the organization as a whole. Remuneration and gender (providing a comparative breakdown of information on salary by type of position, duties performed, and level of responsibility for females relative to males).

Unfortunately, some studies show that the trend which started with General Rule No. 341 has continued with General Rule No. 386, in the sense that issuers have continued with a formalistic approach rather than taking a real opportunity to improve their corporate governance standards.[17]

[17] *Centro de Gobierno Corporativo* of the Pontificia Universidad Católica de Chile, comments made to the CMF in connection to the amendment of General Rule No. 30.

5 The Future of Corporate Governance in Chile: Conclusion and Challenges

5.1 Corporate Governance as Part of the ESG Strategy and Disclosure Obligations

In early 2020 the CMF started a process to reformulate General Rule No. 386, proposing to incorporate to the Annual Report a "Sustainability Report", which included several ESG elements. The public consultation for reformulation was open until March 2020 and the in-depth discussion was scheduled to be held in April and May 2020. However, discussions were put on hold due to the COVID-19 pandemic. In January 2021, the CMF announced its intention to reopen the debate of General Rule No. 386 but with the announced intention of completely reformulating the non-financial reporting rules for listed companies, which also include elements of corporate governing.

In March 2021, the CMF published for consultation a regulation that modernizes and improves the *environmental, social and governance* (ESG) standards that listed companies must include in their Annual Reports. The regulatory proposal involves restructuring the current Annual Report, integrally incorporating ESG issues in its content, including corporate government arrangements and best practices.

The new Report will allow us to know how entities structure their corporate governance; define the strategies to achieve their goals; and how they determine, identify, and manage materially relevant risks. According to the CMF, the proposal under public consultation *aims to reconcile the need for more information on ESG policies, practices and goals adopted by issuers of publicly traded securities with the difficulties or additional costs that reporting such information could entail.*

In its current state, the consultation repeals not only General Rule No. 386, but also General Rule No. 385 and the "Corporate Governance Code" as it is known today. In this context, corporate governance best practices will no longer have an autonomy status, but they will be part of a non-financial information disclosure, this change can have two outputs: or it increases focus as ESG disclosure becomes more relevant or it dilutes its importance in the much broader concept of disclosure of non-financial information.

5.2 *Discussion of the Board Composition*

In recent years there have been discussions over the possibility to include a gender quota for boards in Chile. In 2018 a Bill proposed introducing mandatory gender quotas in all Chilean boards. However, the Bill was only partially taken up as it is now being discussed whether to include gender quotas in State-owned enterprises. In late 2020, the *Corporate Governance Centre* at Pontificia Universidad Católica de Chile published a comprehensive study, concluding that, despite the positive effects of incorporating women on the board (mainly as a spill-over effect), there is as yet no conclusive evidence whether gender has any material effect on a company's financial results in Chile, or in other countries, notwithstanding other multiple positive externalities arising from diversity on boards.

Recently there have also been discussions on the possibility of including employee representatives on the board. While some have argued that the experience in Germany and other countries may be a good example to follow, others argue that employees at board level may go against the very nature of the board as conceptualized in Chile (being representatives of the shareholders) and add little value either to the shareholders or the labor force itself. The discussion is in early stages and there are currently no Bills or draft regulation proposing such changes. However, it is important to follow such discussions, especially in times of constitutional changes in the country.

5.3 *The Challenge of a Private Corporate Governance Code*

As can be seen, the concern to raise corporate governance practices and standards has been present in Chile for many years. This presence is a mixture of corporate governing scandals and corporate governance reforms that are in constant confrontation and evolution. This confrontation has since led to the embedding of corporate governance regulation in law which, while giving security to market participants, especially international ones, restrict companies' flexibility. This may also be an obstacle for economic growth.

As things stand, where attempts at developing a Corporate Governance Code may flounder along with the obligation to form part of the non-financial companies' disclosures in their Annual Reports, it is worth questioning what will be the future of corporate governing in Chile. The feeling after the attempts of General Rules No. 341 and 385 is that these have not been useful tools in improving corporate governance practices and generating a culture of best practices in corporate governance disclosure. The "Code" added little. It has been seen to be more of a *ticking-the-box* exercise rather than an opportunity to promote true best practices and to learn from peers.

In this context, is it worth trying again to push for a Corporate Governance Code this time that emerges from the private sector? Is the local corporate governing culture strong enough to create a code with the conviction of being a useful tool? Is there a "change fatigue" regarding corporate governance regulations? As yet, any answer to these questions is uncertain, but the discussion is certainly underway.

References

Cárdenas, J. (2016). Enredando a las elites empresariales en América Latina: Análisis de redes de interlocking directorates y propiedad en México, Chile, Perú y Brasil. *América Latina Hoy, 73*, 15–44. Universidad de Salamanca, Salamanca, España.

Centro de Gobierno Corporativo UC. (2020a). *Diversidad de género en la dirección de las empresas en Chile*. Retrieved from: https://centrogobiernocorporativo.uc.cl/informes/39-diversidad-de-genero-en-la-alta-direccion-de-las-empresas-en-chile/file

Centro de Gobierno Corporativo UC. (2020b). *Comentario Normativa en Consulta que Modifica NCG 30, en aquellas materias incorporadas por la NCG 386*. Retrieved from: https://centrogobiernocorporativo.uc.cl/informes/37-comentarios-cgcuc-consulta-normativa-cmf-ncg-30/file

Clarke, A., & Barsallo, C. (2009) *Reforming corporate governance: Experiences with public takeover bids in Chile and Panama*. International Finance Corporation. Retrieved from: https://www.ifc.org/wps/wcm/connect/e919718a-3a4a-4cc8%968eeb-ecced1e0882a/Focus6_Eng_B.pdf?MOD=AJPERES&CVID=jtCwuzn

De la Torre, A., Gozzi, J. C., & Schmukler, S. L. (2007). *Capital Market Development: Whither Latin America?* World Bank Policy Research Working Paper. Retrieved from: https://openknowledge.worldbank.org/bitstream/handle/10986/7205/wps4156.pdf?sequence=1&isAllowed=y

Espinosa, P. (2012). Corporate governance in Mexico and the evaluation of risk in bond issuance. In G. Nuñez & A. Oneto (Eds.), *Corporate governance in Brazil, Chile, Colombia, Mexico, and Peru*. Retrieved from: https://repositorio.cepal.org/bitstream/handle/11362/39772/S1420667_en.pdf?sequence=1

Godoy, M., Walker, E., & Zegers M. (2018, enero - abril). Análisis del primer intento de imponer autorregulación sobre gobierno corporativo en Chile: resultados de un oxímoron, *Revista Chilena de Derecho, 45*(1), 179–210

International Monetary Fund. (2016). *Stock Market Liquidity in Chile.* IMF Working Paper No. 16/223 by Brandao Marques, Luis. Retrieved from: https://www.imf.org/external/pubs/ft/wp/2016/wp16223.pdf

La Porta, R., López, F., & Shlleifer, A. (1999). Corporate ownership around the world. *The Journal of Finance, 54*(2), 471–517.

Lefort, F. (2005). Ownership structure and corporate governance in Latin America. *Revista Abante, 8*(1), 55–84.

Lefort, F. (2010). *Business groups in Chile.* In A. Colpan, T. Hikino, & J. Lincoln (Eds.), *Oxford handbook of business groups.* Oxford University Press. http://dx.doi.org/10.1093/oxfordhb/9780199552863.003.0014

Lefort, F., & González, R. (2008). "Hacia un Mejor Gobierno Corporativo en Chile," Abante, Escuela de Administracion. *Pontificia Universidad Católica De Chile, 11*(1), 19–45.

Lefort, F., & Urzúa, F. (2008). Board independence, firm performance and ownership concentration: Evidence from Chile. *Journal of Business Research, 61*(6), 615–622.

Lefort, F., & Walker, E. (2000). The Effects of Economic and Political Shocks on Corporate Governance Systems in Chile. *Abante, 2*(2), 183–206.

Losada-Otálora, M., & Andonova, V. (2017). Multilatinas: Where do we find them? *Cambridge University Press.* https://doi.org/10.1017/9781316417706.002pp11-34

OECD. (2011a). *Corporate Governance in Chile.* Corporate Governance, OECD Publishing. Retrieved from: http://dx.doi.org/10.1787/9789264095953-en

OECD. (2011b). *Achieving effective boards: A comparative study of corporate governance frameworks and board practices in Argentina, Brazil, Chile, Colombia, Mexico, Panama, and Peru.* Retrieved from: https://www.oecd.org/brazil/48510039.pdf

OECD. (2016). *Strengthening corporate governance codes in Latin America.* Report prepared for the 2016 Meeting of the Latin American Corporate Governance Roundtable Retrieved from: https://www.oecd.org/daf/ca/LART-2016-Strengthening-Corporate-Governance-Codes-Latin-America.pdf

OECD. (2019a). *Equity market development in Latin America: Chile.* Report prepared for 2018 meeting of the Task Force on Latin American Equity Market Development. Retrieved from: https://www.oecd.org/corporate/ca/Chile-Latin-America-Equity-Markets.pdf

OECD. (2019b). *Equity market development in Latin America: Enhancing access to corporate finance.* Retrieved from: https://www.oecd.org/corporate/ca/Latin-American-Equity-Markets-2019a.pdf

OECD. (2021a). *The future of corporate governance in capital markets following the COVID-19 crisis*. Retrieved from: https://www.oecd.org/corporate/the-future-of-corporate-governance-in-capital-markets-following-the-covid-19-crisis-efb2013c-en.htm

OECD. (2021b). *OECD Corporate Governance Factbook 2021b*. Retrieved from: https://www.oecd.org/corporate/corporate-governance-factbook.htm

OECD. (2021c). *OECD economic surveys: Chile 2021c*. OECD Publishing. Retrieved from: https://doi.org/10.1787/19990847

Salvaj, E., & Couyoumdjian, J. (2016). 'Interlocked' business groups and the state in Chile (1970–2010). *Business History, 58*(1), 129–148.

World Bank. (2003). *Chile—Report on the Observance of Standards and Codes (ROSC): Corporate governance country assessment (English)*. World Bank. Retrieved from: http://documents.worldbank.org/curated/en/769111468022464847/Chile-Report-on-the-Observance-of-Standards-and-Codes-ROSC-corporate-governance-country-assessment

CHAPTER 9

Colombia

Eulalia Sanín and Óscar Armando Pardo Aragón

1 Introduction

Corporate governance is both a system by which companies are directed and controlled, and a series of relationships between the governing executive body of a company, its board, its shareholders, and other stakeholders.[1] "Good" corporate governance practices are those processes, procedures, and standards that help these four types of actors to interact appropriately for the benefit of the company and all those involved. In Colombia, evolving corporate governance standards and "good" practice have arrived via different mechanisms and through relevant key actors.

[1] European Commission. Green Book. The EU corporate governance regulations (2011), page 2.

E. Sanín (✉)
Kearney, Bogota, Colombia
e-mail: eulalia.sanin@atkearney.com

Ó. A. Pardo Aragón
Faculty of Business Administration, Center of Studies in Comparative Governance, Universidad de Los Andes, Bogotá, Colombia
e-mail: oscarapardo@gmail.com

J. Callund et al. (eds.), *Corporate Governing in Latin America*,
https://doi.org/10.1007/978-3-030-85780-6_9

The recent history of corporate governance in Colombia is composed of two preponderant influences: the advancement of regulations and evolving international practice adopted into the normative and regulatory framework[2]; and the influence of corporate actors such as directors, officers, and companies themselves (what we will call "institutional entrepreneurs") that have also largely implemented and fostered "good" corporate governance practices above and beyond what the normative and regulatory framework of the day has required. These two "forces" have marked out a particular route in Colombia, influencing the corporate environment through a "network effect", where linkages between companies, boards of directors, and economic groups have played an important role, through, among other effects, the increase of external, independent members on boards and the proliferation of board interlocks.

The purpose of this chapter is to first explore how international normative advances were adopted over time by the Colombian normative and regulatory entities and their impact on the Colombian business environment, touching on the actors that took initiative and promoted the advancement of "good" corporate governance practices and the type of instruments that make it possible to show progress in implementation in a group of large corporate players. Second, this chapter explores the network effects that are particularly evident in the role of interlocks among Colombian economic groups, composed mostly of *large cap* and *medium cap* companies. The effect of interlocks as a mechanism of acceleration of adoption of "good" corporate governance practices is examined. Finally, we present evidence of advanced practices that are being carried out in Colombian company boards and argue that these have been aided by the network effect of board interlocks.

2 Institutional and Regulatory Framework and Context

The study of institutional determinants in corporate governance has focused on three main categories: informal restrictions, formal rules, and enforcement (Bebchuk & Weisbach, 2009; Boytsun, 2009). The category that has received the most attention in the literature has been formal

[2] Colombia is a country of civil-law tradition, where laws and rules have had a high importance in moving corporate topics (governance, among others) toward good practices.

rules. The legal approach has facilitated the study of the impact of the law on corporate governance. The evidence in this body of research has shown how legal developments have affected the legal norms that protect investors, and these, in turn, have been shown to have an impact on the concentration of ownership, participation patterns, and development of debt and equity markets (Boytsun et al., 2011). On the other hand, another research group has focused on the lack of legal frameworks and its consequences in the corporate world. Baysinger and Butler (1985) have shown that the absence of governmental direction, and the resulting lack of uniformity in key board dimensions, encourage certain shareholder abuses commonly attributed to the separation of ownership and control in large corporations.

Another current in corporate governance research has focused on the role of enforcement, especially in countries with weak institutions such as emerging markets (Berglöf & Pajuste, 2003; Berglöf & von Thadden, 1999; Pistor, 2000; Pistor et al., 2000). For instance, Berkowitz et al. (2003) have shown in these scenarios of institutional weakness, if there is not enough effort to adapt to social conditions; it is not possible to have substantial progress in corporate governing.

In the analysis of corporate governance in Colombia, it is evident that the legal development that comes from international standards and its adaptive process are elements that are explained by the formal rules of studies. Similarly, the efforts of regulatory entities and the leadership of certain Colombian companies are part of the enforcement study line.

First regulations on corporate governance in Colombia were incorporated into commercial law[3] in 1995. These first regulatory efforts are due to the need to adjust the rules to the business reality of the country. It was clear that business groups and different types of shareholders, for example, had to adjust to a dynamic that had previously not existed. In the same way, in the mirroring international developments, the concept of corporate governance practices first appears in Law 222 of 1995, as seen through its inclusion of provisions on shareholders' rights, information disclosure, creditors rights, duties of the board of directors and executive officers. Later, in 1998, new regulations[4] granted rights and protection mechanisms to minority shareholders. These first steps opened

[3] The Commercial Code (Código de Comercio, ley 222 de 1995).

[4] Law 446 of 1998.

an awareness of the importance of Corporate Governance but were only a component of commercial law, so other sectors did not feel the effect of these changes.

OECD Principles were first issued in 1999 with the purpose of an international implementation among OECD and non-OECD countries. According to the financial stability board, they were recommended to be incorporated in national regulations to contribute to sound financial markets. Those corporate governance principles were integrated into the new internatoinal financial architecture, jointly with regulations on fiscal and monetary policy, banking and financial regulation and supervision, and institutional and market infrastructure. As such, this structure specifically promoted improvements in corporate governing in the area of market infrastructure. This was the first concrete initiative taken to promote an international legal framework approach to a country's environment, which commenced with a general orientation, but also emphasized the specific importance on the financial legal framework.

"Modern" history in Colombian corporate governance begins in 1999–2000 when Colombia underwent a severe financial crisis linked to mortgages. Mounting inflation in the years before the crisis raised the amount of mortgage payments and principals, because their calculation model[5] was linked to inflation. The mortgage crisis has a significant impact on the financial system and, when combined with other economic issues, affected the whole economy. The Central Bank and the national government needed advisory and financial aid from the IMF in 1999, when they signed an *External Fund Facility* (EFF) agreement which implied measures and commitments on fiscal and monetary policy. From then on, Colombian government and institutions were monitored internationally and increasingly nudged to become compliant with higher quality standards and to greater integration with the new financial architecture. The financial crisis of 1999–2000, with the onset of IMF and international oversight, opened a window to reflection and discussions on the good corporate governing behaviors and guidelines to be followed in the Colombian financial system.

Following the mortgage crisis, the Colombian government began to focus on the protection of investor rights, seeking to support their intention to invest in local companies. In 2001, the securities market

[5] The model was expressed in a payment unit called UPAC (*Unidad de Poder Adquisitivo Constante*), linked to inflation.

supervisory agency[6] regulated corporate governance codes for public companies to promote voluntary good practices into the Colombian stock market. The focus was on provisions for companies that wanted to receive investments from the pension funds.

In 2002 global economic and systemic effects of the highly recognized market and corporate crashes of ENRON, PARMALAT, and WORLDCOM, among others also reached Latin America. In response, the CAF[7] also issued its voluntary framework—the guidelines for an Andean Corporate Governance Code—and the OECD issued a White Paper for Latin America. The publication of these guidelines pointed to the need for improvement in corporate governing practice and regulation across Latin America. Both policy documents were aligned in the type of practices and recommendations for the adaptation of legal and regulatory codes, as well as for the adoption of voluntary standards.

In 2003 the IMF and WORLD BANK evaluated the observance of Standards and Codes in Colombia (IMF, 2003). They issued the *Report on the Observance of Standards and Codes*—ROSC, including recommendations on different aspects such as accounting and auditing, institutional and capital markets frameworks as well as corporate governance. The summary of policy recommendations also included interesting aspects for future development. They were grouped into five categories for the report purposes: (i) The rights of shareholders; (ii) Equitable treatment of shareholders, (iii) Role of Stakeholders in Corporate Governance, (iv) Disclosure and transparency, and (v) Responsibilities of the board.

Some relevant recommendations in the 2003 ROSC included: rights to shareholders' participation in fundamental decisions, disproportionate control disclosure, equal treatment for all shareholders, prohibition of insider trading, boards/officers' disclosure of interests, implementation of high-quality accounting/auditing standards, and key functions of the board, among others. As will explained throughout the rest of this chapter, since then the regulations have progressively incorporated those recommendations.

In contrast to other countries in the Latin American region, Colombia fared quite well in relative terms through the international financial

[6] The *SUPERINTENDENCIA DE VALORES*, which were substituted by the *SUPERINTENDENCIA FINANCIERA* in 2005. The *SUPERINTENDENCIA FINANCIERA* included securities and banking supervision functions.

[7] The *CORPORACIÓN ANDINA DE FOMENTO*, a Latin American development Bank.

crisis of 2008–2009, having already undergone its own mortgage crisis earlier in 1999–2000 and having adjusted its economy accordingly in response. Thus, despite the dire international circumstances, the start of the twenty-first century found large Colombian companies relatively strong candidates for mergers and acquisitions activity. Secondly, and perhaps most important to the theme of corporate governance, was the increased interest of institutional investors to participate in the Colombian market and hence the emerging need to communicate a target corporation's status and development in environment, sustainability, and governance (ESG)-relatted matters. The IPO[8] of 10.1% of ECOPETROL equity in 2007; the increasing participation of international institutional investors in Colombian firms, as well as the access of firms to the NEW YORK STOCK EXCHANGE through ADRs (American depository receipts): BANCOLOMBIA in positions in comparison with other firms in the region, and the appetite for growth and regional expansion soon became evident. The internationalization of Colombian firms had two components: first, the expansion in the region through M&A—ECOPETROL in 2008, and NUTRESA in 2009, among others, signaled the start of a decade that would see many changes in the way shareholders, investors, the government, and related groups in general would assess the attractiveness, solidity, and sustainability of large Colombian enterprises.[9]

According to Trujillo and Guzman (2017), some representative Colombian firms had already implemented "good" corporate governance practices long before the government issued regulations on the topic. Some firms, as is the case of MLC[10], Carvajal, or the companies of the multi-industry system of corporate crossholdings, known informally today

[8] Initial Public Offering of ECOPETROL stocks in 2007. Previously it was a fully state-owned firm.

[9] At the start of 2010, Colombia had 181 companies listed in the stock market, the BVC (*BOLSA DE VALORES DE COLOMBIA*), yet it is estimated that only about 10% of these stocks had high liquidity levels. Despite a high growth in total market capitalization due to higher valuations of previously listed companies, issuances of private debt heavily outweighed listing activity, as well as much trading beyond a small core of very large companies. Market capitalization as a proportion of GDP grew over 20% annually over the decade to a level of 40% in 2019, and the stock market value of corporate debt increased at a 17% annual rate to reach 6,4% of GDP (Clavijo, González & Vera, 2011; Sanín & Arteaga, 2012).

[10] MLC the initials of *Multi-Latin Companies*, or *multilatinas*—firms that have expanded to other Latin-American countries.

as GEA[11], were already conscious about stakeholder equitable treatment, transparency, ethics, and corporate principles as far back as the 1960's and 1970's. However, the first regulatory initiatives regarding shareholder rights and regulating inappropriate practices in securities trading were passed in 2002, with the issuing of resolutions 116 and 157. Law 964, which contains mandatory rules for public companies relating to investor protections and information disclosure, was passed in 2004.

After the legal initiatives described above, the FINANCIAL SUPERINTENDENCY took the lead, together with other economic actors, in developing the Country Code initiative in 2007. Their arguments were that better governing practices are to the benefit of the shareholders in different ways. For example, through enhanced value generation and improved risk management, and by gaining access to better financial conditions, through the lower perception of risks by creditors and investors. In this sense, the supervisor suggested that good corporate governance need not be understood as an end in itself, but rather as a means to achieving these aims. On the other hand, it argued that international experience has shown that improving good governance practices requires the concerted action of government authorities, companies, and investors, in combining mandatory standards with self-regulation and voluntary compliance schemes. For this reason, a committee made up of a broad base of entities was formed to draft the Code of Best Corporate Practices for issuers of Colombian securities. The Code was structured in such a way as to set out concrete measures to be adopted by issuers of securities in their daily activity, covering the following broad topics: (i) General Shareholders' Meeting, (ii) Board of directors, (iii) Disclosure of Financial and Non-Financial Information, and (iv) Dispute Resolution. The corporate governance code was issued under a "comply or explain" model.

Regulation was issued as Código País provides voluntary guidelines for supervised firms. Furthermore, in 2008 the company regulator[12]

[11] GEA initials of what is known informally as *Grupo Empresarial Antioqueño*, not formally an economic group in itself, but rather a system of corporate crossholdings between three economic groups: GRUPO SURA, GRUPO NUTRESA, and GRUPO ARGOS, headquartered in the traditionally industrial city of Medellín, capital of Antioquia, giving origin to the informal name GEA.

[12] *SUPERINTENDENCIA DE SOCIEDADES*, or SUPERSOCIEDADES—the supervisory and regulatory body of publicly traded companies in Colombia.

implemented the *"National Survey of Corporate Governance and Corporate Social Responsibility"*, as a tool to diagnose the level of corporate governing in privately owned firms. Subsequently, SUPERSOCIEDADES jointly with leading trade unions[13] issued guidelines on corporate governance for both privately and family-owned firms.

Despite advances in legal and regulatory initiatives and firms' voluntary efforts on corporate governing improvement, Colombia also had an emblematic case of corporate governance failure—INTERBOLSA, a fast-growing stock brokerage firm went bankrupt in 2013, and several directors landed in jail having been the posterchild for the risks of merely "esthetic" corporate governance. INTERBOLSA was among the top scorers in the 2009 Código País report. What could explain the emergence of this emblematic case in Colombia despite the normative and regulatory framework? There are several hypotheses for this: Firstly, there was never any real awareness of the importance and consequences of not adhering to the framework of Corporate Governance. Alternatively, international cases seemed so very far removed, and it could be assumed that they not typical of these Latin American realities. However, when the scandal broke, along with the real consequences of board members being sent to jail, it quickly became clear to other board members, and not only from the financial sector, but in other sectors too, that what had happened could have happened to anyone; and it was therefore important to act on the matter.

A second version of the corporate governance code was issued in 2014. The renewed version included recommendations from the OECD, ROSC,[14] FSAP,[15] and CAF.[16] Dimensions of corporate governance included in this version were: internal control architectures; the rights and equitable treatment of shareholders; transparency and the disclosure

[13] CONFECÁMARAS, LA CÁMARA DE COMERCIO DE BOGOTÁ.

[14] *Report on the Observance of Standards and Codes* (ROSC): an initiative from the WORLD BANK and the INTERNATIONAL MONETARY FUND to monitor compliance with high-quality standards included into the structure of the international financial architecture.

[15] *Financial Sector Assessment Program* (FSAP): an initiative from the IMF and World Bank to assess and develop the countries' financial sector.

[16] The CAF (CORPORACIÓN ANDINA DE FOMENTO, currently BANCO DE DESARROLLO DE AMÉRICA LATINA): a development bank of Latin America.

of financial and non-financial information; the structure and functioning of the board of directors; and, general meeting recommendations.

The questions that arise are: have these Country Code efforts in their different versions and surveys, been worth it?; have they been useful in some way?; and, have they improved corporate governance? An annual comparison of the rates of compliance with key parameters covered by the different versions of the Country Code is useful in trying to answer these questions.

3 The Impact of Country Codes and Other Business Measurement Initiatives

In terms of measurement of progress, results from the 2009 *Encuesta Código País*[17] pointed to a still low level of compliance with the recommendations in different areas: among 174 respondents (of 181 invited to participate), overall scores stood at just 45.8% adoption on Shareholder Meeting recommendations, 54.2% on Board structures and procedures, 55.9% on transparency and the disclosure of financial and non-financial information, and 39.4% for dispute resolution guidelines. Table 1 shows the breakdown of firms who presented compliance reports in the first stage of corporate governance code (2007–2014).

It presents evidence of a permanent commitment to participation in companies in the financial sector and a decrease in participation over the years of companies in the real (non-financial) sector. Its explanation may lie in the strict standards and regulatory requirements faced by the financial sector, while in other sectors compliance is voluntary.

According to the financial sector supervisory body, the results in 2019 show increased levels of commitment to best corporate governance practices among financial services entities and the issuers of securities. Firms have gone ahead with the implementation of improved management standards, greater transparency, higher economic benefits for companies, increasing confidence levels, and better mechanisms to avoid economic losses. There has been an improvement in the efficiency of financial holding companies, which saw how higher performance boards of directors and board committees improved their decision-making processes.

[17] The survey act as compliance report on country corporate governance code that firms submit every year to the regulator, the SUPERFINANCIERA.

Table 1 Description of respondents to the corporate governance survey (*Encuesta Código País*)

Sector	*Issuer category*	*2007*	*2008*	*2009*	*2010*	*2011*	*2012*	*2013*	*2014*
Financial	Banks	19	20	20	22	27	26	27	28
	Trade financial firms (Leasing companies)	22	24	23	18	19	17	18	16
	Other financial companies	13	16	18	18	17	17	17	16
	Financial sector	**54**	**60**	**61**	**58**	**63**	**60**	**62**	**60**
Real	Diverse (other)	44	44	42	40	38	37	34	31
	Utilities	29	27	27	24	21	21	20	19
	Food and beverage	17	18	17	17	17	17	15	13
	Investment companies	14	14	14	13	14	11	11	9
	Construction	13	14	13	8	8	10	10	9
	Trade	5	6	7	5	4	4	4	4
	Real sector	**122**	**123**	**120**	**107**	**102**	**100**	**94**	**85**
Total		**176**	**183**	**181**	**165**	**165**	**160**	**156**	**145**

Source Authors' analysis of *Codigo Pais* data

Firms have good practices regarding shareholder rights protections, appropriate control environments, and risk management processes with responsibilities assigned clearly to identified officers. Colombian firms can deal in complex transactions because they now have robust information mechanisms and alternative sources to access market information.

Table 2 lists the firms that reported levels of compliance greater than 75% in 2009. In addition to strong improvements in companies from the financial sector, the table shows great progress in a state-owned company in the Colombian electricity sector (ISAGEN) as well as in companies belonging to business groups such as the Bolívar and the GEA business groups. These improvements reflect the voluntary commitment—beyond rules and regulations—by organizations that are in the real sector of the Colombian economy. One should also note, however, that Interbolsa, which caused one of the most notorious cases of corporate governing failure, as explained before, also appears in the ranking with one of the highest scores. The façade of "good" practice can also be created and upheld for a while, but the effects of poor governance eventually show through.

In recent years, Colombian corporate governance standards and practices have been fostered in public, state-owned, and private-owned firms, especially those related to the role of independent directors, board diversity, compensation schemes, the professional profiles of board members, independent board assessments, and self-assessments in promoting more efficient and effective boards of directors.

Table 3 shows that in 2019 there are more firms with higher levels of implementation of the recommendations of the corporate governance code. Most of them belong to the financial sector, which, as explained before, has more legally enforced corporate governance rules than the real sector. In 2019, the level of compliance are the highest in the decade, and under some criteria are fully (or almost fully) implemented by issuers. It is also noteworthy that there are many business groups and companies in general that have assumed a serious and consistent commitment, over and beyond the rules and regulations. Most noteworthy is the implementation of higher transparency, higher independence requirements for board members, and innovative voluntary compliance schemes.

Additionally, Sanín and Arteaga (2012) carried out and in-depth analysis of a sample of the very large leading Colombian companies which had adopted and implemented more advanced corporate governance measures than those that had been reported in their publicly available corporate governance reports and bylaws. In fact, the application of the VALOR Index, a CAF, ECLAC, and IADB corporate governance measurement tool, using in-depth information (interviews, review of documented practices in Board and Shareholder Meeting Minutes) resulted in scores almost double those resulting when measuring the companies based only on publicly available corporate governance information. The study concluded that "*the standards set by the indicator proposed by (CAF, ECLAC and IADB) to evaluate companies indicate that the four companies analyzed, whilst successful and in compliance with local norms – and in some cases, also with U.S. market norms- are still distant from the proposed best practice VALOR benchmark value, especially with regards to [the implementation of corporate governance practices for] Board Committees. A point also noted was that some of these best practices [although in implementation] are in fact 'buried' in internal procedures and documents, hindering their verification*" Sanín and Arteaga (2012, p. 153).

Table 2 Issuers with more over 75% compliance levels in 2009

	Issuer name	*Compliance rating*	*Sector*
1	ISAGEN S.A. E.S. P.	92.68	Real sector
2	CFC Leasing Bolivar	90.24	Financial sector
3	Bolsa de Valores de Colombia S.A.	90.24	Financial sector
4	Sociedades Bolívar S.A.	87.80	Real sector
5	Grupo Nutresa	87.80	Real sector
6	Banco BBVA Colombia	87.80	Financial sector
7	Factoring Bancolombia S.A. C.F.C.	87.80	Financial sector
8	Compañía Colombiana de Inversiones S.A. E.S.P.	85.37	Real sector
9	Interbolsa S.A.	82.93	Financial sector
10	Protección S.A.F.	82.93	Financial sector
11	Davivienda	82.93	Financial sector
12	Interconexión Eléctrica S.A. E.S.P.	80.49	Real sector
13	Edatel S.A. E.S.P.	80.49	Real sector
14	Promigas S.A. E.S.P.	80.49	Real sector
15	Banco de Crédito	80.49	Financial sector
16	Banca de Inversión Bancolombia S.A.	80.49	Financial sector
17	Giros y Finanzas C.F.C.	80.49	Financial sector
18	Leasing Bancolombia S.A. C.F.C.	80.49	Financial sector
19	Confiar- Cooperativa Financiera	80.49	Financial sector

(continued)

Table 2 (continued)

	Issuer name	*Compliance rating*	*Sector*
20	Ecopetrol S.A.	78.05	Real sector
21	Inversiones Argos S.A.	75.61	Real sector
22	C.F.C. Sufinanciamiento	75.61	Financial sector

Source Authors' analysis from Código País data

Simultaneously with the CAF/ECLAC/IADB study, three among four companies analyzed—all had in common the rapid growth in their internationalization of both operations and capital sources—had begun measuring themselves internally using the ROBECO SAM *Dow Jones Sustainability Index* (DJSI) benchmark, which, among other ESG components, asked detailed questions regarding the implementation of corporate governance practices. The DJSI reviews and the CAF, ECLAC, and IADB study flagged the opportunity to step up to more sophisticated governance practices, especially relating to the external assessment of the board of directors, a chapter still not touched upon by the first country corporate governance code nor mentioned in any local standard as a corporate governance best practice at the time. Internationalization, and in particular the need to better communicate standards to international institutional investors, thus, was the spark of what would become a distinctive characteristic of Colombian corporate practice, which is the focus on the board of directors as the key lever to further value through corporate governance.

In 2012, a set of representative Colombian firms began the practice of regularly assessing effectiveness and performance of their Boards of Directors with the help of an external, expert, independent third party. This practice was propelled, without a doubt, by the direct question in the DJSI questionnaire—does your board of directors undergo a regular external and independent assessment of effectiveness? Sanín (2012) identified this motivation in three among four cases analyzed in the CAF/ECLAC/BID study. Furthermore, designing the first standardized, comparable methodology in Latin America for the external, independent assessment of board of director's effectiveness. Nutresa,

Table 3 Issuers with high compliance levels in 2019 (higher than 75% of provisions implemented)

	Issuer name	*Compliance rating*	*Sector*
1	Banco Bilbao Vizcaya Argentaria Colombia S.A. BBVA Colombia	97.973	Financial Sector
2	Almacenes Éxito S.A.	97.297	Real Sector
3	Grupo Nutresa S.A.	96.622	Real Sector
4	Grupo De Inversiones Suramericana S.A.	95.946	Real Sector
5	Bancolombia S.A.	95.946	Financial Sector
6	Interconexión Eléctrica S.A. E.S.P.	94.595	Real Sector
7	Constructora Conconcreto S.A.	93.919	Real Sector
8	Empresa de Energía de Bogotá S.A. E.S.P.	93.243	Real Sector
9	Administradora de Fondos de Pensiones y Cesantías Protección	93.243	Financial Sector
10	Grupo Bolívar S.A.	91.892	Financial Sector
11	Banco de Comercio Exterior de Colombia S.A.	91.216	Financial Sector
12	Grupo Argos S.A.	91.216	Real Sector
13	Ecopetrol S.A.	90.541	Real Sector
14	Suramericana S.A.	89.865	Financial Sector
15	Banco W S.A.	89.189	Financial Sector
16	Banco de las Microfinanzas Bancamía S.A.	87.838	Financial Sector
17	Construcciones el Condor S.A.	87.162	Real Sector
18	Compañía de Financiamiento Tuya S.A.	85.811	Financial Sector
19	Corporación de Ferias y Exposiciones S.A. Usua	84.459	Real Sector
20	Banco Coomeva S.A.	84.459	Financial Sector
21	Credifamilia Compañía de Financiamiento Comercial	84.459	Financial Sector
22	Bolsa de Valores de Colombia S.A.	83.784	Financial Sector
23	Celsia S.A. E.S.P.	83.784	Real Sector
24	Carvajal Empaques S.A.	82.432	Real Sector
25	Leasing Bancoldex S.A. Compañía de Financiamiento	81.757	Financial Sector
26	Isagen S.A. E.S.P.	81.081	Real Sector
27	Mineros S.A.	80.405	Real Sector
28	Banco Santander de Negocios Colombia S.A.	79.730	Financial Sector
29	Titularizadora Colombiana S.A. Hitos	79.730	Financial Sector
30	Empresas Públicas de Medellín E.S.P.	79.730	Real Sector

(continued)

Table 3 (continued)

	Issuer name	*Compliance rating*	*Sector*
31	Banco Mundo Mujer S.A. - Mundo Mujer el Banco de la Comunidad	79.730	Financial Sector
32	Banco de Bogotá S. A.	78.378	Financial Sector
33	RCI Colombia S.A. Compañía de Financiamiento	78.378	Financial Sector
34	Banco de Occidente S.A.	78.378	Financial Sector
35	Cementos Argos S.A.	77.703	Real Sector
36	Financiera de Desarrollo Territorial S.A.	76.351	Financial Sector
37	Banco Davivienda S.A.	76.351	Financial Sector
38	Banco Serfinanza	76.351	Financial Sector

Note Issuers with high levels of compliance (>75%) of corporate governance provisions in 2019. Authors' analysis from Código País data

CELSIA, and CEMENTOS ARGOS,[18] as well as PROMIGAS undertook the first formal external assessments of Board performance documented in Colombia in 2012, swiftly followed by GRUPO ARGOS (holding company of CEMENTOS ARGOS and CELSIA), ECOPETROL and its subsidiaries. Evidence of the undertaking of these exercises is registered in the Annual Reports presented at the Annual Shareholder Meetings. Interesting findings presented in these reports are clearly the good practices that have been adopted from the internationalization processes of companies; but also, an internal effect has been the practice of having interlocked directors who have disseminated good corporate governing initiatives through different boards. It is therefore essential to go more in depth in the analysis of interlocks in boards.

4 FROM INTERNATIONALIZATION TO THE NETWORK EFFECTS OF INTERLOCKING BOARDS

Interlocks are a particularly interesting aspect of Colombian corporate governance, because of the high level of interlocked boards among Colombian issuers, and network effect they contribute to create among

[18] These three listed companies are part of the system of corporate crossholdings of mostly listed companies known informally as GEA (Grupo Empresarial Antioqueño, though not formally a company group); their boards were at the time interlocked

firms and economic groups which generates shared practices and perspectives on advancing good corporate governance implementation.

An *interlock* occurs when an individual belongs to the board of directors of two or more companies. *Interlocks* can be direct or indirect. A *direct* interlock exists when one or more directors of a company serve on the board of another company. An *indirect* interlock exists when directors of two different companies serve on the board of a third company, often with the intention of coordinating the activities of the firms involved (Daft & Weick, 1984; Zahra & Pearce, 1989). Pennings (1980) concludes that interlocks have a strong favorable effect on company performance because they provide valuable advantages such as horizontal coordination among firms that have the same value chain, vertical coordination, and enhancing corporate reputation through networking (Schoorman et al., 1981). These advantages help in reducing environmental uncertainty, enhance the status of the firm in the business community, and, on occasion, reduce transaction costs (Zahra & Pearce, 1989). In the end, directors are likely to use and cross-fertilize the knowledge structures they develop from their experience on other boards. Involvement of directors on different boards provides direct strategic experience as well as key indirect information through the social contacts with other directors (Carpenter & Westphal, 2001).

Moreover, building on *Social Network Theory*, director interlocks have the potential to facilitate political cohesion among and across corporations and corporate elites. Potential divisions rooted in individual firms or industries' different positions are reconciled or overcome through consensus building mechanisms that are embedded in social networks, such as those formed through interlocking directorates (Burris, 2005).

Resource Dependence Theory (Pfeffer & Salancik, 1978) suggests that interlocking directors may offer organizations several advantages. First, interlocks facilitate the ready exchange of information across firms (Haunschild & Beckman, 1998; Pennings, 1980). Second, interlocks allow one organization's regular input into another firm's decision-making, thus asserting power and influence (Carpenter & Westphal, 2001; Renneboog & Zhao, 2011; Zajac & Westphal, 1996). Finally, interlocks may enable firms to co-opt sources of environmental uncertainty and secure more resources, thus potentially leading to better performance (Boyd, 1990; Burt, 1983; Haynes & Hillman, 2010).

As an important conclusion from the reviews of literature, it can be observed that interlocks between boards of directors play an important role in implementation of transparency, decision-making, duty, and power-balancing practices in firms. Moreover, interlocked directors may foster new corporate governance practices in firms when they are part of the board. Looking at the Colombian case, it has been possible to show that the high degree of interlocks among the Boards of leading Colombian companies propelled the voluntary implementation of assessment, with a speed that hitherto might have only been expected through regulatory pressure. The positive experience of carrying out a serious and yet constructive process of assessment and feedback had significant effects not only on the Boards and Executive teams of companies, but also on the Directors themselves. One of the first Boards evaluated included two CEOs and two Chairs from other leading firms, companies which in turn undertook external Board assessments themselves within less than 18 months of that first experience.

Colombian firms exhibit at least four different styles of interlocks: (i) firms into the same holding company, (ii) mixed (private and state equity owned) companies, (iii) firms with a high number of independent directors, and (iv) incipient interlocks.

Table 4 shows a summary of interlocks on the board of directors in Colombian firms in 2019.

- ***Type I interlocks*** are evident in firms that belong to the same parent holding. The parent holding extends its practices to affiliates and affiliates share practices among them. Examples of this type of interlock could be observed in companies, such as AVAL, companies of the GEA system (not formally a holding, as we describe above), GRUPO BOLIVAR, and CARVAJAL. Firms in those holdings are large participants in the stock market and have an undeniable impact on the corporate governance culture in Colombia. Within this group of companies, we also find what we call ***institutional entrepreneurs*** or some of the larger Colombian firms, mostly (if not exclusively) who trade in the Colombian Stock market, that have voluntarily adopted best practices ahead of regulation and have had a positive network effect over other connected (via ownership or board interlocks) and smaller companies.

Table 4 Interlocks of the board of directors in Colombian companies in 2019

Entity	*Score*	*Board connections*	*Type of interlocks*
Banco BBVA Colombia	97.97	BBVA	International bank
Almacenes Éxito S.A.	97.30	Éxito	Business group
Grupo Nutresa	96.62	NAS	Business group
Grupo de Inversiones Suramericana S.A.	95.95	NAS	Business group
Bancolombia S.A.	95.95	NAS, Bancolombia	Business group
Interconexión Eléctrica S.A. E.S.P.	94.59	National state-mixed owned	Mixed companies
Constructora Conconcretó S.A.	93.92	NAS	high participation of independents
Empresa de Energía de Bogotá S.A. E.S.P.	93.24	The State of Bogotá	Mixed companies
Protección S.A.	93.24	NAS	Business group
Sociedades Bolívar S.A.	91.89	Bolívar	Business group
Banco De Comercio Exterior de Colombia S.A.	91.22	National state-mixed owned	Mixed companies
Grupo Argos S.A.	91.22	NAS	Business group
Ecopetrol S.A.	90.54	National state-mixed owned	Mixed companies
Suramericana S.A.	89.86	NAS	Business group
Banco W S.A.	89.19		High participation of independents
Banco de las Microfinanzas Bancamía S.A.	87.84		Incipient interlocks

Entity	*Score*	*Board connections*	*Type of interlocks*
Construcciones el Condor S.A.	87.16		high participation of independents
Compañía de Financiamiento Tuya S.A.	85.81	NAS, Bancolombia, Éxito	Business group
Ferias y Exposiciones S.A. Operador Zona Franca	84.46		high participation of independents
Banco Coomeva S.A.	84.46		Business group
Credifamilia Compañía de Financiamiento Comercial	84.46		Incipient interlocks
Bolsa de Valores de Colombia S.A.	83.78	Bancolombia, Aval, others	Business group, high participation of independents
Celsia S.A. E.S.P.	83.78	NAS	Business group
Carvajal Empaques S.A.	82.43	Carvajal	Business group
Leasing Bancoldex S.A. Compañía de Financiamiento	81.76	National state-mixed owned	Mixed companies
Isagen S.A. E.S.P.	81.08	National state-mixed owned	Mixed companies
Mineros S.A.	80.41	Bancolombia, Colpatria, others	high participation of independents
Banco Santander de Negocios Colombia S.A.	79.73		International bank

(continued)

Table 4 (continued)

Entity	*Score*	*Board connections*	*Type of interlocks*
Titularizadora Colombiana S.A. Hitos	79.73	Aval, Colpatria, Bancolombia	high participation of independents
Empresas Públicas de Medellín E.S.P.	79.73	Regional state-mixed owned	state company
Banco Mundo Mujer S.A. -	79.73		Incipient interlocks
Banco De Bogotá S. A	78.38	Aval	Business group
RCI Colombia S.A. Compañía de Financiamiento	78.38		International bank
Banco De Occidente S.A.	78.38	Aval	Business group
Cementos Argos S.A.	77.70	NAS	Business group
Financiera de Desarrollo Territorial S.A.	76.35	National state	State company
Davivienda	76.35	Bolívar	Business group
Banco Serfinanza	76.35		

Note Compliance with corporate governance code and board interlocks in the most representative Colombian firms in 2019

- ***Type II interlocks*** are evident in mixed companies, such as ISA or ECOPETROL, where the State is the controlling shareholder. Corporate governance reforms in the last decade implied an increase of independent directors as State representatives, also a suggestion from the OECD to improve state-owned firms' corporate governance. Both patrimony (in this case, government representatives) as well as independent directors generate an interlock between these companies and extend the impact of best corporate governance among them. The movement in Colombia toward the establishment of economic groups of holdings of sector-related State-owned enterprises, such as GRUPO FINANCIERO BICENTENARIO (created in 2019, and which brings together the financial sector enterprises of the Colombian government under one holding company or conglomerate), also furthers the deepening of interlocks.
- ***Type III interlocks*** occur in firms where independent directors had previously belonged to business groups as executives or directors and form a majority on the Board. Companies with most independent directors, whose previous expertise in parent holdings is a key fact for corporate governance improvement. Among those firms, the BVC (the stock market) MINEROS or CONCONCRETO.
- Finally, ***Type IV interlocks*** occur in firms where the boards of directors are small, but with an important participation of independents, with previous experience in larger firms. Those boards of directors have the required human capital to bring about improvements in the corporate governance practices at those companies. Examples of type IV interlocks are BANCA MUNDO MUJER or CREDIFAMILIA.

Analyzing the progress of corporate governance through the action of interlock directors and their different typologies according to the type of company, it can be concluded that the effects on business groups tend to be more permanent and generate a diffusion effect throughout the spectrum of their companies. When it comes to state companies, the effect of interlock directors is seen to be accompanied by independent members and this is only replicated in companies that are generally listed on the stock market or compete in industrial sectors where there is private competition. It is also seen with greater force in companies of a mixed nature or industrial and commercial of the state.

On the other hand, companies with a large component of independents with group experience, it is clear that the improvement and consistency in good governance practices, their great weight, is supported by the dissemination of good practices of this class of members.

Finally, with respect to small companies with boards with incipient interlock directors, as we have called it, the effects of improvements in corporate governing and their permanence over time can be attributed to the leadership of the Chairs of their boards, their company managers, and the impulses of the few independent board members who are also interlocks.

Evidence of interlocked boards and higher implementation of corporate governance standards is not the only novel analysis that the Colombian case can provide. The authors' work with corporate firms and board performance evaluations also provides a perspective of how the adoption of corporate governance standards has been evolving and how the network effect of interlocks aids that adoption.

5 The Evolution of Good Corporate Governance Practices in Institutional Entrepreneurs

The study of the boards of directors has been referred to as one done from outside the black box, as most approaches to analyzing board activity or impact study the board indirectly or remotely or analyze the individual perspective of board members. These employ a traditional input–output approach to indirectly study group performance (Pettigrew, 1997), for instance investigating the number and length of board meetings as indicators of board activity and diligence (e.g., Brown & Caylor, 2006). Moreover, insider studies of boards focus on the role of the individual rather than the nature of the group's dynamics (Pye, 2001). For instance, Parker (2007) explored the effort of individual directors in promoting strategies in organizations. Later, the effort to explore the black box has led to a tendency to use group behavior analysis. Research on groups focuses on the dynamics and interactions of group behavior and their relationship with their performance (Plugiese et al., 2015). For instance, studies exploring participation and consensus building, the functioning of the board and the way they interact to develop strategies that ultimately lead to an effective group, are good examples of that tendency (Huisman, 2001; Jehn et al., 1999; Westphal & Bednar, 2005). This last trend is what has allowed us to approach different companies and explore their operations, functioning, and relationships with their strategies and group perceptions in the corporate world in Colombia.

Perhaps one of the most salient characteristics of Colombia's path in the institutionalization of corporate governance practices has been the focus on the functioning and operation of the board of directors as the key organizational lever from which corporate governing has led from theory to practice. As mentioned before, a convergence of market-led nudges, regulatory advances, and a high degree of interlocks in the boards of leading companies propelled corporate and controlling shareholders' interest into understanding how governing could be furthered through the board itself. Board performance assessments provided by third party experts and advisors evolved from barely nonexistent in 2010 to generalized and regular practice as committed in board charters, and even in corporate bylaws in some listed companies, as well as burgeoning exercises in privately and family held companies. An informal survey applied to Colombia's most recognized corporate governance practitioners' points on an accelerated growth of board advisory and services, much focused around the improvement of the Boards as collegiate bodies over the last decade.

An example of the effort to improve the performance and effectiveness of boards of directors can be seen in the ongoing evaluation efforts presented below. The following table summarizes the results of comparable *Board Assessments* carried out between 2012 and 2018. Company names are sanitized, yet all companies in the sample are either listed or privately held and within the top ten companies of their sector according to size, ensuring the relevance and generalization of results to the set of public firms in the country.

In Table 5, the percentage of achievement in each category is the result of the objective measurement of not only compliance but implementation of specific indicator measures (45 indicators, in total) of progress in a stages-of-excellence scale that describes international regulatory and applied best practice. 50% achievement, thus, describes bare compliance with local regulation based on the in force corporate governance code; 75% achievement describes reaching international best practice levels based on a compilation of leading international corporate governance practice codes, and a score of over 75% indicates the observed implementation of board *best-in-class* organizational and cultural practices, as described in the specialized literature.

An analysis of these results focuses on the next interesting topics: first, boards that undergo these types of structured, in-depth assessments tend to already have high degrees of implementation of regulatory standards.

Table 5 Aggregated results of board effectiveness assessments

Measurement	*Structure and governance*				*Coordination*	
	Composition	*Functions*	*Meetings*	*Committees*	*Information management*	*External communication*
Mean	68.8%	80.1%	71.5%	80.5%	69.2%	92.7%
SSD	0.47	0.14	0.35	0.36	0.31	0.20

Measurement	*Internal interaction and dynamics*					*Strategic focus*		
	Participation	*Among directors*	*Among directors and COB*	*Among directors—CEO—COB*	*Among the board and executive officers*	*Agenda*	*Discussion/Decision making*	*Strategic goals*
Mean	87.2%					53.8%	81.4%	70.7%
SSD	0.36					0.85	0.44	0.54

Source Eulalia Sanín, Prospecta, Kearney. Analysis by the authors

The mean scores of the components (themselves made up of specific, measurable indicators) of the board effectiveness dimension *Governance* and *Structure* show the highest results, as well as low dispersion in scores relating to Board functions, Meetings and Committees. Board composition shows more dispersion and opportunities, particularly with regard to the best-in-class definition of what an Independent Director means, the proportion of independent directors on the board, board diversity (in profiles as well as other aspects such as gender and background), and, with much emphasis, the role of the board Chair.

The component of coordination (board process and information), points to strengths in communicating to external audiences and opportunities in reviewing and bettering practices in internal information used by the board (pre-readings, presentations, board and committee minutes, and tools for internal board communication on work fronts).

A note on the third dimension—*Internal Interaction and Dynamics*—measured board dynamics and interaction over time—and with infrequent deviations—served to confirm that a different tool would be needed to measure board interactions. This led to the development of the *Exponential Conversations Board Coaching* methodology, developed jointly between KORN FERRY and KEARNEY (Duque & Sanín, 2018).

The initial rounds of application of this advanced board coaching tool in boards that had previously been measured with the aforementioned methodology, despite ranking very high in terms of relationships, pointed to common development opportunities in the following behaviors and dynamics:

- Focus on priorities, influence in prioritizing the board agenda to dedicate the right amount of time to critical topics.
- Inquisitive spirit, curiosity, asking questions that go below the surface.
- Frank exchanges of opinions, active involvement in discussions, debate.
- Active and respectful listening, attention to all interventions, the avoidance of distractors [including electronic devices], promotion of the active listening of all board members.

The fourth area of assessment, *Strategic Focus*, points to a markedly important area of opportunity in planning and prioritizing the board

Agenda. The design of a board plan and a session agenda that follows this plan yet allows for the incorporation of key urgent topics is the central tool for ensuring the board's fiduciary responsibility. Agendas that are pushed solely by the executive run the risk of over focusing on the operations and overlooking the tough questions raised by a board's fiduciary responsibility. From a behavioral perspective, as mentioned above, this is also a key area of board conduct to be improved. This, together with the evident opportunity to upgrade the role and impact of the Chair of board, point to the next generation of value aggregation in the sphere of corporate governance, given while the *style of governing* adapts well to regulation and local best practice, value is best created through the *governing function*.

Other studies contribute additional findings about the quality of corporate governing in Colombian firms. AFE[19] and ANDESCO[20] also carried out such research in the field over the last decade.

According to the AFE study, prior experience of directors is positively associated with perception of firm and board effectiveness. But, for small non-profit organizations this is not a relevant attribute, especially due to the directors' characteristics of those firms, who have little or no prior experience. Family firm directors have more experience than non-profit ones. Gender diversity is also a matter of attention, because the presence of women on boards in Colombia is still very low. Board interlocks are also viewed as having a positive influence on performance.

Another interesting issue for directors in non-profit family and independent firms is the related bylaws or protocols for selecting the chairperson. The perception is that more transparency is required in this process and that clear and adequate rules of selection are determinant in good firm performance, given the key role the Chair of the Board plays in leading the Board in its stewardship of a firm‘s strategy.

Additionally, most family and non-profit firms still do not understand the advantages of an adequate system of compensation for directors. Many provide no compensation to their directors, while other compensation is very low (small amounts paid per meeting attended). However, companies and directors do perceive board compensation as a practice

[19] AFE initials of *Asociación de Fundaciones Empresariales y Familiares*, an association of non-profit and family firms.

[20] ANDESCO are the initials of *Asociación Nacional de Empresas de Servicios Públicos y Comunicaciones*, an association of utilities and telecommunications companies.

that impacts positively on performance, because it allows them to hire more qualified directors. As empiric evidence has demonstrated, education, experience, and the diversity of boards is advantageous for firm's strategic success and board performance.

Moreover, the ANDESCO study has also interesting findings about corporate governance in its associates, who are mainly larger utilities and telecommunications companies. Firstly, regarding how directors' coalitions (or subgroups) could have positive effects on board performance, conversely to some *a priori* perceptions. Those coalitions act as informal agreements between board members to support as a group certain decisions or positions. Evidence from this study also supports the positive impact of board diversity (gender, education, and experience) and board interlocks.

Financial performance also showed a positive relationship with board effectiveness in the ANDESCO study. Performance measures used were ROA and ROE, as traditionally is found in corporate governance literature. Other financial performance measures, such as volatility, or abnormal returns, are not useful in the Colombian case, due mainly to the low liquidity of the stock market. Despite Colombia being an emerging market, the number of liquid companies is still very low (about 22 larger companies).

6 Summary and Conclusions

Colombian corporate governance practices were implemented both because of regulatory requirements and voluntary decisions of institutional entrepreneurs. During the twenty-first century, Colombia has experienced a great improvement in corporate governance practices. The first voluntary code was issued in 2007 and a renewed version in 2014. The second version of the country's corporate governance code incorporated a higher level of compliance with OECD principles than the first version. As a result, the level of compliance to recommended corporate governance practices has had a continuously increasing trend, as evidenced by level of compliance of the corporate governance code, but also by the results of applying external assessments of board performance, which track the real implementation of key measures. We observe that organizations that have performed well in corporate governance in Colombia have different types of interlocks (by business group, by state participation, by participation of independents or incipient formations of independents), which regardless of their type, seem to make these corporate governance practices "stick" over time. The presence of interlocks in business groups is an effective way to disseminate new corporate governance practices via horizontal (corporate) and vertical (subsidiaries and investments) network effects. In joint ventures and medium-sized companies, the role of the independent directors combined with interlocks is essential to spread, apply, and persevere in corporate governance.

We conclude that in Colombia corporate governance is a practice being advanced ahead of regulation by "institutional entrepreneurs"—officers and directors interlocked in economic groups and leading companies; that the network effect benefits subsidiary and affiliated companies and is sustained over time, and that a certain contagion effect, via interlocked board members, causes it to also spill over into other business environments, including evidence of spill over to privately owned, family and state-owned enterprises. Therefore, we argue, identifying and showcasing these institutional entrepreneurs or corporate governance "champions" (directors, officers, and companies) is important in order to promote the network effect; and that further study and accompaniment of this positive externality is desirable in order to accelerate the adoption of better practices in privately, family, and state-owned enterprises.

References

Baysinger, B., & Butler, H. (1985). Corporate governance and the board of directors: Performance effects of changes in board composition. *Journal of Law, Economics, & Organization.*

Bebchuk, L. A., & Weisbach, M. S. (2009). *The state of corporate governance research* (NBER working paper 15537). National Bureau of Economic Research, Cambridge, MA.

Berglöf, E., & Pajuste, A. (2003). *Emerging owners, eclipsing markets? Corporate governance in Central and Eastern Europe* (SITE working paper). Stockholm School of Economics, Stockholm, Sweden.

Berglöf, E., & von Thadden, E.-L. (1999). *The changing corporate governance paradigm: Implications for transition and developing countries* (William Davidson Institute working paper 263). University of Michigan, Ann Arbor, MI.

Berkowitz, D., Pistor, K., & Richard, J.-F. (2003). Economic development, legality, and the transplant effect. *European Economic Review, 47*, 165–195.

Boytsun, A. (2009). *Institutional determinants of corporate governance: The role of informal rules* (PhD dissertation). University of Antwerp, Belgium.

Boytsun, A., Deloof, M., & Matthyssens, P. (2011). Social norms, social cohesion, and corporate governance. *Corporate Governance, An International Review, 19*(1), 41–60.

Boyd, B. (1990). Corporate linkages and organizational environment: A test of the resource dependence model. *Strategic Management Journal, 11*(6), 419–430.

Brown, L. D., & Caylor, M. L. (2006). Corporate governance and firm valuation. *Journal of Accounting and Public Policy, 25*, 409–434.

Burris, V. (2005). Interlocking directorates and political cohesion among corporate elites. *American Journal of Sociology.*

Burt, R. (1983). *Corporate profits and cooptation.* Academic Paper.

Clavijo, S., González, A., & Vera, A. (2011). *El mercado bursátil colombiano: profundidad y nuevos emisores.* Enfoque Mercado de Capitales No. 51, extracted 3 June 2011 from www.deceval.com/InstructivosBoletines/Enfoque51-11.pdf

Carpenter, M. A., & Westphal, J. D. (2001). The strategic context of external network ties: Examining the impact of director appointments on board involvement in strategic decision making. *Academy of Management Journal, 44*(4), 639–660. https://doi.org/10.2307/3069408

Daft, R., & Weick, K. (1984). Toward a model of organizations as interpretation systems. *Academy of Management Review*, W, 284±95.

Fich, E., & Shivdasani, A. (2006). Are busy boards effective monitors? *The Journal of Finance, 61*(2), 689–724.

Haynes, K. T., & Hillman, A. (2010, November). The effect of board capital and CEO power on strategic change. *Strategic Management Journal, 31.*

Haunschild, P. R., & Beckman, C. M. (1998). When do interlocks matter? Alternate sources of information and interlock influence. *Administrative Science Quarterly*, 815–844.

Huisman, M. (2001). Decision-making in meetings as talk-in interaction. *International Studies of Management and Organization, 31*, 69–79.

IMF, W. B. (2003). *Report on the observance of Standards and Codes (ROSC).* http://www.elsevier.com/locate/scpMizruchi. (1996). Cohesion, Structural Equivalence, and Similarity of Behavior: An Approach to the Study of Corporate Political Power. *Sociological Theory, 22*, 271–298.

Jehn, K. A., Northcraft, G. B., & Neale, M. A. (1999). Why differences make a difference: A field study of diversity, conflict and performance in workgroups. *Administrative Science Quarterly, 44*, 741–763.

Parker, L. D. (2007). Boardroom strategizing in professional associations—Processual and institutional perspective. *Journal of Management Studies, 44*, 1454–2148.

Pfeffer, J., & Salancik, G. R. (1978). *The external control of organizations: A resource dependency perspective.* Harper and Row.

Pennings. (1980). *Interlocking directorates: Origins and consequences of connections among organizations' boards of directors, Jossey-Bass, San Francisco.*
Pettigrew, A. M. (1997). What is a processual analysis? *Scandinavian Journal of Management, 13*, 337–348.
Plugiese, A., Nicholson, G., & Bezemer J. (2015). An observational analysis of the impact of board dynamics and directors' participation on perceived board effectiveness. *British Journal of Management.*
Pistor, K. (2000). *Patterns of legal change: Shareholder and creditor rights in transition economies* (EBRD working paper 49/2000). European Bank for Reconstruction and Development, London.
Pistor, K., Raiser, M., & Gelfer, S. (2000). Law and finance in transition economies. *Economics of Transition, 8*, 325–368.
Pye, A. (2001). A study in studying corporate boards over time: Looking backwards to move forwards. *British Journal of Management, 12*, 33–45.
Renneboog, L., & Zhao, Y. (2011). Us knows us in the UK: On director networks and CEO compensation. *Journal of Corporate Finance.*
Sanín, E., & Arteaga, S. (2012). *Gobernanza corporativa y emisión de instrumentos de deuda corporativa en Colombia, in Gobernanza corporativa en el Brasil.* Colombia y México, edited by Georgina Núñez and Andrés Oneto. Santiago de Chile, United Nations, 111–153.
Schoorman, F. D., Bazerman, M. H., & Atkin, R. S. (1981). Interlocking directorates: A Strategy for reducing environmental uncertainty. Academy of Management Review, 6, 243-251.
Westphal, J., & Bednar, M. (2005). Pluralistic ignorance in corporate boards and firms' strategic persistence in response to low firm performance. *Administrative Science Quarterly, 50*(2), 262–298.
Zahra, S. A., & Pearce, J. A. (1989). Boards of directors and corporate financial performance: A review and integrative model. *Journal of Management, 15*, 291–334.
Zajac, E. J., & Westphal, J. D. (1996). *Director reputation, C/Board power, and the dynamics of board interlocks.* Academy of Management Proceedings.

CHAPTER 10

Mexico

Edgar Rogelio Ramírez-Solís, Verónica Ilián Baños-Monroy, and Fernando Sandoval

1 Introduction

Mexico is one interesting case, given its historical and economic characteristics. Mexico was the first Spanish colony to break away from Spain and pave the way for more independence wars in Latin America. The population is primarily a racial mix between the Spanish and indigenous cultures. Mexico has a traditionalist society where family, religion, and culture play a fundamental role. Industrial activity is limited by the government

E. R. Ramírez-Solís (✉) · V. I. Baños-Monroy
Tecnológico de Monterrey, Monterrey, Mexico
e-mail: edgar.ramirez@tec.mx

V. I. Baños-Monroy
e-mail: veronica.banos@tec.mx

F. Sandoval
Institute of Business Families for Mexico and Latin America, Tecnológico de Monterrey, Monterrey, Mexico
e-mail: fsandoval@tec.mx

J. Callund et al. (eds.), *Corporate Governing in Latin America*,
https://doi.org/10.1007/978-3-030-85780-6_10

and local interest groups, such as unions, political parties, chambers of commerce, and private family businesses.

Around 40% of the largest firms in Latin America are family-controlled (Vázquez et al., 2020). Fourteen of the top 37 Latin American family businesses are Mexican firms; two of them are in the top 10: AMÉRICA MÓVIL, which belongs to the Slim family (No. 1), and CEMEX, controlled by the Zambrano family (No. 10)[1] (E.Y., 2017). In addition, some of the oldest family businesses in Latin America are in Mexico; the oldest family business in the continent is JOSÉ CUERVO, founded in 1758 (Cuervo, 2020). Another example is TARDAN HERMANOS SUCESORES S.A., founded in 1847, which belongs to the Tardan family and still manufactures and sells hats and caps (Tardan, 2020).

Mexico's development was tied to an import substitution model in the '70s and '80s of the last century. Mexican industry would grow to meet the needs of its internal markets. As a result, its markets were highly protected from foreign competition, and foreign ownership in Mexican companies was usually restricted to a 49% share (Husted & Serrano, 2002). State-owned enterprises dominated many agricultural and industrial sectors. Mexican companies were assured attractive margins in highly oligopolistic markets, and unsuccessful companies could count on government bailouts. The moral hazard problems created by such an environment created an atmosphere in which political skills were often more critical to success than were business skills. Consequently, corporate governance was not on the agenda of either business or government leaders.

During the 1994 economic crisis, the Mexican banking system drastically curtailed its credit supply to firms, and bank lending to enterprises plummeted from 15.4 to 2.9% of Gross Domestic Product (GDP) between 1995 and 2000. The subsequent recovery was moderate, and by 2010, it only represented one-third of the amount recorded in 1994 (Espinosa, 2012). Since then, concern about corporate governance has increased throughout the world, and Mexico is no exception. The forces behind the current interest in good corporate governance are mainly due to the demands of international investors, the pressures faced by newly privatized companies, and processes of mimetic

[1] Per the annual report, although the Zambrano family only owns around 2.25% of shares, it maintains and continues to control the company.

isomorphism within Mexico (Deloitte, 2018). Therefore, Mexican businesspeople respond to governance movements in the United States, Japan, UK, and the EUROPEAN UNION.

Mexico is part of the 15 largest economies worldwide and the second-largest economy in Latin America (World Bank, 2021). Since 1994, this country has been part of the *North American Free Trade Agreement*, formerly NAFTA, now known as the USMCA or the *United States-Mexico-Canada Agreement*. In addition, Mexico is a member of the WORLD TRADE ORGANIZATION (WTO), ASIA–PACIFIC ECONOMIC COOPERATION (APEC), G-20, and OECD. With a GDP of USD10,118. Mexico's 2.5% average annual GDP growth rate has been slower than most emerging markets, due partly to its high rates of labor informality (57%), poverty (43%), and declining oil production. Moreover, with the deepening of the COVID-19 pandemic and economic contraction in world markets, some analysts foresee a reduction in Mexican GDP of 10% to 12%t by 2021 (ITA, 2021).

This chapter presents the evolution and current state of corporate governance practices and their application in Mexican family businesses. Family-owned companies are the leading way of forming business organizations in Latin America, even among large, listed companies.

2 CORPORATE GOVERNANCE IN FAMILY BUSINESSES

In Mexico, small and medium-sized (SMEs) enterprises represent 99.8% of the total businesses, contribute 52% of the GDP and generate more than 71.9% of the jobs; 57% of these companies have been in the market for less than five years, and are conformed of one family and several non-related workers (INEGI, 2019). Therefore, family firms are smaller and younger than their counterparts in the rest of the world; 66% of them are, in fact, first-generation, 29% second generation, and only 4% of Mexican family firms are third generation (San Martín-Reyna & Durán-Encalada, 2017). Research shows a lack of strategic planning and centralized decision-making (Burgoa et al., 2013; Durán & San Martín, 2013; Sandoval-Arzaga, 2021).

83% of Mexican firms could be considered family businesses (San Martín-Reyna & Durán-Encalada, 2017). Regardless of size, the most dominant companies are owned and managed by one or more families or descendants of the founding family. Six of the top twelve biggest companies in Mexico are family businesses. These companies are AMÉRICA

Móvil, Femsa, Alfa, BIMBO, and CEMEX (Expansión, 2020). Despite being one of the 15 largest economies globally, Mexico occupies the 20th spot regarding stock market capitalization and the 25th in listed companies (OECD, 2019). The market for corporate control is scarce. The corporate governance code is voluntary.

It is worth mentioning that the Mexican corporate system has more in common with the European or Latin American corporate governance models than with the Anglo-Saxon ones (San Martín-Reyna & Durán-Encalada, 2012). In Mexican companies, as in other European or Latin American enterprises, ownership is relatively more concentrated in single families, but this could be advantageous. In a recent study, family-controlled firms outperform non-family companies because the intimate entrepreneurial environment benefits corporate results, promoting long-term relationships and responsible management (Watkins-Fassler & Briano-Torrent, 2019).

Another characteristic of the Latin American corporate governance model (compared with the Anglo-Saxons) is its low stakeholder orientation. Stakeholder orientation is a construct that refers to a concern about the groups that can influence the supply of the resources to the firm's operations (Dhaliwal et al., 2012). The construct is composed of four factors: (1) the legal protection of labor rights, (2) laws requiring mandatory disclosure, (3) public awareness based on the number of non-governmental organizations and number of CSR reports issued, and (4) corporate awareness of stakeholder issues, as measured by opinion surveys regarding sustainable development, ethical practice, and social responsibility of leaders. Some Latin American countries, like Brazil, Chile, and Mexico, are all low in the stakeholder orientation index, meaning that businesses and the law are generally more concerned with stockholders than other stakeholders (Husted & De Sousa-Filho, 2019).

In most family-owned unlisted firms, which are generally medium-sized, some of them follow good corporate governance practices. In a recent study of the Instituto de Familias Empresarias de México y Latinoamérica of the Tecnológico de Monterrey, out of 884 Mexican companies, 34% report that they have a board of directors (Sandoval-Arzaga, 2021). The most common corporate governance body in unlisted companies is the *Top Management Team*, which is present in 32% of firms. There are family councils in 18%, and 15% have *shareholder assemblies*. Besides that, only 7% of family businesses have a family *protocol* or family *constitution* (San Martín-Reyna & Durán-Encalada,

2017). Besides this, 67% of family businesses do not have a training plan to integrate family members or employees into their governance bodies (Ibid.).

In another study of 407 family businesses from 8 Latin American countries, researchers found that for Mexico, only 12% have a *Board of Advisors* and 13% have a formal *board of directors*. The same investigation found the following characteristics in the board of directors: only 10% were external directors, and just 6% had members unrelated to the owning family. Only 10% of firms had formal succession plans. On average, Mexican family businesses use 2.3 of these corporate governance mechanisms simultaneously, while the global standard (includes 33 countries in the world) is 2.1. However, with better performance use 3 or 4 such tools on average (STEP Project for Family Enterprising, 2019).

A lack of formal driving organs in Mexican family businesses is usual, as the *board of directors* are found in 21% of Mexican firms (San Martín-Reyna & Durán-Encalada, 2017), or just 13% of the companies, according to STEP Project (2019). Either way, nepotism prevails in the few established boards when they come to select managers. The selection of managers and directors in family firms is often strongly influenced by personal friendship or family ties (Songini et al., 2013). The board should be the space where the strategy is defined, and this fact reveals that the owners' decisions are reactive and that partners probably do not communicate properly. There is much to be done in terms of the institutionalization of family businesses.

3 The Legal Context

In Mexico, legal protection is weaker than that found in Europe and the United States, and capital markets are less developed. However, this situation has been improving over the last two decades. Moreover, Mexico has been one of the most proactive countries regarding corporate governance matters. This situation arises because Mexico is one of the few OECD member countries in Latin America (only Mexico, Chile, and Colombia are members) and it was the first to join in 1994 (OECD, 2020).

The two fundamental laws affecting Corporate Governance in Mexico are the Company Law (*Ley General de Sociedades Mercantiles*, or LGSM) and the Securities Market Law (*Ley del Mercado de Valores,* or LMV). The LGSM, published in 1934 and amended in 1996, establishes the minimum legal structure for companies together with shareholder rights.

The LMV regulated public companies and was introduced in 1975, but significant amendments were made in 2001. The new version of the Securities Markets Law was enacted in 2006. This version of LMV changed the securities market framework in three areas. First, it expanded the CNBV's authority and introduced significant changes in publicly listed companies' corporate governance; it created two new vehicles designed to facilitate SMEs to raise capital and transition to become publicly listed companies (Fabre, 2008).

The legal system in Mexico still lacks the proper protections for the small investor, whether stock or debt holders. Regarding equity investor rights, the LGSM is the primary piece of legislation dealing with the creation of a limited liability firm, "*Sociedad Anónima*." It also establishes investors' property rights and regulates the firm's different oversight/counseling bodies, such as the board of Directors, the Shareholder Assembly, and the Commissioner. In the case of listed corporations, special regulations were established in the "Law of Securities Markets" enacted in 1975 and in the "Rules of the Law for Promoting and Regulating Foreign Investment" from 1989.

Many requirements that promote more reliable and transparent financial reporting have been made legally enforceable through amendments to the Securities Market Law (*Ley del Mercado de Valores* or LMV). The LMV, which regulates public companies, was published in 1975, but significant amendments went into effect in 2001 and 2003. CNBV has issued several regulations ("*circulares*") covering corporate governance aspects, including disclosure obligations. In 2003, these "circulares" were reissued and updated in the form of an "issuers manual" as the *Circular Única* (ROSC, 2003).

These amendments to the Securities Market Law were designed to change management's behavior to improve the information presented in annual reports. Specifically, the new rules have: (1) better defined the structure and duties of the board of directors and audit committee, (2) established guidelines for the protection of the rights of minority shareholders, and (3) implemented procedures related to the independence of external auditors, as well as internal control provisions (Machuga & Teitel, 2007).

Another player in the Mexican legal context is the Mexican Institute of Public Accountants (*Instituto Mexicano de Contadores Públicos*, or IMCP), a federation founded in 1923; they have more than 22,000 associated Public Accountants throughout the country. IMCP issues *Generally*

Accepted Accounting Standards and Generally Accepted Auditing Standards (GAAP) (IMCP, 2020). Mexican GAAP differs in certain respects from International Accounting Standards (IAS), and IAS is supposed to be applied when Mexican GAAP does not provide a specific standard. The Accounting and Auditing (ROSC, 2003) revealed shortcomings in the actual application of accounting regulation.

In 2003, a *Report on Standards and Codes* benchmarked Mexico's corporate governance observance against the OECD's *Principles for Corporate Governance.* According to this report and another report made by the Institute of International Finance released the same year, Mexico has made significant progress establishing a successful structure for good corporate governance. However, both reports cautioned that real Mexican corporate governing progress must account for many Mexican firms' concentrated ownership and control structure (Fabre, 2008).

As we can see, Mexican legislation provides the primary means necessary for an effective defense of the rights of minority shareholders. However, the lack of specificity in Mexican laws leaves open the possibility of majority shareholders applying them in their favor and to the detriment of the minority group. Although Mexico has made reforms to its statute of "securities," this does not necessarily imply better investor protection (Castro et al., 2009).

4 The Financial System

More than 3,000 registered financial entities integrate the Mexican financial system. Federal authorities oversee the regulation and supervision of the system. It is one of the most comprehensive and sophisticated economic systems globally, considering its number and diversity of actors, products, services, and consumers (SHCP-CNBV, 2018).

One of the most important organisms of the Mexican financial system is the National Banking and Securities Commission (*Comisión Nacional Bancaria y de Valores* or CNBV), regulating the banking and brokerage sectors. CNBV is an independent agency of the Ministry of Finance and Public Credit (SHCP), with technical autonomy and executive powers over the Mexican financial system. Its central role is to supervise and regulate the Mexican financial system (ibid.).

The Mexican Stock Exchange (*Bolsa Mexicana de Valores* or BMV) is a public institution under a concession granted by the

Ministry of Finance (SHCP), observing the Mexican Securities Law. One hundred seventy companies were listed at year-end 2002, and only 147 in 2017 (Santiago, 2017). Continuing the downward trend, in 2021, there were only 148 companies in total. Despite the decline in listed companies, BMV is the second-largest stock exchange in Latin America (only after São Paulo, based in Brazil), with a total market capitalization of over USD 530 billion (BMV, 2021). According to San Martín-Reyna (2018), out of a sample of 67 companies listed, 54% have family ownership concentration. Still, a study by Watkins-Fassler and Briano-Torrent (2019) with a selection of 89 non-financial companies listed in BMV showed that 77% of these firms are family controlled.

BMV is an integrated group that operates cash, listed derivatives, and OTC markets for multiple asset classes, including equities, fixed income, and exchange-traded funds, as well as custody, clearing, settlement facilities, and data products for the local and international financial community (BMV, 2021). Teléfonos de México (Telmex) accounts for over 11% of market capitalization, and about 61% of market capitalization comes from the largest ten companies (most of them family-owned). The BMV is nominally a *Self-Regulatory Organization* but operates under the supervision of the CNBV. Free float averages 12 to 15% of capital (ROSC, 2003).

In most firms listed in BMV, one class of shares gives full voting rights to the family controllers, while others have limited or no voting rights. Financial and business groups have been vital in Mexican economic development. Business groups are characterized by vertical, horizontal, or conglomerate integration (ROSC, 2003). Usually, conglomerates are controlled by investors or a local family, using crossholdings or dual-class shares (San Martín-Reyna & Durán-Encalada, 2012). In 2014, 98% of the listed companies in BMV were part of a business group (OECD, 2015). Holding companies make the most critical decisions, including financing, dividend policy, fixed assets, and top managers hiring.

Business groups respond to various factors that seek to improve the competitive positions of growing companies by evolving and seeking international expansion and economic power and involve more significant amounts and types of stakeholders (Correa-García et al., 2020). Mexican business groups are characterized by the presence of a well-established social structure among participating firms. Hence, interlocking directorates tend to be more frequent and powerful (Uddin & Choudhury, 2008). An interlock is formed when an individual initially affiliated with one firm (e.g., in the role of Chair of the Board or CEO) joins the Board of another firm. About 50% of the Chairs of 52 listed Mexican family firms participated in business networks, simultaneously holding up to six positions on different boards. Regarding CEO interlocks, these were observed in 24% of the same sample, where CEOs were found to hold positions in up to three boards of directors (Watkins-Fassler & Briano-Torrent, 2019).

The lack of transparency in many Mexican family firms and the loose requirements of the CNBV make it virtually impossible to obtain detailed information about the degree of equity concentration in listed firms. Some financial analysts and observers claim that the only complex data available is derived from the concept of "related stockholders," published by the BMV. "Related stockholders" is a concept that refers to individuals with at least 10% of the firms' equity who are frequently involved in the firm's decision-making. It should be clear that this classification does not allow us to identify whether we are dealing with one owner or several significant minorities. Babatz (1997) mentioned that "related stockholders" (79.3% of the firms listed in the BMV) own at least 50% of the equity in those firms.

Shareholder activism is uncommon. Small shareholders have few mechanisms to defend their interests in court. Veto power is nil. Only "minorities" holding at least 33% of voting rights can delay any decision for three days to get more information and then ask a judge to stop any resolution considered against company regulations. Besides the difficulties to prove an explicit fraud in an environment of lax laws and lack of transparency, only "minorities" can sue the administration in a civil demand (Castro et al., 2009).

Even in firms listed on the stock market, the information requirements are not very transparent. In particular, the statement of expenditures is not adequately broken up, and firms are not obliged to declare investments, sales, or acquisitions involving individuals related to the company.

There is a high concentration of control rights in large Mexican firms, not only because family members own extensive holdings of stocks but also because it is common to issue "no-voting" shares. No-voting shareholders are not entitled to vote on the company's majority decisions, but they may be entitled to vote on individual choices. This device allows Mexican business groups to give relatively few monitoring rights to small investors and other stakeholders. Mexico's standard practice is a dual-stock structure, where firms issue some of their equity in the domestic market through non-voting rights stocks. A law passed in 1990 allows a firm to give at most 25% of its equity in non-voting stock (Fabre, 2008).

5 Corporate Governance in Listed Companies

In Mexico, families play an essential part in defining corporate governance practices. For example, most Mexican companies' board members' purpose is to control shareholders through family ties, friendship, business relationships, and labor contracts (Espinoza & Espinoza, 2012). In addition, Husted and Serrano (2002) show that 53% of a company's managers or senior executives are managers of other companies of the same group or relatives of the company's executives. Therefore, CEOs and owners practically have no opposition from independent board members.

One difference must be noted between corporate governance in publicly listed firms compared with the unlisted ones. Public companies are more concerned with the relationship between boards and external shareholders. At the same time, the unlisted businesses want to ensure their long-term sustainability by attracting funds and solving issues between shareholders and other stakeholders, using corporate governing organisms. According to Poletti-Hughes and Williams (2019), there is a conflict with good corporate governance practices in Mexico, when families or family connections tend to sit on the Board and manage the company, limiting minority shareholders' involvement is the duality effect. The Board's Chair is the principal stockholder and the general manager in most Mexican firms. They, therefore, experience little in the way of opposition from independent board members. However, Castañeda (2000) shows that, on average, only 20% of firms allow most external members on the board. This fact does not necessarily mean independence since those external members can also be involved with another company within the same business group. Also, an average of 35.2% of board members belong to the Chair's family; 38.7% are executive managers, and around 57% are employees or relatives of the Chair.

In their research, Castro et al. (2009) show that 40% of the family firms do not have independent CEOs. Eight out of nine board members were insiders (people with a family relationship to key shareholders). A recent study shows that 69% of the CEOs are part of the owner family, and 85% of CEOs are also members of the Board, while CEO duality is 38% in the most prominent family firms listed. Which is not a good practice of corporate governance. Mexico also has a large percentage of family

Chairs in family firms (92%) as well as the lowest female representation on boards, with only 6% (Vázquez et al., 2020).

Castrillo and San Martín (2007) highlight the relationship between corporate governing mechanisms and managerial discretion using a sample of companies listed on the Mexican Stock Exchange. The authors wonder whether the company's ownership structure conditions these mechanisms; the results suggest less managerial discretion in family firms than non-family firms. Boards of Directors in Latin America, especially in Mexico, are not as independent as those in developed countries, making them less effective in monitoring managers' decisions (Lefort, 2005; Santiago -Castro & Baek, 2004).

Sáenz González and García-Meca (2013) examined the relationship between the internal mechanisms of *Corporate Governance and Earnings Management* as measured by discretionary accrual in a sample of 435 listed Latin American non-financial companies from 2006 to 2009. Their results showed that in the region, external directors' role is limited. Besides, ownership concentration might be a manipulative practice/constrictor when the principal shareholders' ownership is moderate. On the other side, not always the concentration of family members in Board positions is something wrong. "Partners know that long-tenured, influential family members offer stability and thus can be held accountable for transgressions. That would be less true in most non-family firms where CEOs are more temporary, identify less with the business, and have less authority from shareholders to resolve significant disputes" (Miller & Le Breton-Miller, 2020).

We agree with Jara et al. (2019) when they conclude that power distribution is related to board of directors' dynamics. Listed family companies that professionalize their management by hiring a non-family CEO tend to retain control of the firm by appointing a family member as Chair of the Board. Therefore, directors representing institutional investors or independent directors tasked with defending minority shareholder interests may positively influence the decision-making process. Furthermore, the research of Watkins-Fassler and Briano-Torrent (2019) suggests that a transition to external CEOs with better networks and experience within the Boards of Directors of other family firms could improve the profitability of family firms listed on the Mexican Stock Exchange. On the other hand, it is easier to reduce opportunistic behaviors through a CEO family member, resulting in efficient resource and risk management. In the end, the firm performance depends on its specific situation.

Regarding the board of directors in Mexican companies, a fundamental flaw is that the Board is integrated by inviting friends or relatives of the owner's family. The relative absence of independent external auditors inside the boards (like an audit committee) prevents the protection of minority shareholders. 65% of family businesses in Mexico do not have an audit committee (KPMG, 2013). Likewise, small shareholders have minimal channels to state their positions and to participate in decision-making. To summon a stockholder assembly, it is necessary to have at least 33% voting rights. Besides, voting by mail is not allowed, and the discussion agenda, usually received only a few days in advance, is very vague.

In big companies, the board of directors represents a block of large shareholders' interests rather than comprising autonomous external auditors, monitoring small shareholder interests. According to Babatz (1997), separation of the rule one-stock-one-vote occurs in 60% of the 121 Mexican public firms of the BMV. The 60% has decreased in recent years to 16% for 2013 (Poletti-Hughes & Williams., 2019). On the contrary, the dual-stock structure is sporadic in industrialized countries with a highly developed stock market. The corresponding percentages for Canada, Japan, the UK, and the United States are 10%, 1%, 1%, and 4%, respectively (Castañeda, 2000). There are three basic regulatory models to deal with dual-class shares: (a) prohibitions, existing in countries like the UK, Germany, Spain, Colombia, or Argentina; (b) the permissive model, present in Canada, Sweden, the Netherlands, and particularly the United States; and (c) the restrictive approach recently implemented in Hong Kong and Singapore (Gurrea-Martínez, 2021).

6 The Code of Best Corporate Governance Practices

In 1999, at the same time, the OECD launched its Code of conduct for corporate governance. A private-sector group (*Consejo Coordinador Empresarial* or CCE) issued voluntarily the code of best corporate governance practices (*Código de Mejores Prácticas Corporativas*, or the Code). The Committee was named: *Best Corporate Practices*, formed inside the CCE, the Mexican Institute of Public Accountants, and other industrial, government, financial, and services organizations. The Committee studied various existing international corporate governance models and adopted the principles they believed to fit into the Mexican economy and culture (Hernández & Conejo, 2003). The first version of the Code was launched in 1999 and includes recommendations on Board organization, functions, and the protection of minority rights.

The same Committee (CCE) asked the CNBV to issue provisions so that the companies whose shares are listed on the Mexican Stock Exchange (BMV) reveal their degree of adherence to the suggested practices. If a public company does not follow such procedures, it will indicate why it does not follow them and the alternative mechanism to suppress them. In October 1999, CNBV issued a circular requiring that companies file "comply or explain" reports on compliance with the Code.

One objective of the Code is to improve the board of directors' oversight and reveal more information to shareholders by including detailed information regarding the Board's structure and functions. As we mentioned, the business environment is characterized by controlling family ownership and weak legal protection of property rights. Machuga and Teitel (2009) examine whether earnings quality has increased in Mexico, surrounding the Code's implementation using various earnings quality characteristics: board composition disclosure, family concentrated ownership, and shared directors. For the sample of firms trading only on the Mexican Stock Exchange, their results across all earnings quality are consistent with management decreasing mechanisms to manipulate earnings, thereby improving earnings quality.

The Code's recommendations apply to all companies, whether of a civil, commercial, or social assistance nature, without distinguishing their size, shareholding composition, or whether they are listed on the stock market. Still, only certain firms must adhere to these recommendations, like listed companies, financial institutions, and trust funds. Although the Code is voluntary, the Mexican National Banking and Securities Commission (CNBV) issued a circular in October 1999 requiring listed companies to indicate their degree of compliance with several provisions of the Code.

Regarding gender equity, San Martín-Reyna and Durán-Encalada (2017) found that women run only 23% of family businesses in Mexico, and only 8% are large firms; women usually only run SMEs. Furthermore, women are almost absent in the corporate governance bodies: less than 28% in top management teams and only 18% in the board of directors. The STEP Project report on Mexico shows that the participation of women on the Board is 13%, while at the global level, it is 31% (Sandoval-Arzaga et al., 2020). That is why a new recommendation of the Code is to incorporate women into the board of directors, because 51% of the

Boards in Mexico do not have a woman among their members; furthermore, out of the 49% who include women, 43% have only one on the Board (Deloitte, 2018). Thus, Mexico is far from being an equity gender society, at least in corporate governance matters.

In 2004, the OECD published a revised version of its *Corporate Governance Principles*. Then, late in September 2015, the *G-20 Corporate Governance Principles* were published. On this basis, the member countries updated their *Principles and Good Practices of Corporate Governance*. That was the reason that in 2018, Mexico launched a new version of the Code. First, the name changed to *Código de Principios y Mejores Prácticas de Gobierno Corporativo* (*Code of Principles and Best Practices of Corporate Governance*), to include the "principles" concept. The Code now includes a new "*Principle of honest and responsible management of the company*" and a best practice about preventing and resolving disputes between shareholders and Board members. Other additions of the Code are recommendations for the selection, hiring, evaluation, and compensation of directors, developing a Family Agreement for representation in governance bodies; and a new Risk and Compliance function in one Corporate Governance Committee. The Code also includes a recommendation for companies to issue codes of ethics and social responsibility (CCE, 2018).

Nevertheless, there are still pending issues in the new version of the code. According to the Code (CCE, 2018), inside the board of directors must include independent members. However, the Code does not mention in-law relatives (those wedded to individuals from the controlling family) or the ties of "*compadrazgo*," very significant in Mexico. "*Compadrazgo*" alludes to the connection between the parents and godparents of a youngster. Godparents are emblematically received as members of a Mexican family. Often "*compadres*" are closer than siblings. Unfortunately, it is challenging to discover "*compadrazgo*" relationships because of their informal nature. A review of the publicly available information on the 90 largest companies in Mexico reveals that 53% of directors are top executives, the firm's group, or relatives of such executives.

Nevertheless, it is almost impossible to determine which of the other board members belong to one of the different categories of "insiders," mentioned by the Code, not to mention the presence of political or "*compadrazgo*" relationships (Husted & Serrano, 2002). The "*compadrazgo*" could mislead investors, especially if they are unaware of Mexico's "familial" practices. This situation could lead to a simulation practice in the decision-making process: There may be no concrete counterweight to the decisions of the owning-founder of the family business.

7 Conclusions

We need to acknowledge that most owners of SMEs and family-controlled companies have limited knowledge of how to implement corporate governance principles and procedures in Mexico. Also, the uniqueness of Mexico's capital structure, legal framework, litigation environments, the lack of compliance with rules, and informal relationships inside the Boards may have limited the *Code of Principles and Best Practices of Corporate Governance* to improve corporate governing to its fullest potential.

First, concerning capital structure, as we mentioned earlier, most Mexican companies are family-controlled, with family members in key management positions and occupying important places on the board of directors. Besides, most companies issue two classes of shares—*common* shares, with voting rights, and *preferred* shares, that do not allow voting for directors. Finally, owners/managers serve on each other's boards, making it questionable whether directors are truly independent (Pliego, 2001). These capital structure features may facilitate opportunistic earnings management, resulting in lower-quality earnings. Although the Code requires a firm's ownership structure to be disclosed in the annual report, the *Report on Observance of Standards and Codes* (ROSC, 2003) and a review of our sample firms' annual reports reveal that compliance with ownership disclosure is infrequent.

Second, the Mexican legal framework is based on the civil law tradition. There is no procedure for class action or shareholder derivative lawsuits. This situation makes it difficult for minority shareholders to enforce their rights against management, directors, or controlling shareholders.

Third, Ball et al. (2013) emphasize that earnings management is inversely related to the strength of the regulation and litigation environment. As it applies to publicly traded companies, the Securities Market Law regulation is performed by the CNBV. The CNBV is responsible for reviewing and enforcing disclosure compliance in listed firms' financial statements, including the Code's provisions. The CNBV has authority to institute administrative proceedings, impose administrative sanctions, fines, suspensions, and debarments of directors, and management and report market abuse offenses to the Attorney General. Prison penalties for management, directors, and auditors are up to 10 years. According to ROSC (2003), however, there is no public record of any sanctions for accounting, reporting, or auditing requirements violations.

Fourth, there is a problem with the lack of compliance with rules requiring voting rights disclosure and failures to provide complete information on related-party transactions. The investor community has a mixed perception of the quality of financial reporting. On the one hand, Mexico is now perceived by the market as rising to meet international standards. The quality, quantity, and delivery of disclosed information have improved. This situation is evidenced by the fact that 30 companies were admonished for non-compliance with quarterly information disclosure requirements in 1999, while only three were fined in 2002. Today the leading companies have investor relations departments. However, the Accounting and Auditing ROSC (2003) indicates that enforcement has focused on legal issues until recently rather than content.

One policy recommendation following the ROSC (2003) review is to strengthen enforcement mechanisms. Although the CNBV monitors adherence to accounting standards, effective sanctions for infractions are challenging to impose within the Mexican legal framework. Under the laws covering commercial activities in Mexico, there are no civil or criminal penalties to deter fraudulent or erroneous financial reporting by the board of directors. High-quality corporate financial reporting can only be achieved through proper enforcement of the established standards.

Fifth, due to informal relationships like "*compadres*" within the board of directors of most companies, in Mexico, we cannot observe at this point whether corporate boards might become influential decision-making bodies in the near future. Also, it is crucial to increase the use of tools and mechanisms and the participation of women in the Boards to improve them, modernize them, and break tradition with modern corporate governing.

In conclusion, as in other Latin American countries, external corporate governance mechanisms (e.g., laws and regulations) in Mexico do not function as efficiently as in developed economies (Chong & López-de-Silanes, 2007). Businesses rely more on internal governance schemes (e.g., family ownership) for stakeholder protection and investor confidence (Steier, 2009). In that sense, families' reputation is a crucial element for companies' long-term success. Families are more concerned with passing the business to their future generations than wealth; so, the firm's survival is a more significant concern. In short, Mexican family businesses use gaps and deficiencies in applying corporate governing to their advantage to achieve better performance standards.

References

Babatz, G. (1997). *Agency problems, ownership structure, and voting structure under lax corporate governance rules: The case of Mexico* (Ph.D. thesis). Harvard University.

Ball, R. (2013). Accounting informs investors and earnings management is rife: Two questionable beliefs. *Accounting Horizons*, *27*(4), 847–853.

BMV Group. (2021). *About us*. https://www.bmv.com.mx/en/bmv-group/about-us. Accessed 21 May 2021.

Burgoa, T., Herrera, E., & Treviño, J. (2013). Study on family business administration in Mexico: Main problems and challenges confronted. *International Journal of Good Conscience, 8*(2), 01–22.

Castañeda, G. (2000). *Corporate governance in Mexico*. Conference in the Latin American Corporate Governance Roundtable. São Paulo, Brazil.

Castrillo, L., & San Martín, J. (2007). La propiedad familiar como mecanismo de gobierno disciplinador de la dirección en las empresas mexicanas, una evidencia empírica. *Contaduría y Administración*, May August *222*, 59–82.

Castro, S., Brown, M., & Báez-Díaz, A. (2009). Prácticas de gobierno corporativo en América Latina. Academia. *Revista Latinoamericana de Administración, 43*, 26–40. https://www.redalyc.org/articulo.oa?id=71612112003

CCE. (2018). *Código de Mejores Prácticas Corporativas*. Available at: https://eslex.mx/cce/cce-codigo-gobierno-corporativo/f. Accessed 19 February 2021.

Correa-García, J. A., García-Benau, M. A., & García-Meca, E. (2020). Corporate governance and its implications for sustainability reporting quality in Latin American business groups. *Journal of Cleaner Production, 260*, 121142.

Chong, A., & López-de-Silanes, F. (2007). Corporate governance and firm value in Mexico. *Investor protection and corporate governance: Firm-level evidence across Latin America*, 397–481.

Cuervo. (2020). *Official website*. https://cuervo.com/. Accessed 19 February 2020.

Deloitte. (2018). *Sexto estudio de Mejores Prácticas en Gobierno Corporativo*. https://www2.deloitte.com/mx/es/pages/risk/articles/6to-estudio-de-mejores-practicas-en-gobierno-corporativo.html. Accessed 15 January 2021.

Dhaliwal, D. S., Radhakrishnan, S., Tsang, A., & Yang, Y. G. (2012). Nonfinancial disclosure and analyst forecast accuracy: International evidence on corporate social responsibility disclosure. *The Accounting Review, 87*(3), 723–759.

Durán, J. A., & San Martín, J. M. (2013). Estudio comparativo de la empresa familiar mexicana en el contexto mundial. *Revista de Contaduría, Administración e Informática. Año 2, No. 5*(septiembre–diciembre), 21–54.

Espinosa, P. (2012). Corporate governance in Mexico and the evaluation of risk in bond issuance. In G. Nuñez & A. Oneto, *Corporate governance in Brazil, Chile, Colombia, Mexico, and Peru*. https://repositorio.cepal.org/bitstream/handle/11362/39772/S1420667_en.pdf?sequence=1. Accessed 10 January 2021.

Espinoza, T. I., & Espinoza, N. C. (2012). Family business performance: Evidence from Mexico. *Cuaderno de Administración de Servicios Organizacionales, 25*(44), 39–61.

Expansión. (2020). *Official website*. https://expansion.mx/empresas/2020/07/15/estas-son-las-500-empresas-mas-importantes-de-mexico-2020. Accessed 9 April 2021.

E.Y. (2017). *Family business yearbook*. https://familybusiness.ey-vx.com/fb-yearbook-flipbook-2017/mobile/index.html#p=146. Accessed 19 February 2020.

Fabre, J. (2008). *The role of institutional investors in promoting good corporate governance practices in Latin America: The case of Mexico*. World Bank and OECD Report. https://www.oecd.org/corporate/ca/corporategovernanceprinciples/42098080.pdf. Accessed 16 May 2021.

Gurrea-Martínez, A. (2021). Theory, evidence, and policy on dual-class shares: A country-specific response to a global debate. *European Business Organization Law Review*. https://link.springer.com/article/10.1007/s40804-021-00212-4. Accessed 26 May 2021.

Hernández, P., & Conejo, J. (2003). Mexico takes on corporate governance challenges. *International Financial Law Review*, 62–64.

Husted, B., & Serrano, C. (2002). Corporate governance in México. *Journal of Business Ethics., 37*(3), 337–348.

Husted, B. W., & de Sousa-Filho, J. M. (2019). Board structure and environmental, social, and governance disclosure in Latin America. *Journal of Business Research, 102*, 220–227.

IMCP. (2020). *Official website of the Instituto Mexicano de Contadores Públicos*. https://imcp.org.mx/que-es-el-imcp/. Accessed 24 December 2020.

INEGI. (2019). *Censos Económicos 2019*. https://www.inegi.org.mx/programas/ce/2019/. Accessed 19 February 2020.

ITA. (2021). *Mexico—Country commercial guide*. International Trade Administration. https://www.trade.gov/knowledge-product/exporting-mexico-market-overview. Accessed 17 May 2021.

Jara, M., López-Iturriaga, F., San-Martín, P., & Saona, P. (2019). Corporate governance in Latin American firms: Contestability of control and firm value. *BRQ Business Research Quarterly, 22*(4), 257–274.
KPMG. (2013). *Empresas familiares en México: El desafío de crecer, madurar y permanecer*. KPMG de México. https://assets.kpmg/content/dam/kpmg/mx/pdf/2016/12/Empresas%20Familiares%20en%20M%C3%A9xico%20el%20desaf%C3%ADo%20de%20crecer%20madurar%20y%20permanecer.pdf. Accessed 19 February 2020.
Lefort, F. (2005). Ownership structure and corporate governance in Latin America. *Revista Abante, 8*, 55–84.
Machuga, S., & Teitel, K. (2007). Changes in the quality of earnings and its components surrounding the implementation of the Mexican Corporate Governance Code. *Journal of International Accounting Research, 6*, 37–55.
Machuga, S., & Teitel, K. (2009). Board of director characteristics and earnings quality surrounding the implementation of a corporate governance code in Mexico. *Journal of International Accounting, Auditing, and Taxation, 18*, 1–13.
Miller, D., & Le Breton-Miller, I. (2020). Family firms: A breed of extremes? *Entrepreneurship Theory and Practice*. https://doi.org/10.1177/1042258720964186
OECD. (2015). *Corporate governance of company groups in Latin America, corporate governance*. OECD Publishing. https://doi.org/10.1787/9789264241725-en. Accessed 12 April 2021.
OECD. (2019). *Equity market development in Latin America: Mexico*. https://www.oecd.org/corporate/ca/Mexico-Latin-America-Equity-Markets.pdf. Accessed 12 April 2021.
OECD. (2020). *Global OECD welcomes Colombia as its 37th member*. https://www.oecd.org/newsroom/global-oecd-welcomes-colombia-as-its-37th-member.htm#:~:text=The%20OECD's%2037%20members%20are,Poland%2C%20Portugal%2C%20Slovak%20Republic%2C. Accessed 12 May 2021.
Poletti-Hughes, J., & Williams, J. (2019). The effect of family control on value and risk-taking in Mexico: A socioemotional wealth approach. *International Review of Financial Analysis, 63*, 369–381.
Pliego, R. (2001). The brave new world of corporate Governance. *Latin Finance*, 61–62.
ROSC. (2003). *Report on the observance of standards and codes*. Corporate Governance Country Assessment. Mexico. https://documents.worldbank.org/en/publication/documents-reports/documentdetail/373691468286248818/mexico-report-on-the-observance-of-standards-and-codes-rosc-corporate-governance-country-assessment. Accessed 22 December 2020.

Sáenz González, J., & García-Meca, E. (2013). Does corporate governance influence earnings management in Latin American markets? *Journal of Business Ethics, 121*, 419–440.

Santiago, J. (2017). "En México la BMV tiene apenas 146 empresas públicas". El Economista, retrieved from: https://www.eleconomista.com.mx/mercados/En-Mexico-la-BMV-tiene-apenas-146-empresaspublicas20170716-0074.html. Accessed 19 October 2020.

Santiago-Castro, M., & Baek, H.Y. (2004). 'Board composition and firm performance of large Latin American firms: An exploratory view.' *Latin American Business Review*, *4*(2): 1–19.

San Martín-Reyna, J. M., & Durán-Encalada, J. A. (2012). The relationship among family business, corporate governance, and firm performance: Evidence from the Mexican stock exchange. *Journal of Family Business Strategy, 3*(2), 106–117. https://doi.org/10.1016/j.jfbs.2012.03.001

San Martín-Reyna, J. M., & Durán-Encalada, J. A. (2017). *Radiografía de la Empresa Familiar en México.* San Andrés Cholula, Fundación Universidad de las Américas Puebla, Puebla México. https://www.udlap.mx/empresasfamiliares/assets/files/radiografiaEmpresaFamMex.pdf. Accessed 22 May 2021.

San Martín-Reyna, J. M. (2018). The effect of ownership composition on earnings management: Evidence for the Mexican stock exchange. *Journal of Economics, Finance and Administrative Science, 23*(46), 289–305. https://doi.org/10.1108/JEFAS-01-2017-0011

Sandoval-Arzaga, et al., (2020). "El impacto en los cambios demográficos en la gobernanza y la sucesión de la empresa familiar en México". *Resultados de la Encuesta STEP Project for Family Enterprise 2019.* https://ifem.tec.mx/. Accessed 20 December 2020.

Sandoval-Arzaga, F. (2021). *Radiografía de la Empresa Familiar Latinoamericana.* Estudio Preliminar. Instituto de Familias Empresarias para México y Latinoamérica, Escuela de Negocios, Tecnológico de Monterrey.

SHCP-CNBV. (2018). *Overview of the Mexican financial system and its AML/CFT regulation and supervision.* https://www.gob.mx/cms/uploads/attachment/file/196042/SFM_230217.pdf. Accessed 20 December 2020.

Steier, L. P. (2009). Familial capitalism in global institutional contexts: Implications for corporate governance and entrepreneurship in East Asia. *Asia Pacific Journal of Management*, *26*(3), 513–535.

STEP Project. (2019). *El proceso de sucesión en empresas de Familia de Latinoamérica.* STEP Project for Family Enterprising. https://ifem.tec.mx/es/publicaciones

Songini, L., Gnan, L., & Malmi, T. (2013). The role and impact of accounting in the family business. *Journal of Family Business Strategy, 4*, 71–83. https://doi.org/10.1016/j.jfbs.2013.04.002

Tardan. (2020). *Official website*. https://tardan.com.mx/nosotros/. Accessed 19 February 2020.

The World Bank. (2021). *Official website*. https://www.worldbank.org/en/country/mexico/overview. Accessed 9 April 2021.

Uddin, S., & Choudhury, J. (2008). Rationality, traditionalism, and the state of corporate governance mechanisms: Illustrations from a less developed country. *Accounting, Auditing and Accountability Journal, 21*(7), 1026–1105. https://doi.org/10.1108/09513570810907465

Vázquez, P., Carrera, A., & Cornejo, M. (2020). Corporate governance in the largest family firms in Latin America. *Cross-Cultural & Strategic Management, 27*(2), 137–163.

Watkins-Fassler, K., & Briano-Torrent, G. (2019). Succession and performance of family firms listed on the Mexican stock exchange. *Contaduría y Administración, 64* (4), Especial Gobierno Corporativo, 1–16.

CHAPTER 11

Peru

Enrique Díaz Ortega

1 Introduction

This chapter discusses the evolution of corporate governing in Peruvian companies over the last 20 to 25 years, focusing on companies listed on the Lima Stock Exchange (LSE or BVL for its acronym in Spanish). By concentrating on this segment, we can provide a consistent and deeper analysis, not only because there is more and better information available, but also because this segment deals with the companies representing the largest share of the country's GDP. That said, such a focus does not prevent us from recognizing the efforts being made to improve corporate governance practices in other activities and areas in the economy. Additionally, the securities market is the business environment which has

E. Díaz Ortega (✉)
ASCLA (Latin America Corporate Secretaries Association), Lima, Peru
e-mail: ediaz@mcifperu.com

J. Callund et al. (eds.), *Corporate Governing in Latin America*,
https://doi.org/10.1007/978-3-030-85780-6_11

led the initiatives to improve corporate governance in Peru, which in turn serve as a point of reference for other sectors in the country.[1]

The central idea is to identify the main factors that might explain the progress and limitations relating to the application of better corporate governance standards. By standards, we allude to the description and promotion of best existing practices, usually going beyond mere compliance with legal requirements. Good governance codes help to compile these practices, although the practices continue to evolve over time and can leave these codes out of date.

To understand the strategies that companies have been adopting regarding their governance, we direct our analysis toward the main external elements influencing such governance. In this way, certain aspects of the economic, institutional, or legal/regulatory environment are relevant for the discussion, as we will state. Also, to make our analysis more specific, we choose the boards as our center of attention, as a critical instance to reflect the changes in corporate governance, and as a catalyst for these changes as well. As Gillan (2006) has remarked, "*many view boards of directors as the lynchpin of corporate governance*". Along these lines, the composition of the board acquires considerable relevance, and even the aspiration to have a professional board is seen as an alternative consistent with good governance (Pozen, 2010).

1.1 The Approach

It is increasingly accepted that corporate governing can be analyzed from the perspective of different professional fields, such as economics, finance, administration, law, sociology, political science, among others.

[1] Another relevant sector is that of state-owned companies; where the holding company, FONAFE (National Fund for the Financing of State Business Activity), has been Promoting different standards and initiatives to improve corporate governance, starting with ad hoc codes of good governance, issued in 2005 and then revised in 2013. The work of the Banking Superintendency (SBS in short for its acronym in Spanish. Extended name: Superintendencia de Bancos, Seguros y AFPs) has also been relevant, which has issued various measures on corporate governance for the different types of entities under its supervision, such as the Pension Funds Administrators (AFPs), Cajas Municipales (Municipal owned Financial Institutions), Cooperatives and Financial Institutions in general. We will mention the pertinent cases when it relates to our focus of analysis.

We start by understanding "Corporate Governance" in a traditional way, as the structure of rights and responsibilities between the different parties related to the organization.[2] Associated with this, governing is exercised through management and control practices by the parties.

Such practices are evolutionary and usually reflect the conjunction of two streams: on the one hand, the idiosyncrasy and institutional rules applied by companies in each country; and on the other hand, the proposals for change and innovation aimed at implementing the best practices that have been identified.[3] The performance of the companies' corporate governance will be determined through the balance of these forces.

In particular, the will to change depends on the incentives/disincentives faced by companies which, in turn, may be linked to both internal and external factors. Internally, among other aspects, there will be the ownership structure, a company's type of economic activity, and its organizational structure. While externally, the primary influences will be the conditions of the economic, social, legal, and institutional environments.

In this way, to complement our perspective we turn to Institutional Theory, since "*...it complements under socialized views of corporate governance by addressing the embeddedness of corporations in a nexus of formal and informal rules*" as noted by Aguilera and Jackson (2003). In this way, following Jiménez-Seminario and Pyper (2019), we embrace elements linked to related theories:

- New Institutional Economics: where the effects of economic, social, and political institutions on economic behavior and market performance are analyzed.[4] Governance mechanisms are the incentives and monitoring arrangements that guide behaviors toward economic and social goals.

[2] For a thorough discussion on the concept of Corporate Governance, see Zingales, L. (1998).

[3] This contrast can be understood in terms of the definitions of *Corporate Embeddedness* and *Corporate Agency* proposed by Hyun Park, Sun; Zhang Yanlong and Keister Lisa (2020).

[4] Institutions are defined as "the humanly devised constraints that shape human interaction" (North, 1990).

- New Institutional Theory: highlights the relevance of institutional logic as the cultural matrix defining appropriate practices of organization, behavior, and governance. It also relies on cultural and meaning systems to guide social actions, as well as structures and policies.

1.2 Methodology

The analysis carried out is based mainly on a historical review of public information available on macroeconomic and stock market statistics, as well as the main components of the regulatory framework. In the same way, the main corporate and administrative characteristics of the corporate governance of companies is also reviewed.

The chapter ends with an assessment of qualitative information obtained from in-depth interviews with a sample of company directors, who were chosen because of their long tenure as board members of select and relevant companies in the Peruvian market.[5]

2 Understanding the Context

2.1 Macroeconomic and Institutional Conditions

As indicated, environmental factors largely constrain the development of corporate governing. For that purpose, we concentrate on macroeconomic conditions and the institutional framework (including relevant legal and regulatory matters).

In the first half of the 1990s, Peru underwent a radical transformation in its macroeconomic policies, as well as in the legislative framework that regulated the performance of the state, the relationship of the state with the private sector, as well as the conditions for the performance of the

[5] The interviews were carried out by the author on condition that the names of the directors will not be disclosed. The number of interviews was limited, but sufficient to gather valuable information on the configuration and performance of the boards on which they sit. Several qualitative insights that have been shared were gleaned from these interviews. The predetermined profile of the board member selected for interview is an individual with over 20 years of experience as a director; who is/or has been a member of several listed companies on the Lima Stock Exchange (LSE); and where the companies form(ed) part of the General Index of the LSE; and finally, where their appointments was as an independent board member.

businesses. Both the economic conditions and the institutional framework were revamped as a result of these reforms.[6]

While macroeconomic stability was achieved (after a period of hyper-inflation), the Peruvian economy was liberalized, leaving it subject more to the predominance of market forces, with a state that was withdrawing a great deal from economic activity, with multiple incentives to promote private investment and welcome foreign investment, as well as opening the economy to the rest of the world. The multiple exchange rate system was left behind, and a *managed float* regime was adopted, in turn Peru embraced the free movement of capital.

Regarding the normative framework, the Constitution was abolished and replaced by another in which the favoring of the market economy and the subsidiary role of the state were clarified. Barriers to international trade and the flow of capital were drastically reduced. Along the same lines, a new Companies Law—Law N°26.887 (*Ley General de Sociedades*) (LGS)—was enacted, which set out the primary conditions for the functioning of the main organs of a company. Likewise, free market competition rules were issued giving rise to a new supervisory body for the defense of the consumer and free competition (INDECOPI).[7]

At the same time, the Government carried out an aggressive privatization program, transferring ownership of companies established in various sectors, such as banking, mining, telecommunications, industrial, and energy. In several cases, this implied the entry of international operators that maintained investments in various countries, and that in turn applied the management and control policies originated in their parent companies. The Government also reordered the management of companies that remained under its control with the creation of a specialized holding company (FONAFE[8]).

[6] Our description is only a summary of the reforms carried out. The subject of reforms and liberalization of the Peruvian economy has been dealt with at length in other publications, such as World Bank Group (2015).

[7] As part of the strategy of incorporating competition policies and liberalizing the economy, the government had issued Legislative Decree No. 701, the Law for the Elimination of Monopolistic, Controlling and Restrictive Practices on Free Competition, at the end of 1991. The validity of said law was conditioned to the establishment of the National Commission of Free Competition. This Commission was not created, and that gap was filled with the creation of INDECOPI. See INDECOPI (2013).

[8] Acronym in Spanish for "*Fondo Nacional de Financiamiento de la Actividad Empresarial del Estado*".

In addition, reforms were enacted to the capital market, the banking and financial system, all at the same time as the private pension system was being created (Individual accounts managed by Fund Administrators. An AFP[9] scheme, similar to that of other countries, and inspired by the radical approach to public pensions taken by Chile in 1980). The capital market reform fostered the emergence of new players (such as a *Central Depository Agency*, independent risk rating agencies, mutual fund managers, and securitization intermediaries) but, above all, the possibility that companies could find new sources of financing under the conditions that public markets offering securities require greater transparency, risk management, and better corporate governance.

Regarding transparency, it is as well to note that the reforms related to the capital market led to a demand for better standards from corporations. These new issuers of securities needed to disclose more financial and non-financial information that hitherto, while the AFPs needed to assess their investment risks by drawing on various sources of information, and not only from the issuers, but also from independent risk rating agencies, investment banks, or other specialized agents. In 1993, Peru began adopting the *International Accounting Standards*, and more recently the *International Financial Information Standards*, through resolutions issued by the "*Consejo Normativo de Contabilidad*" (Accounting Regulatory Council).

The banking system reform promoted greater solvency and better prudential control by the supervised institutions. The Central Bank Law was reformulated, giving it much greater autonomy, prohibiting it from lending money to the Government, and establishing the control of inflation as its main objective (inflation target scheme). As a consequence, the supervisory bodies were reinforced in their functions and capacities (CONASEV[10] and SBS[11]). In regulatory matters, the reforms did not

[9] AFP is acronym for "*ADMINISTRADORA DE FONDOS DE PENSIONES*", the regulated pension fund management company investing members' mandatory social security savings and reporting and administering their individual capitalization accounts.

[10] NATIONAL SUPERVISORY COMMISSION OF COMPANIES AND SECURITIES (CONASEV), which will later become the SUPERINTENDENCY OF SECURITIES MARKET (SMV for its acronym in Spanish. Extended name: SUPERINTEDENCIA DE MERCADO DE VALORES).

[11] *SUPERINTENDENCIA DE BANCA, SEGUROS Y AFP* – The BANK, INSURANCE AND PENSIONS SUPERINTENDENCY.

explicitly consider aspects related to corporate governance, which have only appeared gradually over the last 20 years.

In the following years, the central lines of macroeconomic policies held their course, which delivered annual inflation of around 2%, accompanied by fiscal and monetary policies that were prudent. The country began accumulating international reserves and sufficient fiscal savings to face future crises.

The impact these reforms generated in the Peruvian economy is summarized in Table 1, but the principal elements can be summarized as:

- Sustained GDP growth (Approx. 7% annual GDP growth in dollars).
- Trade openness (Exports plus imports) almost doubled with respect to the GDP.
- Foreign direct investment (FDI) successively multiplied by 5 to 6 times over five-year periods.
- Participation of foreign investors in the LSE reached 40% of the market capitalization.
- Revenues to the Treasury from the effect of privatizations were around USD9 billion in the 1990s, falling off subsequently, but still remaining a relevant source of public funding.
- The stock market capitalization has multiplied ten-times compared to the start of the 1990s.
- The pension funds managed by the AFPs accumulated portfolios greater than 50% of GDP.
- Credit from the financial system to the private sector more than doubled (% of GDP).

Given this focuses on companies listed in the LSE, it is as well to highlight some aspects of the evolution of this stock exchange. As seen in Table 1, although the stock market grew in terms of market capitalization, the actual number of companies listed did not grow and the amounts traded had an evolution that ceased to grow and even decreased in recent years.

Table 1 Peru: Selected macroeconomic indicators (1990–2019)

Concept	*1990*	*1995*	*2000*	*2005*	*2010*	*2015*	*2019*
Amounts (millions $)							
GDP	29,408	51,407	50,432	74,240	149,036	191,323	230,809
Foreign investment (accumulated last 5 years)	180	6521	10,004	8813	30,766	43,375	37,293
Privatization flows (accumulated last 5 years)	n/a	4958	3941	1177	908	349	911
Stock market capitalization - LSE	810	11,702	13,648	36,196	160,982	90,577	162,329
Yearly amount traded (average last 5 years)—LSE	336	2566	7330	2843	7782	6015	6296
Initial Public Offerings (average last 5 years)—LSE	n/a	180	957	700	635	1523	1877
Number of listed companies—LSE	n/a	236	230	235	263	275	260
Private Pension Funds (AFP)	n/a	1094	2674	9394	30,761	36,067	52,302
Ratios (%)							
(X + M)/PBI	21.09%	25.72%	28.38%	39.67%	43.36%	37.50%	38.46%
Equity investments by foreigners in BVL	n/a	n/a	n/a	34.18%	40.04%	29.66%	32.73%
Equity investments by AFPs in BVL	n/a	2.98%	5.84%	9.56%	6.13%	2.86%	3.74%
Financial system credit to private sector/GDP	n/a	17.57%	27.72%	21.93%	30.42%	42.01%	43.15%

Sources BCRP, BVL, SMV, SBS, PROINVERSIÓN

As the OECD (2019a, b)[12] points out, companies did not resort to the capital market to issue more shares, preferring rather to issue bonds.[13] In addition, the heightened concentration of the banking sector has naturally encouraged corporations to take traditional credits rather than support them through access to the capital market.

In this way, the market has not achieved the necessary breadth or depth, remaining a market with low levels of liquidity.[14] There have been many diverse efforts to counteract this, the most notable being the attempt at integrating several markets in the region—Chile, Colombia, Mexico, and Peru—into a single market to ensure greater trading volumes, known as MILA.[15] This initiative, however, never achieved its ambitious aims, despite some advances in accessibility to the other markets that are part of this agreement. This may be due to factors such as the lack of operational alignment between the clearing, settlement, and custody processes, which have tended to restrict cross-border trading.[16]

As such, the market capitalization has remained concentrated in a small proportion of listed companies; the same companies that, as will be seen, are usually also those that stand out in terms of better corporate governance practices. By international standards, this shortage of large traded corporate stocks has meant that Peru remains at risk of losing its "*emerging market*" status and going back to being a "*frontier market*", as defined by the methodology of the MSCI indexes.[17] Were this to happen,

[12] Organization for Economic Cooperation and Development (2019). "*Equity Market Development in Latin America: Enhancing Access to Corporate Finance – Chapter Peru*".

[13] Statistically, for the study period, almost 100% of the IPOs correspond to the issuance of bonds or short-term debt instruments.

[14] This feature has also been relieved in OECD publication (2019a, b), referring to the "*Capital Markets Development Degree Indicator*" produced by the Peruvian Central Bank.

[15] MILA ("*Mercado Integrado Latinoamericano*" for its acronym in Spanish) is the initiative of transnational stock market integration without merger or corporate integration, and that rather resorts to the use of technological tools and the adaptation and harmonization of the regulation for the negotiation of markets of capital and custody of titles. It is made up of the stock exchanges of Chile, Colombia, Mexico, and Peru.

[16] As noted by the World Bank Group (2019) in "*Documento de Apoyo para el desarrollo de una Hoja de Ruta para fortalecer el rol el mercado de valores peruano de cara al financiamiento del sector corporativo*".

[17] MSCI prepares various international indices, among which there are some made up of portfolios of groups of countries such as "emerging" or "border", which are classified

the impact on the LSE's trading and liquidity would be dire, as there would then be significantly less foreign investor interest to invest in the Peruvian market.

Despite the key indicators of economic growth, these market characteristics ensure the heightened relevance of corporate governance of Peruvian companies. That said, the Peruvian economy still exhibits other negative factors that limit its economic development. On the one hand, according to Machado (2014), the informal economy produces between 35% and 60% of GDP and employs around 60% of the economically active population. Moreover, Peru also ranks as one of the countries with high levels of corruption.[18] Both these elements are clearly harmful to the promotion of better corporate governance practices, imposing important barriers to improvements in market standards.

2.2 Regulatory Framework

The legal framework related to corporate governance has not changed structurally in recent years; the Companies Law dates from the mid-1990s,[19] while the Securities Market Law makes no explicit reference to corporate governance—it has subsequently been modified to enhance board members' responsibilities regarding issues of money laundering and corruption.

In 2001, a special Task Force was formed to discuss a draft *Code of Good Corporate Governance* for large corporations. This initiative was led by CONASEV and handled by groups of organizations representing the capital market.[20] In this way, Peru gradually aligned itself with the global

according to different factors such as the number of listed companies that exceed a certain market capitalization, or the proportion of stock trading on behalf of foreign investors, etc. See https://www.msci.com/index-methodology.

[18] It ranks 101 among 198 countries, according to the *Corruption Perception Index* (2019), published by Transparency International.

[19] It should be noted that since 2014, the Ministry of Justice has appointed work committees to propose changes to the Companies Law and collect the proposals that exist in this regard. The idea is to update the law to the new socioeconomic conditions, and improve competitiveness based on efficient business organization rules. This reform is pending approval.

[20] MEF, SBS, BVL, Procapitales, ASBANC, CONFIEP, and MCIF. Procapitales is a business association that brings together entities linked to the capital market. ASBANC is the association of private banks. CONFIEP is the union of business associations in the

trends in establishing a national Code in accordance with the guidelines launched by the OECD in 1999.[21]

At the initiative of the SMV, this Code was updated in 2013 and has been supported by both private and public entities. This new version covers areas of control, risk, and compliance. In addition, incorporated conditions to improve directors' ethical behavior as well as recommendations and reinforcement of the structure and overall performance of the board.

Since 2005, CONASEV has established that all listed companies should include a statement in their Annual Report explaining, principle by principle, whether they comply with the Code (*self-assessment*), applying—on a voluntary basis—the "comply or explain" approach it promotes. In 2014 this regulation was also updated with the aim of improving the self-assessments, as much more specific questions have since been incorporated to encourage greater details in issuer explanations.

In 2008, the LSE created a specific index for companies that demonstrate good corporate governance standards (the *Corporate Governance Index*). To be part of the index, self-assessment on the compliance of the Code should be reviewed by independent specialized entities ("*Validadoras*"). To consolidate this program, since 2014 the LSE has begun publishing the results in a survey denominated "The Voice of the Market" ("*La Voz del Mercado*"). With this, only those companies that have not been vetoed by the market in the survey can be recognized as with the title *Good Corporate Governance* (GCG). In this way, the model "*has complemented an issuer-driven model in which companies have to report their progress, with a market demand-driven based on polling market participants*".[22]

The Bank Superintendency (SBS) subsequently took a similar approach to the LSE *Good Corporate Governance* (GCG) categorization, creating the *Comprehensive Risk Management* criteria in 2017, which are applicable to all financial institutions and insurance companies. The provisions focus their attention on the board and on the issues of control and risk management. The SBS includes the review of these matters in the

different economic sectors. MCIF is a consulting firm specialized in Corporate Governance issues.

[21] Since updated (OECD, 2015).

[22] See "*Strengthening Corporate Governance Codes in Latin America*", OECD (2016).

regular inspections it carries out on the entities. More recently, the SBS has begun to promote consolidated supervision of economic groups, and the SMV is about to join that trend.

Toward the year 2012, the law of the *Private Pension System* (SPP) was modified in several extremes, and among them it was included that within the fiduciary responsibilities of the AFPs they should incorporate principles of corporate governance. Likewise, the Administrators were required to include two independent directors on their boards. On the other hand, at the end of 2017, the SBS incorporated the appointment of directors in companies where they have sufficient shareholding to give them the right to propose such board members into its guideline regulations for the AFPs.

For its part, SMV, aiming at a more rigorous oversight, started in 2017 the issuance of inductive notes ("*Oficios Circulares*") that required companies to explain in more detail some specific issues of their self-assessment (board operations, independent directors, internal audit, code of ethics, transactions between related parties, etc.), and where the answers they provided were also disseminated as "*Hechos de importancia*".

Efforts to continue improving capital market conditions are ongoing. Thus, in 2018, the SMV, in conjunction with some associations, such as PROCAPITALES, promoted the constitution of the *Advisory Council on the Peruvian Capital Market*. This Council organized its activities through several working groups to focus efforts on specific issues. At the same time, with the support of the WORLD BANK, it was possible to define the lines of action to be followed, including precisely "Strengthening and / or dissemination of the corporate governance supervision program". The progress and achievements of these actions have yet to be seen.[23]

With a view to providing a better perspective of the legal aspects, Figure 1—Evolution of Capital Market and Corporate Governance Regulations in Peru (1992–2017)—provides a "Timeline of relevant regulations" and the most important regulatory milestones in assessing progress, both in terms of important changes in the economic environment, and those relating directly to corporate governance. The evolution is still

[23] See Grupo Banco Mundial (2019), ibid.

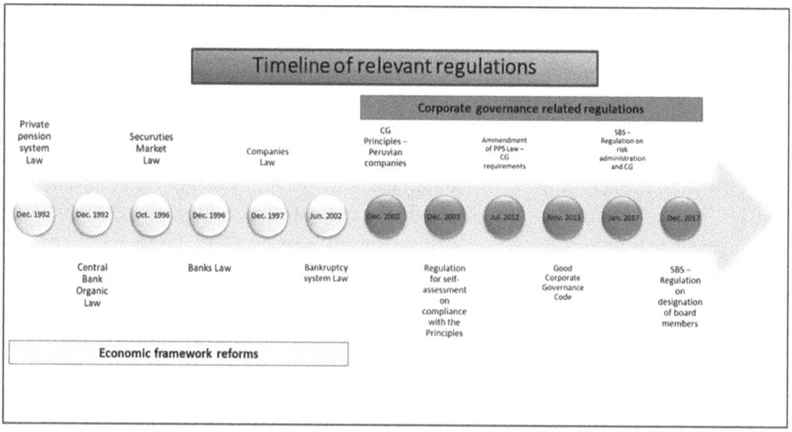

Fig. 1 Evolution of capital market and corporate governance regulations in Peru (1992–2017)

ongoing, as seen with the incorporation of ESG and sustainability criteria and their expected impact on the Peruvian market.[24]

3 Corporate Governing Evolution: Progress and Challenges

Although the evolution of corporate governing encompasses several dimensions, as shown by the different Corporate Governance Codes or set of GCG principles (transparency, shareholder rights, boards, management, stakeholders, ethics, control, risk management, among others), for a more accurate assessment, we opted to study the board as a key institution in looking under the hood of corporate governance in a company, as expressed by Adams et al. (2009): "Understanding the role of boards is vital both for our understanding of corporate behavior and with respect to setting policy to regulate corporate activities". In turn, we apply the idea raised by Kose and Lemma (1997) that the effectiveness of the board depends on its size, independence, and composition.

[24] For the purposes of analysis, we focus on the times when the laws or regulations were originally issued. There is no expectation to monitor the details of all modifications or updates to these regulations.

Regarding boards, only some features or facts are public knowledge,[25] while other aspects can only be gathered from the experience of the actors.[26]

3.1 Code Compliance Evaluations

The self-assessments on compliance with the Code are the most relevant references about the GC standards of listed companies. They have generated new elements of information about the company, contributing in principle to heightened market transparency that has also thrown into relief other corporate governance issues, such as stakeholder relationships, risk management procedures, and internal controls.

From a formal perspective, companies have reacted positively, approving a variety of new documents and policies. Let us emphasize that formalities are relevant insofar as they lay foundations for contractual commitments and arrangements, essential for governance by reducing agency costs (Jensen & Meckling, 1976). However, there are indications that the implementation of what was approved has not been entirely effective. Along the same lines, as the OECD study (2019a, b) points out, companies perceive their own corporate governing as substantially better than the market's own appreciation, for each dimension of said governance.

A case in point is that less than 10% of listed companies opt every year for the specialized revisions (validation) required to be considered as part of the *Corporate Governance Index* (CGI).[27] This indicates that the conditions for entering the CGI have been unattractive. The above should not ignore the fact that companies seeking recognition in the LSE have various motivates for doing so, one of the main ones being the fact

[25] As an element of support, the historical evolution of about 35 companies (reference or short list) has been analyzed, corresponding mainly to the components of the General Index of the LSE. Also, the main banks were included as well as those companies that have been part of the CG Index over time. These companies represent 64% of the LSE market cap.

[26] For these other factors we have relied on the author's own long experience, as well as on interviews with experienced board members.

[27] The statistical data on the boards of the companies listed in the LSE that we will cite on several occasions are taken from the document "*El Perfil de los Directorios en el Perú – Edición 2019*", published by *Mercados de Capitales, Inversiones y Finanzas* (2020).

that investors value this recognition positively, as analyzed by Fuenzalida and Mongrut (2013).

This is verified, for example, when by comparing the evolution of the LSE Indices (*Good Governance Index*—GCGI with the *General Index*–GI)—a highlighted in Fig. 2 above, where the accumulated performance of companies with good corporate governance exceeds, by a good margin, the average of listed companies. Along the same line of reasoning, Skare and Hasic (2015) also point out "compliance with the standards of good corporate governance helps to enhance the decision-making process", which is especially relevant for boards.

On the other hand, the concentration of ownership is a characteristic of Peruvian (and many other Latin American) companies. In this regard, recent studies establish that the adoption of good corporate governing practices, through the Codes and their compliance, helps to mitigate the agency problems between the controlling shareholders and minority shareholders (see del Briano-Turrent & Rodriguez-Ariza, 2016).

In any case, a telling factor is that the apparent advances in corporate governance did not avert some corporate scandals from occurring, even from companies that belonged to the Corporate Governance Index,

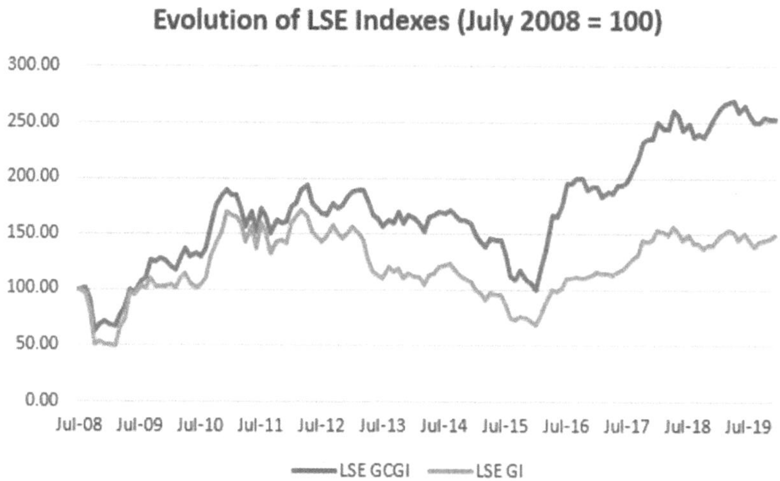

Fig. 2 Companies with *Good Governance Index* and the *General Index* on the Lima Stock Exchange

similar to those occurring in the global markets, as pointed out by Paulina da Costa (2016). These events have been linked to cases of corruption in megaprojects with the government, undisclosed support for political campaigns; or financial maneuvers to affect minority shareholders. Companies have reacted by adjusting part of their corporate governance standards; but the corresponding penalties that the authorities had to issue have not occurred with the necessary severity or timeliness. In this way, some form of self-regulation took place, where it was sought to correct the insufficiency of information and improve the compliance mechanisms; seeking above all to manage reputational risk. In turn, institutional investors (AFPs) required adjustments and responses from the companies involved.

3.2 *Ownership*

A central characteristic in the Peruvian companies is the concentration of ownership.[28] At the beginning of the 1990s, said ownership was exercised mainly by the state (through state-owned enterprises) or by family business groups.

Due to macroeconomic reforms, a dynamic started for the companies listed in the stock exchange in which the interest of maintaining control, both in property and in management, was contrary to the proposals being made to develop the capital market and better integrate the economy to international markets.

Consequently, the shareholding was opened but only partially, which is reflected in the lack of IPOs as well as in the reduced flotations[29] of the existing shares. As new shareholders are housed, investor protection becomes a bigger concern.[30] Such protection should be given through the exercise of control rights, as Shleifer and Vishny (1996) have outlined. However, when legal frameworks are weak, reforms take place slowly, and

[28] The concentration of ownership is not unique to Peru, as evidenced by the OECD in its publication "*Owners of the World's listed Companies*" (2019a). Several Latin American countries exhibit high concentration indices such as Argentina, Brazil, Chile, or Mexico (the main 3 shareholders own more than 50% of the shareholding of listed companies).

[29] The process of offering a company's shares for sale on the stock market for the first time.

[30] Cadbury (2022) shares a reflection on the implications on corporate governance of these changes.

rules are not duly enforced; investors remain more exposed, particularly minorities, as highlighted long ago by La Porta and López-de-Silanes (2000). For a shallow market such as Peru's, corporate governance emerges as a valuable option to improve investor protections and thus seeks to make that market more attractive.

Nowadays, after more than 25 years, the condition of concentration in the ownership of companies has not changed for the most part, identifying some patterns of evolution such as:

- Companies that were privatized and transferred control from the state to private agents (e.g., BBVA, Siderperu, Telefónica, Casa Grande, Refineria la Pampilla, Interbank, and ENEL).
- Private companies that maintained a high level of ownership concentration, without modifying the controlling shareholder (e.g., Cementos Pacasmayo, Minsur, Rimac Seguros y Reaseguros, Unacem, San Ignacio de Morococha, El Brocal, Aluminos Record, Banco de Crédito, and ENGIE).
- Private companies, which manage the control with a percentage lower than half of the capital, due to a certain dispersion in ownership (e.g., Buenaventura, Alicorp, Corporación Aceros Arequipa, Graña y Montero, and Credicorp).
- Private companies whose ownership was transferred to foreign investors, who now concentrate ownership (e.g., Scotiabank, Nexa resources, Southern,[31] Austral, Backus, and Lindley).
- Companies that were created during the period of analysis and that have controlling shareholders (e.g., Pesquera Exalmar, Intercorp Financial Services, and Inretail).

The fact that the most important companies prefer maintaining controlling shareholders shows a structural feature of the way companies are managed in Peru; but also reflects the mistrust of existing institutions, the same that could eventually affect the property rights of shareholders.[32]

[31] In this case, the owner was already a foreign company and switched to another foreign investor.

[32] One of the concerns that the study of the Bolsa de Valores de Lima–EY (2017) picks up on among investors is that equal treatment is required for the minority shareholder, in view of the advantages that the controlling shareholders would have.

In the few notorious cases, where controlling majority shareholders are absent (Ferreycorp, Buenaventura), they have been superseded by other features, such as the stability/longevity in the positions of management or board members.

During the period of analysis, the AFPs have emerged as relevant market players with the potential to significantly alter the ownership structures of listed companies as well as the possibility of promoting improvements in corporate governance of listed companies.[33] However, the participation of AFPs (with the sizeable pool of pensions funds they manage) in terms of the market capitalization on the LSE, remains insignificant,[34] having tended to focus on a small number of companies with larger capitalization and liquid shares.[35] This has been the case with pension fund holdings predominantly of Ferreycorp, Cementos Pacasmayo, Buenaventura, Credicorp, and ENGIE. Hitherto, Graña y Montero was also in this group until its crisis. All these companies were also part of the *Corporate Governance Index*.

Several authors argue that the involvement of institutional investors in monitoring or controlling company activities where they invest has the potential to constrain agency problems, as summarized by Gillan and Starks (2003). However, at the same time, the presence of a controlling shareholder "*moves the focus of agency costs from executive management to the controlling shareholder*" as pointed out in Schlimm, et al. (2010). In this case, board independence becomes more critical. In this regard, as noted by Trujillo et al. (2015), the study of board practices in exercising its critical functions refocuses attention on a board's composition and operations.

[33] For instance, the OECD (2019b) publication refers to Peruvian institutional investors consider that improvements in CG would allow them to expand their investments into local equities.

[34] According to the OECD (2019a) publication, average participation of institutional investors as shareholders of the listed companies represents 41%. In Peru, this participation was less than 10%. However, it was higher for specific cases. This likely reflects the scarcity of options in the stock market, as there are no large companies that allow them to host large investors, such as the AFPs in their shareholding.

[35] In certain circumstances, liquidity can have an adverse effect on corporate governance improvements. Institutional investors can influence the CG of issuers through their "voice" or their purchases or sales of shares ("exit"). The incentive to use the "voice" (greater activism) is reduced with the degree of liquidity of the market or of the action (better chance to exit). See Edmans (2017).

3.3 *Board Composition*

In the late 1990s and early 2000s, in a context where most companies were family-owned, the controlling shareholder's decisions were often vertical and discretionary, including those of appointment of the board members.

In this way, the boards used to be established by little formality, where the directors were chosen within the owner's circle of trust, by close personal references, or by being people with high exposure in the business world, serving in this last case more like a good image issue for the company. The search for suitable competencies was not essential.

From the director's point of view, the appointment was seen more as a prize, and little was expected of their roles or attention paid to their responsibilities. The CEOs and team managed the agendas of the sessions, and they were reluctant to share information very openly with external members of the board, preferring to do so in a limited way.

As such, boards had a low turnover, and it was common to maintain the presence of some board members almost permanently.

If we shift our attention to the formation of the boards nowadays[36], we will notice that there is already more interest in searches for greater professionalization, for proven accumulated experience, as well as for expanded diversity; even though this process is still only partial. In this regard, the LSE–EY study (2017) agrees with this impression, as it registers as one of its findings that "A more professional board of directors with independents is required".

The first trait of diversity that has been adopted is that of independence. The proportion of independent directors has reached 30% in the year 2019, having grown from 22% in 2014. Table 2 shows some selected indicators related to boards and corporate governance standards.

The most regulated sectors (the banks and AFPs), as well as those companies participating in the *Corporate Governance Index*, maintain a better proportion of independent directors. The need for a more professional boards of directors with independence was also stressed in the BVL-EY study (2017).

Although independence seeks to incorporate elements of greater objectivity in decision-making, it is not straightforward to assess the true independence of a board member. In this regard, consider the following:

[36] As inspired by contributions such as the Carter & Lorsch, (2004).

Table 2 Selected indicators on corporate governance compliance in Peru

Concept	*General average*	*LSE General Index*	*LSE Corporate Governance Index*
Board size	6.0	7.4	8.0
Independent directors/board size	30.1%	34.9%	41.3%
Number of *Board Committees*	2.1	2.5	3.4
Have established an *Audit Committee*	60.4%	86.2%	100%
Have established a *Risk Committee*	49.7%	50.0%	60%
Perform board self-evaluations	45.7%	58.7%	70%
Perform external board evaluations	16.9%	34.5%	70%
Regulates the boards compensation policy	48.4%	55.2%	90%
Regulates a policy on related-party transactions	55.9%	86.2%	90%
Regulates a policy on risk management	71.4%	79.3%	80%
Regulates an information policy	68.3%	75.9%	80%

Source Prepared by the author based on the self-assessment on compliance of the Code (2019)

- Independence qualification is based mainly on the characteristic of the absence of a property or business relationship, as well as a family relationship with the controlling shareholders or with management.[37] This formal verification allows us to identify external directors, but whose independence can only be observed in the exercise of their function.
- The figures confirm that most board members are considered "not independent". In most cases, the controlling shareholder has preferred to remain on the board or has also appointed officials of the company or the business group. The independent board member

[37] Precisely, the SMV, through its regulations, has sought to provide criteria to classify a director as independent; the most recent regulation being Resolution 016-2019-SMV/01, "Guidelines for the Qualification of Independent Directors".

must know how to deal in this context. Otherwise, the independent directors only end up adapting to the will of the control group ("establishment").

- The average tenure period of a board member is 7 years (in some sectors in might stretch to 8 years), denoting limited rotation. This would imply that certain board members initially appointed as independent, lose this condition over time, due to their prolonged contact with the company and/or its management team.

In general, despite the apparent intention to incorporate greater independence, the selection process itself conditions the outcomes. It is still common that newly appointed directors come from sources, such as previous professional or commercial relationships with the control group; members of law firms; and public officials who have recently held high positions, etc. This characteristic is confirmed by the publication of "*Semana Económica*" (2017), which revealed that the candidates for directors are chosen mainly based on the recommendations of the shareholders or the current members of the board. In turn, from an academic point of view, authors such as Lefort (2005) have observed that the concentration of ownership limits the independence of the boards, making them rather more a consultative instance.

Even the AFPs have not been able to compensate for this predominant situation. Rather, the AFPs were expected to place greater emphasis on the corporate governance of the companies where they invest, since AFP regulations indicate that when they propose board members, they should make sure that these members are given the appropriate induction to promote the LSE's *Good Corporate Governance* (GCG) within the company. Furthermore, in the beginning, the board members appointed at the suggestion of the AFPs faced certain resistance on the part of the rest of the board, which was linked to the controlling shareholder. In this context, the information did not flow to them in a sufficient or timely manner.

The diversity objective has also pointed toward the variety of competencies in the board.[38] While a couple of decades ago, having repeated professions on the board was rarely challenged; now there is an effort to

[38] Again, we refer to the LSE–EY survey, which revealed the requirement of a methodical and periodic evaluation of the board members in order to have directors that add value to the company.

diversify and the most required professions on the boards are: business administrators (26.6%), economists (20.8%), lawyers (13.0%), industrial engineer (9.9%), civil engineer (4.6%), and accountant (3.2%).

Another element of diversity that is becoming more relevant is that of gender. In this regard, we note that there is a large gap to be resolved in this case. Currently, women represent only 10% of board positions.

In addition, at the beginning of the century, the boards used to be more numerous, and the most recent data indicates that the size is decreasing.[39] In 2019, the size of the average board of directors was six, diminishing compared to previous years, where it had been seven. This possibly reflects the incremental responsibilities of the boards and the search for professionalization, which has since led to targeting the type of talent being sought.

3.4 *Availability of Board Members*

Expanding diversity on the board, particularly in terms of independent members, requires that a proper offer of board members be available—chicken and egg. In an economy such as the Peruvian, it is usual to argue that there is a short supply of appropriate professionals, which supports the justification for selecting directors from a limited pool of potential board members. Indeed, in absolute terms, the amount of independent board members has grown slowly (in the last 5 years, only 0.3 members per company). Rather, it can be verified that conservative attitudes of the companies determine these outcomes. This situation is supported by the following market information:

- 22% of board members are already incumbents on the boards of at least one other listed company.
- There is a limited pool of qualified professionals who fully satisfy the conditions of an appointment, as one of the recurring requirements is to have experience as a board member in similar-sized companies. Hence, several hold a seat on different boards, or they rotate among the listed companies. Only recently have a few companies started

[39] In the short list of companies, we have analyzed, it was not unusual to have boards with more than 10 members: reaching 16 members in some cases. Currently, only a few maintain large boards.

incorporating foreigners as independent nominee directors to their boards.

- Consistent with the above, the average age of board members has been increasing. Thus, Directors over 55 years of age are predominant. There are almost no directors under the age of 35.
- Companies make little use of "Headhunters" to find candidates for their boards. This practice recently emerged, and only partially, among the AFPs when they have had to propose board members. This also coincides with the findings of the "*Semana Econòmica*" survey (2017).
- Interlocking board memberships can also be found among companies belonging to the same economic groups.

Despite these findings, the opportunity to make new board members available has not gone unnoticed by business schools and other organizations looking to develop programs as well as in forming networks for board members and company secretaries. These initiatives have only arisen over the last 5 years, as yet they show few favorable results in terms of positioning relevant numbers of new board members.

3.5 Board Engagement

Currently, the degree of engagement of the board members has increased. This refers to dedication in time and involvement in key issues of the company. Although there are differences between companies from different economic sectors, in general the rules and regulations stressing the responsibilities of board members have been tightening, which increases the risk of this function.

Board members now respond with their personal assets in cases of company fraud, or even in situations of tax avoidance when the appropriate tax policies have not been adopted, for example. In the financial sector, boards are required to establish and monitor audit and risk management policies. The rules on the prevention of money laundering have also been expanded, to mention some important ones. All of this has contributed to the Compliance function becoming more effective due to the boards' own requirements.

One of the ways in which the greater involvement of the boards is noted is in the gradual increase of the established committees. On average, the companies listed in the LSE have two committees. Even though the number can be considered low for international standards, small growth has been observed in recent years (in 2016 the average was 1.5).

The fact that the audit committee is the most common among companies shows that control issues are important for boards. Nevertheless, the study related to "La Voz del Mercado 2016" highlights that according to investors the control and prevention environment still needs to improve.

Other relevant aspects are capturing more the attention of the boards:

- 81% have a *Code of Ethics*.
- 71% have a risk management policy.
- 62% have approved information policies.
- 56% regulate operations with related parties.

It is true that having the policies does not ensure compliance, since there is no independent supervision of this, except in the case of financial institutions closely monitored by SBS. Similarly, ethics is a difficult subject to monitor, and it is perceived that checking on aspects such as the management of conflicts of interest, is far from being ideal. Regarding this last aspect, the study of BVL–EY (2017) also stresses the importance to manage conflicts of interest better; a problem that is exacerbated by the existence of controlling shareholders. Likewise, the "*Semana econòmica*" (2017) also reveals that most boards only devote a small part of their time to analyzing ethical issues, and it even confirmed that very few companies have an ethics committee.

On the other hand, there are other issues that still reveal insufficient progress:

- Slightly more than 18% have *Corporate Governance Committees*. This could be revealing the lack of strategic view on corporate governing, or even the absence of the board's leadership in this regard.
- Only 27% have a *Nomination* or *Compensation Committee*. A common flaw related to this issue is the virtual absence of succession plans for the main executives. Likewise, compensation policies for board members are often set aside.
- Just 16% of them perform external evaluations of the board (even though 46% indicate that they do carry out self-evaluations). None of them discloses the results. Boards are still reluctant to formally

identify paths of improvement in their performance. This aspect deserves more attention from companies, even more so when there are several valuable contributions on how to approach the analysis of the effectiveness and performance of the board.[40]

In contrast, the companies that belong to the *Corporate Governance Index* exhibit better indicators for all these aspects: 70% of them do perform board's external evaluations, and 60% of these companies have a *Corporate Goverance Committees* as well as a *Compensation Committees.*

3.6 Internationalization

One of the most effective external incentives in terms of corporate governance improvements has been the internationalization to which some companies have been exposed. The internationalization referred to here the trading of a company's securities in more developed refer (most commonly in USA). Other companies that receive similar influences are the subsidiaries of companies established in more developed markets, although in these cases the influence will depend mostly on whether the foreign controlling shareholder has its shares listed on the stock exchange of their home country.[41]

Consequently, as those Peruvian companies' securities are traded in those markets, they have applied more demanding corporate governance standards. This is reflected in matters such as transparency and communication with shareholders; composition of the boards with the inclusion of at least one-third of independent members; or with the formation of board committees under the presidency of independent directors.

Thus, we have companies whose shares (or their ADRs) are traded on the NYSE; as well as companies whose shares have become part of an ETF that is traded in the USA; or also companies that have issued bonds internationally. In this way, we have the following cases:

[40] See, for example, Nicholson & Keil (2004); Van den Berghe & Levrau (2004).

[41] The LSE–EY survey (2017) also reaffirms these ideas by identifying that, for investors, the best ranked companies are those with securities that are listed on foreign exchanges or whose parent company is located abroad.

- Companies whose shares or ADRs are traded on the NYSE: Buenaventura, Cementos Pacasmayo, Credicorp, Graña y Montero.[42]
- Companies that have issued international bonds[43]: Alicorp, Ferreycorp, BBVA, Banco de Crédito, Cementos Pacasmayo, Exalmar, In Retail, International Financial Services, Interbank, Telefónica del Perú, Southern Copper.
- Companies whose shares are part of the ETF called EPU[44]: Graña y Montero, Credicorp, Buenaventura, Southern Copper, Volcán, Alicorp, Intercorp, Minsur, Cerro Verde, Ferreycorp, Cementos Pacasmayo, Luz del Sur, Nexa, BBVA, Unacem, ENEL, Casagrande, Relapasa, Aceros Arequipa, Siderperu, and Brocal.
- Companies acquired by foreign companies whose shares are listed on the stock exchange of their country: Austral, BBVA, Relapasa, Scotiabank, Backus, and ENEL.

It is observed that some of these companies appear in more than one of the indicated segments. These different groups of companies do not necessarily face the same degree of corporate governance requirements, but they do tend to have greater scrutiny from investors or other groups of interest. Those companies with shares listed on the NYSE must meet greater demands as they must certify that they comply with the corporate governance standards of said stock exchange, particularly in terms of the composition of their boards. For their part, international bond issuers must be risk rated, and they must also meet greater information requirements. As for those that are only part of the EPU, they will have somewhat less severe requirements, while there is an ETF Administrator who must ensure that the information of the companies that make up the portfolio flows to the market. Finally, for those companies whose new controlling shareholder is a foreign company whose shares are listed on the stock exchange of their country; an indirect influence

[42] The company has faced serious problems due to allegations of corruption and consequent legal problems.

[43] There is an additional group of Peruvian companies that issued bonds internationally. They are not listed on the LSE or that are not part of our short list for analysis.

[44] EPU tracks a market-cap-weighted index of Peruvian firms.

would be exerted in the corporate governing of the Peruvian company as a subsidiary of the former.

The internationalization described does not of itself provide more robust corporate governance assurances. There are cases where not enough progress is observed, for example, in the composition of the boards of directors regarding the appointment of independent directors. This is the case of companies where the majority foreign shareholder is not listed in its country of origin (e.g., NEXA and CERRO VERDE), or companies where foreign shareholders do list but do not have a majority shareholding (e.g., VOLCÁN).

In other cases, where even though independent directors had been appointed, insufficient autonomy has been noted on the board, either because the required special committees were not formed according to best practices, or because various relevant policies had not been approved by the board (e.g., LINDLEY and LUZ DEL SUR).[45]

On the other hand, internationalization can also be seen in a small group of companies[46] that have been included in the *Dow Jones Sustainability MILA Pacific Alliance Index*,[47] for which they have had to demonstrate high ESG[48] standards.[49]

3.7 *Combining Factors*

In order to clarify how the corporate governance standards of Peruvian companies differ, we established a set of verification criteria. The idea being to combine external factors to which the company has been subjected (i.e., internationalization and AFPs), with internal decision-making factors that the company has decided to adopt (i.e., *Corporate*

[45] This information is corroborated with the review of the self-assessment of compliance with the GC Code.

[46] These companies are FERREYCORP, CEMENTOS PACASMAYO, RIMAC SEGUROS, UNACEM, and SOUTHERN COPPER.

[47] The Dow Jones Sustainability MILA Pacific Alliance Index is a float-adjusted market capitalization weighted index that measures the performance of Chilean, Colombian, Mexican, and Peruvian companies selected with ESG (Environmental, Social, and Governance) criteria using a best-in-class approach.

[48] Environment, Social and Governance.

[49] The SMV has already issued a regulation requiring companies to provide a simplified report on the adoption of ESG practices. Companies seem to be paying more attention to it, in particular because of the interest regarding the so-called "green financing".

Governance Index, independent directors, board assessments, committees on special issues,and policies governing special issues). These internal factors have been identified as those that companies are slow to adopt or involve more advanced stages in their corporate governance.

Table 3 shows the results of an exercise, where companies have been grouped from the best corporate governance standard (Group 1) to those with the lowest corporate governance standard (Group 4), based on the criteria outlined in Table 4.

From here we can conclude:

- Very few companies fully satisfy all the criteria.
- Being part of the *Corporate Governance Index* does not guarantee to have the optimal corporate governance standards. Some specific aspects remain under-addressed, even though the companies in this Index satisfactorily cover most of the GCG criteria.
- The shortcomings in the companies' corporate governance performance include: proportion of independent directors, board evaluations, establishment of some special committees such as *Corporate Governance* or *Nominations* and *Compensation*, approval of special policies such as board compensation.

4 Final Remarks

We have sought to know some features of the evolution of corporate governance in Peruvian companies. For this, we have focused on the companies listed in the Lima Stock Exchange (LSE), and, in particular, on the boards of these companies. This approach has sought to concentrate on identifying elements external to these companies, and to gauge their impact on the adoption of the country's Good Corporate Governance standards byin these same companies

The economic reforms and the economic progress achieved by Peru since the 1990s established an environment conducive to fostering better business standards, including those of *Good Corporate Governance* (GCG).

In this way, the initiatives to advance in GCG have been led by regulatory bodies, supported in part by the LSE. More than deep legal reforms, it has been subsidiary regulations of the supervisory bodies (SMV and SBS) themselves that have predominated. There are no mandatory

Table 3 Companies grouped according to corporate governance standards being met in Peru (2019)

Group	*Corporate Governance Criteria*	Companies *Assessed to Meet the Criteria*	
Group 1	Complies with the *Corporate Governance Index*	BBVA	
	External exposure: Shares or bond issues	Cementos Pacasmayo	
	Other external exposure: at least one condition	Ferreycorp	
	At least 2 conditions of Relevant board issues	Buenaventura	
	Majority of committees on special issues		
	Policies on special issues: Board compensation and any of these policies		
Group 2	Complies with the *Corporate Governance Index* and with one condition international exposure	Alicorp	Credicorp
	Does not comply with the *Corporate Governance Index*. Satisfies at least two conditions of external exposure	Graña y Montero	Telefónica del Perú
	At least one condition of relevant board issues	Rimac Seguros	Exalmar
	At least one committee on special issues	Scotiabank	

(continued)

Table 3 (continued)

Group	*Corporate Governance Criteria*	COMPANIES *A*SSESSED TO *M*EET THE CRITERIA		
	At least one policy on special issues	UNACEM		
Group 3	May or not comply with the *Corporate Governance Index*	MINSUR	AUSTRAL	INTERBANK
	External exposure: At least one condition	CORPORACIÓN ACEROS AREQUIPA	REFINERIA LA PAMPILLA	ENGIE
	At least one condition on relevant board features or on committees on special issues	CASA GRANDE	LINDLEY	INTERCORP
	At least one policy on special issues	IN RETAIL	BANCO DE CRÉDITO	CERRO VERDE
Group 4	Do not meet the set of minimum conditions of the other groups	ALUMINIOS RECORD LUZ DEL SUR ENEL	NEXA SIDERPERU VOLCÁN	

Source Prepared by the author based on the self-assessment on compliance of the Code (2019)

standards for listed companies, but rather a self-assessment regarding compliance with the Code, which is disclosed to the market. For their part, the institutions of the financial system must comply with a regulations of the SBS that focuses on certain aspects of the board, as well as on internal control and risk management issues. Furthermore, compliance with the standards of both regulatory bodies by financial institutions sometimes becomes more complex because the regulations of the SMV and the SBS have not always been compatible (e.g., different scope in the independent director criteria).

However, regulatory incentives to improve corporate governance have been unable to sway other structural patterns of Peruvian companies, predominantly due to their close concentration of ownership. This characteristic has been maintained throughout the years, even though several companies have been privatized, and that foreign capital has taken control of other private companies. When such concentration is not observed, there has been long stability in the management of the company, with executives or board members remaining in their positions for extended

Table 4 Criteria used to group companies according to their corporate governance standards

Corporate Governance Index	*Companies that were component of the Corporate Governance Index and others validated for GCG. Last 5 years*
External exposure	Shares (ADR) traded in exchanges of more developed markets
	International bond issues
	Foreign company–majority shareholder listed in its country of origin. More developed market
	Included in EPU Portfolio
	Included in ESG MILA Index
	Shares as part of AFPs Portfolios
Relevant board features	Independent directors: more than 30% of the board
	Board evaluation: self-assessment
	Board evaluation: external assessment
Committees on special issues	Risks management
	Corporate governance
	Nomination/Compensation
Policies on special issues	Board compensation
	Related-party Transactions (RPTs)
	Information management

Source Prepared by the author, based on public information of the self-evaluations of compliance with the Code; and another disclosed by the company

periods. The concentration of ownership has tended to act as an insurance policy, so allowing companies to retain control of their property rights, in a context of a fragile and potentially changing institutional framework.

This has led to gradual progress in terms of GCG, confirming the companies' conservative attitudes, that can be verified as follows:

- Less than 10% of listed companies have turned to specialized external companies to validate their self-assessments regarding compliance with the Code (*Corporate Governance Index* procedure).
- Although the participation of independent directors on the boards has increased, in general, the process of board member selection has privileged specific criteria with respect to candidates, such as having already served as a director in companies of a similar size, have had prior professional or business contact with the company, belong to a recognized law firm, have served as a high-level public official;

and generally, enjoy the confidence of the controlling shareholder. Likewise, the use of "headhunters" in these processes is still rare.

- On the contrary, most of the board members are not independent, reflecting the intention of the shareholders to remain present on the boards.
- The tenures of the board members are still long (seven years on average) by international comparisons, reflecting slow dynamics of change and innovation.[50] This observation goes hand in hand with the fact that the average age of directors has been increasing.
- A small portion of companies carry out external evaluation of their boards, even though a little less than half of the listed companies indicate that they do carry out board self-assessments.

Even when some corporate scandals have taken place, it has been the self-imposed remedies by the companies that has prevailed rather than the financial or penal penalties or legal reforms that might have arisen directly following such experiences.

We also note that despite the emergence of the AFPs as shareholders, no significant corrections have been seen to this trend. Furthermore, depending on their objectives, the AFPs concentrated their investments in a limited number of companies, focusing on those with the largest market cap and shares with good liquidity, also passing through a favorable corporate governance standard. The AFPs might also have contributed to incorporating headhunters in the board member selection processes; even when this practice is still limited.

The incremental responsibility that board members assume in fulfilling their role is one of the external factors that have contributed to certain improvements in corporate governance. Several regulations have since established criminal liability for directors or even exposed their assets as a result of incorrectly exercising the function of director. In response to this, board engagement has been expanded, either through increasing the number of special committees (although the average is still low) or through the approval of policies relating to ethics, risk, or control issues.

Internationalization, mainly relating to the negotiation of securities issued by Peruvian companies in more advanced capital markets is another

[50] The publication of "Semana Econòmica" (2017) also shows that the majority of the directors surveyed have remained in that position for 10 years or more.

external factor that has helped them to display better corporate governance standards than their peers. This entails a greater demand on the quality of the information they disseminate, and, in general, a more exhaustive scrutiny on the part of market agents. This scrutiny also extends to the composition of the board itself, particularly regarding the integration of independent members. At the same time, there are differences in degree between the demands faced by companies that are internationalizing; the most rigorous being the case where the shares of the Peruvian company (or its ADRs) are traded, followed by the case where it has issued international bonds.

In short, the progress of the listed companies in terms of corporate governance has been gradual and is still only partial, and even focused on certain companies more than others. Precisely, a verification exercise, with a set of specific criteria, led us to the discovery that only a few companies comply fully with the best corporate governance standards. Most companies show progress, more of a formal nature, consistent with the self-assessment of compliance with the Code that they carry out annually. However, there are still shortcomings in aspects that usually require greater commitment or require a deeper understanding of complex or sensitive issues for the company.

In this regard, from an internal perspective, companies should review whether they have sufficient incentives to advance their corporate governance standards. Then, From an external viewpoint, the regulators (as well as the LSE) should evaluate appropriate mechanisms to promote those aspects that are being less well attended to in corporate governance by the listed companies. For their part, the roles institutional investors should be playing in demanding better corporate governance standards also need tightening up.

Making progress on all the above-mentioned aspects is transcendental, firstly to improve minority shareholder protections and those of financing intermediaries in general, largely due to the predominance and persistency of high concentrations of share ownership. Moreover, this is key to facilitating enhanced transparency, control, or risk management issues, all of which are essential for a company's sustainability and the robustness and stability of the market in general.

References

Adams, R., Hermalin, B., & Weisbach, M. (2009). *The role of board of directors in corporate governance: A conceptual framework and survey*. ECGI Working Paper.

Aguilera, R., & Jackson, G. (2003). The cross-national diversity of corporate governance: Dimensions and determinants. *Academy of Management Review, 28*(3), 447–465.

Bolsa de Valores de Lima & EY. (2017). Los retos del Gobierno Corporativo en el Perú de cara a la Alianza del Pacífico: Análisis de los resultados de La Voz del Mercado 2016.

Cadbury, A. (2022). *Corporate governance and chairmanship: A personal view*. Oxford University Press.

Carter, C., & Lorsch, J. (2004). *Back to the drawing board*. Harvard Business School Press.

Briano-Turrent, G., & Rodriguez-Ariza, L. (2016). Corporate governance ratings on listed companies: An institutional perspective in Latin America. *European Journal of Management and Business Economics*, *25*(2), 63–75.

Edmans, A., & Holderness, C. (2017). *Blockholders: A survey of theory and evidence*. ECGI Working Paper.

Fuenzalida, D., & Mongrut S. (2013). Good corporate governance: Does it pay in Peru? *Journal of Business Research, 66*(10), 1759–1770.

Gillan, S. (2006). Recent developments in corporate governance: An overview. *Journal of Corporate Finance, 12*(3), 381–402.

Gillan, S., & Starks, L. (2003). Corporate governance, corporate ownership and the role of institutional investors: A global perspective. *Journal of Applied Finance*.

Hyun, P., Zhang, Y., & Keister, L. (2020). Governance innovations in emerging markets. *Journal Academy of Management Perspectives, 34*(2), 226–239.

INDECOPI. (2013). *Libre competencia: Análisis de las funciones del INDECOPI a la luz de las decisiones de sus órganos resolutivos*.

Jensen, M. C., & Meckling, W. H. (1976). Theory of the firm: Managerial behavior, agency costs, and ownership structure.

Jimenez-Seminario, G., & Pyper, N. (2019). *Governing as minding the institutional gap*. Conference: British Academy of Management 2019.

Kose, J., & Lemma, S. W. (1997). *Corporate governance and board effectiveness*. NYU Stern, Department of Finance, Working paper series.

La Porta, R., López-de-Silanes, F., Shleifer, A., & Vishny, R. (2000). Investor protection and corporate governance. *Journal of Financial Economics, 58*(1–2), 3–27.

Lefort, F. (2005). Ownership structure and corporate governance in Latin America. *Abante Magazine*.

Machado, R. (2014). *The informal economy in Peru: Magnitude and determinants, 1980–2011.* Centro de Investigación de la Universidad del Pacífico.

Mercados de Capitales, Inversiones y Finanzas. (2020). *El Perfil de los Directorios en el Perú.* Edición 2019.

Mundial, G. B. (2019). Documento de Apoyo para el desarrollo de una Hoja de Ruta para fortalecer el rol el mercado de valores peruano de cara al financiamiento del sector corporativo.

Nicholson, G. C., & Kiel, G. C. (2004). A framework for diagnosing board effectiveness. *Corporate Governance: An International Review, 12*(4), 442–460.

North, D. C. (1990). *Institutions, institutional change and economic performance.* Cambridge University Press.

Organization for Economic Cooperation and Development. (1999). *Principles of corporate governance.* OECD.

Organization for Economic Cooperation and Development. (2015). *G20/OECD principles of corporate governance.* OECD.

Organization for Economic Cooperation and Development. (2016). *Strengthening corporate governance codes in Latin America.* OECD.

Organization for Economic Cooperation and Development. (2019a). *Owners of the world's listed companies.* OECD.

Organization for Economic Cooperation and Development. (2019b). *Equity market development in latin america: Enhancing access to corporate finance—Chapter Peru.* OECD.

Paulina da Costa, A. M. (2016). Corporate governance and fraud: Evolution and considerations. In O. L. Emeagwali (Ed.), *Corporate governance and strategic decision making.* https://www.intechopen.com/books/5968.

Pozen, R. (2010). The case for professional boards: It's time to get more engagement from your directors. *Harvard Business Review.*

Schlimm, D., Mezzetti, L., & Sharfman, B. (2010). Corporate governance and the impact of controlling shareholders. *Corporate Governance Advisor, 18*(1), 1–10.

Semana económica. (2017). Un Nuevo directorio: Una nueva agenda. Auspiciado por KPMG y PAD.

Shleifer, A., & Vishny, R. (1996). *A survey on corporate governance.* NBER Working Paper.

Skare, M., & Hasic, T. (2015). Corporate governance, firm performance and economic growth—Theoretical analysis. *Journal of Business Economics and Management, 17*(1), 35–51.

Trujillo, M. A., Guzman, A., & Prada, F. (2015). *Juntas directivas en el desarrollo del gobierno corporativo.* CESA – SECO – IFC.

Van den Berghe, L., & Levrau, A. (2004). Evaluating boards of directors: What constitutes a good corporate board? *Corporate Governance: An International Review, 12*(4), 461–478.

World Bank Group. (2015). *Peru building on success*. Document of the World Bank.

Zingales, L. (1998). Corporate governance. In P. Newman (Ed.), *The New Palgrave dictionary of economics and the law*. Springer.

Index

J. Callund et al. (eds.), *Corporate Governing in Latin America*, https://doi.org/10.1007/978-3-030-85780-6

B

C

D

E

FSC
www.fsc.org
MIX
Papier | Fördert
gute Waldnutzung
FSC® C083411

Kolibri 360 GmbH
Ferdinand-Jühlke-Straße 7
99095 Erfurt, Deutschland
produktsicherheit@kolibri360.de